DIVORCE & DISSOLUTION OF CIVIL PARTNERSHIP IN THE SHERIFF COURT

DIVORCE & DISSOLUTION OF CIVIL PARTNERSHIP IN THE SHERIFF COURT

An exposition of the law and practice
relating to divorce & dissolution of
civil partnership in the sheriff court

Eighth Edition

by

S. A. Bennett, LL.B. (Hons)
Advocate

Barnstoneworth Press
2007

First published, 1984
Second edition, 1987
Third edition, 1991
Fourth edition, 1994
Fifth edition, 1997
Sixth edition, 2000
Seventh edition, 2005
Eighth edition, 2007

© S. A. Bennett

ISBN 978-0-9534152-7-4

Published by S. A. Bennett, Advocate, Advocates' Library,
Parliament House, Edinburgh EH1 1RF
under the name 'Barnstoneworth Press'.

Website: www.barnstoneworthpress.com

Typeset by Initial Typesetting Services, Edinburgh
Printed by Inglis Allen (UK) Limited, Kirkcaldy

CONTENTS

TABLE OF CASES

A page number in **bold type** indicates that a digest of the case is printed on that page.

TABLE OF STATUTES

TABLE OF STATUTORY INSTRUMENTS

TABLE OF ORDINARY CAUSE RULES

CHAPTER 1

SPECIAL RULES OF PROCEDURE

THE ordinary cause rules include special provisions applicable to actions of divorce[1] and, where indicated, actions for dissolution of a civil partnership. Some of these rules are drawn to the attention of practitioners under the relevant subject heading (*e.g.* mental disorder). Others are mentioned in this chapter.

CITATION AND INTIMATION

Citation

Except where the address of the defender is not known to the pursuer and cannot reasonably be ascertained, citation of the defender in an action of divorce or dissolution of a civil partnership requires to be in Form F15 or Form CP15, as the case may be, which must be attached to a copy of the initial writ and warrant of citation in Form F14 or Form CP14 and must have appended to it a notice of intention to defend in Form F26 or Form CP16.[2] The certificate of citation requires to be in Form F16 or Form CP17, which must be attached to the initial writ.[3]

Where the address of the defender is not known to the pursuer and cannot reasonably be ascertained, citation of the defender in such actions is effected in accordance with rule 5.6,[4] which provides as follows:

"(1) Where the address of a person to be cited or served with a document is not known and cannot reasonably be ascertained,

---

[1] For the purpose of this Chapter, "divorce" is taken to include other family actions (as defined in r. 33.1(1)), as appropriate.

[2] rr. 33.10 and 33.11(1) or 33A.10 and 33A.11(1). Unless the sheriff otherwise directs, no warrant for citation may be granted without there being produced with the initial writ an extract of the relevant entry in the register of marriages or an equivalent document, or an extract of the relevant entry in the civil partnership register or an equivalent document, as the case may be – r. 33.9(a) or r. 33A.9(1) and (2)(a). See also Chap. 6, text accompanying n. 54. As to service in cases of mental disorder of defender, see r. 33.13 or 33A.13 (set forth in Chap. 2, n. 42).

[3] r. 33.11(2) or 33A.11(2).

[4] r. 5.6 applies to all ordinary causes. In actions of divorce and other family actions and actions of dissolution of civil partnership, there is the additional requirement of intimation in terms of r. 33.7(1)(*a*) and (6) or r. 33A.7(1)(a) and (6) (as to which, see text accompanying nn. 11 and 30 *infra*). The pursuer must also aver in the condescendence what steps have been taken to ascertain the defender's present whereabouts — r. 3.1(6).

1

the sheriff shall grant warrant for citation or service upon that person —

    (a) by the publication of an advertisement in Form G3 in a specified newspaper circulating in the area of the last known address of that person, or

    (b) by displaying on the walls of court a copy of the instance and crave of the initial writ, the warrant of citation and a notice in Form G4;

and the period of notice fixed by the sheriff shall run from the date of publication of the advertisement or display on the walls of court, as the case may be.

(2) Where service requires to be executed under paragraph (1), the pursuer shall lodge a service copy of the initial writ and a copy of any warrant of citation with the sheriff clerk from whom they may be uplifted by the person for whom they are intended.

(3) Where a person has been cited or served in accordance with paragraph (1) and, after the cause has commenced, his address becomes known, the sheriff may allow the initial writ to be amended subject to such conditions as to re-service, intimation, expenses or transfer of the cause as he thinks fit.

(4) Where advertisement in a newspaper is required for the purpose of citation or service under this rule, a copy of the newspaper containing the advertisement shall be lodged with the sheriff clerk by the pursuer.

(5) Where display on the walls of court is required under paragraph (1)(b), the pursuer shall supply to the sheriff clerk for that purpose a certified copy of the instance and crave of the initial writ and any warrant of citation."

Intimation

The sheriff may, at any time, (i) order intimation of an action of divorce or dissolution of a civil partnership[5] to be made to such person as he thinks fit; (ii) postpone intimation, where he considers that such postponement is appropriate and, in that case, make such order in respect of postponement of intimation as he thinks fit; or (iii) dispense with intimation, where he considers that such dispensation is

---

[5] Intimation of motions and other matters falls to be made in terms of, *e.g.* rr. 33.25 or 33A.26, 33.69(2) or 33A.62(2) and 33.70(2) or 33A.63(2). The requirement to intimate motions does not apply in an action of divorce or dissolution of a civil partnership where no notice of intention to defend has been lodged or insofar as it proceeds as undefended — r. 33.33 and r. 33A.33.

appropriate.[6] A crave[7] or motion[8] to dispense with intimation may be granted by him.

The pursuer requires to include in the initial writ[9] a crave for a warrant for intimation —

(a) in an action for divorce or dissolution of a civil partnership where the address of the defender is not known to the pursuer and cannot reasonably be ascertained, to —

    (i) every child of the marriage between the parties who has reached the age of 16 years or every child of the family (within the meaning of section 101(7) of the Civil Partnership Act 2004[10]), as the case may be, and

    (ii) one of the next-of-kin of the defender who has reached that age,

unless the address of such a person is not known to the pursuer and cannot reasonably be ascertained, and a notice of intimation in Form F1 or Form CP1 must be attached to the copy of the initial writ intimated to any such person[11];

(b) in an action for divorce where the pursuer alleges that the defender has committed adultery with another person, to that person, unless—

    (i) that person is not named in the initial writ and, if the adultery is relied on for the purposes of section 1(2)(a) of the Divorce (Scotland) Act 1976 (irretrievable breakdown of marriage by reason of adultery), the initial writ contains

---

[6] r. 33.15(1) or r. 33A.15(1). In terms of r. 33.12(3) or r. 33A.12(3) the sheriff may, if he thinks fit, order intimation to a local authority (such intimation requiring to be in Form F8 or Form CP6). Whenever he considers it necessary for the proper disposal of an action of divorce, the sheriff must direct that the action be brought to the notice of the Lord Advocate in order that he may determine whether he should enter appearance therein — Sheriff Courts (Scotland) Act 1907, s. 38B(1). No expenses are claimable by or against the Lord Advocate in any action in which he has entered appearance under that section — Sheriff Courts (Scotland) Act 1907, s. 38B(2).

[7] r. 33.7(5) or r. 33A.7(5), applicable to pursuers (see text accompanying n. 28 *infra*) and r. 33.15(3) or r. 33A.15(3), applicable to any party (see text accompanying nn. 27 and 28). See also r. 33.7(7) or r. 33A.7(7), n. 19 *infra*.

[8] r. 33.7(6) or r. 33A.7(6), applicable to any party (see text accompanying n. 30 *infra*). See also r. 33.8 or r. 33A.8 (see nn. 31–34 *infra* and accompanying text).

[9] In the event that the pursuer makes a crave or averment which, had it been made in the initial writ, would have required a warrant for intimation under r. 33.7 or r. 33A.7, she requires to include in her writ a crave for a warrant for intimation or to dispense with such intimation; and r. 33.7 or r. 33A.7, with the necessary modifications, applies to such a crave as it applies to a crave under the rule — r. 33.15(3) or r. 33A.15(3).

[10] See Chap. 4, n. 7.

[11] r. 33.7(1)(a) or r. 33A.7(1)(a).

an averment that his or her identity is not known to the pursuer and cannot reasonably be ascertained; or

   (ii) the pursuer alleges that the defender has been guilty of rape upon or incest with, that named person,

and a notice of intimation in Form F2 must be attached to the copy of the initial writ intimated to any such person[12];

(c) in an action for divorce or dissolution of a civil partnership where the defender is a person who is suffering from a mental disorder[13], to —

   (i) those persons mentioned in sub-paragraph (a)(i) and (ii), *supra*, unless the address of such person is not known to the pursuer and cannot reasonably be ascertained,

   (ii) the *curator bonis* to the defender, if one has been appointed; and

   (iii) any person holding the office of guardian or continuing or welfare attorney to the defender under or by virtue of the Adults with Incapacity (Scotland) Act 2000,

and a notice of intimation in Form F3 or Form CP2 must be attached to the copy of the initial writ intimated to any such person[14];

(d) in an action for divorce relating to a marriage which was entered into under a law which permits polygamy where—

   (i) one of the decrees specified in section 2(2) of the Matrimonial Proceedings (Polygamous Marriages) Act 1972 is sought; and

   (ii) either party to the marriage in question has any spouse additional to the other party,

to any such additional spouse, and a notice of intimation in Form F4 must be attached to the initial writ intimated to any such person;[15]

(e) in an action for divorce or dissolution of a civil partnership where the sheriff may make a section 11 order in respect of a child —

   (i) who is in the care of a local authority, to that authority and a notice of intimation in Form F5 or Form CP3 must be attached to the initial writ intimated to that authority;

   (ii) who, being a child of one party to the marriage or one

---

[12] r. 33.7(1)(b).

[13] "Mental disorder" has the meaning assigned in section 328 of the Mental Health (Care and Treatment) (Scotland) Act 2003 (as to which, see Chap. 2, n. 41)—r. 33.1(2) and r. 33A.1(2).

[14] r. 33.7(1)(c) or r. 33A.7(1)(b).

[15] r. 33.7(1)(d).

party to the civil partnership, as the case may be, has been accepted as a child of the family by the other party to the marriage or the other party to the civil partnership, as the case may be, and who is liable to be maintained by a third party, to that third party, and a notice of intimation in Form F5 or Form CP3 must be attached to the initial writ intimated to that third party; or

    (iii) in respect of whom a third party in fact exercises care or control, to that third party, and a notice of intimation in Form F6 or Form CP4 must be attached to the initial writ intimated to that third party[16];

(f) in an action for divorce or dissolution of a civil partnership where the pursuer craves a section 11 order, to any parent or guardian of the child who is not a party to the action, and a notice of intimation in Form F7 or Form CP5 must be attached to the initial writ intimated to any such parent or guardian[17];

(g) in an action for divorce or dissolution of a civil partnership where the pursuer craves a residence order in respect of a child and the pursuer is —

    (i) not a parent of that child, and

    (ii) resident in Scotland when the initial writ is lodged,

to the local authority within which area the pursuer resides, and a notice of intimation in Form F8 or Form CP6 must be attached to the initial writ intimated to that authority[18];

(h) in an action for divorce or dissolution of a civil partnership which includes a crave for a section 11 order, to the child to whom such an order would relate if not a party to the action, and a notice of intimation in Form F9 or Form CP7 must be intimated to that child[19];

(i) in an action for divorce or dissolution of a civil partnership where the pursuer makes an application for an order under

---

[16] r. 33.7(1)(e) or r. 33A.7(1)(c).

[17] r. 33.7(1)(f) or r. 33A.7(1)(d).

[18] r. 33.7(1)(g) or r. 33A.7(1)(e). Rule 33.7(4) or rule 33A.7(4) requires a pursuer not resident in Scotland when the initial writ is lodged for warranting who craves a residence order in respect of a child of which he or she is not a parent to include a crave for an order for intimation in Form F8 or Form CP6 to such local authority as the sheriff thinks fit. Note that r. 33.12(3) or r. 33A.12(3) bestows upon the sheriff a general discretionary power to order intimation to a local authority (in Form F8 or Form CP6).

[19] r. 33.7(1)(h) or r. 33A.7(1)(f), subject to r. 33.(7)(7) or r. 33A.7(7), which provides that where a pursuer considers that to order such intimation is inappropriate, he or she must (a) include a crave in the initial writ to dispense with intimation to that child, and (b) include in the initial writ averments setting out the reasons why such intimation is inappropriate, and the sheriff may dispense with such intimation or make such other order as he or she thinks fit. Where younger children are involved or where there is a risk

section 8(1)(aa) of the Family Law (Scotland) Act 1985 (transfer of property) and —
  (i) the consent of a third party to such a transfer is necessary by virtue of an obligation, enactment or rule of law, or
  (ii) the property is subject to a security,
to the third party or creditor, as the case may be, and a notice of intimation in Form F10 or Form CP8 must be attached to the initial writ intimated to any such person[20];

(j) in an action for divorce or dissolution of a civil partnership where the pursuer makes an application for an order under section 18 of the 1985 Act (which relates to avoidance transactions), to —
  (i) any third party in whose favour the transfer of, or transaction involving, the property is to be or was made, and
  (ii) any other person having an interest in the transfer of, or transaction involving, the property,
and a notice of intimation in Form F11 or Form CP9 must be attached to the initial writ intimated to any such person[21];

(k) in an action for divorce or dissolution of a civil partnership where the pursuer makes an application for an order under the Matrimonial Homes (Family Protection) (Scotland) Act 1981, where the application is under section 3(1), 3(2), 4, 7, 13 or 18 of that Act, and the entitled spouse is a tenant or occupies the matrimonial home by permission of a third party or the pursuer makes an application for an order under Chapter 3 of Part 3 of the Civil Partnership Act, where the application is under section 103(1), 103(2), 104, 107 or 112 of that Act, and the entitled civil partner is a tenant or occupies the family home by permission of a third party, as the case may be, to the landlord or the third party, as the case may be, and a notice

---

of upsetting the child, other methods of intimation than the formal process of intimation in terms of Form F9 or Form CP7 may well be preferable — *S v. S*, 2002 S.C. 246 at p. 250. See Chap. 6, nn. 22–24 and accompanying text. *Cf. Gallacher v. Gallacher*, 1997 S.L.T. (Sh.Ct.) 42 (sheriff expected to see crave in initial writ for dispensation of intimation to six-year-old child)). The court should not dispense with intimation unless there is a crave to that effect — *H v. H*, 2000 Fam. L.R. 73 at p. 75. In terms of r. 33.15(2) or r. 33A.15(2), where the sheriff is considering whether to make a s. 11 order by virtue of s. 12 of the 1995 Act (restrictions on decrees of divorce affecting children), he requires to order intimation in Form F9 or Form CP7 to the child to whom the order would relate unless intimation has already been given or the sheriff considers that the child is not of sufficient age or maturity to express his views. Note that the initial writ itself does not fall to be intimated in terms of either r. 33.7(1)(h) or r. 33A.7(1)(f) or r. 33.15(2) or r. 33A.15(2).
[20] r. 33.7(1)(i) or r. 33A.7(1)(g).
[21] r. 33.7(1)(j) or r. 33A.7(1)(h).

of intimation in Form F12 or Form CP10 must be attached to the initial writ intimated to any such person[22];

(l)　in an action for divorce or dissolution of a civil partnership where the pursuer makes an application for an order under section 8(1)(ba) of the Family Law (Scotland) Act 1985 (orders under section 12A of the 1985 Act for pension lump sum), to the person responsible for the pension arrangement and a notice of intimation in Form F12A or Form CP11 must be attached to the initial writ intimated to any such person;[23] and

(m)　in an action for divorce or dissolution of a civil partnership where a pursuer makes an application for an order under section 8(1)(baa) of the Act of 1985 (pension sharing orders), to the person responsible for the pension arrangement and a notice of intimation in Form F12B or Form CP12 must be attached to the initial writ intimated to any such person.[24]

Each notice of intimation must be on a period of notice of 21 days unless the sheriff otherwise orders; but the sheriff cannot order a period of notice of less than two days.[25]

Where a defender intends to make an application for a section 11 order which, had it been made in an initial writ, would have required a warrant for intimation under rule 33.7 or rule 33A.7, he must include a crave in his notice of intention to defend for a warrant for intimation or to dispense with such intimation.[26]

Where a party makes a crave or averment which, had it been made in an initial writ, would have required a warrant for intimation under rule 33.7 or rule 33A.7, that party must include a crave in his writ for a warrant for intimation or to dispense with such intimation.[27]

Where the address of a person mentioned in paragraphs (b), (d), (e), (f), (h), (i), (j), (k), (l) or (m) *supra* is not known and cannot reasonably be ascertained, there must be included in the writ of the party concerned a crave to dispense with intimation; and the sheriff may grant that crave or make such other order as he thinks fit.[28]

Where the identity or address of any person in respect of whom a warrant for intimation requires to be applied for is not known and

---

[22]　r. 33.7(1)(k) or r. 33A.7(1)(i).

[23]　r. 33.7(1)(l) or r. 33A.7(1)(j).

[24]　r. 33.7(1)(m) or r. 33A.7(1)(k).

[25]　r. 33.7(3) or r. 33A.7(3).

[26]　r. 33.34(3) or r. 33A.34(3), also providing that r. 33.7 or r. 33A.7, with the necessary modifications, applies to a crave for a warrant under r. 33.34(3) or r. 33A.34(3) as it applies to a crave for a warrant under that rule.

[27]　r. 33.15(3) or r. 33A.15(3), also providing that r. 33.7 or r. 33A.7 with the necessary modifications, applies to a crave for a warrant under r. 33.15(3) or r. 33A.15(3) as it applies to a crave for a warrant under that rule.

[28]　rr. 33.7(5) or 33A.7(5) (pursuer) and 33.15(3) or 33A.15(3) (any party).

cannot reasonably be ascertained, the party required to apply for the warrant must include in his pleadings an averment of that fact and averments setting out what steps have been taken to ascertain the identity or address, as the case may be, of that person.[29]

Where the identity or address of a person to whom intimation is required becomes known during the course of the action, the party who would have been required to insert a crave for warrant for intimation to that person must lodge a motion for a warrant for intimation to that person or to dispense with such intimation.[30]

In an action for divorce or dissolution of a civil partnership in which the pursuer founds upon an alleged association[31] between the defender and another named person, the pursuer must, immediately after the expiry of the period of notice, lodge a motion for an order for intimation to that person or to dispense with intimation.[32] In determining the motion, the sheriff may—(a) make such order as he thinks fit; (b) dispense with intimation; and (c) where he dispenses with intimation, order that the name of that person be deleted from the condescendence of the initial writ.[33] Where intimation is ordered, a copy of the initial writ and an intimation in Form F13 or Form CP13 must be intimated to the named person.[34]

UNDEFENDED ACTIONS

The requirement of proof

In an action of divorce or dissolution of civil partnership, whether or not appearance has been entered for the defender, no decree or judgment in favour of the pursuer may be pronounced until the grounds of action have been established by evidence.[35]

As a consequence of this requirement of proof, default by the defender in an action of divorce or dissolution of civil partnership, entitles the sheriff only to allow the case to proceed as undefended.[36]

Affidavits

In actions for divorce or dissolution of a civil partnership to which

---

[29] r. 33.4 or r. 33A.4.

[30] r. 33.7(6) or 33A.7(6).

[31] "Association", in the case of divorce, means "sodomy, incest or any homosexual relationship" and, in the case of dissolution of civil partnership, means "sodomy, incest or any homosexual or heterosexual relationship"—r. 33.8(4) or r. 33A.8(4).

[32] r. 33.8(1) or r. 33A.8(1).

[33] r. 33.8(2) or r. 33A.8(2).

[34] r. 33.8(3) or r. 33A.8(3).

[35] Civil Evidence (Scotland) Act 1988, s. 8(1) and (2), as amended by the Civil Partnership Act 2004, Sched. 28, para. 55.

[36] r. 33.37(2)(a) r. 33A.37(2)(a).

rule 33.28 or rule 33A.29 applies, evidence requires to be given by affidavit, unless the sheriff otherwise directs.[37]

The foregoing rules apply to—

(a) actions in which no notice of intention to defend has been lodged;

(b) an action in which a curator *ad litem* has been appointed under rule 33.16 or rule 33A.16 where the curator *ad litem* to the defender has lodged a minute intimating that he does not intend to lodge defences;

(c) any action which proceeds at any stage as undefended where the sheriff so directs; and

(d) the merits of an action which is undefended on the merits where the sheriff so directs, notwithstanding that the action is defended on an ancillary matter.[38]

Where the foregoing rules apply, unless the sheriff otherwise directs, evidence relating to the welfare of a child must be given by affidavit, at least one affidavit being emitted by a person other than a parent or party to the action.[39]

At any time after the expiry of the period for lodging a notice of intention to defend, the pursuer then requires to (a) lodge in process the affidavit evidence; and (b) endorse a minute in Form F27 or Form CP27 on the initial writ[40] as follows:

"(*Insert name of solicitor for the pursuer*) having considered the evidence contained in the affidavits and the other documents[41] all as specified in the Schedule hereto and being satisfied that upon

---

[37] r. 33.28(2) or r. 33A.29(2). The Practice Note relative to affidavits in family actions (reproduced in App. IV) should be consulted before affidavit evidence is presented to the court. An affidavit sworn prior to the raising of the action is admissible only insofar as it relates to events which occurred before the action was raised (*McInnes v. McInnes*, 1990 S.C.L.R. 327). Rule 33.28(4) or r. 33A.29(4) provides that evidence in the form of a written statement bearing to be the professional opinion of a duly qualified medical practitioner, which has been signed by him and lodged in process, shall be admissible in place of parole evidence by him. Note that at any proof in an undefended action, it is not necessary to record the evidence — r. 33.32 or r. 33A.32.

[38] r. 33.28(1) or r. 33A.29(1).

[39] r. 33.28(3) or r. 33A.29(3). Where a child is in the care of a local authority it is sufficient to tender evidence of that fact by affidavit from a person qualified to speak to that fact (*Hunter v. Hunter*, 1979 S.L.T. (Notes) 2).

[40] r. 33.29(1) or r. 33A.30(1).

[41] Other documents include any marriage or civil partnership certificate and birth certificate requiring to be lodged with the initial writ in terms of r. 33.9 or r. 33A.9, as well as any notice of consent, joint minute, extract decree, extract conviction, photograph, medical report or other production relevant to the case.

the evidence a motion for decree (in terms of the crave(s)[42] of the initial writ) [*or in such restricted terms as may be appropriate*][43] may properly be made, moves the court accordingly.

> In respect whereof
> Signed
>
> Solicitor for the pursuer (*add designation and business address*)

SCHEDULE
(*Number and specify documents considered*)."

The sheriff may at any time after the pursuer has complied with the foregoing,[44] without requiring the appearance of parties, grant decree in terms of the motion for decree; or may remit the cause for such further procedure, including proof by parole evidence, as he thinks fit.[45]

The sheriff may accept evidence by affidavit at any hearing for an order or interim order.[46]

DEFENDED ACTIONS

Part III of Chapter 33 and Part III of Chapter 33A of the ordinary cause rules comprise rules applicable to actions for divorce and dissolution of civil partnership which are defended.

Rule 33.34 makes provision regarding notices of intention to defend and defences, applying[47] where the defender seeks —

---

[42] Note that r. 33.26 or r. 33A.27 entitles the sheriff to grant decree in respect of those parts of a joint minute in relation to which he could otherwise make an order, whether or not such a decree would include a matter for which there was no crave.

[43] Illustrations of "restricted terms" are as follows:

  (i)   ... for decree in terms of the first, third and fourth craves of the initial writ ...

  (ii) ... for decree in terms of the first crave and the joint minute no. 10 of process ...

  (iii) ... for decree in terms of the first and second craves, and in relation to the third crave (for a periodical allowance) for the sum craved or for such other sum as the court thinks fit ...

[44] Subject to the rule of law that an action falls if no procedure has followed within a year and a day of the expiry of the period of notice — *McCulloch v. McCulloch*, 1990 S.L.T. (Sh. Ct.) 63 and *Dunnett v. Dunnett*, 1990 S.C.L.R. 135 (*cf. Donnelly v. Donnelly*, 1991 S.L.T. (Sh. Ct.) 9 (rule of law inapplicable where action defended for a time) and *The Royal Bank of Scotland plc v. Mason*, 1995 S.L.T. (Sh. Ct.) 32 (rule of law inapplicable where motion enrolled for decree in absence, albeit unsuccessfully)). Note that an action also falls if no service of the initial writ is effected within a year and a day of the granting of the warrant for citation of service — *Diaz v. Diaz*, 1999 S.C.L.R. 329.

[45] r. 33.29(2) or r. 33A.30(2).

[46] r. 33.27 or r. 33A.28.

[47] r. 33.34(1) or r. 33A.34(1).

(a) to oppose any crave in the initial writ;
(b) to make a claim for —
 (i) aliment[48];
 (ii) an order for financial provision within the meaning of section 8(3) of the Family Law (Scotland) Act 1985[49]; or
 (iii) a section 11 order[50];
(c) an order —
 (i) under section 16(1)(b) or (3) of the 1985 Act (setting aside or varying agreement as to financial provision)[51];
 (ii) under section 18 of the 1985 Act (which relates to avoidance provisions)[52]; or
 (iii) under the Matrimonial Homes (Family Protection) (Scotland) Act 1981 or under Chapter 3 or Chapter 4 of Part 3 of the Civil Partnership Act 2004; or
(d) to challenge the jurisdiction of the court.

In such an action, the defender must —

(a) lodge a notice of intention to defend in Form F26 or Form CP16 before the expiry of the period of notice; and
(b) make any claim or seek any order, as above referred to, in those defences by setting out in his defences —
 (i) craves;
 (ii) averments in the answers to the condescendence in support of those craves; and
 (iii) appropriate pleas-in-law.[53]

---

[48] Also provided for by r. 33.39(1)(a) and (2)(b) or r. 33A.39(1)(a) and (2)(b).

[49] Also provided for by r. 33.48(1)(a) and (2)(a) or r. 33A.45(1)(a) and (2)(a).

[50] Also provided for by r. 33.39(1)(a) and (2)(a) or r. 33A.39(1)(a) and (2)(a). But see r. 9.6(3), mentioned in n. 53 *infra*.

[51] Also provided for by r. 33.48(1)(a) and (2)(b) or r. 33A.45(1)(a) and (2)(b).

[52] Also provided for by r. 33.48(1)(a) and (2)(c) or r. 33A.45(1)(a) and (2)(c).

[53] r. 33.34(2) or r. 33A.34(2). But see r. 9.6(3) (neither crave nor averments need be made in defences which relate to s. 11 order). It has been suggested that when the defender seeks to make a relevant claim against the pursuer, which he must do by lodging defences with appropriate craves, followed by answers to the condescendence and appropriate pleas-in-law, all in response to the pursuer's craves *and* in support of his own craves, he should in his answers, as well as responding to the pursuer's averments, include, where appropriate, averments in support of his craves; and where the defender is making a claim which it is not possible to deal with in an answer to an article of condescendence (because the pursuer is not making a similar claim or at least has made no averments in relation to that matter), he should insert *additional* answers in his answers to the condescendence in support of his claim, allowing the pursuer during the adjustment period to insert *additional* articles of condescendence to respond to those additional answers — *Bell v. MacPherson*, 1997 S.L.T. (Sh. Ct.) 62 at p. 63.

Notwithstanding abandonment by a pursuer, the court may allow a defender to pursue an order or claim sought in his defences; and the proceedings in relation to that order or claim shall continue in dependence as if a separate cause.[54]

Parties to a defended action require, except on cause shown, to attend personally at the Options Hearing.[55] Failure by a party to attend, however, attracts no sanction provided that he or she is represented at the diet.[56]

Provision is made by rule 33.37 or rule 33A.37 for the granting of decree by default, the rule applying[57] in an action in which the defender has lodged a notice of intention to defend where a party fails —

(a) to lodge, or intimate the lodging of, any production or part of process,

(b) to implement an order of the sheriff within a specified period,

(c) to appear or be represented at any diet, or

(d) otherwise to comply with any requirement imposed upon that party by the rules.

Where a party has so failed, and is thereby in default, the sheriff may —

(i)   allow the action to proceed as undefended under Part 2 of Chapter 33 or Chapter 33A of the rules; or

(ii) grant decree of absolvitor; or

(iii) dismiss the action or any claim made or order sought; or

(iv) make such other order as he thinks fit to secure the expeditious progress of the cause; and

(v)   award expenses.[58]

Where no party appears at a diet, the sheriff may dismiss the action.[59]

The sheriff may, on cause shown, prorogate the time for lodging any production or part of process, or for intimating or implementing any order.[60]

SIMPLIFIED PROCEDURE

Simplified divorce applications and simplified dissolution of civil partnership applications may be made if, but only if —

---

[54] r. 33.35 or r. 33A.35.

[55] r. 33.36 or r. 33A.36. The parties are similarly obliged to attend any Child Welfare Hearing (along with any child who has indicated his or her wish to attend) — r. 33.22A(5) or r. 33A.23(5). As to such hearings, see Chap. 6, text accompanying nn. 57–62.

[56] *Grimes v. Grimes*, 1995 S.C.L.R. 268.

[57] r. 33.37(1) or r. 33A.37(1).

[58] r. 33.37(2) or r. 33A.37(2).

[59] r. 33.37(3) or r. 33A.37(3).

[60] r. 33.37(4) or r. 33A.37(4).

(a)   the applicant relies on the facts set out in section 1(2)(d) of the Divorce (Scotland) Act 1976 or section 117(3)(c) of the Civil Partnership Act 2004 (no cohabitation for one year with consent of defender to decree), or section 1(2)(e) of the 1976 Act or section 117(3)(d) of the 2004 Act (no cohabitation for two years) or section 1(1)(b) of the 1976 Act or section 117(2)(b) of the 2004 Act (issue of interim gender recognition certificate);

(b)   in an application under section 1(2)(d) of the 1976 Act or section 117(3)(c) of the 2004 Act, the other party consents to decree of divorce or of dissolution of civil partnership being granted;

(c)   no other proceedings are pending in any court which could have the effect of bringing the marriage or civil partnership to an end;

(d)   there are no children of the marriage or child of the family (as defined in section 101(7) of the 2004 Act) under the age of 16 years;

(e)   neither party to the marriage or civil partnership applies for an order for financial provision on divorce or dissolution of civil partnership; and

(f)   neither party to the marriage or civil partnership suffers from mental disorder.[61]

If an application ceases to be one to which the foregoing applies at any time before the final decree, it is deemed to be abandoned and must be dismissed.[62]

A simplified application must be made in Form F31 or Form CP29 (no cohabitation for one year with consent of defender to decree) or Form F33 or Form CP30 (no cohabitation for two years) or Form F33A or Form CP31 (issue of interim gender recognition certificate) and must be signed by the applicant.[63]

It is the duty of the sheriff clerk to cite any person and intimate any document in connection with a simplified application.[64]

Any person on whom service or intimation of a simplified application has been made may give notice by letter sent to the sheriff clerk that he challenges the jurisdiction of the court[65] or opposes the

---

[61]   r. 33.73(1) and (3) or r. 33A.66(1) and (3). In the case of a simplified divorce application, there must also be no religious impediment to the remarriage of either party — r. 33.73(1)(g).

[62]   r. 33.73(2) or r. 33A.66(2).

[63]   r. 33.74 or r. 33A.67. The applicant also to send an extract or certified copy of the marriage certificate or of the civil partnership certificate and the appropriate fee — r. 33.75 or r. 33A.68.

[64]   r. 33.76(2) or r. 33A.69(2).

[65]   The sending of such a letter does not imply acceptance of the jurisdiction of the court — r. 33.78(4) or r. 33A.71(4).

grant of decree of divorce or dissolution of civil partnership and giving the reasons for his opposition to the application[66]; and in that event, the sheriff must dismiss the application unless he is satisfied that the reasons given for the opposition are frivolous.[67]

Parole evidence cannot be given in a simplified application.[68]

Any appeal against an interlocutor granting decree in terms of the simplified application may be made, within 14 days after the date of decree, by sending a letter to the court giving reasons for the appeal.[69]

Any application to the court after decree has been granted in a simplified application which could have been made if it had been made in an action of divorce or dissolution of civil partnership requires to be made by minute.[70]

---

[66] r. 33.78(1) or r. 33A.71(1).

[67] r. 33.78(2) or r. 33A.71(2). As to "frivolous", see *Waugh v. Waugh*, 1992 S.L.T. (Sh. Ct.) 17. An application was dismissed where a question arose as to the validity of the marriage in *Aranda v. Aranda*, 1990 S.L.T. (Sh. Ct.) 101.

[68] r. 33.79 or r. 33A.72.

[69] r. 33.81 or r. 33A.74. As to "reasons for the appeal", see *Colville v. Colville*, 1988 S.L.T. (Sh. Ct.) 23 and *Norris v. Norris*, 1992 S.L.T. (Sh. Ct.) 51.

[70] r. 33.82 or r. 33A.75.

CHAPTER 2

MISCELLANEOUS TOPICS

Miscellaneous topics of significance in the law and practice relating to divorce and dissolution of civil partnership are considered in this chapter.

JURISDICTION

A sheriff court has jurisdiction by virtue of section 8(2) of the Domicile and Matrimonial Proceedings Act 1973[1] to entertain an action for divorce if (and only if[2])

  (a) either —
        (i) the Scottish courts have jurisdiction under the Council Regulation;[3] or
       (ii) the action is an excluded action[4] and either party to the marriage in question is domiciled in Scotland at the date when the action is begun.[5]

---

[1] As amended by the Divorce Jurisdiction, Court Fees and Legal Aid (Scotland) Act 1983, Sched. 1, para. 18, The European Communities (Matrimonial Jurisdiction and Judgments) (Scotland) Regulations 2001 (S.S.I. 2001 No. 36), reg. 2(3)(a) and The European Communities (Matrimonial and Parental Responsibility Jurisdiction and Judgments) (Scotland) Regulations 2005 (S.S.I. 2005 No. 42), reg. 2(3).

[2] Prorogation, for example, is not a ground of jurisdiction in actions of divorce — *Singh v. Singh*, 1988 S.C.L.R. 541.

[3] "The Council Regulation" means Council Regulation (EC) No. 2201/2003 concerning jurisdiction and the recognition and enforcement of judgments in matrimonial matters and the matters of parental responsibility — 1973 Act, s. 12(5)(c), as amended by The European Communities (Matrimonial and Parental Responsibility Jurisdiction and Judgments) (Scotland) Regulations 2005 (S.S.I. 2005 No. 42), reg. 2(6)(b).

[4] "Excluded action" means an action in respect of which no court of a Contracting State has jurisdiction under the Council Regulation and the defender is not a person who is — (i) a national of a Contracting State (other than the United Kingdom or Ireland); or (ii) domiciled in Ireland — 1973 Act, s. 12(5)(d), as amended by The European Communities (Matrimonial Jurisdiction and Judgments) (Scotland) Regulations 2001 (S.S.I. 2001 No. 36), reg. 2(5)(b). "Contracting State" means Belgium, Cyprus, Czech Republic, Germany, Greece, Spain, Estonia, France, Hungary, Ireland, Italy, Latvia, Lithuania, Luxembourg, Malta, Netherlands, Austria, Poland, Portugal, Slovak Republic, Slovenia, Finland, Sweden and the United Kingdom — 1973 Act, s. 12(5)(b), as amended by The European Communities (Matrimonial and Parental Responsibility Jurisdiction and Judgments) (Scotland) Regulations 2005 (S.S.I. 2005 No. 42), reg. 2(6)(a).

[5] *Cf. City of Edinburgh District Council v. Davis*, 1987 S.L.T. (Sh. Ct.) 33 (action "raised" when citation of defender effected).

and

(b) either party to the marriage —
    (i) was resident in the sheriffdom[6] for a period of 40 days ending with that date,[7] or
    (ii) was resident in the sheriffdom for a period of not less than 40 days ending not more than 40 days before the said date and has no known residence in Scotland at that date.[8]

The Scottish courts have jurisdiction under the Council Regulation in accordance with article 3 thereof, which provides as follows:

"1. In matters relating to divorce, legal separation or marriage annulment, jurisdiction shall lie with the courts of the Member State:

(a) in whose territory:
– the spouses are habitually resident,[9] or
– the spouses were last habitually resident, in so far as one of them still resides there, or
– the respondent is habitually resident, or
– in the event of a joint application, either of the spouses is habitually resident, or
– the applicant is habitually resident if he or she resided there for at least a year immediately before the application was made, or
– the applicant is habitually resident if he or she resided there for at least six months immediately before the application was made and is either a national of the Member State in question or, in the case of the United Kingdom and Ireland, has his 'domicile' there.

---

[6] There seems to be nothing as a matter of law to require the raising of the action in the *sheriff court* in which the party was resident. As a matter of practice, however, special cause must be shown to obtain warrant for citation from any court within a sheriffdom other than that in which the cause would normally fall to be dealt, namely the court within the district of which the relevant party was resident (see *Simpson v. Bruce*, 1984 S.L.T. (Sh. Ct.) 38).

[7] Residence within the sheriffdom thereafter cannot be taken into account in determining whether or not there is jurisdiction — *McNeill v. McNeill*, 1960 S.C. 30.

[8] There would appear to be no room to interpret s. 8(2)(b)(ii) in anything other than a literal fashion: *cf. McNeill v. McNeill*, 1960 S.C. 30; *Fraser v. Macfadyen* (1940) 56 Sh. Ct. Rep. 66; and *Hutchison v. Goodale*, 1940 S.L.T. (Sh. Ct.) 24.

[9] "Habitual residence ... is a question of fact [which] encompasses the idea of where the person normally lives" (*per* the Sheriff Principal in *Morris v. Morris*, 1993 S.C.L.R. 144 at p. 145). In the context of the Child Abduction and Custody Act 1985, a habitual residence was "one which is being enjoyed voluntarily for the time being and with the settled intention that it should continue for some time ... A person can, we think, have only one habitual residence at any one time" (*per* the Lord President in *Dickson v. Dickson*, 1990 S.C.L.R. 692 at p. 703). *Cf. Cameron v. Cameron*, 1996 S.L.T. 306.

(b) of the nationality of both spouses or, in the case of the United Kingdom, and Ireland, of the 'domicile' of both spouses.

2. For the purpose of this regulation, 'domicile' shall have the same meaning as it has under the legal systems of the United Kingdom and Ireland."[10]

A sheriff court also has jurisdiction to entertain an action for divorce (notwithstanding that jurisdiction would not be exercisable under section 8(2)) if it is begun at a time when an original action is pending in respect of the marriage; and for this purpose "original action" means an action in respect of which the court has jurisdiction by virtue of section 8(2) or (3), but this does not give the court jurisdiction to entertain an action in contravention of Article 6 of the Council Regulation.[11] The foregoing provisions are without prejudice to any sheriff court's jurisdiction to entertain an action of divorce remitted to it in pursuance of any enactment or rule of court, provided that entertaining the action would not contravene Article 6 of the Council Regulation.[12]

The sheriff has jurisdiction to entertain an action for the dissolution of a civil partnership if (and only if)

---

[10] "Domicile ... is an idea of law. It is the relation which the law creates between an individual and a particular locality or country. To every adult person the law ascribes a domicile, and that domicile remains his fixed attribute until a new and different attribute takes its place" (*per* Lord Westbury in *Bell v. Kennedy* (1869) 6 M (H.L.) 69 at p. 78). A person becomes capable of having a domicile when he attains the age of 16 years (Age of Legal Capacity (Scotland) Act 1991, s. 7). This is a "domicile of choice", which is a "conclusion or inference which the law derives from the fact of a man fixing voluntarily his sole or chief residence in a particular place, with the unlimited intention of continuing to reside there" (*per* Lord Westbury in *Udny v. Udny* (1869) 7 M (H.L.) 89 at p. 99).

[11] 1973 Act, s. 8(3A), as inserted by The European Communities (Matrimonial Jurisdiction and Judgments) (Scotland) Regulations 2001 (S.S.I. 2001 No. 36), reg. 2(3)(b) and amended by The European Communities (Matrimonial and Parental Responsibility Jurisdiction and Judgments) (Scotland) Regulations 2005 (S.S.I. 2005 No. 42), reg. 2(3)(b). Article 6 states that a spouse who (a) is habitually resident in the territory of a Member State; or (b) is a national of a Member State or, in the case of the United Kingdom and Ireland, has his or her 'domicile' in the territory of one of the latter Member States, may be sued in another Member State only in accordance with Articles 3, 4 and 5. The terms of Article 3 are reproduced *supra*. Article 4 states that the court in which proceedings are pending on the basis of Article 3 shall also have jurisdiction to examine a counterclaim, insofar as the latter comes within the scope of the Council Regulation. Article 5 states that without prejudice to Article 3, a court of a Member State that has given judgment on a legal separation shall also have jurisdiction for converting that judgment into a divorce, if the law of that Member State so provides.

[12] 1973 Act, s. 8(4), as amended by The European Communities (Matrimonial Jurisdiction and Judgments) (Scotland) Regulations 2001 (S.S.I. 2001 No. 36), reg. 2(3)(c) and The European Communities (Matrimonial and Parental Responsibility Jurisdiction and Judgments) (Scotland) Regulations 2005 (S.S.I. 2005 No. 42), reg. 2(3)(b). An example of an action of divorce remitted to the sheriff court is *Gribb v. Gribb*, 1992 S.C.L.R. 776.

(a)   the court has jurisdiction under section 219 regulations (*viz.* regulations issued under section 219 of the Civil Partnership Act 2004); or

(b)   no court has, or is recognised as having, jurisdiction under section 219 regulations and either civil partner is domiciled in Scotland on the date when the proceedings are begun

and either civil partner—

(a)   was resident in the sheriffdom for a period of 40 days ending with the date when the action is begun; or

(b)   had been resident in the sheriffdom for a period of not less than 40 days ending not more than 40 days before that date and has no known residence in Scotland at that date.[13]

The regulations issued under section 219 of the Civil Partnership Act 2004 are The Civil Partnership (Jurisdiction and Recognition of Judgments) (Scotland) Regulations 2005.[14] Regulation 4 thereof provides:

"The courts in Scotland shall have jurisdiction in relation to proceedings for the dissolution ... of a civil partnership ... where—

(a)   both civil partners are habitually resident in Scotland;

(b)   both civil partners were last habitually in Scotland and one of the civil partners continues to reside there;

(c)   the defender is habitually resident in Scotland;

(d)   the pursuer is habitually resident in Scotland and has resided there for at least one year immediately preceding the date on which the action is begun; or

(e)   the pursuer is domiciled and habitually resident in Scotland and has resided there for at least six months immediately preceding the date on which the action is begun."

CONCURRENT PROCEEDINGS

Where more than one legal system has jurisdiction to grant decree of divorce or dissolution of civil partnership, complex rules are required to avoid conflicts of jurisdiction.

These rules are to be found in Schedule 3 to the Domicile and Matrimonial Proceedings Act 1973 and in rules of court corresponding thereto made by virtue of section 226 of the Civil Partnership Act

---

[13] Civil Partnership Act 2004, ss. 225(1)(a) and (b) and (2)(a) and (b).
[14] S.S.I. 2005 No. 629.

2004, namely Part XIII of Chapter 33A of the Ordinary Cause Rules.[15] They require the parties to actions of divorce and dissolution of civil partnership to tell the court about any proceedings continuing outwith Scotland which are in respect of the marriage or civil partnership or capable of affecting its validity (hereinafter referred to as "concurrent proceedings") and they make provision regarding mandatory and discretionary sists by the Scottish court where there are concurrent proceedings elsewhere.

The duty on parties to inform the court of any concurrent proceedings subsists while the action is pending and until proof in the action has begun.[16] Failure of a person to perform this duty prolongs the time within which the court has a discretion to sist the cause (which discretion would otherwise cease to be exercisable at the beginning of the proof).[17]

Ordinary cause rule 33.2 or 33A.2 provides the machinery whereby each party may discharge this duty.

The pursuer must state in the condescendence of the initial writ whether to her knowledge any proceedings are continuing[18] in Scotland or in any other country which are in respect of the marriage or civil partnership to which the initial writ relates or are capable of affecting its validity or subsistence.[19]

Where such proceedings are continuing, the pursuer must also state:

 (a) the court, tribunal or authority before which they have been commenced;
 (b) the date of commencement;
 (c) the names of the parties;
 (d) the date or expected date of any proof (or its equivalent) in the proceedings; and

---

[15] Schedule 3 is subject to Article 19 of the Council Regulation — 1973 Act, s. 11(2), as inserted by The European Communities (Matrimonial and Parental Responsibility Jurisdiction and Judgments) (Scotland) Regulations 2005 (S.S.I. 2005 No. 42), reg. 2(5)(b). Article 19 *inter alia* states that where proceedings relating *inter alia* to divorce between the same parties are brought before courts of different Member States, the court second seised shall of its own motion stay its proceedings until such times as the jurisdiction of the court first seised is established; that where the jurisdiction of the court first seised is established, the court second seised shall decline jurisdiction in favour of that court; and that in that case, the party who brought the relevant action before the court second seised may bring that action before the court first seised.

[16] Sched. 3, para. 7 or r. 33A.80. Neither the taking of evidence on commission nor a separate proof relating to any preliminary plea is to be regarded as part of the proof in the action: Sched. 3, para. 4(a) or r. 33A.79(3).

[17] Sched. 3, para. 9(1) and (4) or r. 33A.82(1) and (4); there is no other sanction in respect of such failure; para. 9(4) or r. 33A.82(4).

[18] Proceedings are "continuing" at any time after they have commenced and before they have been finally disposed of — r. 33.1(3) or r. 33A.1(3).

[19] r. 33.2(2)(a) or r. 33A.2(2)(a).

(e)   such other facts as may be relevant to the question of whether or not the action before the sheriff should be sisted under Schedule 3 to the 1973 Act or Article 19 of the Council Regulation, or under Part XIII of Chapter 33A of the Ordinary Cause Rules.[20]

Where such proceedings are continuing; the action before the sheriff is defended; and either (i) the initial writ does not contain the statement anent those proceedings above referred to, or (ii) the particulars mentioned in (a) to (e) above are incomplete or incorrect, any defences or minute, as the case may be, lodged by any person to the action must include that statement and, where appropriate, the further or correct particulars.[21]

Mandatory sists

Where before the beginning of the proof in a continuing action of divorce or dissolution of civil partnership it appears to the court, on the application[22] of a party to the marriage or civil partnership, that proceedings in respect of that marriage for divorce or nullity of marriage or for dissolution or nullity of civil partnership are continuing in a related jurisdiction (*i.e.* another country within the United Kingdom[23]) and certain other conditions are satisfied, the court *must* sist the action.[24]

These other conditions are that it appears to the court:

(1)   that the parties to the marriage or civil partnership have resided together after the marriage was contracted or the civil partnership was formed or treated as having been formed within the meaning of section 1(1) of the Civil Partnership Act 2004;

(2)   that the place where they resided together when the action in the Scots court was begun (or, if they did not then reside together, where they last resided together before that date) is in that related jurisdiction; and

(3)   that either party was habitually resident in that related jurisdiction throughout the year ending with the date on which they last resided together before the action in the Scots court was begun.

---

[20] r. 33.2(2)(b) or r. 33A.2(2)(b). As to Article 19 of the Council Regulation, see n. 15 *supra*.

[21] r. 33.2(3) or r. 33A.2(3).

[22] Application for a sist or the recall of a sist under Schedule 3 to the 1973 Act must be made by written motion — r. 33.17 or r. 33A.17.

[23] Namely, England, Wales, Northern Ireland, Jersey, Guernsey (including Alderney and Stark) and the Isle of Man — para. 3(2) or r. 33A.79(2).

[24] Sched. 3, para. 8 or r. 33A.81.

Where an action has been sisted by reference to proceedings in a related jurisdiction, the Scots court loses the power to make a "relevant order" in that action, namely an interim order relating to aliment or children.[25] Any such order already made ceases to have effect three months from the date of the sisting of the action (unless the order or the sist has by then been recalled).[26] These provisions are subject to the court's power to make, or extend the duration of, a relevant order if the court considers such to be necessary "as a matter of necessity and urgency."[27]

If at the time of the sisting of the Scots action there is in force, or if thereafter there comes into force, in the proceedings elsewhere an order in relation to any of certain specified matters, that order supersedes any similar order in the Scots action that has been, or might be, made.[28] These matters are periodical payments for a spouse or party to a civil partnership, periodical payments for a child, arrangements to be made concerning with whom a child is to live, contact with a child, and any other matter relating to parental responsibilities within the meaning of section 1(3) of the Children (Scotland) Act 1995 or parental rights within the meaning of section 2(4) of that Act.

These provisions have no effect on the power of the court to make relevant orders once the sist has been recalled; to vary or recall relevant orders still in force; or to enforce any relevant order as respects any period when it is or was in force.[29]

The court may on the application of a party to the action recall a mandatory sist if it appears to the court that the proceedings elsewhere are sisted or concluded or that the prosecution of them has been unreasonably delayed.[30] Once the sist has been recalled, the rule on mandatory sists has no further application.[31]

Discretionary sists

Where before the beginning of the proof[32] in a continuing action of divorce or dissolution of civil partnership it appears to the court that there are concurrent proceedings in another jurisdiction (*i.e.* outwith the United Kingdom) the court *may* sist the action.[33]

---

[25] Sched. 3, para. 11(2)(a) or r. 33A.84(2)(a); "relevant order" is defined in para. 11(1) or r. 33A.84(1).

[26] Sched. 3, para. 11(2)(b) or r. 33A.84(2)(b).

[27] Sched. 3, para. 11(2)(c) or r. 33A.84(2)(c).

[28] Sched. 3, para. 11(3) or r. 33A.84(3), including any order judged to be necessary as a matter of necessity and urgency.

[29] Sched. 3, para. 11(4) or r. 33A.84(4).

[30] Sched. 3, para. 10(1) or r. 33A.83(1). As to the mode of application, see n. 22 *supra*.

[31] Sched. 3, para. 10(2) or r. 33A.83(2).

[32] See n. 16 *supra*.

[33] Sched. 3, para. 9(1) or r. 33A.82(1). Cf. n. 15 *supra*.

Its discretion to do so is to be exercised if it appears to the court that the balance of fairness (including convenience) as between the parties to the marriage or civil partnership is such that it is appropriate for those other proceedings to be disposed of before further steps are taken in the Scots action.[34] In considering the balance of fairness and convenience, the court requires to have regard to all factors appearing to be relevant, including the convenience of witnesses and any delay or expense which may result from the proceedings being sisted, or not being sisted.[35] The proper initial approach to the question of the balance of fairness (including convenience) is to consider the overall connection of the marriage or civil partnership with the jurisdictions in question; and if the overall connection of the marriage or civil partnership is prima facie with Scotland, the court would only be entitled to grant the sist if it were to take the view that there were, nevertheless, other circumstances by reason of which justice required that a sist should be granted.[36]

The court may on the application of a party to the action recall a discretionary sist if it appears to the court that the proceedings elsewhere are sisted or concluded or that the prosecution of them has been unreasonably delayed.[37]

MENTAL DISORDER

Mentally disordered pursuer

An insane person cannot competently pursue an action of divorce.[38] Mental disorder falling short of insanity does not of itself preclude the raising of an action of divorce; the pursuer must however have the capacity to give instructions for the raising and prosecution of the action.[39] A preliminary proof as to the pursuer's mental condition is competent; the onus on the defender to establish incapacity is a heavy one.[40]

Mentally disordered defender

In an action where the defender is a person who is suffering from a mental disorder,[41] intimation requires to be made in accordance with

---

[34] *ibid.*

[35] Sched. 3, para. 9(2) or r. 33A.82(2).

[36] *Mitchell v. Mitchell*, 1992 S.C. 372. See also *De Dampierre v. De Dampierre* [1988] A.C. 92.

[37] Sched. 3, para. 10(1) or r. 33A.83(1). As to the mode of application, see n. 22 *supra*.

[38] *Thomson v. Thomson* (1887) 14 R. 634.

[39] *Gibson v. Gibson*, 1970 S.L.T. (Notes) 60.

[40] *AB v. CB*, 1937 S.C. 408.

[41] "Mental disorder" has the meaning assigned in section 328 of the Mental Health (Care and Treatment) (Scotland) Act 2003—r. 33.1(2). In terms of s. 328(1), "mental disorder"

rule 33.7(1)(c) or rule 33A.7(1)(b); and where the defender is also resident in a hospital or other similar institution, citation requires to be effected in accordance with rule 33.13 or rule 33A.13.[42]

Rule 33.16 or rule 33A.16 applies where it appears to the court that the defender is suffering from a mental disorder. In that event, the sheriff must:

(a) appoint a curator *ad litem* to the defender;

(b) where the facts set out in section 1(2)(d) of the Divorce (Scotland) Act 1976 or section 117(3)(c) of the Civil Partnership Act 2004 (no cohabitation for one year with consent of defender to decree) are relied on —

    (i) make an order for intimation of the ground of the action to the Mental Welfare Commission for Scotland; and

    (ii) include in such an order a requirement that the Commission sends to the sheriff clerk a report indicating whether in its opinion the defender is capable of deciding whether or not to give consent to the granting of decree.[43]

---

means any—(a) mental illness; (b) personality disorder; or (c) learning disability, however caused or manifested. By virtue of s. 328(2), a person is not mentally disordered by reason only of any of the following—(a) sexual orientation; (b) sexual deviancy; (c) transsexualism; (d) transvestism; (e) dependence on, or use of, alcohol or drugs; (f) behaviour that causes, or is likely to cause, harassment, alarm or distress to any other person; (g) acting as no prudent person would act.

[42] As to r. 33.7(1)(c) or r. 33A7(1)(b), see Chap. 1 (text accompanying n. 14). Rule 33.13 or 33A.13 requires citation to be executed by registered post or the first class recorded delivery service addressed to the medical officer in charge of that hospital or institution; and there requires to be included with the copy of the initial writ —
(a) a citation in Form F15 or Form CP15;
(b) any notice required by r. 33.14(1) or r. 33A.14(1) (see Chap. 3, nn. 29 and 37 and accompanying text);
(c) a request in Form F17 or Form CP18;
(d) a form of certificate in Form F18 or Form CP19 requesting the medical officer to —
    (i) deliver and explain the initial writ, citation and any notice or form of notice of consent required under r. 33.14(1) or r. 33A.14(1) personally to the defender; or
    (ii) certify that such delivery or explanation would be dangerous to the health or mental condition of the defender; and
(e) a stamped envelope addressed for return of that certificate to the pursuer or his solicitor, if he has one.
The medical officer must send the certificate in Form F18 or Form CP19 duly completed to the pursuer or his solicitor, as the case may be, and that certificate must be attached to the certificate of citation (r. 33.13(2) and (3) or r. 33A.13(2) and (3)).
Where such a certificate bears that the initial writ has not been delivered to the defender, the sheriff may, at any time before decree —
(a) order such further medical inquiry, and
(b) make such order for further service or intimation, as he thinks fit (r. 33.13 (4) or r. 33A.13(4)).

[43] r. 33.16(2) or r. 33A.16(2).

Within seven days after the appointment of a curator *ad litem*, the pursuer must send to him —

(a) a copy of the initial writ and any defences (including any adjustments and amendments) lodged; and

(b) a copy of any notice in Form G5 sent to him by the sheriff clerk.[44]

On receipt of a report from the Commission, the sheriff clerk must —

(a) lodge the report in process; and

(b) intimate that this has been done to —

    (i) the pursuer;

    (ii) the solicitor for the defender, if known; and

    (iii) the curator *ad litem*.[45]

The curator *ad litem* requires to lodge in process within 14 days after the report of the Commission has been lodged in process or, where no such report is required, within 21 days after the date of his appointment, one of the following:

(a) a notice of intention to defend;

(b) defences to the action;

(c) a minute adopting defences already lodged; or

(d) a minute stating that the curator *ad litem* does not intend to lodge defences.[46]

Notwithstanding that he has lodged a minute stating that he does not intend to lodge defences, a curator *ad litem* may appear at any stage of the action to protect the interests of the defender.[47] If, at any time, it appears to the curator *ad litem* that the defender is not suffering from mental disorder, he may report that fact to the court and seek his own discharge.[48]

The pursuer is responsible, in the first instance, for payment of the fees and outlays of the curator *ad litem* incurred during the period from his appointment until —

(a) he lodges a minute stating that he does not intend to lodge defences;

(b) he decides to instruct the lodging of defences or a minute adopting defences already lodged; or

(c) being satisfied after investigation that the defender is not suffering from mental disorder, he is discharged.[49]

---

[44] r. 33.16(3) or r. 33A.16(3).

[45] r. 33.16(4) or r. 33A.16(4).

[46] r. 33.16(5) and (6) or r. 33A.16(5) and (6).

[47] r. 33.16(7) or r. 33A.16(7).

[48] r. 33.16(8) or r. 33A.16(8).

[49] r. 33.16(9) or r. 33A.16(9).

The effect of mental disorder on the use of affidavit procedure and the simplified procedure is noted in Chapter 1.[50]

PUBLICITY OF PROCEEDINGS[51]

Section 1(1) of the Judicial Proceedings (Regulation of Reports) Act 1926 provides:

"It shall not be lawful[52] to print or publish, or cause or procure to be printed or published—

(a) in relation to any judicial proceedings any indecent matter or indecent medical, surgical or physiological details being matters or details the publication of which would be calculated to injure public morals;

(b) in relation to any judicial proceedings for dissolution of marriage, any particulars other than the following, that is to say:—

  (i) the names, addresses and occupations of the parties and witnesses;

  (ii) a concise statement of the charges, defences and counter-charges in support of which evidence has been given;

  (iii) submissions on any point of law arising in the course of the proceedings, and the decision of the court thereon;

  (iv) the summing-up of the judge and the finding of the jury (if any) and the judgment of the court and observations made by the judge in giving judgment:

Provided that nothing in this part of this subsection shall be held to permit the publication of anything contrary to the provisions of paragraph (a) of this subsection."

---

[50] See Chap. 1, text accompanying nn. 38 and 61.

[51] See also Chap. 6, n. 32.

[52] The Act does not apply to material printed or published for purposes of judicial proceedings, nor to bona fide law reports, nor to publications "of a technical character bona fide intended for circulation among members of the legal or medical professions" — s. 1(4). No person, other than a proprietor, editor, master printer or publisher, is liable to be convicted under it — s. 1(2). The Act does not give a divorce litigant any civil law right to recover damages for its breach – *Nicol v. Caledonian Newspapers Ltd,* 2003 S.L.T. 109.

CHAPTER 3

THE MERITS

The grounds upon which the court may grant decree for divorce or the dissolution of a civil partnership, namely (a) the irretrievable breakdown of the marriage or civil partnership; or (b) the issue of an interim gender recognition certificate under the Gender Recognition Act 2004, are examined in this chapter. The court's powers in certain cases of irretrievable breakdown to postpone the grant of decree are considered first.

POSTPONEMENT OF DECREE

Reconciliation

One of the aims of the Divorce (Scotland) Act 1976, according to its long title, is to "facilitate reconciliation of the parties in consistorial causes."

To that end the court is empowered in appropriate cases to continue any pending action of divorce for such period as it thinks proper to enable attempts to be made to effect reconciliation (and any co-habitation during this period is disregarded for the purposes of that action).[1] A similar provision exists with respect to actions for dissolution of civil partnership.[2]

Religious impediment to remarriage

Notwithstanding that irretrievable breakdown of a marriage has been established in an action of divorce, the court may—(a) on the application of a party; and (b) if satisfied—(i) that the applicant is prevented from entering into a religious marriage[3] by virtue of a requirement of the religion of that marriage; and the other party can

---

[1] Divorce (Scotland) Act 1976, s. 2(1).

[2] Civil Partnership Act 2004, s. 118.

[3] "Religious marriage" means a marriage solemnised by a marriage celebrant of a prescribed religious body, and "religion of that marriage" is construed accordingly—1976 Act, s. 3A(7), as inserted by the Family Law (Scotland) Act 2006, s. 15. Any Hebrew Congregation is a religious body for the purposes of s. 3A(7) by virtue of regulation 2 of The Divorce (Religious Bodies) (Scotland) Regulations 2006 (S.S.I. 2006 No. 253). A marriage celebrant of a prescribed religious body is a reference to—(a) a minister,

act so as to remove, or enable or contribute to the removal of, the impediment which prevents that marriage; and (ii) that it is just and reasonable to do so, postpone the grant of decree until it is satisfied that the other party has so acted.[4]

The court may, whether or not on the application of a party, recall such a postponement and may, before doing so, order the other party to produce a certificate from a relevant religious body confirming that the other party has acted as above described.[5]

IRRETRIEVABLE BREAKDOWN

In an action for divorce, on the application of the pursuer,[6] the court may grant decree if it is established[7] that the marriage has broken down irretrievably.[8] Likewise, in an action for dissolution of a civil partnership, on the application of the pursuer, the court may grant decree if it is established[7] that the civil partnership has broken down irretrievably.[9]

In terms of section 1(2) of the Divorce (Scotland) Act 1976, the irretrievable breakdown of a marriage is taken to be established in an action of divorce if—

---

clergyman, pastor or priest of such a body; (b) a person who has, on the nomination of such a body, been registered under section 9 of the Marriage (Scotland) Act 1977 as empowered to solemnise marriages; or (c) any person who is recognised by such a body as entitled to solemnise marriages on its behalf—1976 Act, s. 3A(8), as inserted by the Family Law (Scotland) Act 2006, s. 15.

[4] 1976 Act, s. 3A(1), (2) and (3), as inserted by the Family Law (Scotland) Act 2006, s. 15. Any application for such postponement must be made by minute in the process to which the application relates—r. 33.27A.

[5] 1976 Act, s. 3A(4) and (5), as inserted by the Family Law (Scotland) Act 2006, s. 15. A religious body is "relevant" for these purposes if the applicant considers the body competent to provide the aforesaid confirmation—1976 Act, s. 3A(6), as inserted by the Family Law (Scotland) Act 2006, s. 15. Any application for recall of such postponement must be made by minute in the process to which the application relates—r. 33.27A.

[6] A counter claim for divorce is incompetent (*Farley v. Farley,* 1990 S.C. 279).

[7] The onus of proving irretrievable breakdown is on the pursuer – *Paterson v. Paterson,* 1938 S.C. 251 at p. 256; *Ross v. Ross,* 1997 S.L.T. (Sh. Ct.) 51 at p. 53. The evidence establishing the grounds must consist of or include evidence other than that of a party to the marriage or civil partnership – Civil Evidence (Scotland) Act 1988, s. 8(3), (3A) and (4), as amended by the 2004 Act, Sched. 28, para. 55. The court has power to allow futher proof in the event of failure to lead evidence from a witness other than the parties – *Symanski v. Symanski,* 2005 Fam. L.R. 6. The standard of proof required to establish the ground of action is on the balance of probability – 1976 Act, s. 1(6); 2004 Act, s. 117(8).

[8] 1976 Act, s. 1(1)(a).

[9] 2004 Act s. 117(2)(a).

"(a) since the date of the marriage the defender has committed adultery; or

(b) since the date of the marriage the defender has at any time behaved (whether or not as a result of mental abnormality and whether such behaviour has been active or passive) in such a way that the pursuer cannot reasonably be expected to cohabit with the defender; or

(d) there has been no cohabitation between the parties at any time during a continuous period of one year after the date of the marriage and immediately preceding the bringing of the action and the defender consents to the granting of decree of divorce; or

(e) there has been no cohabitation between the parties at any time during a continuous period of two years after the date of the marriage and immediately preceding the bringing of the action."

In terms of section 117(3) of the Civil Partnership Act 2004, the irretrievable breakdown of a civil partnership is taken to be established in an action for the dissolution of a civil partnership if—

"(a) since the date of registration of the civil partnership the defender has at any time behaved (whether or not as a result of mental abnormality and whether such behaviour has been active or passive) in such a way that the pursuer cannot reasonably be expected to cohabit with the defender; or

(c) there has been no cohabitation between the civil partners at any time during a continuous period of one year after the date of registration of the civil partnership and immediately preceding the bringing of the action and the defender consents to the granting of decree of dissolution of the civil partnership; or

(d) there has been no cohabitation between the civil partners at any time during a continuous period of two years after that date and immediately preceding the bringing of the action."

Each of the foregoing grounds is considered in turn.

Adultery

Adultery is:

"sexual intercourse or carnal connexion between a consenting spouse and a member of the opposite sex who is not the other spouse ..."[10]

---

[10] *MacLennan v. MacLennan*, 1958 S.C. 105 at p. 109.

One act of adultery is sufficient. How the offended spouse responds to it or perceives it is immaterial.[11] Whether or not the marriage partners were cohabiting at the time is irrelevant. Good faith (*e.g.* committing adultery in the genuine belief that the marriage partner is dead) is not a defence.[12]

Adminicles of evidence relevant to proof of adultery include admissions of adultery,[13] "opportunity plus",[14] diaries and letters,[15] fathering or mothering a child by a third party[16] and other sexual behaviour on the part of the offending spouse.[17]

Irretrievable breakdown is not to be taken to be established if the adultery has been connived at in such a way as to raise the defence of *lenocinium*.[18] The essence of this defence is that the pursuer has actively promoted the adultery in question.[19]

Irretrievable breakdown is also not to be taken to be established if the adultery has been condoned by the pursuer's cohabitation with the defender in the knowledge or belief that the defender has committed the adultery; and adultery will not be held to have been so condoned by reason only of the fact that after the commission of the adultery the pursuer has continued or resumed cohabitation with the defender, provided that the pursuer has not cohabited with the defender at any time after the end of the period of three months from the date on which cohabitation was continued or resumed with the aforesaid knowledge or belief.[20]

Intimation of an adultery action and of an adultery allegation falls to be made in accordance with rules 33.7(1)(b) and 33.15(3), respectively.[21]

Behaviour

The question as to whether the pursuer can reasonably be expected to cohabit with the defender is a question as to the position at the date of

---

[11] *Stewart v. Stewart*, 1987 S.L.T. (Sh. Ct.) 48 at p. 50.
[12] *Hunter v. Hunter* (1900) 2 F 774.
[13] *Sinclair v. Sinclair*, 1986 S.L.T. (Sh. Ct.) 54 at p. 56.
[14] *Hannah v. Hannah*, 1931 S.C. 275 (shared hotel bedroom); *Hall v. Hall*, 1958 S.C. 206 (late night home visits).
[15] *Creasey v. Creasey*, 1931 S.C. 9 and *Argyll v. Argyll*, 1963 S.L.T. (Notes) 42 (diary); *Rattray v. Rattray* (1897) 25 R 315 (letter).
[16] *MacKay v. MacKay*, 1946 S.C. 78 (wife having child by another man); *Campbell v. Campbell* (1860) 23 D 99 (husband having child by another woman).
[17] *Collins v. Collins* (1884) 11 R (H.L.) 19 at pp. 29, 33 (condoned adultery); *Whyte v. Whyte* (1884) 11 R 710 (husband behaving indecently towards another woman); *Wilson v. Wilson*, 1955 S.L.T. (Notes) 81 (wife embracing another man).
[18] 1976 Act, s. 1(3).
[19] Scottish Law Commission, *Report on Family Law* (Scot. Law Com. No. 135, 1992), para. 13.2. An example is where the husband has encouraged the wife to prostitute herself (*Marshall v. Marshall* (1881) 8 R 702).
[20] 1976 Act, ss. 1(3) and 2(2).
[21] See Chap. 1, text accompanying nn. 12 and 27.

proof and the court is entitled to take into account the pursuer's circumstances at that date and the changes that will have occurred in the parties' lives since they separated.[22] Irretrievable breakdown is however only to be taken to be established where the fact that the pursuer cannot reasonably be expected to cohabit with the defender flows, in a causal sense, from the nature of the relevant behaviour of the defender.[23]

Whereas

> "adultery is based on objective fact and affords a ground for divorce however the offended spouse responds to it or perceives it … in relation to s. 1(2)(b) of the 1976 Act, the effective question is how the offended spouse could reasonably be expected to react to specific behaviour on the part of the other spouse".[24]

The more obvious examples of behaviour establishing irretrievable breakdown include habitual abuse of alcohol or drugs, violence directed at the pursuer (including attempted and threatened violence) and extra-marital sexual activity.[25] Relevant conduct may be persistent, or cumulative, or (exceptionally) neither:

> "… conduct on the part of a defender, by word or act, may be of such a nature that even if there is no risk of a repetition it is so destructive of a marriage relationship as to make it unreasonable to expect the pursuer to cohabit with the defender."[26]

Where the defender has been convicted of a criminal offence upon which the pursuer wishes to found (*e.g.* assault upon her), she may rely upon section 10 of the Law Reform (Miscellaneous Provisions) (Scotland) Act 1968 to establish the commission of the offence:

> "(1) In any civil proceedings, the fact that a person has been convicted of an offence by or before any court in the United

---

[22] *Findlay v. Findlay*, 1991 S.L.T. 457.

[23] *Findlay v. Findlay*, 1991 S.L.T. 457. See also *Knox v. Knox*, 1993 S.C.L.R. 381 and *Smith v. Smith*, 1994 S.C.L.R. 244.

[24] *Stewart v. Stewart*, 1987 S.L.T. (Sh. Ct.) 48 at p. 50 (admission of extra-marital "association" after persistent late homecoming justified divorce).

[25] Where the pursuer founds upon an alleged association between the defender and another named person, r. 33.8 or r. 33A.8 applies. See Chap. 1, text accompanying nn. 31–34.

[26] *Hastie v. Hastie*, 1985 S.L.T. 146 at p. 148 (false accusations of infidelity and of an incestuous association).

Kingdom or by a court-martial there or elsewhere shall ... be admissible in evidence for the purpose of proving, where to do so is relevant to any issue in those proceedings, that he committed that offence, whether or not he was so convicted upon a plea of guilty or otherwise and whether or not he is a party to the civil proceedings; but no conviction other than a subsisting one shall be admissible in evidence by virtue of this section.

(2) In any civil proceedings in which by virtue of this section a person is proved to have been convicted of an offence by or before any court in the United Kingdom or by a court-martial there or elsewhere —

    (a) he shall be taken to have committed that offence unless the contrary is proved, and

    (b) without prejudice to the reception of any other admissible evidence for the purpose of identifying the facts which constituted that offence, the contents of any document which is admissible as evidence of the conviction, and the contents of the complaint, information, indictment or charge-sheet on which the person was convicted, shall be admissible in evidence for that purpose ...

(4) Where in any civil proceedings the contents of any document are admissible in evidence by virtue of subsection (2) of this section, a copy of that document, or of the material part thereof, purporting to be certified or otherwise authenticated by or on behalf of the court or authority having custody of that document, shall be admissible in evidence and shall be taken to be a true copy of that document or part unless the contrary is shown ..."

Non-cohabitation

In cases of one year's non-cohabitation with the defender's consent to the granting of decree and of two years' non-cohabitation, it must be averred and proved that the parties have not cohabited for the requisite period of time.[27]

In considering whether or not a period of non-cohabitation has been continuous no account is to be taken of any period (or periods) not

---

[27] An action raised before the expiry of the requisite period of non-cohabitation is "manifestly groundless" — *Matthews v. Matthews*, 1985 S.L.T. (Sh. Ct.) 68. Conversion of an action, whether for divorce or for dissolution of civil partnership, based on other grounds, to a one-year or two-year action by amendment after the expiry of the requisite period of non-cohabitation is competent — *Duncan v. Duncan*, 1986 S.L.T. 17.

exceeding six months in all during which the parties cohabited with one another, any such period (or periods) however not counting as part of the period of non-cohabitation.[28]

Ordinary cause rules 33.14 or 33A.14 and 33.18 or 33A.18 provide the machinery for the giving and the withdrawal of consent to the granting of decree of divorce or dissolution of a civil partnership.

The pursuer requires to attach to the copy initial writ served upon the defender a notice in Form F19 or Form CP20 and a notice of consent in Form F20 or Form CP21.[29] The defender thereafter indicates to the court his consent by giving notice in writing in Form F20 or Form CP21 to the sheriff clerk.[30] The evidence of one witness is sufficient for the purpose of establishing that the signature on the notice of consent is that of the defender.[31]

The defender is entitled to withdraw his consent at any time and for any reason. Where the initial writ contains an averment that the defender consents to the grant of decree, he may give notice in writing to the court that he has not consented to decree being granted or that he withdraws any consent which he has already given.[32] Where he does so, the sheriff clerk must intimate the terms of the letter to the pursuer who is required within 14 days after the date of the intimation, if none of the other facts mentioned in section 1(2) of the Divorce (Scotland) Act 1976 (or section 117(3) of the Civil Partnership Act 2004, as the case may be) is averred in the initial writ, to lodge a motion for the action to be sisted.[33] If no such motion is lodged, the pursuer shall be deemed to have abandoned the action and the action must be dismissed.[34] If the motion is granted and the sist is not recalled or renewed within a period of six months from the date of the interlocutor granting the sist, the pursuer is deemed to have abandoned

---

[28] 1976 Act, s. 2(4) and 2004 Act, s. 119(3). *C.f.* s. 13(2) of the 1976 Act (parties to a marriage held to cohabit with one another only when they are in fact living together as man and wife, and cohabitation to be construed accordingly).

[29] r. 33.14(1)(a)(i) and r. 33A.14(1)(a)(i). The certificate of citation must state which notice or form has been attached in the initial writ — r. 33.14(2) and r. 33A.14(2). See also text accompanying Chap. 1, n. 2.

[30] r. 33.18(1) and 33A.18(1). The defender is free to deliver the notice of consent personally or have an intermediary (*e.g.* the pursuer's solicitor) deliver it — *Taylor v. Taylor*, 1988 S.C.L.R. 60. Where a defender sought to indicate his consent in oral evidence, decree was refused in *Rodgers v. Rodgers*, 1994 S.C.L.R. 750.

[31] r. 33.18(2) and 33A.18(2). It has been held that where a lengthy period of time has elapsed since the date of the defender's signature the sheriff has a discretion as to whether or not to treat the consent form as valid — *Donnelly v. Donnelly*, 1991 S.L.T. (Sh. Ct.) 9.

[32] r. 33.18(3) and r. 33A.18(3).

[33] r. 33.18(4) and (5) and r. 33A.18(4) and (5).

[34] r. 33.18(6) and r. 33A.18(6).

the action and the action must be dismissed.[35] In any case where the defender has not given or has withdrawn his consent, it is incompetent or at least inappropriate for the court to pronounce any interlocutor in the process, save as already mentioned.[36]

The pursuer in a two-year case requires to send with the copy initial writ served upon the defender a notice as nearly as may be in terms of Form F23 or Form CP24.[37]

INTERIM GENDER RECOGNITION CERTIFICATE

In an action for divorce the court may grant decree if an interim gender recognition certificate under the Gender Recognition Act 2004 has, after the date of the marriage, been issued to either party of the marriage.[38] Likewise, in an action for dissolution of a civil partnership the court may grant decree if an interim gender recognition certificate has, after the date of the registration of the civil partnership, been issued to either of the civil partners.[39]

A gender recognition certificate is issued by the Gender Recognition Panel upon an application under section 1(1) of the Act. Such an application may be made by a person of either gender who is aged at

---

[35] r. 33.18(7) and r. 33A.18(7).

[36] *Boyle v. Boyle*, 1977 S.L.T. (Notes) 69.

[37] r. 33.14(1)(b)(i) and r. 33A.14(1)(b)(i). The certificate of citation must state which notice or form has been attached to the initial writ — r. 33.14(2) and r. 33A.14(2). See also text accompanying Chap. 1, n. 2.

[38] 1976 Act, s. 1(1)(b). Unless the sheriff otherwise directs, a warrant of citation shall not be granted without there being produced with the initial writ—(a) where the pursuer is the subject of the interim gender recognition certificate, the interim gender recognition certificate or, failing that, a certified copy of the interim gender recognition certificate; or (b) where the pursuer is the spouse of the person who is the subject of the interim gender recognition certificate, a certified copy of the interim gender recognition certificate (r. 33.9A(1) and (2)). For the purposes of the foregoing, a certified copy of an interim gender recognition certificate shall be a copy of that certificate sealed with the seal of the Gender Recognition Panels and certified to be a true copy by an officer authorised by the President of Gender Recognition Panels (r. 33.9A(3)).

[39] Civil Partnership Act 2004, s. 117(2)(b). Unless the sheriff otherwise directs, a warrant of citation shall not be granted without there being produced with the initial writ—(a) where the pursuer is the subject of the interim gender recognition certificate, the interim gender recognition certificate or, failing that, a certified copy of the interim gender recognition certificate; or (b) where the pursuer is the civil partner of the person who is the subject of the interim gender recognition certificate, a certified copy of the interim gender recognition certificate (r. 33A.9(1) and (2)). For the purposes of the foregoing, a certified copy of an interim gender recognition certificate shall be a copy of that certificate sealed with the seal of the Gender Recognition Panels and certified to be a true copy by an officer authorised by the President of Gender Recognition Panels (r. 33A.9(4)).

least 18 on the basis of (a) living in the other gender; or (b) having changed gender under the law of a country or territory outside the United Kingdom.[40] Unless the applicant is married or a civil partner, any certificate so issued is to be a full gender recognition certificate.[41] If the applicant is married or a civil partner, the certificate is to be an interim gender recognition certificate.[42]

A court which grants a decree of divorce or a decree of dissolution of a civil partnership on the ground that an interim gender recognition certificate has been issued to a party to the marriage or the civil partnership must, on doing so, issue a full gender recognition certificate to that party and send a copy to the Secretary of State.[43]

---

[40] Gender Recognition Act 2004, s. 1(1).
[41] 2004 Act, s. 4(1) and (2), as amended by the Civil Partnership Act 2004, s. 250(2)(b).
[42] 2004 Act, s. 4(1) and (3), as amended by the Civil Partnership Act 2004, s. 250(2)(b).
[43] 2004 Act, ss. 5(1)(b) and 5A(1)(b), as amended by the Civil Partnership Act 2004, s. 250(4).

CHAPTER 4

PROTECTIVE MEASURES

In this chapter various measures for the protection of a party's position in an action of divorce or dissolution of a civil partnership are discussed. These range in importance and effect from the accommodation address to interdicts and interim exclusion orders.

ACCOMMODATION ADDRESS

Where the pursuer does not wish to disclose her whereabouts to the defender, she may be designed as care of her solicitors in the instance of the initial writ. Use of an accommodation address is however a privilege, for, when a party's true address is not given, he is not properly designed, and accordingly the initial writ is not properly framed.[1]

There are circumstances in which the court will allow the use of an accommodation address (*e.g.* where there would otherwise be a risk of abuse); facts to justify the privilege must however be fully stated in the initial writ.[2] Application may be made to the court by motion to ordain a party using an accommodation address to reveal his or her true address.[3]

INTERDICTS

The court may grant interdicts in the context of actions for divorce ('matrimonial interdicts') or dissolution of civil partnership ('relevant interdicts').

An interdict is a matrimonial interdict if it is:

"an interdict including an interim interdict which —
    (a)   restrains or prohibits any conduct of one spouse towards the other spouse or a child of the family,[4] or

---

[1] *Doughton v. Doughton*, 1958 S.L.T. (Notes) 34.
[2] *ibid.*
[3] As in *Stein v. Stein*, 1936 S.L.T. 103.
[4] "Child of the family" includes any child or grandchild of either spouse, and any person who has been brought up or treated by either spouse as if he were a child of that spouse,

    (b)   prohibits a spouse from entering or remaining in—
- (i)   a matrimonial home;[5]
- (ii) any other residence occupied by the applicant spouse;
- (iii) any place of work of the applicant spouse;
- (iv) any school attended by a child in the permanent or temporary care of the applicant spouse."[6]

An interdict is a relevant interdict if it is:

"an interdict, including an interim interdict, which—
    (a)   restrains or prohibits any conduct of one civil partner towards the other civil partner or a child of the family,[7] or
    (b)   prohibits a civil partner from entering or remaining in—
- (i)   a family home;[8]

---

whatever the age of such a child, grandchild or person may be—Matrimonial Homes (Family Protection) (Scotland) Act 1981, s. 22, as amended by the Children (Scotland) Act 1995, s. 105(4) and Sched. 4, para. 30.

[5] "Matrimonial home" means any house, caravan, houseboat or other structure which has been provided or has been made available by one or both of the spouses as, or has become, a family residence and includes any garden or other ground or building usually occupied with, or otherwise required for the amenity or convenience of, the house, caravan, houseboat or other structure but does not include a residence provided or made available by a person for one spouse to reside in, whether with any child of the family or not, separately from the other spouse—1981 Act, s. 22, as amended by the Law Reform (Miscellaneous Provisions) (Scotland) Act 1985, s. 13(10) and the Family Law (Scotland) Act 2006, s. 9 and Sched. 3. If the tenancy of a matrimonial home is transferred from one spouse to the other by agreement or under any enactment, and following the transfer, the spouse to whom the tenancy was transferred occupies the home but the other spouse does not, the home shall, on such transfer, cease to be a matrimonial home—1981 Act, s. 22, as amended by the 2006 Act, s. 9.

[6] Matrimonial Homes (Family Protection) (Scotland) Act 1981, s. 14(2), as amended by the Family Law (Scotland) Act 2006, s. 10. "Applicant spouse" means the spouse who has applied for the interdict; and "non-applicant spouse" is to be construed accordingly—1981 Act, s. 14(6), as inserted by the Family Law (Scotland) Act 2006, s. 10(3).

[7] "Child of the family" means any child or grandchild of either civil partner, and any person who has been brought up or treated by either civil partner as if the person were a child of that partner, whatever the age of such a child, grandchild or person, and "family" means the civil partners in the civil partnership, together with any child, grandchild or person so treated by them—Civil Partnership Act 2004, s. 101(7), as amended by the Family Law (Scotland) Act 2006, Sched. 1, para. 3.

[8] "Family home" means any house, caravan, houseboat or other structure which has been provided or has been made available by one or both of the civil partners as, or has become, a family residence and includes any garden or other ground or building usually occupied with, or otherwise required for the amenity or convenience of, the house, caravan, houseboat or other structure but does not include a residence provided or made available by a person for one civil partner to reside in, whether with any child of the family or not, separately from the other civil partner—2004 Act, s. 135, as amended by the Family Law

    (ii) any other residence occupied by the applicant civil partner;

    (iii) any place of work of the applicant civil partner;

    (iv) any school attended by a child in the permanent or temporary care of the applicant civil partner."[9]

If the non-applicant spouse is an entitled spouse or has occupancy rights, the court may only grant a matrimonial interdict prohibiting him or her from entering or remaining in the matrimonial home if the interdict is ancillary to an exclusion order or by virtue of s. 1(3) of the Matrimonial Homes (Family Protection) (Scotland) Act 1981 the court refuses leave to exercise occupancy rights.[10]

If the non-applicant civil partner is an entitled partner or has occupancy rights, the court may only grant a relevant interdict prohibiting him or her from entering or remaining in the family home if the interdict is ancillary to an exclusion order or by virtue of s. 101(4) of the Civil Partnership Act 2004 the court refuses leave to exercise occupancy rights.[11]

The terms of any matrimonial or relevant interdict must be no wider than are necessary to curb the illegal actings complained of, and so precise and clear that the person interdicted is left in no doubt what he is forbidden to do[12]; and must be justified by the applicant's pleadings.[13]

Where there is no information of a wrong actually being committed by the defender against the pursuer, there must be reasonable apprehension that the defender may, in the future, do the illegal acts which the pursuer seeks to have him restrained from doing in her crave.[14]

(Scotland) Act 2006, Sched. 1, para. 12. If the tenancy of a family home is transferred from one civil partner to the other by agreement or under any enactment, and following the transfer, the civil partner to whom the tenancy was transferred occupies the home but the other civil partner does not, the home shall, on such transfer, cease to be a family home—*ibid.*

[9] Civil Partnership Act 2004, s. 113(2), as amended by the Family Law (Scotland) Act 2006, Sched. 1, para. 8. "Applicant civil partner" means the civil partner who has applied for the interdict; and "non-applicant civil partner" is to be construed accordingly—2004 Act, s. 113(6), as inserted by the 2006 Act, Sched. 1, para. 8.

[10] Matrimonial Homes (Family Protection) (Scotland) Act 1981, s. 14(3), (4) and (5), as inserted by the Family Law (Scotland) Act 2006, s. 10(3). As to the meaning of "non-applicant spouse" see n. 6 *supra.*

[11] Civil Partnership 2004, s. 113(3), (4) and (5), as inserted by the Family Law (Scotland) Act 2006, Sched. 1, para. 8. As to the meaning of "non-applicant civil partner", see n. 9 *supra.*

[12] *Murdoch v. Murdoch*, 1973 S.L.T. (Notes) 13.

[13] See, *e.g. McKenna v. McKenna*, 1984 S.L.T. (Sh. Ct.) 92.

[14] *Bailey v. Bailey*, 1987 S.C.L.R. 1 at p. 4.

In any application for perpetual interdict, whether or not the action is defended, it is the duty of the court to exercise a sound judicial discretion in deciding whether interdict should be granted; and such grant can only be made on strong or at least reasonable grounds.[15]

Breach of interdict

When an interim interdict is claimed to have been breached, a minute may be lodged containing detailed averments in support of a crave for the court to ordain the defender to appear at the bar to explain his actings.[16] A breach of interdict constitutes a contempt of court which may lead to punishment, and it is necessary in the interests of fairness that the alleged contempt should be clearly and distinctly averred and that the proceedings for contempt be confined to the averments.[17]

Such a minute may be presented with the concurrence of the procurator fiscal concerned with any criminal proceedings which may be taken as a result of the actings in question.[18] If the alleged breach is denied, answers may be ordered and a proof held. The standard of proof is proof beyond reasonable doubt.[19] Proceedings for breach of interdict are civil proceedings to which section 1 of the Civil Evidence (Scotland) Act 1988 applies.[20] If the breach is admitted or proved, the defender is liable to punishment by fine or imprisonment.[21]

Where perpetual interdict is claimed to have been breached, procedure is by way of initial writ.[22] Proceedings taken by way of initial writ for breach of interdict are civil proceedings to which the appeal provisions of the Sheriff Courts (Scotland) Act 1907 apply.[23]

---

[15] *Bailey v. Bailey*, 1987 S.C.L.R. 1; *Cunningham v. Cunningham,* 2001 Fam.L.R. 12; *S v. Q,* 2005 S.L.T. 53 (see also *Gunn v. Gunn*, 1955 S.L.T. (Notes) 69 and *Morton v. Morton,* 1996 G.W.D. 22–1276).

[16] See *Gribben v. Gribben*, 1976 S.L.T. 266. Note that an interim interdict ceases to be operative when the action ceases to be pending (*Stewart v. Stallard*, 1995 S.C.L.R. 167).

[17] *Byrne v. Ross*, 1992 S.C. 498.

[18] *Gribben v. Gribben*, 1976 S.L.T. 266.

[19] *Gribben v. Gribben*, 1976 S.L.T. 266.

[20] *Byrne v. Ross*, 1992 S.C. 498.

[21] *Byrne v. Ross*, 1992 S.C. 498. In *Forbes v. Forbes*, 1993 S.C. 271, at p. 275, the Inner House observed that it is proper not to call on the minuter in hearing submissions as to penalty, except with respect to matters of competency.

[22] *Forbes v. Forbes*, 1993 S.C. 271.

[23] *Maciver v. Maciver*, 1996 S.L.T. 733.

POWERS OF ARREST

In the case of an interdict which is—

(a) a matrimonial interdict which is ancillary to (i) an exclusion order within the meaning of section 4(1) of the Matrimonial Homes (Family Protection) (Scotland) Act 1981; or (ii) an interim order under section 4(6) of the 1981 Act; or

(b) a relevant interdict which is ancillary to (i) an exclusion order within the meaning of 104(1) of the Civil Partnership Act 2004; or (ii) an interim order under section 104(6) of the 2004 Act,

the court must, on an application under section 1 of the Protection from Abuse (Scotland) Act 2001, attach a power of arrest to the interdict.[24]

In the case of any other interdict, the court must, on such application, attach a power of arrest to the interdict if satisfied that—(a) the interdicted person has been given the opportunity to be heard by, or represented before, the court; and (b) attaching the power of arrest is necessary to protect the applicant from a risk of abuse in breach of the interdict.[25]

Application for attachment of a power of arrest to an interdict requires to be made by way of crave in the initial writ or defences in which the interdict to which it relates is applied for, or, if made after the application for interdict, by motion in the process of the action in which interdict was sought, or by minute, with answers if appropriate, should the sheriff so order.[26]

The court, on attaching a power of arrest, must specify a date of expiry for the power, being a date not later than three years after the date when the power is attached.[27]

A power of arrest comes into effect only when it has been served on the interdicted person along with such documents as may be prescribed.[28] In terms of r. 41.2(2), where the sheriff attaches a power of arrest to an interdict as aforesaid, the documents to be served on the interdicted person are the following:

(a) a copy of the application for interdict;

---

[24] Protection from Abuse (Scotland) Act 2001, s. 1(1) and (1A), as amended by the Family Law (Scotland) Act 2006, s. 32(1) and (2).

[25] 2001 Act, s. 1(1) and (2), as amended by the 2006 Act, s. 32(1) and (3). Intimation is also required in terms of r. 41.2(1)(b). "Abuse" includes violence, harassment, threatening conduct, and any other conduct giving rise, or likely to give rise, to physical or mental injury, fear, alarm or distress; and "conduct" includes – (a) speech; and (b) presence in a specified place or area – 2001 Act, s. 7.

[26] r. 41.2(1)(a).

[27] 2001 Act, s. 1(3).

[28] 2001 Act, s. 2(1).

(b)   a copy of the interlocutor granting interdict;

(c)   where the application to attach the power of arrest was made after the interdict was granted, a copy of the certificate of service of the interdict.

As soon as possible after a power of arrest has been served, the person who obtained it, or such other person as may be prescribed, must deliver such documents as may be prescribed to the chief constable of any police area in which the relevant interdict has effect.[29] In terms of r. 41.2(3), after the power of arrest has been served, the documents to be delivered by the person who obtained the power of arrest to the chief constable are the following:

(a)   a copy of the application for interdict;

(b)   a copy of the interlocutor granting interdict;

(c)   a copy of the certificate of service of the interdict; and

(d)   where the application to attach the power of arrest was made after the interdict was granted—

    (i)   a copy of the application for the power of arrest;

    (ii)   a copy of the interlocutor granting it;

    (iii) a copy of the certificate of service of the power of arrest and the documents that required to be served along with it.

Such person must, after such compliance, lodge in process a certificate of delivery in Form PA1.[30]

A power of arrest ceases to have effect—(a) on the date of expiry specified by the court; (b) when it is recalled by the court; or (c) when the interdict to which the power is attached is varied or recalled whichever is the earliest.[31]

The duration of a power of arrest must, on the application of the person who obtained it, be extended by the court, if satisfied that—(a) the interdicted person has been given an opportunity to be heard by, or represented before, the court, and (b) the extension is necessary to protect the applicant from a risk of abuse in breach of the interdict.[32] Such application falls to be made by minute in the process of the action in which the power of arrest was attached.[33]

The court, on extending or further extending the duration of a power of arrest, must specify a new date of expiry for the power,

---

[29] 2001 Act, s. 3(1). "Relevant interdict" means the interdict to which the power of arrest is or was attached—2001 Act, s. 3(2).

[30] r. 41.5.

[31] 2001 Act, s. 2(2).

[32] 2001 Act, s. 2(3).

[33] r. 41.3(1).

being a date not later than three years after the date when the extension is granted.[34]

Where the duration of a power of arrest has been extended, or further extended, the extension or further extension comes into effect only when it has been served on the interdicted person along with such documents as may be prescribed.[35] In terms of r. 41.3(2), when the sheriff extends the duration of a power of arrest, the person who obtained the extension must deliver a copy of the interlocutor granting the extension to the chief constable of any police area in which the interdict has effect. Such person must, after such compliance, lodge in process a certificate of delivery in Form PA1.[36]

A power of arrest must be recalled by the court if—(a) the person who obtained it applies for recall; or (b) the interdicted person applies for recall and the court is satisfied that—(i) the person who obtained the power has been given an opportunity to be heard by, or represented before, the court; and (ii) the power is no longer necessary to protect that person from a risk of abuse in breach of the interdict.[37] Such application requires to be made by minute in the process of the action in which the power of arrest was attached.[38]

In terms of r. 41.3(2), where the sheriff recalls a power of arrest, the person who obtained the recall must deliver a copy of the interlocutor recalling the interdict to the chief constable of any police area in which the relevant interdict has effect.

Where an interdict to which a power of arrest has been attached is varied or recalled, the person who obtained the variation or recall must deliver a copy of the interlocutor varying or recalling the interdict to the chief constable of any police area in which the interdict has effect.[39] Such person must, after such compliance, lodge in process a certificate of delivery in Form PA1.[40]

Where a power of arrest attached to an interdict has effect a constable may arrest the interdicted person without warrant if the constable— (a) has reasonable cause for suspecting that person of being in breach of interdict; and (b) considers that there would, if that person were not arrested, be a risk of abuse or further abuse by that person in breach of the interdict.[41]

---

[34] 2001 Act, s. 2(4) and (6).
[35] 2001 Act, s. 2(5) and (6).
[36] r. 41.5.
[37] 2001 Act, s.2(7).
[38] r. 41.3(1).
[39] r. 41.4.
[40] r. 41.5.
[41] 2001 Act, s. 4(1). Police powers and procedure thereafter are set forth in ss. 4(2) to (6) and 5.

INTERIM EXCLUSION ORDERS[42]

Where there is an entitled and a non-entitled spouse,[43] or where both spouses are entitled, or permitted by a third party, to occupy a matrimonial home,[44] either spouse, whether or not in occupation at the time of the application, may apply to the court for an order (an "exclusion order") suspending the occupancy rights of the other spouse in the matrimonial home.[45]

Where there is an entitled and non-entitled partner,[46] or where both partners are entitled, or permitted by a third party, to occupy a family home,[47] either partner, whether or not that partner is in occupation at the time of the application, may apply to the court for an exclusion

---

[42] "Interim exclusion order" is not a term found in the 1981 Act; it is used here to denote an interim order granted in terms of s. 4(6) of the Act. Since exclusion orders cease to have effect upon termination of the marriage (1981 Act, s. 5(1)(a)), or upon dissolution of the civil partnership (Civil Partnership Act 2004, s. 105(2)(a)) it seems appropriate when discussing the exclusion of a party to an action for divorce or dissolution of civil partnership from a matrimonial home or family home to concentrate upon such orders *ad interim*. Different considerations apply in respect of the court's power, on or after granting decree, to grant an incidental order excluding a party to the marriage or civil partnership from occupation of a matrimonial home or family home (as to which, see Chap. 7, n.147 and accompanying text). The tests applicable to the making of exclusion orders (text accompanying nn. 51 to 55 *infra*) apply also to the making of interim exclusion orders (*Bell v. Bell*, 1983 S.C. 182 and *Ward v. Ward*, 1983 S.L.T. 472).

[43] A "non-entitled spouse" is a spouse who, apart from the provisions of the 1981 Act, is not entitled, or permitted by a third party, to occupy a matrimonial home; such a spouse has the right (a) if in occupation, to continue to occupy the matrimonial home, together with any child of the family, and (b) if not in occupation, with leave of the court to enter into and occupy the matrimonial home, together with any child of the family — 1981 Act, s. 1(1), and (1A), as amended by the Law Reform (Miscellaneous Provisions) (Scotland) Act 1985, s. 13(2) and (3). If there has been no cohabitation between an entitled spouse and a non-entitled spouse during a continuous period of two years and during that period the non-entitled spouse has not occupied the matrimonial home, the non-entitled spouse shall, on the expiry of that period, cease to have occupancy rights in the matrimonial home—1981 Act, s. 1(7), as inserted by the Family Law (Scotland) Act 2006, s. 5.

[44] As to the meaning of "matrimonial home", see n. 5 *supra*.

[45] 1981 Act, s. 4(1), as amended by the Law Reform (Miscellaneous Provisions) (Scotland) Act 1985, s. 13(5).

[46] A "non-entitled partner" is a partner in a civil partnership who apart from the provisions of the Civil Partnership Act 2004 is not entitled, or permitted by a third party, to occupy a family home of the civil partnership; such a civil partner has the right (a) if in occupation, to continue to occupy the family home, together with any child of the family; (b) if not in occupation, to enter into and occupy the family home, together with any child of the family—2004 Act, s. 101(1) and (2). If there has been no cohabitation between an entitled partner and a non-entitled partner during a continuous period of two years and during that period the non-entitled partner has not occupied the family home, the non-entitled partner shall, on the expiry of that period, cease to have occupancy rights in the family home—2004 Act, s. l01(6A), as inserted by the Family Law (Scotland) Act 2006, Sched. 1, para. 3.

[47] As to the meaning of "family home", see n. 8 *supra*.

order suspending the occupancy rights of the other partner in the family home.[48]

Application for an interim exclusion order requires to be made by motion.[49] An interim order may only be made if the non-applicant spouse or non-applicant partner has been afforded an opportunity of being heard by or represented before the court.[50]

The court requires to make the order if it appears to the court that the making of the order is necessary for the protection of the applicant or any child of the family[51] from any conduct or threatened or reasonably apprehended conduct[52] of the non-applicant spouse or partner which is or would be injurious to the physical or mental health of the applicant or child.[53]

The court must not however make the order:

> If it appears to the court that the making of the order would be unjustified or unreasonable ... having regard to all the circumstances of the case including ...[54]
>
> > (*a*) the conduct of the spouses or partners, in relation to each other and otherwise;
> >
> > (*b*) the respective needs and financial resources of the spouses or partners;

---

[48] Civil Partnership Act 2004, s. 104(1).

[49] r. 33.69(1)(b) or r. 33A.62(1)(b). In terms of s. 4(6) of the 1981 Act and s. 104(6) of the 2004 Act, an interim exclusion order may be made by the court "pending the making of an exclusion order". It seems, therefore, that the final order should be craved (in the initial writ or the defences, as the case may be — rr. 33.67(1)(b), 33.34(1)(c)(iii) and 33.34(2)(b)(i) or rr. 33A.60(1)(b), 33A.34(1)(c)(iii) and 33A.34(2)(b)(i)) on the footing that decree may be sought in the event that divorce or dissolution of civil partnership, as the case may be, is not granted.

[50] 1981 Act, s. 4(6) or 2004 Act, s. 104(7). Failure to intimate the motion for an interim exclusion order to the non-applicant precludes the sheriff from granting it (*Nelson v. Nelson*, 1988 S.L.T. (Sh. Ct.) 26). The non-applicant should ordinarily be given an opportunity to lodge affidavits (*Armitage v. Armitage*, 1993 S.C.L.R. 173). Rule 33.69(2) or r. 33A.62(2) requires intimation of the motion also to be given, where the entitled spouse or entitled partner is a tenant or occupies the matrimonial home by the permission of a third party, to the landlord or third party, as the case may be; and, in any event, to any other person to whom intimation is required by the sheriff to be made.

[51] As to the meaning of "child of the family", see nn. 4 & 7 *supra*.

[52] As to "conduct" see *Matheson v. Matheson*, 1986 S.L.T. (Sh. Ct.) 2. The fact that the parties are not at the time of the motion living together is not a bar to the obtaining of an order (*Brown v. Brown*, 1985 S.L.T. 376), even where they have been separated for a lengthy period (*Millar v. Millar*, 1991 S.C.L.R. 649).

[53] 1981 Act, s. 4(2) or 2004 Act, s. 104(2). The court does not require, before granting an interim exclusion order, to be satisfied that the applicant would be in immediate danger of suffering irreparable harm (*McCafferty v. McCafferty*, 1986 S.C. 178 at p. 182).

[54] 1981 Act, s. 4(3) or 2004 Act, s. 104(3).

(c)   the needs of any child of the family;

(d)   the extent (if any) to which the matrimonial home or family home is used in connection with a trade, business or profession of either spouse or partner;

(e)   whether the entitled spouse or entitled partner offers or has offered to make available to the non-entitled spouse or non-entitled partner any suitable alternative accommodation; and

(f)   where the matrimonial home or family home is or is part of an agricultural holding ... or is let, or is a home in respect of which possession is given, to the non-applicant spouse or to both spouses or to the non-applicant partner or to both partners by an employer as an incident of employment, subject to a requirement of residence [therein] ... that requirement and the likely consequences of the exclusion of the non-applicant spouse or partner from the matrimonial home or family home.[55]

The court has a discretion as to whether or not to make an interim exclusion order; an appellate court could only interfere with any decision taken in exercise of this discretion if it were to be satisfied that the judge of first instance had misdirected himself and had erred in law, or, if he had applied the correct test, that he had reached an unwarranted conclusion.[56] If it appears to the court that an interim interdict (with or without the attachment of a power of arrest, as the case may be) is providing or would provide adequate protection to the applicant spouse or partner, an interim exclusion order will not be granted.[57]

---

[55] 1981 Act, ss. 3(3) and 4(3) or 2004 Act, s. 103(3) and 104(3).

[56] *McCafferty v. McCafferty*, 1986 S.C. 178. See also *Bell v. Bell*, 1983 S.C. 182, *Brown v. Brown*, 1985 S.L.T. 376, and *Coster v. Coster*, 1992 S.C.L.R. 210. An appeal can competently be taken without leave of the sheriff against the award of an interim exclusion order where an ancillary interim interdict has also been granted (*Oliver v. Oliver*, 1989 S.L.T. (Sh. Ct.) 1) even where leave to appeal that award has been refused by the sheriff (*Anthony v. Anthony*, 1996 G.W.D. 11–671). Failure by the defender to lodge a notice of intention to defend does not mean that he has no locus to appeal (*Nelson v. Nelson*, 1988 S.L.T. (Sh. Ct.) 26). An interim exclusion order is an exception to the general rule that the effect of an appeal is to sist execution on a decree (*Orr v. Orr*, 1980 G.W.D. 12–506).

[57] *Bell v. Bell*, 1983 S.C. 182. If the sheriff has applied the correct test and taken into account all relevant factors in granting an interim exclusion order, failure on his part to state that an interim interdict preventing abuse would be insufficient to protect the applicant would seem not to justify recall of the order by the appellate court: *Brown v. Brown*, 1985 S.L.T. 376 (*cf. Colagiacomo v. Colagiacomo*, 1983 S.L.T. 559 at p. 561). For illustrations of circumstances in which means other than an interim exclusion order would be unlikely to secure the desired degree of protection, see *Ward v. Ward*, 1983 S.L.T. 472 (drink-related course of conduct over a long period) and *Robertson v. Robertson*, 1999 S.L.T. 38 (unreasonably intrusive and jealous behaviour).

The court cannot be satisfied that the making of the order is necessary on the basis of *ex parte* statements alone — there must be sufficient material for the court to be satisfied on a prima facie basis that the pursuer required the protection of such an order.[58] Appropriate "material" includes the following:

(i) affidavits[59];

(ii) extract convictions (where relevant);

(iii) medical reports.

What quantity and quality of material is sufficient will depend on the circumstances of each case.[60]

In making an interim exclusion order the court *must*, on the application of the applicant:

(i) grant a warrant for the summary ejection of the non-applicant from the matrimonial home or family home, unless the non-applicant satisfies the court that it is unnecessary to grant such a warrant[61]; and

(ii) grant an interdict prohibiting the non-applicant from entering the matrimonial home or family home without the express permission of the applicant[62];

(iii) grant an interdict prohibiting the removal by the non-applicant, except with the written consent of the applicant or by a further order of the court, of any furniture and plenishings in the matrimonial home or family home, unless the non-applicant satisfies the court that it is unnecessary to grant such an interdict.[63]

In making an interim exclusion order the court *may*:

(a) grant an interdict prohibiting the non-applicant from

---

[58] *Ward v. Ward*, 1983 S.L.T. 472, at p. 475. The court in *Ward* relied on material presented in an independent report ordered by the court in connection with a dispute between the parties over custody of their children. Alternatively the court may order a preliminary proof, as was done in *Assar v. Assar*, 1994 G.W.D. 2–102 (on minute and answers).

[59] r. 33.27 or r. 33A.28.

[60] See, *e.g. Colagiacomo v. Colagiacomo*, 1985 S.L.T. 559; *Boyle v. Boyle*, 1986 S.L.T. 656; and *Coster v. Coster*, 1992 S.C.L.R. 210.

[61] 1981 Act, s. 4(4)(a) and 2004 Act, 104(4)(a). See, *e.g. Mather v. Mather*, 1987 S.L.T. 565 (interim exclusion order granted but suspended for three months to allow husband to find alternative accommodation).

[62] 1981 Act, s. 4(4)(b) and 2004 Act, s. 104(4)(b).

[63] 1981 Act, s. 4(4)(c) and 2004 Act, 104(4)(c). "Furniture and plenishings" means any article situated in a matrimonial home which (a) is owned or hired by either spouse or is being acquired by either spouse under a hire-purchase agreement or conditional sale agreement; and (b) is reasonably necessary to enable the home to be used as a family residence, but does not include any vehicle, caravan, houseboat or other structure as is mentioned in the definitions of "matrimonial home" or "family home" (nn. 5 and 8 *supra*).

entering or remaining in a specified area in the vicinity of the matrimonial home or family home[64];

(b) where the warrant for the summary ejection of the non-applicant has been granted in his or her absence, give directions as to the preservation of the non-applicant's goods and effects which remain in the matrimonial home or family home[65];

(c) on the application of either spouse or partner, make an interim exclusion order, or the warrant or interdict mentioned in (i), (ii), (iii) or (a) *supra*, subject to such terms and conditions as the court may prescribe[66]; and

(d) on the application of either spouse or partner, make such other order as it may consider necessary for the proper enforcement of any of the foregoing orders.[67]

Applications for variation or recall of any order suspending occupancy rights require to be made by minute intimated: (a) to the other spouse or partner; (b) where the entitled spouse or entitled partner is a tenant or occupies the matrimonial home by the permission of a third party, to the landlord or third party, as the case may be, and (c) to any other person to whom intimation is ordered by the sheriff to be made.[68]

ORDERS RELATING TO AVOIDANCE TRANSACTIONS

Where an application for an order for financial provision, or for variation of or recall of such order, has been made in a divorce action, the person making the claim may, not later than one year from the date of the disposal of the claim, apply[69] to the court for an order —

(i) setting aside[70] or varying any transfer of, or transaction involving, property effected by the other party not more than five years before the date of the making of the claim; or

---

[64] 1981 Act, s. 4(5)(a) and 2004 Act, s. 104(5)(a).

[65] 1981 Act, s. 4(5)(b) and 2004 Act, s. 104(5)(b).

[66] 1981 Act, s. 4(5)(c) and 2004 Act, s. 104(5)(c).

[67] 1981 Act, s. 4(5)(d) and 2004 Act, s. 104(5)(d).

[68] r. 33.70 or r. 33A.63, giving effect to 1981 Act, s. 5(1) and 2004 Act, s. 105(1).

[69] Application must be made by a crave in the initial writ or defences, as the case may be, except that an application after final decree requires to be made by minute in the process of the action to which the application relates — rr. 33.48(1)(a) and (2)(c) and 33.52(b) or r. 33.53(1) and (2), or rr. 33A.45(1)(a) and (2)(c) and 33A.49(b) or r. 33A.50(1) and (2).

[70] The power to "set aside" a transaction implies a power to reduce a writing or deed by which the transaction is effected — *Hernandez-Cimorra v. Hernandez-Cimorra*, 1992 S.C.L.R. 611 (*cf. Harris v. Harris*, 1988 S.L.T. 101). A letter purporting to acknowledge a loan was set aside in *Tahir v. Tahir (No. 2)*, 1995 S.L.T. 451.

(ii)   interdicting the other party from effecting any such transfer or transaction.[71]

If the court is satisfied that the transfer or transaction had the effect of, or is likely to have the effect of, defeating in whole or in part the applicant's claim, it may make the order applied for or such other order as it thinks fit.[72] The court may include in the order such terms and conditions as it thinks fit and may make any ancillary order which it considers expedient to ensure that the order is effective.[73]

The order must not prejudice any rights of a third party in or to the property where that third party:

(a)   has in good faith acquired the property or any of it or any rights in relation to it for value; or

(b)   derives title to such property or rights from any person who has done so.[74]

Intimation therefore requires to be given in accordance with rules 33.7(1)(j) or 33A.7(1)(h) and 33.15(3) or 33A.15(3).[75]

DILIGENCE ON THE DEPENDENCE

Circumstances may arise in actions of divorce where a financial claim is being made by one spouse against the other in which some security for the claim would be desirable. Inhibition and arrestment on the dependence of the action may be very effective remedies for this purpose. They have been described by the Scottish Law Commission as follows:

"Inhibition is a procedure whereby the defender in an action can be prevented, pending the disposal of the action, from disposing of his heritable property. Arrestment on the dependence is a procedure whereby a third party holding moveable property for the defender or owing money to the defender can be prevented from parting with the property or money pending the disposal of the action."[76]

---

[71] Family Law (Scotland) Act 1985, s. 18(1), as amended by the Civil Partnership Act 2004, Sched. 28, para. 24. See also *Wilson v. Wilson*, 1999 S.L.T. 249 (order refused after proof in the absence of any real grounds in equity or otherwise to grant it).

[72] 1985 Act, s. 18(2). In *Tahir v. Tahir (No. 2)*, 1995 S.L.T. 451, the Lord Ordinary reduced a sheriff court decree in order to give effect to the setting aside of a fictitious borrowing transaction.

[73] 1985 Act, s. 18(4).

[74] 1985 Act, s. 18(3). (As to onus, *cf. Leslie v. Leslie*, 1983 S.L.T. 186 and 1987 S.L.T. 232.)

[75] See Chap. 1, text accompanying nn. 21 and 27.

[76] *Report on Aliment and Financial Provision* (Scot. Law Com. No. 67, 1981), para. 3–152.

Where a claim for aliment or for an order for financial provision has been made, the sheriff has power, on cause shown,[77] to grant warrant for arrestment on the dependence of the action in which the claim is made and, if he or she thinks fit, to limit the arrestment to any particular property or to funds not exceeding a specified value.[78] Application for a warrant for inhibition requires to be made to the Court of Session, that court having power, on cause shown, to grant such warrant and, if it thinks fit, to limit the inhibition to any particular property.[79] Inhibition has been judicially observed to be a more effective and more suitable method of protection than interdict against the disposal of a heritable property.[80]

---

[77] Such would include where the defender is verging on insolvency, or is outside Scotland, or is about to decamp, or is depleting his assets to defeat the pursuer's claim — *Ellison v. Ellison* (1901) 4 F 257; *Stuart v. Stuart*, 1926 S.L.T. 31; *Gillanders v. Gillanders*, 1966 S.C. 54; *Brash v. Brash*, 1966 S.C. 56; *Wilson v. Wilson*, 1981 S.L.T. 101; *Pow v. Pow*, 1987 S.C. 95. Warrant to arrest on the dependence was recalled in *Matheson v. Matheson*, 1995 S.L.T. 765 on the basis that arrestments interfering with the legitimate business operation of the defender unduly hampered and frustrated his ordinary trading activities without legitimate advantage to the pursuer, the recall being subject to full disclosure of the transactions entered into and of the application of all sums thus realised.

[78] Family Law (Scotland) Act 1985, s. 19(1) and (2). The Scottish Law Commission in its *Report on Diligence on the Dependence and Admiralty Arrestments* (Scot. Law Com. No. 164, 1998), para. 3.89, recommends that their recommendations on warrants for diligence on the dependence securing debts already due, liability for wrongful or unjustified diligence and related matters, should extend to diligence on the dependence securing future or contingent debts, including aliment and financial provision on divorce and should replace s. 19 of the Family Law (Scotland) Act 1985.

[79] 1985 Act, s. 19(1) and (2). In terms of R.C.S. 59.1(5) an application for letters of inhibition on the dependence of an action to which a claim under s. 19 of the Family Law (Scotland) Act 1985 applies, requires to be placed before the Lord Ordinary, whose decision thereon is final and not subject to review. For an illustration of circumstances in which the court's power would not be exercised, see *Thom v. Thom*, 1990 S.C.L.R. 800. The Scottish Law Commission in its *Report on Diligence on the Dependence and Admiralty Arrestments* (Scot. Law Com. No. 164, 1998), para. 3.97, recommends that jurisdiction should be conferred on the sheriff to grant warrant for inhibition on the dependence.

[80] *Wilson v. Wilson*, 1981 S.L.T. 101 at p. 102.

CHAPTER 5

PROPERTY ORDERS

The sheriff is empowered by statute to make various orders, described herein as "property orders", relative to a matrimonial home or a family home.[1] The more important of these (excepting exclusion orders and related remedies[2]) are discussed in this chapter.[3]

ORDERS REGULATING OCCUPANCY RIGHTS

The Matrimonial Homes (Family Protection) (Scotland) Act 1981 and the Civil Partnership Act 2004 provide for the granting of certain orders concerning the occupancy rights[4] of spouses and civil partners as follows:

(i)   declaring the occupancy rights of the applicant;
(ii) enforcing the occupancy rights of the applicant;
(iii) restricting the occupancy rights of the non-applicant;
(iv) regulating the exercise by either spouse or partner of his or her occupancy rights;
(v)   protecting the occupancy rights of the applicant in relation to the non-applicant; and

---

[1] The Matrimonial Homes (Family Protection) (Scotland) Act 1981 and the Civil Partnership Act 2004. As to the court's power under the Family Law (Scotland) Act 1985 to make an incidental order regulating the occupation of the matrimonial home or family home and the use of furniture and plenishings therein, or regulating liability, as between the parties, for outgoings in respect of the matrimonial home or family home and furniture or plenishings therein, see Chap. 7, nn. 147 and 148 and accompanying text.
[2] As to which, see Chap. 4.
[3] Orders under the 1981 Act, s. 2(1)(e) and (4)(a) and the 2004 Act, s. 102(1)(e) and (4)(a) (authorisation of non-entitled spouse or civil partner to carry out non-essential repairs and improvements to matrimonial home) and under the 1981 Act, s. 2(3), (4)(b), (5)(b) and (6) and the 2004 Act, s. 102(3), (4)(b), (5)(b) and (6) (apportionment between spouses or civil partners of certain expenditure relating to home) (cf. *Porter v. Porter*, 1990 S.C.L.R. 752 and *Wilson v. Wilson*, 2001 S.L.T. (Sh.Ct.) 55) are not discussed herein.
[4] Occupancy rights are those enjoyed by a non-entitled spouse or a non-entitled partner (a) if in occupation, to continue to occupy the matrimonial home or family home, as the case may be, together with any child of the family; (b) if not in occupation, to enter and occupy the matrimonial home or family home, as the case may be, together with any child of the family — 1981 Act, s. 1(1) and 1(1A) and 2004 Act, s. 101(1) and (2).

(vi) granting to a spouse or partner with occupancy rights the possession or use of furniture and plenishings in a matrimonial home or family home owned, hired or being acquired by the other spouse or partner.[5]

An order in category (i) must be granted if it appears to the court that the application relates to a matrimonial home or a family home, as the case may be.[6] The court may make such order relating to an application[7] within the remaining categories as appears to it to be just and reasonable having regard to all the circumstances of the case, including the matters specified in paragraphs (a) to (e) of section 3(3) of the 1981 Act or of section 103(3) of the 2004 Act,[8] except that no such order may be made if it appears that the effect of the order would be to exclude the non-applicant from the matrimonial home or family home, as the case may be.[9]

Since the granting of decree automatically terminates occupancy rights,[10] the criteria for the making of interim orders regulating such rights are of greater practical significance for present purposes. These criteria are "necessity" and "expediency", the court being empowered to make such interim order as it may consider necessary or expedient in relation to —

(a) the residence of either spouse or partner in the home to which the application relates;
(b) the personal effects of either spouse or partner or of any child of the family; or
(c) the furniture and plenishings.[11]

An interim order may only be made if the non-applicant has had an opportunity of being heard by or represented before the court.[12]

---

[5] 1981 Act, s. 3(1) and (2) and 2004 Act, s. 103(1) and (2). *Cf.* n. 24 *infra.*
[6] 1981 Act, s. 3(3) and 2004 Act, s. 103(3). Such an order is accordingly appropriately craved where there is any question as to whether or not any particular property is a matrimonial home or family home, as the case may be.
[7] An application by a pursuer or a defender must be made by a crave in the initial writ or in defences, as the case may be (rr. 33.67(1)(b) and 33.34(1)(c)(iii) and (2)(b)(i)), intimated in accordance with rr. 33.7(1)(k) and 33.15(3) or rr. 33A.60(1)(b) and 33A.34(1)(c)(iii) and (2)(b)(i), intimated in accordance with rr. 33A.7(1)(i) and 33A.15(3) (see Chap. 1, text accompanying nn. 22 and 27).
[8] Paras. (a) to (e) are set forth in n. 21 *infra.*
[9] 1981 Act, s. 3(5) and 2004 Act, s. 103(5).
[10] *Cf.* n. 4 *supra.*
[11] 1981 Act, s. 3(4) and 2004 Act, s. 103(4).
[12] *ibid.*

Application for an interim order must be made by motion.[13] The court may vary or recall an order regulating occupancy rights upon an application therefor made by minute.[14]

ORDERS DISPENSING WITH CONSENT TO DEALING

The continued exercise of occupancy rights conferred on a non-entitled spouse or non-entitled partner in respect of a matrimonial home or family home, as the case may be, cannot be prejudiced by reason only of any dealing[15] of the entitled spouse or entitled partner relating to that home; and a third party is not by reason only of any such dealing entitled to occupy that matrimonial home or family home or any part of it.[16] The position is otherwise *inter alia* where:

    (a) the non-entitled spouse or non-entitled partner in writing either—
        (i) consents or has consented to the dealing, the consent being given in the prescribed form; or
        (ii) renounces or has renounced his or her occupancy rights in the particular property to which the dealing relates; or
    (b) the court has made an order under section 7 of the Matrimonial Homes (Family Protection) (Scotland) Act 1981 or section 107 of the Civil Partnership Act 2004 dispensing with the consent of the non-entitled spouse or non-entitled partner, as the case may be, to the dealing.[17]

---

[13] r. 33.69(1)(a) or r. 33A.62(1)(a). Intimation of the motion requires to be made to the non-applicant and if the entitled spouse or entitled partner is a tenant or occupies the matrimonial home or family home by the permission of a third party to the landlord or third party, as the case may be, and to any other person to whom intimation was or is to be made by virtue of rr. 33.7(1)(k) or r. 33A.7(1)(i) or 33.15 or 33A.15 — r. 33.69(2) or 33A.62(2). In terms of the 1981 Act, s. 3(4) and the 2004 Act, s. 103(4) an interim order may be made by the court "pending the making of [a property] order". It seems, therefore, that the final order should be craved (in the initial writ or the defences, as the case may be — rr. 33.67(1)(b), 33.34(1)(c)(iii) and (2)(b)(i) or rr. 33A.60(1)(b) and 33A.34(1)(c)(iii) and (2)(b)(i)) on the footing that decree may be sought in the event that divorce or dissolution of civil partnership is not granted.

[14] 1981 Act, s. 5 and r. 33.70(1)(a) and 2004 Act, s. 105 and r. 33A.63(1). Intimation requires to be made in accordance with the preceding footnote — r. 33.70(2) or r. 33A.63(2).

[15] "Dealing" includes the grant of a heritable security and the creation of a trust—1981 Act, s. 6(2) and 2004 Act, s. 106(2).

[16] 1981 Act, s. 6(1) and 2004 Act, s. 106(1). However, the occupancy rights of a non-entitled spouse or non-entitled partner are not exerciseable where, following a dealing of the entitled spouse or entitled partner relating to the home—(a) a person acquires the home, or an interest in it, in good faith and for value from a person other than the person who is or, as the case may be, was the entitled spouse or entitled partner; or (b) a person derives title to the home from a person who so acquired title—1981 Act, s. 6(1A) and 2004 Act, s. 106(1A).

[17] 1981 Act, s. 6(3)(a) and (b) and 2004 Act, s. 106(3)(a) and (b).

The court may, on the application[18] of an entitled spouse or an entitled partner or any other person having an interest, make an order dispensing with the consent of the non-entitled spouse or non-entitled partner to a dealing which has taken place or a proposed dealing, if—

(a) such consent is unreasonably withheld,[19]

(b) such consent cannot be given by reason of physical or mental disability, or

(c) the non-entitled spouse or non-entitled partner cannot be found after reasonable steps have been taken to trace him or her.[20]

The court in considering whether to make the order must have regard to all the circumstances of the case, including the matters specified in paragraphs (a) to (e) of section 3(3) of the 1981 Act or s. 103(3) of the 2004 Act. [21]

If in relation to a proposed sale—(a) negotiations with a third party have not begun; or (b) negotiations have begun but a price has not been agreed, an order dispensing with consent may be made only if— (a) the price agreed for the sale is no less than such amount as the court specifies in the order; and (b) the contract for the sale is concluded

---

[18] Application is by motion intimated to the other spouse or civil partner and any other person to whom intimation is ordered to be made — r. 33.69(1)(c) and (2)(a) and (c) or r. 33A.62(1)(c) and (2)(a) and (c). As to procedure where relevant and material facts are disputed, see *Longmuir v. Longmuir*, 1985 S.L.T. (Sh. Ct.) 33 at p. 36.

[19] 1981 Act, s. 7(1)(a) and 2004 Act, s. 107(1)(a). The onus is on the applicant to show that consent is being unreasonably withheld—*Hall v. Hall*, 1987 S.L.T. (Sh. Ct.) 15. Consent is taken to be unreasonably withheld where it appears to the court that—(a) the non-entitled spouse or non-entitled partner has led the entitled spouse or entitled partner to believe that such consent would be given and that the non-entitled spouse or non-entitled partner would not be prejudiced by any change in the circumstances of the case since such apparent consent was given, or (b) that the entitled spouse or entitled partner has, having taken all reasonable steps to do so, been unable to obtain an answer to a request for consent— 1981 Act, s. 7(2) and 2004 Act, s. 107(2). In *O'Neill v. O'Neill*, 1987 S.L.T. (Sh. Ct.) 26 consent was held to be withheld unreasonably where the purpose of withholding was not to protect occupancy rights but to attempt to force the other spouse into certain actings in exchange.

[20] 1981 Act, s. 7(1) and 2004 Act, s. 107(1). The court may also make such an order in the case of a non-entitled spouse who is under legal disability by reason of nonage—1981 Act, s. 7(1)(d), as inserted by the Age of Legal Capacity (Scotland) Act 1991, s. 10 and Sched. 1.

[21] 1981 Act, s. 7(3) and 2004 Act, s. 107(3). The matters specified in paras. (a) to (e) are as follows: (a) the conduct of the spouses or partners, whether in relation to each other or otherwise; (b) their respective needs and financial resources; (c) the needs of any child of the family; (d) the extent (if any) to which the matrimonial home or family home is used in connection with a trade, business or profession of either spouse or partner; and (e) whether the entitled spouse or entitled partner offers or has offered to make available to the non-entitled spouse or non-entitled partner any suitable alternative accommodation.

before the expiry of such period as may be so specified.[22] If the proposed dealing is the grant of a heritable security, the order may be made only if—(a) the heritable security is granted for a loan of no more than such amount as the court specifies in the order; and (b) the security is executed before the expiry of such period as maybe so specified.[23]

An application for such an order will be refused where a transfer of property order relative to the matrimonial home is craved by the non-applicant spouse.[24]

If the court refuses an application for an order dispensing with consent to a dealing, it may make an order requiring a non-entitled spouse or non-entitled partner who is or becomes the occupier of the matrimonial home or family home—

(a) to make such payments to the owner of the home in respect of its occupation as may be specified in the order,

(b) to comply with such other conditions relating to the occupation of the matrimonial home or family home as may be so specified.[25]

ORDERS TRANSFERRING TENANCY[26]

A sheriff in an action for divorce or dissolution of civil partnership may, on granting decree or within such period as he may specify on granting decree, make an order:

(i) transferring the tenancy of a matrimonial home or family home to a non-entitled spouse or a non-entitled partner,[27] or

(ii) where the spouses or partners are joint or common tenants of

---

[22] 1981 Act, s. 7(1A) and (1B) and 2004 Act, s. 107(1A) and (B), as inserted by the Family Law (Scotland) Act 2006, s. 7 and Sched. 1, para. 6.

[23] 1981 Act, s. 7(1C) and (1D) and 2004 Act, s. 107(1C) and (1D), as inserted by the Family Law (Scotland) Act 2006, s. 7 and Sched. 1, para. 6.

[24] *Rae v. Rae*, 1991 S.L.T. 454. Where an application is made for an order dispensing with consent to a dealing and an action is or has been raised by a non-entitled spouse or non-entitled partner to enforce occupancy rights, such part of the action as relates to the enforcement of the occupancy rights is to be sisted until the conclusion of the proceedings on the application — 1981 Act, s. 7(4) and r. 33.71 and 2004 Act, s. 107(4) and r. 33A.64.

[25] 1981 Act, s. 7(3A) and 2004 Act, s. l07(3A), as inserted by the Family Law (Scotland) Act 2006, s. 7 and Sched. 1, para. 6.

[26] Applications for these are not competent where the tenancy is a service tenancy, a lease of a farm, croft or similar holding, a long lease or a tenancy-at-will — 1981 Act, s. 13(7) and 2004 Act, s. 112(8). Note also that "tenancy" includes subtenancy, statutory tenancy as defined in s. 3 of the Rent (Scotland) Act 1971 and statutory assured tenancy as defined in s. 16(1) of the Housing (Scotland) Act 1988 — 1981 Act, s. 22 and 2004 Act, s. 135.

[27] 1981 Act, s. 13(1) and (2), as amended by the Family Law (Scotland) Act 1985, Sched. 1, para. 11 and 2004 Act, s. 112(1) and (2).

a matrimonial home or family home, vesting the tenancy in one spouse or partner only.[28]

In either case, the court may provide for payment by the applicant to the other of such compensation as seems just and reasonable in all the circumstances of the case.[29]

The court is required in determining whether or not to grant the order to have regard to all the circumstances of the case, including the matters specified in paragraphs (a) to (e) of section 3(3) of the Matrimonial Homes (Family Protection) (Scotland) Act 1981 and section 103(3) of the Civil Partnership Act 2004 and the suitability of the applicant to become the tenant (or sole tenant, as the case may be) and his or her capacity to perform the obligations under the lease.[30]

The applicant must serve a copy of the application on the landlord who must have an opportunity of being heard by the court before the order may be granted.[31]

The effect of the order is to vest the tenancy (or sole tenancy, as the case may be) in the applicant without intimation to the landlord, subject to all the liabilities under the lease, other than any arrears of rent for the period before the making of the order.[32] The importance of the order lies in the fact that a spouse or partner without a right of tenancy or incidental order entitling his or her occupation is liable to ejection once the marriage is terminated by divorce or the civil partnership is dissolved.

---

[28] 1981 Act, s. 13(9) and (10) and 2004 Act, s. 112(10) and (11).

[29] 1981 Act, s. 13(1) and (9) and 2004 Act s. 112(1) and (10). Where the matrimonial home or family home is a Scottish secure tenancy within the meaning of the Housing (Scotland) Act 2001, no account shall be taken, in assessing the amount of any such compensation of the loss, by virtue of the transfer of the tenancy of the home, of a right to purchase the home under Part III of the Housing (Scotland) Act 1987—1981 Act, s. 13(11) and 2004 Act, s. 112(12).

[30] 1981 Act, s. 13(3) and 2004 Act, s. 112(3). Paras. (a) to (e) are set forth in n. 21 *supra*. For an illustration of circumstances justifying the granting of an order, see *McGowan v. McGowan*, 1986 S.L.T. 112 and *Guyan v. Guyan* 2001 Fam. L.R. 99.

[31] 1981 Act, s. 13(4) and 2004 Act, s. 112(4). Intimation of the application (which is made by a crave in the initial writ or in defences — rr. 33.48(1)(a) and (2)(d) and 33.34(1)(c)(iii) and (2)(b)(i) or r. 33A.45(1(a) and (2)(d) and 33A.34(1)(c)(iii) and (2)(b)(i)) requires to be made to the landlord in accordance with rr. 33.7(1)(k) and 33.15(3) or r. 33A.7(1)(i) and 33A.15(3)) (see Chap. 1, text accompanying nn. 22 and 27).

[32] 1981 Act, s. 13(5) and 2004 Act, s. 112(5).

CHAPTER 6

CHILDREN

The subject of children in the context of the law and practice relating to divorce and dissolution of civil partnership is discussed in this chapter; and the jurisdiction, duties and powers of the court in this connection are considered in turn.

JURISDICTION OF THE COURT

Where an application is competently made to a sheriff court for the making, variation or recall of an order which is ancillary or collateral to an action of divorce and which relates to children, as a general rule[1] if the court has jurisdiction to entertain the action it has jurisdiction to entertain the application.[2] A similar provision exists with respect to actions for dissolution of civil partnership.[3]

---

[1] The court does not have jurisdiction where (a) the court is exercising jurisdiction in the proceedings by virtue of Article 3 of the Council Regulation; and (b) the making or variation of an order in consequence of the application would contravene Article 6 of the Council Regulation—Domicile and Matrimonial Proceedings Act 1973, s. 10(1B), as inserted by The European Communities (Matrimonial Jurisdiction and Judgments) (Scotland) Regulations 2001 (S.S.I. 2001 No. 36), reg. 2(4) and amended by The European Communities (Matrimonial and Parental Responsibility Jurisdiction and Judgments) (Scotland) Regulations 2005 (S.S.I. 2005 No. 42), reg. 2(4). Article 3 of the Council Regulation is reproduced in Chap. 2, text accompanying nn. 9 and 10. As to Article 6, see Chap. 2, n. 11. The court does not have jurisdiction, either, after the dismissal of the action or after decree of absolvitor is granted therein, unless the application for the order relating to the child was made on before such dismissal or the granting of decree of absolvitor—Family Law Act 1986, s. 13(2), as amended by the Children (Scotland) Act 1995, Sched. 4, para. 41(3). See also 1986 Act, s. 13(4) and (5) (court's jurisdiction where refusing principal remedy sought in matrimonial proceedings to entertain an application for variation of an order relating to children if matrimonial proceedings continuing in another court in the United Kingdom) and s. 13(6) (court's power in matrimonial proceedings to decline jurisdiction to entertain an application for an order relating to a child if but for certain statutory provisions another court in Scotland or another part of the United Kingdom would have jurisdiction and more appropriate for matters to be determined there).

[2] Domicile and Matrimonial Proceedings Act 1973, s. 10(1) and (1A), as amended and inserted, respectively, by para. 20(2)(a) and para. 20(2)(b) of Sched. 4 to the Children (Scotland) Act 1995.

[3] Civil Partnership Act, s. 227(1), (2) and (5)

A court which has such jurisdiction may refuse the application in any case where the matter in question has already been determined in other proceedings,[4] or may sist the proceedings on such application at any stage where it appears to the court (a) that proceedings with respect to the matters to which the application relates are continuing outside Scotland or in another court in Scotland; (b) that it would be more appropriate for those matters to be determined in proceedings outside Scotland or in another court in Scotland, and that such proceedings are likely to be taken there; or (c) that it should exercise its powers under Article 15 of the Council Regulation (transfer to a court better placed to hear the case).[5]

DUTIES OF THE COURT

Restrictions on decrees affecting children

In an action for divorce or dissolution of a civil partnership where a child of the family[6] has not reached the age of 16 years,[7] the court is bound to consider (in the light of such information as is before the court as to the arrangements which have been or are proposed to be made for the upbringing of that child) whether to exercise with respect to him certain statutory powers.[8] In all such actions in which there is any such child, therefore, the pursuer should include averments in the initial writ anent the arrangements made or proposed for the child whether or not he or she is seeking any order from the court.

Where the court is of the opinion that (a) the circumstances of the case require or are likely to require it to exercise any such power with respect to the child concerned; (b) it is not in a position to exercise

---

[4] Family Law Act 1986, s. 14(1).

[5] 1986 Act, s. 14(2), as amended by The European Communities (Matrimonial and Parental Responsibility Jurisdiction and Judgments) (Scotland) Regulations 2005 (S.S.I. 2005 No. 42), reg. 4(2)(b). *Cf. Hill v. Hill,* 1991 S.L.T. 189; and *B v. B,* 1998 S.L.T. 1245.

[6] "Child of the family", in relation to the parties to a marriage means (i) a child of both of them; or (ii) any other child, not being a child who is placed with them as foster-parents by a local authority or voluntary organisations, who has been treated by both of them as a child of the family — Children (Scotland) Act 1995, s. 12(4)(a), as amended by the Family Law (Scotland) Act 2006, Sched. 2, para. 8. "Child of the family", in relation to the partners in a civil partnership, means a child who has been treated by both partners as a child of the family which their partnership constitutes—1995 Act, s. 12(4)(b), as so amended.

[7] 1995 Act, s. 12(3). The *punctum temporis* is the date when the question first arises as to whether the court should give such consideration as is mentioned in the provision (*ibid.*).

[8] 1995 Act, s. 12(1), as amended by the Civil Partnership Act 2004, Sched. 28, para. 60(1) and (2). The powers are those conferred by ss. 11 and 54 of the Act (to make, respectively, s. 11 orders and references to the Principal Reporter). As to the sheriff's duty to order intimation to the child when so considering, see r. 33.15(2) or r. 33A.15(2), considered in Chap. 1, n. 19.

that power without giving further consideration to the case; and (c) there are exceptional circumstances which make it desirable in the interests of that child that it should not grant decree in the action until it is in a position to exercise such power, it must postpone its decision on the granting of decree in the action until it is in such a position.[9]

The welfare principle

In considering whether or not to make a statutory order[10] with respect to a child and what order to make, the court must regard the *welfare* of the child concerned[11] as *its paramount consideration*.[12]

The term "welfare" is not statutorily defined but has been judicially explained as follows:

> "'Welfare' is an all encompassing word. It includes material welfare, both in the sense of adequacy of resources to provide a pleasant home and a comfortable standard of living and in the sense of adequacy of care to ensure that good health and due personal pride are maintained. However, while material considerations have their place they are secondary matters. More important are the stability and the security, the loving and understanding care and guidance, the warm and compassionate relationships, that are essential for the full development of the child's own character, personality and talents."[13]

What is in the best interests of any particular child is essentially a question of fact; and since cases vary infinitely on their facts, case law

---

[9] 1995 Act, s. 12(2).

[10] The order in question is that under s. 11(1) of the 1995 Act, considered *infra* (text accompanying nn. 35–42).

[11] *cf. Birmingham City Council v. H (A Minor)* [1994] 2 A.C. 212 (regard not to be had to welfare of 15-year-old mother in application for contact with baby). Where sibling children with competing interests are the subject of an application in the same set of proceedings, and it is impossible to achieve what is in the paramount interests of each child, the court may require to balance the children's interests and achieve the situation of least detriment to all the children — see *Re T and E (Proceedings: Conflicting Interests)* [1995] 1 F.L.R. 581 at p. 587.

[12] 1995 Act, s. 11(7)(a). It is not normally appropriate, where the welfare of children is involved, to dispose of an application solely on the pleadings, and the court will not dispose of the matter, except on a point of law only, without conducting some kind of inquiry into the facts — *O v. O*, 1994 S.C. 569.

[13] *Per* Hardie Boys J. in *Walker v. Walker and Harrison*, noted in [1981] NZ Recent Law 257. See also the statutory list of relevant factors in the equivalent English legislation, the Children Act 1989, s. 1(3), which includes the following: (a) the ascertainable wishes and feelings of the child concerned considered in the light of his age and understanding; (b) his physical, emotional and educational needs; (c) the likely effect on him of any change in his circumstances; (d) his age, sex, background and any characteristics of his which the court considers relevant; (e) any harm which he has suffered or is at risk of suffering; and (f) how capable each of his parents, and any other person in relation to whom the court considers the question to be relevant, is of meeting his needs.

assumes a lesser significance in this area. Worthy of particular note, however, are the judicial expressions of (1) a general preference that the mother should have custody of the very young child[14]; (2) the need for close and anxious attention to the possible effects on the child of any change to existing arrangements[15]; and (3) the desirability of placing very great and usually decisive weight on the wishes of the teenage child.[16]

The *paramountcy* formulation connotes:

> "... a process whereby, when all the facts, relationships, claims and wishes of parents, risks, choices, and other circumstances are taken into account and weighed, the course to be followed will be that which is most in the interests of the child's welfare as that term has now to be understood. That is the ... paramount consideration because it rules on or determines the course to be followed."[17]

There is no onus upon the applicant to demonstrate to the satisfaction of the court that the making of the order sought is in the best interests of the child.[18] The court must consider all the relevant circumstances and decide what in its judgment the welfare of the child requires.[19] The courts of review will only interfere with the judgment of the court of first instance in exceptional circumstances.[20]

The minimum intervention principle

In considering whether or not to make an order with respect to a child and what order to make, the court must not make any such order unless it considers that it would be better for the child if the order were made, rather than that no order be made at all.[21]

---

[14] *Brixey v. Lynas*, 1997 S.C. (H.L.) 1. *Cf. MacMillan v. Brady*, 1997 Fam.L.R. 29.

[15] *J v. C* [1970] A.C. 668 at p. 715.

[16] *Gover v. Gover*, 1969 S.L.T. (Notes) 78 and *Blance v. Blance*, 1978 S.L.T. 74. And see n. 23 *infra*.

[17] *Per* Lord MacDermott in *J v. C* [1970] A.C. 668, at p. 710, under reference to the formulation "its first and paramount consideration", thought to amount to the same thing in *C v. C (A Minor: Custody Appeal)* [1991] 1 F.L.R. 223 at p. 230.

[18] *White v. White*, 2001 S.C. 689.

[19] *Osborne v. Matthan (No. 2)*, 1998 S.C. 682 at pp. 688–689; *Pearson v. Pearson*, 1999 S.L.T. 1364 at p. 1367. The judge of first instance is described in these cases as having no discretion once he has identified what the welfare of the child requires. For the alternative view that a decision of this kind involves the exercise of a discretion, see *Britton v. Central Regional Council*, 1986 S.L.T. 207 at p. 208; *Early v. Early*, 1990 S.L.T. 221 at p. 223; *Brixey v. Lynas*, 1994 S.C. 606 at p. 608; *Osborne v. Matthan*, 1997 S.C. 29 at p. 32; *O'Malley v. O'Malley*, 2004 Fam.L.R. 44; *G v. G (Minors: Custody Appeal)* [1985] 1 W.L.R. 647 at p. 652; *In re K D* [1988] A.C. 806 at p. 819.

[20] *Senna-Cheribbo v. Wood*, 1999 S.C. 328.

[21] 1995 Act, s. 11(7)(a), giving effect to the recommendation of the Scottish Law Commission that the provision was needed to discourage unnecessary orders relating to children (*Report on Family Law* (Scot. Law Com. No. 135, 1992), para. 5.18). *Cf. Potter v. Potter*, 1993 S.L.T. (Sh. Ct.) 51 at p. 52, *Ross v. Ross*, 1997 S.L.T. (Sh. Ct.) 51 at p. 54, *Cunningham v. Cunningham*, 2001 Fam. L.R. 12 and *G v. G*, 2003 Fam. L.R. 118.

Views of the child

In considering whether or not to make an order with respect to a child and what order to make, the court, taking account of the child's age and maturity, must so far as practicable (1) give him or her an opportunity to indicate whether he or she wishes to express his or her views; (2) if he or she does so wish, give him or her an opportunity to express them; and (3) have regard to such views as he or she may express.[22] The duty on the court to comply with the foregoing requirements is one which continues until the relevant order is made and the fact that formal intimation may have been dispensed with as inappropriate in no way relieves the court of complying with that continuing duty, if necessary *ex proprio motu*.[23] So far as affording a child the opportunity to make known his or her views, the only proper and relevant test is one of practicability, and how a child should be given such an opportunity will depend on the circumstances of each case and, in particular, on his or her age:

> "At one extreme, intimation in terms of Form F9 may be appropriate whereas, at the other extreme, a much less formal method will be appropriate. Seeing a child in chambers is, of course, always open to the court but, in the case of a very young child, we do not discount the possibility that his or her views, or the lack of them, could properly be made known to the court through the agency of, for example, a private individual who is well known to the child or perhaps by a child psychologist. But, if, by one method or another it is 'practicable' to give a child the opportunity of expressing his views, then, in our view, the only safe course is to employ that method. What weight is thereafter given to such views as may be expressed is, of course, an entirely different matter. It follows that we do not agree … that the formal process of intimation in terms of Form F9 [or Form CP7] should necessarily be seen as the principal mode of compliance with s. 11(7)(b). In particular, where younger children are involved or

---

[22] 1995 Act, s. 11(7)(b). This provision gives effect to Art. 12 of the United Nations Convention on the Rights of the Child, reproduced in App. V. See *e.g. Brooks v. Brooks*, 1990 G.W.D. 2–62 (child's wishes determinative); *Henderson v. Henderson*, 1997 Fam. L.R. 120 (child's views of importance in conjunction with other factors); *Perendes v. Sim*, 1998 S.L.T. 1382 (children's wishes accorded limited weight); *H v. H*, 2000 Fam. L.R. 73 (child's wishes determinative); *S v. S*, 2002 S.C. 246 (child's wishes determinative); *Ellis v. Ellis*, 2003 Fam.L.R. 77 (children's wishes not given decisive weight); *J v. J*, 2004 Fam.L.R.20 (children's wishes not given decisive weight) and *C v. McM*, 2005 Fam. L.R. 36 (children's views ambivalent). A child who is 12 years or more is presumed to be of sufficient age and maturity to form a view — 1995 Act, s. 11(10). See also n. 27 *infra*.

[23] *S v. S*, 2002 S.C. 246 at p. 250; r. 33.19(3) and r. 33A.19(3). In a case where the parties' children had been interviewed by a social worker at an earlier stage of the proceedings and had shown divided loyalty, the sheriff was held to have correctly exercised his discretion not to give them a further opportunity to express views (*C v. McM*, 2005 Fam. L.R. 36).

where there is a risk of upsetting the child, other methods may well be preferable."[24]

Where a child has returned to the sheriff clerk Form F9 or Form CP7 or otherwise indicated to the court a wish to express views on a matter affecting him or her, the sheriff requires to order such steps to be taken as he or she considers appropriate to ascertain the views of that child.[25] The child is not required to be represented in the proceedings if he or she does not wish to be.[26] He or she may express his or her views personally to the sheriff, orally or in writing.[27] Alternatively, somebody else, who need not be an advocate or a solicitor, may do so on his or her behalf,[28] and the sheriff may appoint somebody for the purpose of recording the views of the child in writing.[29] The sheriff may direct that such views, and any written views, given by a child be sealed in an envelope marked "Views of the child — confidential"; be kept in the court process without being recorded in the inventory of process; be available to a sheriff only; not be opened by any person other than a sheriff; and not form a borrowable part of the process.[30]

Third party rights

The court must, notwithstanding its duties, endeavour to ensure that any order which it makes, or any determination by it not to make an

---

[24] *S v. S,* 2002 S.C. 246 at p. 250. See also *H v. H,* 2000 Fam.L.R. 73.

[25] r. 33.19(1) and (2) or r. 33A.19(1) and (2).

[26] 1995 Act, s. 11(9). In *Fourman v. Fourman,* 1998 Fam.L.R. 98, the parties' 14-year-old daughter became a party minuter in the action. The sheriff observed that she was old enough to instruct a solicitor and be represented; that she had a view and a particular position to adopt although she did not side with either parent; that being represented enabled her to take part in the proceedings but not be directly involved in the argument between her parents; that rather than give oral evidence she lodged an affidavit; and that the procedure adopted of the child becoming a party minuter was entirely appropriate. The sheriff also opined as to the proper procedure for a party minuter to adopt, namely to lodge (i) a minute seeking to be sisted as a party, stating in a statement of facts the grounds on which the minuter wished to become a party; and (ii) defences. The other parties should answer the party minuter's pleadings and the record should incorporate the party minuter's pleadings as well as the other parties' answers to them in their pleadings and any appropriate pleas-in-law. In *H v. H,* 2000 Fam.L.R. 73 the evidence of the parties' child was accepted by affidavit.

[27] r. 33.20 or r. 33A.20. Note that an interview cannot be substituted for a proof — *Macdonald v. Macdonald,* 1985 S.L.T. 244. Note further that careful consideration would always require to be given to the question of whether to embark upon the process of interviewing a child and, if it is to be undertaken, the most appropriate method of approaching this sensitive task — *W v. W,* 2003 S.L.T. 1253 at p. 1259. *Cf. G v. G,* 2003 Fam.L.R. 118.

[28] Sheriff Courts (Scotland) Act 1971, s. 32(j) and Form F9 or Form CP7.

[29] r. 33.20(1) or r. 33A.20(1).

[30] r. 33.20(2) or r. 33A.20(2). The practicalities involved in reconciling the parties' right to a fair hearing and a child's right to express his views are of immense difficulty, best resolved by taking the fundamental principle that a party is entitled to disclosure of all materials as the starting point and next considering whether disclosure would involve a real possibility of significant harm to the child — *McGrath v. McGrath,* 1999 S.L.T. (Sh.Ct.) 90 (*cf. Dosoo v. Dosoo,* 1999 S.L.T. (Sh.Ct.) 86).

order, does not adversely affect the position of a person who has, in good faith and for value, acquired any property of the child concerned, or any right or interest in such property.[31]

POWERS OF THE COURT

The court's powers in connection with the children in divorce actions are wide and include[32] (in addition to power to prevent the removal of children[33] and certain restricted powers to make provision for the maintenance of children[34]) powers to make

---

[31] 1995 Act, s. 11(8).

[32] Note that the court has a statutory power in relation to court proceedings to restrict publicity concerning a person under the age of 17 years (see Children and Young Persons (Scotland) Act 1937, s. 46(1), as amended, and *C v. S*, 1989 S.C. 1).

[33] The sheriff may at any time after the commencement of proceedings (*i.e.* when the warrant of citation is signed), on an application by (a) any party to the proceedings, (b) the guardian of the child concerned, or (c) any other person who has or wishes to obtain the care of a child, grant interdict or interim interdict prohibiting the removal of the child from the United Kingdom or any part thereof, or out of the control of the person in whose care the child is— Family Law Act 1986, s. 35(3) and (5), as amended by the Age of Legal Capacity (Scotland) Act 1991, Sched. 1, para. 47 and the Children (Scotland) Act 1995, Sched. 4, para. 41(8) and Sched. 5. Any such interdict or interim interdict automatically has effect in the rest of the United Kingdom—1986 Act, s. 36. An application by a party to the proceedings requires to be made by motion (r. 33.24(1)(a) or r. 33A.25(1)(a)) and by any other person by minute (r. 33.24(1)(b) or r. 33A.25(1)(b)). The application need not be served or intimated (r. 33.24(2) or r. 33A.25(2)). Interdict was refused in *S v. Q*, 2005 S.L.T. 53. The court granting the interdict or interim interdict may order the surrender of any United Kingdom passport issued to or containing particulars of the child—1986 Act, s. 37(1).

[34] The court's powers to make provision for the maintenance of children have been very largely curtailed by the Child Support Act 1991, as amended by the Child Support Act 1995. The residual role of the court in this respect, prescribed by s. 8 of the Act is, broadly, confined to: (a) revoking maintenance orders (subs. (3)); (b) making maintenance orders giving effect to written agreements (subs. (5)); (c) making top up maintenance orders (subs. (6)); (d) making maintenance orders requiring payees to meet some or all of the expenses incurred in connection with the provision of instruction at an educational establishment or training for a trade, profession or vocation (subs. (7)); (e) making certain maintenance orders in relation to disabled children (subs. (8) and (9)); and (f) making maintenance orders against a person with care of the child (subs. (10)). An adult training centre attended by a handicapped child was held to be an educational establishment for the purposes of s. 8(7) in *McBride v. McBride*, 1995 S.C.L.R. 1021. Applications for aliment require to be made by a crave in the initial writ or defences, as the case may be or, where the applicant is a third party, by minute (r. 33.39(1) and (2)(b) or r. 33A.39(1) and (2)(b)), unless made after decree (in which case the application is made by minute in the original process — r. 33.45(1) or r. 33A.42(1)). Applications for interim aliment in either case are made by motion (rr. 33.43(a) and 33.45(2) or r. 33A.40(a) and 33A.42(2)). An application may be made by a person over 18 years for aliment or interim aliment in terms of r. 33.46 or r. 33A.43. The court's powers to vary an order after decree are restricted to the circumstances described in s. 8(3A), namely to cases where s. 4(10) or s. 7(10) prevents the making of an application for a maintenance assessment (written maintenance agreement made before April 5, 1993 or maintenance order in force, or benefit being paid to parent of child) and no application has been made for a maintenance assessment or such an application has

orders[35] in relation to parental responsibilities[36] and parental rights[37] under section 11(1) (a) and (b) of the Children (Scotland) Act 1995 and to make a reference to the Principal Reporter under section 54 of that Act.

---

been made but no maintenance assessment has been made in response to it. The powers are exercisable upon a material change of circumstances (Family Law (Scotland) Act 1985, s. 5(1)) and may be sought to be invoked by way of minute lodged in the original process (r. 33.45(1) or r. 33A.42(1)) — see *e.g. McGilchrist v. McGilchrist*, 1997 S.L.T. (Sh. Ct.) 2. Such application requires however to be made while the obligation to aliment still exists — *Paterson v. Paterson*, 2002 S.L.T. (Sh. Ct.) 65. The making of a maintenance assessment with respect to a child for whom the decree of aliment was granted constitutes a material change of circumstances for the purposes of s. 5(1) (s. 5(1A)). In that event, the court is not bound to vary the alimentary award precisely in line with the maintenance assessment but is entitled to look at the whole position again (*Stokes v. Stokes*, 1999 S.C.L.R. 327). Where such a minute has been lodged, any party may lodge a motion for an interim order which may be made pending the determination of the application (r. 33.45(2) or r. 33A.42(2)). The court has power to backdate a variation, in terms of s. 5(2) of the 1985 Act, to the date of the application for variation or, on special cause shown, to a date prior to that (see *e.g. Hannah v. Hannah*, 1988 S.L.T. 82; *Dalgleish v. Robinson*, 1991 S.C.L.R. 892; and *Mitchell v. Mitchell*, 1992 S.C.L.R. 553), and in that event to order any sums paid under the decree to be repaid (1985 Act, s. 5(4)). (As to variation of an order for interim aliment in a depending action, see Chap. 7, text accompanying nn. 11–13 and r. 33.43(a) or r. 33A.40(a)). In any action in which an order for aliment is sought, or is sought to be varied or recalled, the pleadings of the applicant must include an averment stating whether and, if so, when and by whom, a maintenance order has been granted in favour of or against that party or of any other person in respect of whom the order is sought (r. 33.5 or r. 33A.5). See also r. 33.6(2) or r. 33A.6(2) with respect to applications for top up maintenance orders; r. 33.6(3) or r. 33A.6(3) in relation to applications not covered by the Child Support Act 1991; and r. 33.6(5) or r. 33A.6(5) with regard to actions involving parties in respect of whom a decision has been made in any application, review or appeal under the 1991 Act relating to any child of those parties.

[35] "Orders" includes interim orders and orders varying or discharging orders — 1995 Act, s. 11(13). When dealing with a motion for an interim order, what the sheriff requires to do is to consider all the material information before him and then decide whether he is satisfied that it would be in the best interests of the child or children to make any order relating to parental rights — *Armstrong v. Gibson*, 1991 S.L.T. 193 at p. 194. See also *G v. G*, 2002 Fam.L.R. 120.

[36] "Parental responsibilities" are the following which a parent has in relation to his or her child —

> "(a) to safeguard and promote the child's health, development and welfare;
> (b) to provide, in a manner appropriate to the stage of development of the child — (i) direction; (ii) guidance, to the child;
> (c) if the child is not living with the parent, to maintain personal relations and direct contact with the child on a regular basis; and
> (d) to act as the child's legal representative, but only in so far as compliance with [the foregoing] is practicable and in the interests of the child."

— 1995 Act s. 1(1). "Child" means, for the purposes of (a), (b)(i), (c) and (d) above, a person under the age of 16 years; and for the purposes of (b)(ii), a person under the age of 18 years — s. 1(2).

[37] "Parental rights" are the following, which a parent has in order to enable him to fulfil his parental responsibilities in relation to his child —

Section 11 orders

In terms of section 11(2) of the Act, the court may[38] make such order in relation to parental responsibilities or parental rights under subsection (1) as it thinks fit; and without prejudice to the generality of that subsection may, in particular, so make any of the following orders[39]:

"(a) an order depriving a person of some or all of his parental responsibilities or parental rights in relation to a child;

(b) an order —

   (i) imposing upon a person (provided he is at least sixteen years of age or is a parent of the child) such responsibilities; and

   (ii) giving that person such rights;

(c) an order regulating the arrangements as to —

   (i) with whom; or

   (ii) if with different persons alternately or periodically, with whom during what periods, a child under the age of

---

"(a) to have the child living with him or otherwise to regulate the child's residence;

(b) to control, direct or guide, in a manner appropriate to the stage of development of the child, the child's upbringing;

(c) if the child is not living with him, to maintain personal relations and direct contact with the child on a regular basis; and

(d) to act as the child's representative."

—1995 Act, s. 2(1). "Child" means a person under the age of 16 years — s. 2(7). Where two or more persons have a parental right as respects a child, each of them may exercise that right without the consent of the other, or, as the case may be, of any of the others, unless any decree or deed conferring the right, or regulating its exercise, otherwise provides — s. 2(2). Without prejudice to any court order, no person is entitled to remove a child habitually resident in Scotland from, or to retain any such child outwith, the United Kingdom without the consent of any person (whether or not a parent of the child) who for the time being has and is exercising in relation to him a right mentioned in (a) or (c) above; except that, where both the child's parents are persons so described, the consent required for his removal or retention must be that of them both — s. 2(3). The fact that a person has parental responsibilities or parental rights in relation to a child does not entitle that person to act in any way which would be incompatible with any court order relating to the child or the child's property, or with any supervision requirement made under s. 70 of the Act — s. 3(4). A person who has parental responsibilities or parental rights in relation to a child cannot abdicate those responsibilities or rights to anyone else, but may arrange for some or all of them to be fulfilled or exercised on his behalf; and without prejudice to that generality any such arrangement may be made with a person who already has parental responsibilities or parental rights in relation to the child concerned — s. 3(5).

[38] The existence of a supervision requirement does not serve to make a crave for a s. 11 order incompetent — *P v. P*, 2000 S.L.T. 781.

[39] Orders in terms of s. 11(2)(g) and (h) of the Act, relating to children's property and guardianship, are not considered herein.

sixteen years is to live (any such order being known as a 'residence order')[40];

(d)   an order regulating the arrangements for maintaining personal relations and direct contact between a child under that age and a person with whom the child is not, or will not be, living (any such order being known as a 'contact order')[41];

(e)   an order regulating any specific question which has arisen, or may arise, in connection with [*inter alia* parental responsibilities or parental rights] (any such order being known as a 'specific issue order')[42];

---

[40] A residence order is intended to regulate where a child is to make his home; and so a contact order is the appropriate order to regulate overnight or longer stays — *McBain v. McIntyre*, 1997 S.C.L.R. 181. Where the court makes a residence order which requires that a child live with a person who, immediately before the order is made, does not have in relation to the child all the parental responsibilities mentioned in s. 1(1)(a), (b) and (d) of the 1995 Act, and the parental rights mentioned in s. 2(1)(b) and (d) of the Act, that person shall, subject to the provisions of the order and of any order made under subs. (1), have the relevant responsibilities and rights while the residence order remains in force — s. 11(12). A joint residence order was held to be competent in *Fourman v. Fourman*, 1998 Fam.L.R. 98, at p. 102.

[41] An award of postal contact was made in *A v. M*, 1999 Fam.L.R. 42. *Quaere* what form an order would take preventing contact altogether (*cf. Nottinghamshire C.C. v. P* [1993] 3 All E.R. 815 and *Re H and Others (Prohibited Steps Order)* [1995] 4 All E.R. 110). In this regard, the right of the child enshrined in Art. 9(3) of the U.N. Convention on the Rights of the Child (App. V) to personal relations and direct contact with both parents on a regular basis requires to be borne in mind, albeit in the context no doubt of the welfare principle (*cf. Sanderson v. McManus*, 1997 S.C. (H.L.) 55). As to the responsibility of the parent with whom the child lives to help make contact orders work, see *Cosh v. Cosh*, 1979 S.L.T. (Notes) 72 at p. 73. Where the sheriff at his or her own instance or on the motion of a party is considering making a contact order or interim contact order subject to supervision by the social work department of a local authority, he or she must ordain the party moving for such an order to intimate to the chief executive of that local authority (where not already a party to the action and represented at the hearing at which the issue arises) (a) the terms of any relevant motion; (b) the intention of the sheriff to order that the contact order be supervised by the social work department of that local authority; and (c) that the local authority shall, within such period as the sheriff has determined (i) notify the sheriff clerk whether it intends to make representations to the sheriff; and (ii) where it intends to make representations in writing, to do so within that period — r. 33.25 or r. 33A.26. An appeal without leave of the sheriff against an interim contact order or the refusal of an application for an interim contact order is incompetent—*Fergus v. Eadie*, 2005 S.C.L.R. 176.

[42] There does not have to be a dispute between the parties in order for the court to have power to make a specific issue order; it is sufficient that there is a question to be answered — *Re H G (Specific Issue Order: Sterilisation)* [1993] 1 F.L.R. 587. In *Fourman v. Fourman*, 1998 Fam.L.R. 98, a mother asked the court to determine as a specific issue whether she would be allowed to remove the parties' children to Australia (her homeland) to live there. In *M v. M*, 2000 Fam.L.R.84, a mother asked the court to determine as a specific issue whether she would be allowed to remove the parties' children to the United States (her homeland) to live there. In *S v. S*, 2002 S.C. 246, a mother sought a specific issue order to enable her to take her child to Australia so that she could pursue a career

(f) an interdict prohibiting the taking of any step of a kind specified in the fulfilment of parental responsibilities or the exercise of parental rights relating to a child or in the administration of a child's property... ."

A section 11 order has the effect of depriving a person of a parental responsibility or parental right only in so far as the order expressly so provides and only to the extent necessary to give effect to the order.[43] The fact that a person has parental responsibilities or parental rights in relation to a child, however, does not entitle that person to act in any way which would be incompatible with any court order relating to the child.[44]

An order may be made (1) upon an application by any person who has parental responsibilities or parental rights in relation to the child in question[45] or who, not having, and never having had, parental responsibilities or parental rights in relation to the child, claims an interest[46]; or (2) in the absence of any application, where the court (even if it declines to make any other order) considers that it should be made.[47]

Application to the court for a section 11 order is made by the pursuer by a crave in the initial writ,[48] accompanied by any appropriate crave for warrant for intimation or to dispense with intimation.[49] Such an

---

opportunity. In *M v. C*, 2002 S.L.T. (Sh. Ct.) 82, a father sought specific issue orders (1) that the mother could not alter the child's surname; and (2) that the child should not be required to attend classes in religious instruction, in each case without the father's consent. In *G v. G*, 2002 Fam.L.R. 120, a mother sought a specific issue order providing that the parties' older child attend a boarding school. In *McShane v. Duryea*, 2006 Fam. L.R. 15, a mother sought a specific issue order allowing her to move to the United States with the parties' child. For other examples of such an order see *Re R (Minor)* (1993) 15 B.M.L.R. 72; *Re R (A Minor)(Blood Transfusion)* [1993] 2 F.L.R. 757; *Re F (Specific Issue: Child Interview)* [1995] 1 F.L.R. 819; *Dawson v. Wearmouth* [1997] 2 F.L.R. 629, affirmed by the House of Lords on 25 March 1999; *Re T (Change of Surname)* [1998] 2 F.L.R. 620; *Re T (Change of Surname)* [1998] 2 F.L.R. 656; and *Re A (Specific Issue Order)* [2001] 1 F.L.R. 121.

[43] 1995 Act, s. 11(11).
[44] 1995 Act, s. 3(4).
[45] 1995 Act, s. 11(3)(a)(ii).
[46] 1995 Act, s. 11(3)(a)(i). Such a person would include, *e.g.* the child's step-parent and, by virtue of s. 11(5) of the Act, the child itself (but not a local authority). A local authority can however competently make representations to the court to the effect that the court should make no order in favour of a party applying for a s.11 order, and may do so by way of a minute — *McLean v. Dornan*, 2001 Fam.L.R. 58.
[47] 1995 Act, s. 11(3)(b).
[48] r. 33.39(1)(a) and (2)(a) or r. 33A.39(1)(a) and (2)(a). Application by a party in an action depending before the court for, or for variation of, a residence order or a contact order must be made by motion — r. 33.43(b) or r. 33A.40(b).
[49] r. 33.7(1)(e) or r. 33A.7(1)(c) (intimation where child in care of local authority or third party or liable to be maintained by third party); r. 33.7(1)(f) or r. 33A.7(1)(d) (intimation where s. 11 order craved and parent not party to the action); r. 33.7(1)(g) or r. 33A.7(1)(e)

application falls to be made by a defender by a crave in the defences,[50] so accompanied,[51] or simply by completing Form F26 (notice of intention to defend in a family action) so as to indicate a wish to obtain a section 11 order.[52] Application for a section 11 order by a person other than the pursuer or defender is made by minute in the cause.[53]

Unless the sheriff on cause shown otherwise directs, a warrant for citation cannot be granted in a divorce action which includes a crave for a section 11 order without there being produced with the initial writ an extract of the relevant entry in the register of births or equivalent document.[54]

A party who makes an application for a section 11 order in respect of a child must include in his or her pleadings averments giving particulars of any other proceedings known to him or her, whether in Scotland or elsewhere and whether concluded or not, which relate to the child in respect of whom the section 11 order is sought.[55] Where such other proceedings are continuing or have taken place, and the averments of the applicant do not contain particulars of the other proceedings, or contain particulars which are incomplete or incorrect, any defences or minute, as the case may be, lodged by any party to the action must include such particulars or such further or correct particulars as are known to him or her.[56]

Where (a) on the lodging of a notice of intention to defend in a divorce action in which the initial writ seeks or includes a crave for a section 11 order, a defender wishes to oppose any such crave or order, or seeks the same order as that craved by the pursuer; (b) on the lodging of a notice of intention to defend in a divorce action, the defender

---

(intimation where residence order craved and pursuer is not parent and is resident in Scotland); r. 33.7(1)(h) or r. 33A.7(1)(f) (intimation to child where s. 11 order craved); r. 33.7(5) or r. 33A.7(5) (intimation dispensed with where address unknown); and r. 33.7(7) or r. 33A.7(7) (intimation dispensed with where inappropriate for child). These rules are reproduced in Chap. 1 (nn. 17–19 and 28 and accompanying text).

[50] rr. 33.34(1)(b)(iii) and (2)(b)(i) or r. 33A.34(1)(b)(iii) and (2)(b)(i), and 33.39(1)(a) and (2)(a) or r. 33A.39(1)(a) and (2)(a). Contrast these provisions with r. 9.6(3) (in divorce action neither crave nor averments need be made in defences which relate to s. 11 order). See also r. 33.43(b) or r. 33A.40(b), mentioned in n. 48 *supra*.

[51] r. 33.15(3) or r. 33A.15(3) (party making crave which would have required warrant under r. 33.7 or r. 33A.7 if sought in initial writ required to include crave for warrant or to dispense with such intimation in his writ).

[52] r. 33.22A(1)(a) and (b) and (4), or r. 33A.23(1)(a) and (b) and (4) and r. 9.6(3).

[53] r. 33.39(1)(b) and (2)(a) or r. 33A.39(1)(b) and (2)(a). See also r. 33.43(b) or r. 33A.40(b), mentioned in n. 48 *supra*; r. 33.7(1)(e)–(h), (5) and (7) or r. 33A.7(1)(c)-(f), (5) and (7), mentioned in n. 49 *supra*; and r. 33.15(3) or r. 33A.15(3), mentioned in n. 51 *supra*. *Cf. Robb v. Gillan,* 2004 Fam.L.R. 120.

[54] r. 33.9(b) or r. 33A.9(3).

[55] r. 33.3(1)(a) or r. 33A.3(1)(a), implementing s. 39 of the Family Law Act 1986.

[56] r. 33.3(2) or r. 33A.3(2).

seeks a section 11 order which is not craved by the pursuer; or (c) in any other circumstances in a divorce action, the sheriff considers that a Child Welfare Hearing should be fixed and makes an order (whether at his own instance or on the motion of a party) that such a hearing be fixed, the sheriff clerk requires to fix a date and time for a Child Welfare Hearing on the first suitable court date occurring not sooner than 21 days after the lodging of such notice of intention to defend, unless the sheriff directs the hearing to be held on an earlier date.[57] On fixing the date for the Child Welfare Hearing, the sheriff clerk must intimate that date in Form F41 or Form CP26 to the parties,[58] whose right to make any other application to the court whether by motion or otherwise is unaffected thereby.[59] At the Child Welfare Hearing (which may be held in private), the sheriff must seek to secure the expeditious resolution of disputes in relation to the child by ascertaining from the parties the matters in dispute and any information relevant to that dispute, and may (a) order such steps to be taken, or (b) make such order, if any, or (c) order further procedure, as he thinks fit.[60] All parties (including a child who has indicated his or her wish to attend) must, except on cause shown, attend the Child Welfare Hearing personally.[61] It is the duty of the parties to provide the sheriff with sufficient information to enable him to conduct the Child Welfare Hearing.[62]

In any action of divorce or dissolution of civil partnership in which an order in relation to parental responsibilities or parental rights is in issue, the sheriff may, at any stage of the action,[63] where he considers

---

[57] r. 33.22A(1) or r. 33A.23(1). Where in an action of divorce the only matters in dispute are an order in terms of s. 11 of the Children (Scotland) Act 1995, or the matters in dispute include an order in terms of s. 11, there is no requirement to fix an Options Hearing insofar as the matters in dispute relate to an order in terms of s. 11(2) of the Act — r. 9.2(1A). Otherwise, the fixing of a Child Welfare Hearing does not obviate the need to fix an Options hearing under r. 9.2 — *Henderson v. Adamson,* 1998 S.C.L.R. 365.

[58] r. 33.22A(2) or r. 33A.23(2).

[59] r. 33.22A(3) or r. 33A.23(3).

[60] r. 33.22A(4) or r. 33A.23(4). The sheriff is entitled under the rule to make a final order at the Child Welfare Hearing without hearing evidence (*Hartnett v. Hartnett,* 1997 S.C.L.R. 525; *Morgan v. Morgan,* 1998 S.C.L.R. 681; *McCulloch v. Riach,* 1999 S.C.L.R. 159; and *O'Malley v. O'Malley,* 2004 Fam.L.R. 44). A sheriff was however held not to have exercised his discretion reasonably in dismissing the action at the Child Welfare Hearing without having given the pursuer any prior indication of any intention to dismiss at that stage — *Ross v. Ross,* 1999 S.C.L.R. 1112. If a proof is held, the evidence should be recorded by a shorthand writer (*Hartnett, supra*).

[61] r. 33.22A(5) or r. 33A.23(5). Failure by a party to attend, however, attracts no sanction provided that he or she is represented at the diet — *McLaren v. Henderson,* 2006 S.L.T. (Sh. Ct.) 68.

[62] r. 33.22A(6) or r. 33A.23(6).

[63] Reference to a mediator may be made after proof (*Harris v. Martin,* 1995 S.C.L.R. 580) but is not a competent disposal as a final order of the court (*Patterson v. Patterson,* 1994 S.C.L.R. 166).

it appropriate to do so, refer that issue to a mediator accredited to a specified family mediation organisation.[64] In general, no information as to what occurred during family mediation is admissible as evidence in any civil proceedings.[65]

Where the court is considering any question relating to the care and upbringing of a child, it may, without prejudice to its power to appoint any other person,[66] not being an officer of the local authority for the purpose, appoint an appropriate local authority to investigate and report to the court on all the circumstances of the child and on the proposed arrangements for the care and upbringing of the child.[67] On making an appointment for such purpose, whether of a local authority or another person, the sheriff requires to direct that the party who sought the appointment or, where the court makes the appointment of its own motion, the pursuer or minuter (as the case may be) must (a) instruct the local authority or reporter, and (b) be responsible, in the first instance, for the fees and outlays of the local authority or reporter appointed.[68] The party who sought the appointment or, where the sheriff makes the appointment of his own motion, the pursuer or minuter (as the case may be) is required, within seven days after the date of the appointment, to intimate the name and address of the local authority or reporter to any local authority to which intimation of the action has been made.[69] On completion of his report, the local authority or reporter, as the case may be, is required to send it, with a copy of it for each party, to the sheriff clerk who must upon receipt send a copy to each party.[70] Where a local authority or reporter has been appointed, an

---

[64] r. 33.22 or r. 33A.22.

[65] Civil Evidence (Family Mediation) (Scotland) Act 1995, s. 1, subject to s. 2 (exceptions, *e.g.* as to contracts and where every participant agrees on admissibility).

[66] Such a person may be an advocate or a solicitor. Such appointment may most appropriately be made in cases of particular urgency, cases involving parties living in different local authority areas and cases where the local authority has already been extensively involved (*cf. O v. O*, 1994 S.C. 569 at p. 572).

[67] Matrimonial Proceedings (Children) Act 1958, s. 11(1), as amended by the Children (Scotland) Act 1995, Sched. 4, para. 9. If on consideration of the report the court, either *ex proprio motu* or on the application of any person concerned, considers it expedient to do so, it may require the person who furnished the report to appear and to be examined on oath regarding any matter dealt with in the report, and such person may be examined or cross-examined accordingly — 1958 Act, s. 11(4). The report is not otherwise evidence in the case and falls to be disregarded — *Whitecross v. Whitecross,* 1977 S.L.T. 225 at p. 227; *Kristiansen v. Kristiansen,* 1987 S.C.L.R. 462; *Bailey v. Bailey,* 2001 Fam.L.R. 133 at p. 137. But see *O v. O,* 1994 S.C. 569 at p. 572 and *McIntyre v. McIntyre,* 1962 S.L.T. (Notes) 70. It has been held that a report prepared in order to be of assistance to the court at the time of the proof should have been considered by the sheriff on its merits before he reached his decision (*Bailey, loc. cit.*).

[68] r. 33.21(2) or r. 33A.21(2).

[69] r. 33.21(3) or r. 33A.21(3).

[70] r. 33.21(4) and (5) or r. 33A.21(4) and (5).

application for a section 11 order in respect of the child concerned cannot be determined until the report has been lodged.[71]

Where in proceedings for or relating to a section 11 order in respect of a child there is not available to the court adequate information as to where the child is, the court may order any person who it has reason to believe may have relevant information to disclose it to the court.[72] Application for the order requires to be made by motion; and the sheriff may ordain the person against whom the order has been made to appear before him or to lodge an affidavit.[73] A person cannot be excused from complying with such an order by reason that to do so may incriminate him or his spouse of an offence; but a statement or admission made in compliance with the order is not admissible in evidence against either of them in proceedings for any offence other than perjury.[74]

Where any parties have reached agreement in relation to a section 11 order, a joint minute may be entered into expressing that agreement; and, subject to rule 33.19(3) or 33A.19(3) (no order before views of child expressed), the sheriff may grant decree in respect of those parts of the joint minute in relation to which he could otherwise make an order, whether or not such a decree would include a matter for which there was no crave.[75] No agreement can however bind the court.[76]

To enforce section 11 orders the court may grant such orders as an order for delivery[77] or for sheriff officers to search for and take possession of a child.[78] Wilful failure to make a child available for the purposes of a contact order may be punishable as a contempt of court. A party alleged to be in breach of an interim order may be ordained to appear at the bar to answer the charge and, in the event of denial, minute and answers may be ordered.[79] Where a final order is claimed to have been breached, procedure is by way of initial writ.[80] If the court is satisfied that the order or interim order has been breached, it may impose a penalty of imprisonment or a fine, or may admonish the party in breach.[81]

---

[71] r. 33.21(6) or r. 33A.21(6).

[72] Family Law Act 1986, s. 33(1). *Cf. Abusaif v. Abusaif*, 1984 S.L.T. 90.

[73] r. 33.23 or r. 33A.24.

[74] 1986 Act, s. 33(2).

[75] r. 33.26 (a) or r. 33A.27(a).

[76] *Robson v. Robson*, 1973 S.L.T. (Notes) 4: *Anderson v. Anderson*, 1989 S.C.L.R. 475; *McKechnie v. McKechnie*, 1990 S.L.T. (Sh. Ct.) 75.

[77] *McEwen v. McEwen,* 2000 Fam.L.R. 116. *Cf. Brown v. Brown*, 1948 S.C. 5 and *Thomson v. Thomson*, 1979 S.L.T. (Sh. Ct.) 11. As to the power of the court to make an order for the delivery of a child by one parent to the other parent other than in implementation of a s. 11 order, see the Family Law Act 1986, s. 17(1).

[78] *cf. Caldwell v. Caldwell*, 1983 S.C. 137.

[79] *Johnston v. Johnston*, 1996 S.L.T. 499.

[80] *Celso v. Celso*, 1992 S.C.L.R. 175.

[81] Note that the standard of proof is proof beyond reasonable doubt (*Johnston v. Johnston*, 1996 S.L.T. 499).

A section 11 order relating to parental responsibilities or parental rights ceases to have effect where a relevant order made outwith Scotland comes into force, so far as it makes provision for any matter for which the same or different provision is made by that order,[82] or in any event once the child reaches the age of 16 years.[83] Where a section 11 order made by a court in Scotland ceases by virtue of the coming into force of a relevant order to have effect so far as it makes provision for any matter, that court has no power to vary it so as to make provision for that matter.[84] Otherwise, the court may vary,[85] or recall, any section 11 order made by it notwithstanding that it would no longer have jurisdiction to make the original order.[86]

Application after final decree for, or for the variation or recall of, a section 11 order or in relation to the enforcement of such an order requires to be made by minute in the process of the action to which the application relates.[87] Where a minute has been lodged, any party may apply by motion for any interim order which may be made pending the determination of the application.[88]

Reference to the Principal Reporter

In terms of section 54(1) of the Children (Scotland) Act 1995, where it appears to the court that any of certain statutory conditions is satisfied with respect to a child, it may refer the matter to the Principal Reporter, specifying the condition. The statutory conditions are those set forth in section 52(2), namely that the child:

---

[82] 1986 Act, s. 15(1), as amended by the Children (Scotland) Act 1995, Sched. 4, para. 41(4) and the European Communities (Matrimonial Jurisdiction and Judgments) (Scotland) Regulations 2001 (S.S.I. 2001 No. 36), reg. 4(2), the relevant orders being an order under Pt. I of the 1986 Act, or an order varying such an order, competently made by another court in any part of the United Kingdom with respect to the child in question; or an order relating to the parental responsibilities or parental rights in relation to that child which is made outside the United Kingdom and recognised in Scotland by virtue of s. 26 of the 1986 Act, or by virtue of the Council Regulation.

[83] In the unlikely case of an order in relation to the parental responsibility to provide guidance to the child (s. 1(1)(b)(ii)), the order would cease to have effect on the child's eighteenth birthday — 1995 Act, s. 1(2)(b).

[84] 1986 Act, s. 15(2).

[85] An order varying an original order means any order made with respect to the same child as the original order was made — s. 15(3).

[86] s. 15(2), subject to ss. 11(1) and 13(4).

[87] r. 33.44(1) or r. 33A.41(1). It is incompetent to proceed by way of separate action — *McEwen v. McEwen,* 2000 Fam.L.R. 116. Note that where the court is asked to consider a variation of a s. 11 order originally granted upon the parties' joint motion, it is of little value to look for a change of circumstances since the agreement was made — *McGhee v. McGhee,* 1998 Fam.L.R. 122. The court is required to decide on the evidence whether it is in the best interests of the child that the original order be varied or recalled — *Thomson v. Thomson,* 2000 G.W.D. 23–874.

[88] r. 33.44(2) or r. 33A.41(2).

"(a) is beyond the control of any relevant person;

(b) is falling into bad association or is exposed to moral danger;

(c) is likely (i) to suffer unnecessarily; or (ii) be impaired in his health or development, due to a lack of parental care;

(d) is a child in respect of whom any of the offences mentioned in Schedule 1 to the Criminal Procedure (Scotland) Act 1975 (offences against children to which special provisions apply) has been committed;

(e) is, or is likely to become, a member of the same household as a child in respect of whom any of the offences referred to in para. (d) above has been committed;

(f) is, or is likely to become, a member of the same household as a person in respect of whom an offence under sections 2A to 2C of the Sexual Offences (Scotland) Act 1976 (incest and intercourse with a child by step-parent or person in position of trust) has been committed by a member of that household;

(g) is, or is likely to become, a member of the same household as a person in respect of whom an offence under sections 1 to 3 of the Criminal Law (Consolidation) (Scotland) Act 1995 (incest and intercourse with a child by step-parent or person in position of trust) has been committed by a member of that household;

(h) has failed to attend school regularly without reasonable excuse;

(i) has committed an offence.

(j) has misused alcohol or any drug, whether or not a controlled drug within the meaning of the Misuse of Drugs Act 1971;

(k) has misused a volatile substance by deliberately inhaling its vapour, other than for medicinal purposes;

(l) is being provided with accommodation by a local authority under section 25, or is the subject of a parental responsibilities order obtained under section 86, of the Act and, in either case, his behaviour is such that special measures are necessary for his adequate supervision in his interest or in the interest of others."

Where the court has referred a matter to the Principal Reporter under section 54(1) he must —

(a) make such investigation as he thinks appropriate; and

(b) if he considers that compulsory measures of supervision[89] are necessary, arrange a children's hearing to consider the case of the child under section 69 of the Act, and section 54(1) applies as if the condition specified by the court thereunder were a ground of referral established in accordance with section 68 of the Act.[90]

---

[89] "Supervision" in relation to compulsory measures of supervision may include measures taken for the protection, guidance, treatment or control of the child — 1995 Act, s. 52(3).

[90] 1995 Act, s. 54(3).

CHAPTER 7

MONEY

The subject of money in the context of the law and practice of divorce and dissolution of civil partnership (excepting maintenance for children) is discussed in this chapter; and the court's power to make orders relative to the subject under the Family Law (Scotland) Act 1985[1] before, upon, and after the granting of decree are examined.

ORDERS MADE BEFORE THE GRANTING OF DECREE

Interim aliment orders

A claim for interim aliment is competent in an action of divorce by either party against the other party, and in an action for dissolution of a civil partnership by either partner against the other partner.[2] Application must be made by motion.[3] Whether or not the claim is disputed, the court may award the sum claimed or any lesser sum or may refuse to make an award.[4] An award of interim aliment must consist of an award of periodical payments payable only until the date of the disposal of the action or such earlier date as the court may specify.[5] It is incompetent to backdate an award of interim aliment.[6]

The court may order either party to provide details of his resources,[7] and may reasonably expect the parties to produce documentary

---

[1] In actions brought before September 1, 1986 (the date of commencement of the Family Law (Scotland) Act 1985) s. 5 of the Divorce (Scotland) Act 1976 continues to operate — 1985 Act, s. 28(3).

[2] 1985 Act, s. 6(1)(b) and (c), as amended by the Civil Partnership Act 2004, Sched. 28, para. 13.

[3] r. 33.50 or r. 33A.47. A crave for interim aliment is therefore inappropriate (compare, *e.g.* r. 33.49(1)(a) or r. 33A.46(1)(a) and r. 33.49(1)(b) or r. 33A.46(1)(b)). For a contrary view, see *Kerr v. Kerr*, 1995 S.C.L.R. 1130.

[4] 1985 Act, s. 6(2).

[5] 1985 Act, s. 6(3).

[6] *Kirk v. Kirk,* 2003 Fam.L.R. 50; *Adamson v. Adamson,* 1996 S.L.T. 427.

[7] 1985 Act, s. 20, considered *infra*. "Resources" means present and foreseeable resources — s. 27(1). Both the benefits of a company car and payment by the company of pension contributions constitute resources which ought to be taken into account, at least to the extent that the recipient's cash income is thereby not subject to such outlays (*Semple v. Semple*, 1995 S.C.L.R. 569).

evidence of their respective net[8] incomes at any hearing on a claim for interim aliment. In deciding what award of interim aliment if any to make, the court may have regard to considerations applicable in determining the amount to award in respect of a claim for aliment, namely needs, earning capacity and general circumstances.[9]

Awards of interim aliment are within the discretion of the sheriff and an appellate court could only interfere with any decision taken in exercise of this discretion if it were to be satisfied that the judge of first instance had erred in law, or that he had failed to notice a relevant factor, or that he had arrived at a wholly unreasonable decision.[10]

An award of interim aliment may be varied or recalled by an order of the court[11] but no such variation or recall can be backdated.[12] It has been held that variation of an award of interim aliment is competent without a change of circumstances having been established, there requiring only to be a sufficient reason to justify a variation.[13]

Incidental orders

An incidental order may be made under section 8(2) of the Act before, as well as on or after, the granting or refusal of decree of divorce

---

[8] As in *Wiseman v. Wiseman*, 1989 S.C.L.R. 757 and *Pryde v. Pryde*, 1991 S.L.T. (Sh. Ct.) 26. But see *MacInnes v. MacInnes*, 1993 S.L.T. 1108.

[9] *McGeachie v. McGeachie*, 1989 S.C.L.R. 99 ("While it is true that the criteria set out in s. 4 of the 1985 Act do not by virtue of the Act apply to interim aliment awards ... these criteria are consistent with pre-existing law and practice in relation to the determination of interim aliment ... [N]eeds, earning capacity and general circumstances are all proper elements to consider when awarding interim aliment" (*per* the Sheriff Principal at p. 100)). As to "needs" see now *McGeoch v. McGeoch*, 1998 Fam.L.R. 130. *Quaere* whether, and if so when, a spouse could reasonably expect to be alimented when cohabiting with a third party (*cf. Brunton v. Brunton*, 1986 S.L.T. 49; *Kavanagh v. Kavanagh*, 1989 S.L.T. 134; and *Atkinson v. Atkinson* [1995] 2 F.L.R. 356). See also *Munro v. Munro*, 1986 S.L.T. 72 and *Henderson v. Henderson*, 1991 G.W.D. 31–1864 (relevance of paying spouse's cohabitant's earnings).

[10] *Begg v. Begg*, 1987 S.C.L.R. 704 at p. 705. See also *Adams v. Adams*, 2002 S.C.L.R. 379 at p. 380 (appellate court not entitled to interfere with judge of first instance's decision unless it could be shown that he had misdirected himself in law, taken into account an irrelevant consideration, left out of account a relevant consideration or reached a decision which was plainly wrong). An appeal without leave of the sheriff against an award of interim aliment or the refusal of an application for interim aliment is incompetent (*Rixson v. Rixson*, 1990 S.L.T. (Sh. Ct.) 5; *Hulme v. Hulme*, 1990 S.L.T. (Sh. Ct.) 25; *Dickson v. Dickson*, 1990 S.L.T. (Sh. Ct.) 80; and *Richardson v. Richardson*, 1991 S.L.T. (Sh. Ct.) 7). The position is otherwise if the sheriff's interlocutor is incompetent — *Kirk v. Kirk*, 2003 Fam.L.R. 50.

[11] 1985 Act, s. 6(4). The provisions of s. 6 apply to an award so varied and the claim therefor as they applied to the original award and the claim therefor — *ibid*. Application for variation or recall must be made by motion — r. 33.50 or r. 33A.47.

[12] *McColl v. McColl*, 1993 S.C. 276.

[13] *Bisset v. Bisset*, 1993 S.C.L.R. 284.

or dissolution of civil partnership.[14] The orders which fall within the definition of an incidental order and the considerations applicable to the making thereof are detailed *infra*. An incidental order may be varied or recalled by subsequent order on cause shown.[15]

Orders for provision of details of resources

By virtue of section 20 of the Act, the court may order either party to provide details of his resources.[16] The power may be exercised even where there is no suggestion that the party called upon to provide details is in some way concealing some resource.[17] If the party so called upon fails to provide details of his present and foreseeable resources he will be in contempt of an order of court.[18] Section 20 does not however give the court power to conduct an inquiry as to the extent of the disclosure.[19] In order to fulfil his obligation, the party ordered must provide a figure for the value of each item of property but does not require to produce documentation vouching the figure.[20] The sheriff is entitled to seek clarification of matters in any list of resources and may appoint the solicitor for the party concerned to appear personally before him.[21] It remains for the party claiming a specific financial provision to formulate and prove the entitlement.[22]

---

[14] 1985 Act, s. 14(1), excepting the orders specified in the text accompanying nn. 147 and 148 *infra*. For illustrations of circumstances in which incidental orders sought *pendente lite* were refused as premature, see *McKeown v. McKeown*, 1988 S.C.L.R. 355 and *Demarco v. Demarco*, 1990 S.C.L.R. 635. A motion for an incidental order for the sale of the jointly owned matrimonial home by a party not craving any financial provision was refused as incompetent in *MacClue v. MacClue*, 1994 S.C.L.R. 933. Application for an incidental order *pendente lite* may be made by motion, except that the sheriff is not bound to determine such a motion if he considers that the application should properly be by a crave in the initial writ or defences, as the case may be — r. 33.49(1) or r. 33A.46(1).

[15] 1985 Act, s. 14(4). Application in a depending action for such variation or recall must be made by minute in the process of the action to which the application relates — r. 33.49(2) or r. 33A.46(2).

[16] "Resources" means present and foreseeable resources — s. 27(1). Note that the power is additional to the power of the court to grant commission and diligence *inter alia* for the recovery of documents relative to a party's financial position (Administration of Justice (Scotland) Act 1972, s. 1(1)).

[17] *Lawrence v. Lawrence*, 1992 S.C.L.R. 199.

[18] *Nelson v. Nelson*, 1993 S.C.L.R. 149.

[19] *ibid.*

[20] *ibid.*

[21] *ibid.*

[22] *Williamson v. Williamson*, 1989 S.L.T. 866 at p. 867. Once documents have been submitted in terms of s. 20, the matter is properly before the court — *MacQueen v. MacQueen*, 1992 G.W.D. 28–1653.

ORDERS MADE UPON THE GRANTING OF DECREE

In terms of section 8(1) of the Act[23]:

> "In an action for divorce, either party to the marriage and in an action for dissolution of a civil partnership, either partner may apply to the court for one or more of the following orders —
> - (*a*)   an order for the payment of a capital sum to him by the other party to the action [capital sum order];
> - (*aa*) an order for the transfer of property to him by the other party to the action [transfer of property order][24];
> - (*b*)   an order for the payment of a periodical allowance to him by the other party to the action [periodical allowance order];
> - (*ba*) an order under section 12A(2) or (3) of this Act [pension lump sum order];
> - (*baa*) a pension sharing order;
> - (*c*)   an incidental order within the meaning of section 14(2) of this Act [incidental order]."

Any such order, defined in the Act as "an order for financial provision",[25] is essentially discretionary and is thus subject to review by an appellate court only if it can be shown that the judge of first instance misdirected himself in law or failed to take into account a relevant and material factor or reached a result which is manifestly inequitable or plainly wrong.[26] The considerations applicable to the various orders for financial provision are now considered in turn.

Capital sum, pension lump sum, pension sharing and transfer of property orders

A capital sum order or a transfer of property order may be made either (a) on granting decree of divorce or of dissolution of a civil partnership, or (b) within such period as the court on granting the

---

[23] As amended by the Law Reform (Miscellaneous Provisions) (Scotland) Act 1990, Sched. 8, para. 34 and Sched. 9; the Pensions Act 1995, s. 167(1); the Welfare Reform and Pensions Act 1999, s. 20(1) and (2); and the Civil Partnership Act 2004, Sched. 28, para. 14.

[24] A transfer of property order subject to a balancing payment was made in *Wallis v. Wallis*, 1993 S.C. (H.L.) 49 and in *Collins v. Collins*, 1997 Fam.L.R. 50.

[25] 1985 Act, s. 8(3).

[26] *Little v. Little*, 1990 S.L.T. 785 at p. 787, approved by the House of Lords in *Jacques v. Jacques*, 1997 S.C. (H.L.) 20. See also *Peacock v. Peacock*, 1993 S.C. 88. Note that there must be material before the court in the light of which that discretion can be exercised, even where the application is not contested — *Ali v. Ali*, 2001 S.C. 618.

decree may specify.[27] The court may stipulate that the order will come into effect at a specified future date.[28] The court, on making a capital sum order, may order that the capital sum will be payable by instalments.[29]

The court, on making an order for payment of a capital sum, may make an order (a "pension lump sum order") in certain circumstances requiring the person responsible for the pension arrangement[30] to pay

---

[27] 1985 Act, s. 12(1) as amended by the Civil Partnership Act 2004, Sched. 28, para. 18. See, for example, *Thomson v. Thomson,* 2003 Fam.L.R. 22 (divorce decree specifying period of 18 months from date of decree for any order in respect of pursuer's crave for sale of matrimonial home). In the event that an application is made but not determined within the specified period, the court's inherent jurisdiction may be invoked to enable the sheriff to do justice between the parties—*Lindsay v. Lindsay,* 2005 S.L.T. (Sh. Ct.) 81.

[28] 1985 Act, s. 12(2). See *e.g. Little v. Little,* 1990 S.L.T. 785 (payment postponed in part until after expected date of sale of matrimonial home); *Dorrian v. Dorrian,* 1991 S.C.L.R. 661; *Gulline v. Gulline,* 1992 S.L.T. (Sh. Ct.) 71; *Bannon v. Bannon,* 1993 S.L.T. 999; *Gracie v. Gracie,* 1997 S.L.T. (Sh. Ct.) 15 (payment postponed in full or in part until date of vesting of pension entitlement); *Shand v. Shand,* 1994 S.L.T. 387 (payment postponed until likely date of conclusion of defender's sequestration); and *Collins v. Collins,* 1997 Fam.L.R. 50 (payment of balancing capital sum postponed until date of death of husband).

[29] 1985 Act, s. 12(3). "Instalment payments may well be appropriate when the capital asset concerned is an income-generating asset. Where there is no such capital asset, for the court to require capital to be created by payment of instalments arising out of income would be quite wrong and contrary to the intention of the Act. To do so would merely be to establish a requirement to pay a periodical allowance for a very extended period but under another name." (*Dorrian v. Dorrian,* 1991 S.C.L.R. 661 at p. 663). Payment by instalments was ordered in *Bell v. Bell,* 1988 S.C.L.R. 457, *Buckle v. Buckle,* 1995 S.C.L.R. 590; *Gracie v. Gracie,* 1997 S.L.T. (Sh. Ct.) 15; *McEwan v. McEwan,* 1997 S.L.T. 118; *McHugh v. McHugh,* 2001 Fam.L.R. 30; *Carrol v. Carrol,* 2003 Fam.L.R. 108; and *Sweeney v. Sweeney (No 2),* 2006 S.C. 82.

[30] The person responsible for the pension arrangement is (a) in the case of an occupational pension scheme or a personal pension scheme, the trustees or managers of the scheme; (b) in the case of a retirement annuity contract or an annuity falling within paragraph (d) or (e) of the definition of "pension arrangement", the provider of the annuity; (c) in the case of an insurance policy falling within para. (d) of the definition of that expression, the insurer — 1985 Act, s. 27(1), as amended by the Welfare Reform and Pensions Act 1999, Sched. 12, para. 12. Where a pension lump sum order imposes any requirement on the person responsible for the pension arrangement ("the first arrangement") and the liable party acquires transfer credits under another arrangement ("the second arrangement") which are derived (directly or indirectly) from a transfer from the first arrangement of all his accrued rights under that arrangement; and the person responsible for the new arrangement has been given notice in accordance with the Divorce etc. (Notification and Treatment of Pensions) (Scotland) Regulations 2000 (S.I. 2000/1050) (App. X), the order has effect as if it had been made in respect of the person responsible for the new arrangement — 1985 Act, s. 12A(6), as amended by the Welfare Reform and Pensions Act 1999, Sched. 12, para. 9. The court may, nonetheless, on an application by any person having an interest, vary a pension lump sum order by substituting for the person responsible for the pension arrangement specified in the order the person responsible for any other pension arrangement under which any pension lump sum is payable to the liable party or in respect of his or her death (see n. 165 *infra*).

the whole or part of a pension lump sum payable to the liable party, when it becomes due, to the other party to the marriage or as the case may be to the other partner as a payment in or towards discharge of the liability under the capital sum order.[31] The relevant circumstances are those where (a) the matrimonial property or the partnership property within the meaning of section 10 of the 1985 Act includes any rights or interest in benefits under a pension arrangement which the liable person has or may have (whether such benefits are payable to him or in respect of his death); and (b) those benefits include a lump sum payable to him or in respect of his death.[32] Where the benefits include a lump sum payable in respect of the death of the liable person, the court, on making the capital sum order, may make an order (a) if the person responsible for the pension arrangement in question has power to determine the person to whom the sum, or any part of it, is to be paid, requiring him to pay the whole or part of that sum, when it becomes due, to the other party; (b) if the liable person has power to nominate the person to whom the sum, or any part of it, is to be paid, requiring the liable person to nominate the other person in respect of the whole or part of that sum; (c) in any other case, requiring the person responsible for the pension arrangement in question to pay the whole or part of that sum, when it

---

[31] 1985 Act, s. 12A(1) and (2), inserted by the Pensions Act 1995, s. 167(3), as amended by the Welfare Reform and Pensions Act 1999, Sched. 12, para. 9, and amended by the Civil Partnership Act 2004, Sched. 28, para. 19. Any such payment discharges so much of the liability of the person responsible for the pension arrangement to or in respect of the liable party as corresponds to the amount of the payment and shall be treated for all purposes as a payment made by the liable party in or towards the discharge of his liability under the capital sum order — 1985 Act, s. 12A(4), as so amended. Where the court makes an order under subs. (2) imposing requirements on the trustees or managers of an occupational pension scheme; and after the making of the order the Board of the Pension Protection Fund gives the trustees or managers of the pension scheme a notice under section 160 of the Pensions Act 2004 or any provisions in force in Northern Ireland corresponding to the provision of that Act in relation to the scheme, the order shall have effect as if references to the trustees or managers of the scheme were references to the Board; and references to any lump sum to which the person with benefits under a pension arrangement is or might become entitled under the scheme were references to the amount of any compensation payable under Chapter 3 of Part 2 of the 2004 Act, or the equivalent Northern Ireland provision, to which that person is or might become entitled in respect of the lump sum—1985 Act, s. 12A(7B) and (7C), as inserted by the Family Law (Scotland) Act 2006, s. 17(4)(a). Note that the court cannot make a pension lump sum order in relation to matrimonial property, or partnership property, consisting of compensation payable under Chapter 3 of Part 2 of the Pensions Act 2004 or any provisions in force in Northern Ireland corresponding to that Chapter—1985 Act, s. 8(4A), as inserted by the Family Law (Scotland) Act 2006, s. 17. As to the power of the court to recall a pension lump sum order, see n. 164 *infra*.

[32] 1985 Act, s. 12A(1), as inserted by the Pensions Act 1995, s. 167(3), as amended by the Welfare Reform and Pensions Act 1999, Sched. 12, para. 9 and as amended by the Civil Partnership Act 2004, Sched. 28, para. 19.

becomes due, to the other person instead of to the person to whom, apart from the order, it would be paid.[33] Where, as regards a pension arrangement, the parties to a marriage or the partners in a civil partnership have in effect a qualifying agreement which contains a term relating to pension sharing, the court cannot make a pension lump sum order unless it also sets aside the agreement or term under section 16(1)(b) of the Act.[34] Where an order under section 8(1)(ba) is applied for, intimation falls to be made to the person responsible for the pension arrangement.[35]

The court may make an order ("a pension sharing order") which (a) provides that one party's (i) shareable rights under a specified pension arrangement; or (ii) shareable state scheme rights, be subject to pension sharing for the benefit of the other party, and (b) specifies the percentage value, or the amount, to be transferred.[36] The transferor's shareable rights under the relevant arrangement become subject to a debit of the appropriate amount and the transferee becomes entitled to

---

[33] 1985 Act, s. 12A(3), as inserted by the Pensions Act 1995, s. 167(3), as amended by the Welfare Reform and Pensions Act 1999, Sched. 12, para. 9 and as amended by the Civil Partnership Act 2004, Sched. 28, para. 19. Where the court makes an order under subs. (3), and after the making of the order the Board of the Pension Protection Fund gives the trustees or managers of the pension scheme a notice under section 160 of the Pensions Act 2004 or any provision in force in Northern Ireland corresponding to the provision of that Act in relation to the scheme, the order shall, on the giving of such notice, be recalled— 1985 Act, s. 12A(7A), as inserted by the Family Law (Scotland) Act 2006, s. 17(4)(a).

[34] 1985 Act, s. 8(5)(a), as inserted by the Welfare Reform and Pensions Act 1999, s. 84 and Sched. 12, paras. 5 and 6 and as amended by the Civil Partnership Act, 2004, Sched. 28, para. 14. As to "qualifying agreement", see n. 41 *infra*.

[35] See Chap. 1, text accompanying n. 23.

[36] 1985 Act, ss. 8(1)(baa) and 27(1), as amended by the Welfare Reform and Pensions Act 1999, s. 20(1) to (3). See, for example, *Galloway v. Galloway,* 2003 Fam.L.R. 10. The reference to shareable rights under a pension arrangement is to rights in relation to which pension sharing is available under Chapter 1 of Part IV of the 1999 Act or under corresponding Northern Ireland legislation, and the reference to shareable state scheme rights is to rights in relation to which pension sharing is available under Chapter II of Part IV of the 1999 Act or under corresponding Northern Ireland legislation — 1985 Act, s. 27(1A), as inserted by the 1999 Act, s. 20(1) and (4). Pension sharing is available under Chapter 1 of Part IV in relation to a persons's shareable rights under any pension arrangement other than an excepted public service pension scheme; and a person's shareable rights under a pension arrangement are any rights of his under the arrangement, other than rights of a description specified by regulations made by the Secretary of State — 1999 Act, s. 27(1) and (2). The rights under a pension arrangement which are not shareable are set forth in reg. 2 of The Pension Sharing (Valuation) Regulations 2000 (S.I. 2000/1052) (App. X). The court cannot make a pension sharing order in relation to matrimonial property, or partnership property, consisting of compensation payable under Chapter 3 of Part 2 of the Pensions Act 2004 or any provision in force in Northern Ireland corresponding to that Chapter—1985 Act, s. 8(4A), as inserted by the Family Law (Scotland) Act 2006, s. 17.

a credit of that amount as against the person responsible for that arrangement, the appropriate amount being (where the order specifies a percentage value to be transferred) the specified percentage of the cash equivalent of the relevant benefits on the valuation day or (where the order specifies an amount to be transferred) the lesser of (a) the specified amount, and (b) the cash equivalent of the relevant benefits on the valuation day.[37] The court cannot, in the same proceedings, make both a pension sharing order and a pension lump sum order in relation to the same pension arrangement.[38] Moreover, the court cannot make a pension sharing order in relation to the rights of a person under a pension arrangement if there is in force a pension lump sum order which relates to benefits or future benefits to which he is entitled under the pension arrangement.[39] If a pension sharing order relates to rights under a pension arrangement, the court may include in the order provision about the apportionment between the parties of any charge under section 41 of the Welfare Reform and Pensions Act 1999 (charges in respect of pension sharing costs) or under corresponding Northern Ireland legislation.[40] Provision which corresponds to the provision which may be made by a pension sharing order may be agreed between the parties to a marriage or between persons who are civil partners of each other where the provision (i) is contained in a qualifying

---

[37] 1999 Act, s. 29(1)–(3). Where the relevant arrangement is an occupational pension scheme and the transferor is in pensionable service under the scheme on the transfer day, the relevant benefits are the benefits or future benefits to which he would be entitled under the scheme by virtue of his shareable rights under it had his pensionable service terminated immediately before that day; and otherwise are the benefits or future benefits to which, immediately before the transfer day, the transferor is entitled under the terms of the relevant arrangement by virtue of his shareable rights under it — 1999 Act, s. 29(4) and (5). The valuation day is such day within the implementation period for the credit as the person responsible for the relevant arrangement may specify by notice in writing to the transferor and transferee — 1999 Act, s. 29(7). The implementation period for a pension credit is the period of four months beginning with the later of (a) the day on which the relevant order or provision takes effect, and (b) the first day on which the person responsible for the pension arrangement to which the relevant order provision relates is in receipt of (i) the relevant matrimonial documents, and (ii) such information relating to the transferor and the transferee as the Secretary of State may prescribe by regulations — 1999 Act, s. 34(1). The implementation period may alter in accordance with The Pension Sharing (Implementation and Discharge of Liability) Regulations 2000 (S.I. 2000/1053) (App. X).

[38] 1985 Act, s. 8(4), as inserted by the Welfare Reform and Pensions Act 1999, s. 84 and Sched. 12, paras. 5 and 6.

[39] 1985 Act, s. 8(6), as inserted by the Welfare Reform and Pensions Act 1999, s. 84 and Sched. 12, paras. 5 and 6.

[40] 1985 Act, s. 8A, as inserted by the Welfare Reform and Pensions Act 1999, s. 84 and Sched. 12, paras. 5 and 7. As to charges in respect of pension sharing costs, see the Pensions on Divorce etc. (Charging) Regulations 2000 (S.I. 2000/1049) (App. X).

agreement;[41] (ii) is in the prescribed form;[42] and (iii) takes effect on the grant, in relation to the marriage, of decree of divorce or (as the case may be) on the grant, in relation to the civil partnership, of decree of dissolution.[43] Where, as regards a pension arrangement, the parties to a marriage or the partners in a civil partnership have in effect a qualifying agreement which contains a term which relates to pension sharing, the court cannot make a pension sharing order unless it also sets aside the agreement or term under section 16(1)(b) of the Family Law (Scotland) Act 1985.[44] A pension sharing order or equivalent provision is deemed never to have taken effect if the person responsible for the pension arrangement to which the order or provision relates (or, in the case of the sharing of state scheme rights, the Secretary of State) does not receive before the end of the period of two months beginning with the relevant date[45] (a) copies of the relevant documents,[46] and (b) such information relating to the transferor and transferee as the Secretary of State may prescribe.[47] The sheriff may, on the application of any person having an interest, make an order (a) extending the foregoing period of two months, and (b) if that period

---

[41] A qualifying agreement is one which (a) has been entered into in such circumstances as the Secretary of State may prescribe by regulations; and (b) is registered in the Books of Council and Session — 1999 Act, ss. 28(3) and 48(3). The prescribed circumstances are set forth in regs. 3 and 5 of The Pensions on Divorce etc. (Pension Sharing) (Scotland) Regulations 2000 (S.I. 2000/1051) (App. X). In the case of the sharing of rights under a pension arrangement, the agreement is not a qualifying agreement if there is in force a pension lump sum order which relates to benefits or future benefits to which the party who is the transferor is entitled under the pension arrangement to which the provision relates — 1999 Act, s. 28(6).

[42] The Secretary of State may prescribe the form of qualifying agreements by regulations — 1999 Act, ss. 28(1)(f)(ii) and 48(1)(f)(ii). The prescribed form is set forth in regulations 2 and 4 of The Pensions on Divorce etc. (Pension Sharing) (Scotland) Regulations 2000 (S.I. 2000/1051) (App. X).

[43] 1999 Act, s. 28(1)(f), as amended by the Civil Partnership Act 2004, Sched. 27, para. 159.

[44] 1985 Act, s. 8(5)(b), as inserted by the Welfare Reform and Pensions Act 1999, s. 84 and Sched. 12, paras. 5 and 6 and amended by the Civil Partnership Act 2004, Sched. 28, para. 14.

[45] The relevant date is the date of the extract of the decree responsible for the divorce or dissolution to which the order or provision relates — 1999 Act, ss. 28(8) and 48(7), as amended by the Civil Partnership Act 2004, Sched. 27, para. 159.

[46] The relevant documents are (a) in the case of a pension sharing order, copies of the order and the decree responsible for the divorce or dissolution to which it relates; and (b) in the case of an equivalent provision, copies of the provision and the decree responsible for the divorce or dissolution to which it relates, and documentary evidence that the agreement containing the provision is one which has been entered into in such circumstances as the Secretary of State may prescribe — 1999 Act, ss. 28(9) and 48(8), as amended by the Civil Partnership Act 2004, Sched. 27, para. 159. As to prescribed circumstances, see n. 41 *supra*.

[47] 1999 Act, ss. 28(7) and 48(6), as amended by the Civil Partnership Act 2004, Sched. 27, para. 159. The prescribed information is set forth in reg. 5 of The Pensions on Divorce etc. (Provision of Information) Regulations 2000 (S.I. 2000/1048) (App. X).

has already expired, providing that, if the person responsible for the arrangement (or, in the case of the sharing of state scheme rights, the Secretary of State) receives the documents and information concerned before the end of the period specified in the order, section 28(7) or 48(6) of the Welfare Reform and Pensions Act 1999 (pension sharing order or equivalent provision deemed never to have taken effect) is to be treated as never having applied.[48] Where an order under section 8(1)(baa) is applied for, intimation falls to be made to the person responsible for the pension arrangement.[49]

The court is bound not to make a transfer of property order if the consent of a third party which is necessary under any obligation, enactment or rule of law has not been obtained.[50] An order for the transfer of property subject to security cannot be made without the consent of the creditor unless he has been given an opportunity of being heard by the court.[51] Where the consent of a third party to such a transfer is necessary by virtue of an obligation, enactment or rule of law, or the property is subject to a security, intimation must be made to the third party or creditor, as the case may be.[52]

Application for a capital sum, transfer of property,[53] pension lump sum or pension sharing order may be made by the pursuer by inserting a crave therefor in the initial writ; and by the defender by inserting a crave in the defences.[54]

---

[48] 1999 Act, ss. 28(10) and 48(9). As to the mode of application, see n. 166 *infra*.

[49] See Chap. 1, text accompanying n. 24.

[50] 1985 Act, s. 15(1). This provision will apply in the case of a property which is subject to a standard security which includes a condition requiring the consent of the security holder to a transfer of the property — *MacNaught v. MacNaught*, 1996 S.C.L.R. 151.

[51] 1985 Act, s. 15(2). This provision will apply in the case of a property which is subject to a standard security which does not include a condition requiring the consent of the security holder to a transfer of the property. It confers upon such a security holder a right, which he would not otherwise have, to appear and be heard by the court in divorce proceedings, and it allows the court, having afforded such an opportunity to the security holder, to make a transfer order even without his consent — *MacNaught v. MacNaught*, 1996 S.C.L.R. 151.

[52] See Chap. 1, text accompanying n. 20.

[53] "...[A] sufficient description of the property should be included in the order which is to be made under section [8(1)(aa)] to satisfy the requirement of the common law, which is to distinguish the subjects from all other lands. In most cases a brief description will be all that is needed. In more complex cases it may be necessary for a more detailed description to be given. The court will expect to be provided with sufficient information by the party who seeks the order to enable this to be done" (*per* the Lord President in *Walker v. Walker*, 1991 S.L.T. 157 at p. 160). It is to be noted that the issue of whether a transfer of property order (i) is an order which itself transfers the property to the other spouse, or (ii) is no more than an order that the spouse having the title to the property should transfer it to the other, has been decided by *Walker* in favour of the latter proposition. A crave for a transfer of property order requires to be framed accordingly (see App. I).

[54] rr. 33.48(1)(a) and (2)(a) or r. 33A.45(1)(a) and (2)(a), and 33.34(1)(b)(ii) and (2)(b) or r. 33A.34(1)(b)(ii) and (2)(b).

Where an application for an order under section 8(1)(a), (aa), (ba) or (baa) has been made, the court must make such order, if any, as is:

"(*a*) justified by the principles set out in section 9 of [the] Act; and
(*b*) reasonable having regard to the resources of the parties."[55]

Section 9(1) of the 1985 Act[56] specifies the principles which the court must apply in deciding what order for financial provision, if any, to make. These are:

"(*a*) the net value of the matrimonial property should be shared fairly between the parties to the marriage or as the case may be the net value of the partnership property should be so shared between the partners in the civil partnership [Principle A];

(*b*) fair account should be taken of any economic advantage derived by either person from contributions by the other, and of any economic disadvantage suffered by either person in the interests of the other person or the family [Principle B];

(*c*) any economic burden of caring, (i) after divorce, for a child of the marriage under the age of 16 years; (ii) after dissolution of the civil partnership, for a child under that age who has been accepted by both partners as a child of the family, should be shared fairly between the persons [Principle C];

(*d*) a person who has been dependent to a substantial degree on the financial support of the other person should be awarded such financial provision as is reasonable to enable him to adjust, over a period of not more than three years from (i) the date of the decree of divorce, to the loss of that support on divorce; (ii) the

---

[55] 1985 Act, s. 8(2), subject to ss. 12–15 of the Act, noted *infra*. As to "resources", see *Cunniff v. Cunniff*, 1999 S.C. 537 (if a person, albeit unemployed, has an early prospect of earning a substantial income, there may be said to be "resources"). Section 8(2) sets out two criteria, but does not in terms direct the court to consider one in advance of, or in isolation from, the other — *McVinnie v. McVinnie (No. 2)*, 1997 S.L.T. (Sh. Ct.) 12 at p. 14. They are cumulative with the result that unless both are satisfied the court has no power to make an order (*Wallis v. Wallis*, 1993 S.C. (H.L.) 49 at p. 56). Accordingly, s. 8(2)(b) does not entitle the court to award any greater amount by way of a capital sum beyond what is justified by the principles set forth in the Act but "can only operate to cut down any sum, otherwise justified, having regard to the current resources of the parties" (*Latter v. Latter*, 1990 S.L.T. 805 at p. 807 — see *e.g. Crockett v. Crockett*, 1992 S.C.L.R 591 and *Sweeney v. Sweeney (No. 2)*, 2006 S.C. 82). Once the nature and value of the assets comprised in the matrimonial property at the relevant date have been established, it is reasonable to assume that they remain substantially the same at the date of proof unless the contrary is proved; and so, if it is desired to prove the contrary, fair notice requires to be given on record so that the matter can be properly investigated and thereafter tested at proof — *Fulton v. Fulton*, 1998 S.L.T. 1262 at pp. 1263–1264. See also *Fraser v. Fraser*, 2002 Fam.L.R. 53.

[56] As amended by the Civil Partnership Act 2004, Sched. 28, para. 15(2).

date of decree of dissolution of the civil partnership, to the loss of that support on dissolution [Principle D];

(*e*) a person who at the time of the divorce or of the dissolution of the civil partnership seems likely to suffer serious financial hardship as a result of the divorce or dissolution should be awarded such financial provision as is reasonable to relieve him of hardship over a reasonable period [Principle E]."

The principles are at this juncture considered individually in relation to other provisions of the Act respecting their application.

Principle A. *The net value of the matrimonial property* should be *shared fairly* between the parties to the marriage and *the net value of the partnership property* should be *shared fairly* between the partners in the civil partnership.

(i) *The matrimonial property* is all the property[57] belonging to the parties or either of them at the relevant date[58] which was acquired by them or him (otherwise than by way of gift[59] or succession from a third party) either (a) before the marriage for use by them as a family home or as furniture or plenishings for such home[60] or (b) during the marriage but before the relevant date.[61] *The partnership property* is all the property[57] belonging to the partners or either of them at the relevant date[58] which was acquired by them or by one of them (otherwise than by way of gift[59]

---

[57] Such may be heritable *or* moveable property (*Petrie v. Petrie*, 1988 S.C.L.R. 390). As to the former, see *Smith v. Smith*, 1992 G.W.D. 23–1324. Property held by a company in which a party has a controlling interest is not matrimonial or partnership property — *Wilson v. Wilson*, 1999 S.L.T. 249.

[58] The "relevant date" is whichever is the earlier of (i) the date on which the parties ceased to cohabit; and (ii) the date of service of the summons (*sic*) in the action for divorce or dissolution of civil partnership — 1985 Act, s. 10(3), as amended by the Civil Partnership Act 2004, Sched. 28, para. 16. The parties to a marriage are held to cohabit with one another only when they are in fact living together as man and wife (s. 27(2), as to which see *Buczynska v. Buczynski*, 1989 S.L.T. 558, *Brown v. Brown,* 1998 Fam.L.R. 81 and *Banks v. Banks,* 2005 Fam.L.R. 116). No account is to be taken of any cessation of cohabitation where the parties thereafter resumed cohabitation (except where the parties ceased to cohabit for a continuous period of 90 days or more before resuming cohabitation for a period or periods of less than 90 days in all) — 1985 Act, s. 10(7). As to s. 10(7), see *Pryde v. Pryde*, 1991 S.L.T. (Sh. Ct.) 26.

[59] As to "gift", see *Whittome v. Whittome (No. 1)*, 1994 S.L.T. 114. Shares were held to be matrimonial property, notwithstanding that their acquisition had been partly financed by means of a gift of money, in *Fulton v. Fulton*, 1998 S.L.T. 1262. The onus of proof is on the party claiming that property was acquired by way of gift or succession — *Wilson v. Wilson*, 1999 S.L.T. 249 and *MacLean v. MacLean*, 2001 Fam.L.R. 118.

[60] In an action of divorce in which the parties had previously married and divorced one another, a matrimonial home acquired during the course of the first marriage for use by the parties as a family home was held to be matrimonial property (*Mitchell v. Mitchell*, 1994 S.C. 601).

[61] 1985 Act, s. 10(4).

or succession from a third party)—(a) before the registration of the partnership for use by them as a family home or as furniture or plenishings for such a home, or (b) during the partnership but before the relevant date.[62] Property must fall within (a) or (b) to constitute matrimonial property or partnership property.[63]

The proportion of any rights or interests of either person (a) under a life policy or similar arrangement; and (b) in any benefits under a pension arrangement[64] which either person has or may have (including such benefits payable in respect of the death of either person), which is referable to the period between the date of the marriage or registration of the partnership and the relevant date is taken to form part of the matrimonial or partnership property, as the case may be.[65] A claim for damages in respect of an accident

---

[62] 1985 Act, s. 10(4A), as inserted by the Civil Partnership Act 2004, Sched. 28, para. 16.

[63] *Maclellan v. Maclellan*, 1988 S.C.L.R. 399 (croft tenancy acquired prior to marriage for use other than as family home not matrimonial property).

[64] "Benefits under a pension arrangement" includes any benefits by way of pension, including relevant state scheme rights, whether under a pension arrangement or not — 1985 Act, s. 27(1), as inserted by the Welfare Reform and Pensions Act 1999, Sched. 12, para. 12. "Pension arrangement" means (a) any occupational pension scheme within the meaning of the Pension Schemes Act 1993; (b) a personal pension scheme within the meaning of that Act; (c) a retirement annuity contract; (d) an annuity or insurance policy purchased or transferred for the purpose of giving effect to rights under an occupational pension scheme or a personal pension scheme; (e) an annuity purchased or entered into for the purpose of discharging liability in respect of a pension credit under s. 26(1)(b) of the Welfare Reform and Pensions Act 1999 or under corresponding Northern Ireland legislation — *ibid*. "Relevant state scheme rights" means (a) entitlement, or prospective entitlement, to a Category A retirement pension by virtue of s. 44(3)(b) of the Social Security Contributions and Benefits Act 1992 or under corresponding Northern Ireland legislation; and (b) entitlement, or prospective entitlement, to a pension under s. 55A of the Social Security Contributions and Benefits Act 1992 (shared additional pension) or under corresponding Northern Ireland legislation — *ibid*. "Retirement annuity contract" means a contract or scheme approved under Chapter III of Part XIV of the Income and Corporation Taxes Act 1988 — *ibid*.

[65] 1985 Act, s. 10(5), as amended by the Pensions Act 1995, s. 167(2)(a), the Welfare Reform and Pensions Act 1999, Sched. 12, para. 8(1) and (2) and the Civil Partnership Act 2004, Sched. 28, para. 16. In terms of s. 10(5A) of the 1985 Act, as amended by the Family Law (Scotland) Act 2006, s. 17(3), where either person is entitled to compensation payable under Chapter 3 of Part 2 of the Pensions Act 2004 or any provision in force in Northern Ireland corresponding to that Chapter, the proportion of the compensation which is referable to the period between the date of the marriage or registration of the partnership and the relevant date is to be taken to form part of the matrimonial or partnership property. Such is valued in accordance with regulation 2 of The Divorce and Dissolution etc. (Pension Protection Fund) (Scotland) Regulations 2006 (S.S.I. 2006 No. 254). Note that the use of the word "referable" is intended to secure that there is not brought into account as matrimonial or partnership property any part of the pension rights which the party can be regarded as already "having" at the date of the marriage or registration of the partnership; and an interest in a pension is referable to the period before marriage or registration of the partnership to the extent that it arises out of membership of the scheme before marriage or registration of the partnership — *Jackson v. Jackson*, 2000 S.C.L.R. 81.

occurring during the marriage or partnership but before the relevant date is matrimonial or partnership property.[66] A claim for a refund in respect of income tax deducted during the marriage or partnership but before the relevant date is matrimonial or partnership property.[67] Shares in a private company issued during the marriage or partnership and derived from a series of gifted shareholdings in five companies, which had become subsidiaries of the company following upon an overall reconstruction are matrimonial or partnership property.[68] Shares in a private company allotted as a bonus issue during the marriage or partnership in respect of a gifted shareholding are matrimonial or partnership property, as are the shares in the public company the registration and flotation of which resulted from the reorganisation of that same private company.[69] A matrimonial home bought in a party's name prior to the date of the marriage or before the registration of the partnership with funds given by that party's relatives to her solicitors prior to settlement is not matrimonial or partnership property.[70] A redundancy payment received after the relevant date is not matrimonial or partnership property.[71] A payment received upon leaving the army after the relevant date is not matrimonial or partnership property.[72]

(ii) *The net value* of the matrimonial or partnership property is the value[73] of the property at the relevant date after deduction of any debts,[74]

---

[66] *Skarpaas v. Skarpaas*, 1993 S.L.T. 343; *Carrol v. Carrol*, 2003 Fam.L.R. 108 (see also *Petrie v. Petrie*, 1988 S.C.L.R. 390).

[67] *MacRitchie v. MacRitchie*, 1994 S.L.T. (Sh. Ct.) 72.

[68] *Latter v. Latter*, 1990 S.L.T. 805. *Cf. Pressley v. Pressley,* 2002 S.C.L.R. 804.

[69] *Whittome v. Whittome (No. 1)*, 1994 S.L.T. 114.

[70] *Latter v. Latter*, 1990 S.L.T. 805.

[71] *Smith v. Smith*, 1989 S.L.T. 668 and *Tyrrell v. Tyrrell*, 1990 S.L.T. 406.

[72] *Gibson v. Gibson*, 1990 G.W.D. 4–213.

[73] For the purpose of calculating the value of the matrimonial or partnership property its market value should not be reduced by the hypothetical incidence of capital gains tax nor by other personal liabilities which remain contingent at the relevant date — *Sweeney v. Sweeney,* 2004 S.C. 372. Where the parties have not agreed the value of an item of matrimonial or partnership property, the court may only make a finding as to such value by reference to the evidence, which failing by selecting a figure falling within the parties' respective estimates — *Pryde v. Pryde*, 1991 S.L.T. (Sh. Ct.) 26.

[74] A contingent tax liability should not be brought into account by way of deduction from the net value of the matrimonial or partnership property (*Sweeney v. Sweeney,* 2004 S.C. 372; *McConnell v. McConnell,* 1997 Fam. L.R. 970). Note however that such a liability might in some cases constitute special circumstances such as to justify departure from the principle of equal sharing—*Sweeney v. Sweeney (No. 2)*, 2006 S.C. 82. Any contingent liability to repay a proportion of the discount on the purchase price of the matrimonial home is not to be regarded as a debt incurred by the parties or either of them which was outstanding at the relevant date — *Stuart v. Stuart,* 2001 S.L.T. (Sh. Ct.). 20. An Irish tax debt which the husband did not intend to pay and was unenforceable in the United Kingdom was held not to be a "debt" in *Cunniff v. Cunniff*, 1999 S.C. 537.

outstanding[75] at that date, incurred by the parties or either of them (a) before the marriage so far as they relate to the matrimonial or partnership property, and (b) during the marriage or partnership.[76] However, in its application to property transferred by virtue of a transfer or property order, the net value of that property is taken to be its value at the 'appropriate valuation date' after deduction of any such debts.[77] The appropriate valuation date is—(a) where the parties to the marriage or, as the case may be, the partners agree on a date, that date; (b) where there is no such agreement, the date of the transfer of property order.[78] If however the court considers that, because of the exceptional circumstances of the case, (b) should not apply, the appropriate valuation date is to be such other date as near as may be to the date of the making of the transfer of property order as the court may determine.[79] Any changes in value after the relevant date must otherwise be left out of account when calculating the value of the matrimonial or partnership property.[80] If there is no net value to be shared, Principle A is not applicable.[81]

The rights or interests of a party under a life policy may be valued on the basis of its surrender value or on the basis of its replacement value.[82] Benefits under a pension arrangement or relevant state scheme rights and shareable rights under a pension arrangement or shareable state scheme rights fall to be valued as prescribed.[83] A claim for damages

---

[75] Income tax due on income earned up to the relevant date but not payable until after that date is a debt outstanding at the relevant date — *McConnell v. McConnell*, 1997 Fam.L.R. 97 at pp. 105–106; *Jackson v. Jackson*, 2000 S.C.L.R. 81 at p. 91; and *Buchan v. Buchan*, 1992 S.C.L.R. 766.

[76] 1985 Act, s. 10(2), as amended by the Civil Partnership Act 2004, Sched. 28, para. 16. In calculating the net value one does not require to be concerned with the question which party owns which items of property or which party is liable for which debts—*Russell v. Russell*, 2005 Fam. L.R. 96. Note that the position is different when one gets to the stage of deciding what order should be made so as to achieve fair sharing of that net value—*ibid.*

[77] 1985 Act, s. 10(2) and (3A), as inserted by the Family Law (Scotland) Act 2006, s. 16.

[78] *ibid.*

[79] *ibid.*

[80] *Wallis v. Wallis*, 1992 S.C. 455 at p. 460 and 1993 S.C. (H.L.) 49 at p. 55.

[81] *Graham v. Graham*, 1997 Fam.L.R. 117.

[82] The surrender value is the amount payable to a person who surrenders a life insurance policy; the replacement value is the amount payable by a person to replace the probable proceeds of a life insurance policy. An equal division of the surrender value of endowment life policies was ordered in *Muir v. Muir*, 1989 S.L.T. (Sh.Ct.) 20 at p. 21.

[83] 1985 Act, s. 10(8), as substituted by the Welfare Reform and Pensions Act 1999, Sched. 12, para. 8(1) and (3), and 1985 Act, s. 10(8A), as inserted by the 1999 Act, Sched. 12, para. 8(4), and the Divorce etc. (Pensions) (Scotland) Regulations 2000 (S.S.I. 2000 No 112), The Pension Sharing (Valuation) Regulations 2000 (S.I. 2000/1052) and The Sharing of State Scheme Rights (Provision of Information and Valuation) (No 2) Regulations 2000 (S.I. 2000/2914) (App. X). The prescribed method of valuation is mandatory — *Miller v. Miller*, 2000 Fam.L.R. 19 and *Stewart v. Stewart*, 2001 S.L.T. (Sh. Ct.) 114. The person responsible for the pension arrangement may be required to provide information as to the

which is yet to be quantified and admitted may be valued on the basis that it will attract less if offered for sale in the market place than the amount awarded by the decree which is obtained at the end of the day.[84] A business may be valued on the basis of a break-up value or a forced sale or on the basis of a value as a going concern.[85] Leased heritable property may be valued on the basis of vacant possession or as subject to tenants' rights.[86] Household contents may be valued on the basis of auction room prices or on a willing buyer/willing seller basis.[87] A debt due to a party to the marriage or partnership may be valued at less than its book value.[88] The court may derive assistance from a table of matrimonial property or partnership property showing values.[89]

(iii) The net value of the matrimonial or partnership property is taken to be *shared fairly* when it is shared equally or in such other proportions as are justified by special circumstances.[90]

Section 10(6) provides that "special circumstances", without prejudice to the generality of the words,[91] may include[92]:

---

value of the benefits or rights and is entitled to recover the administrative expenses of providing such information from either party — The Pensions on Divorce etc. (Provision of Information) Regulations 2000 (S.I. 2000/1048) and The Pensions on Divorce etc. (Charging) Regulations 2000 (S.I. 2000/1049) (App. X).

[84] *Skarpaas v. Skarpaas*, 1993 S.L.T. 343. But see *Carrol v. Carrol*, 2003 Fam.L.R. 108 (court unable to find it proved that claim had a value if offered for sale in market place or what value such a claim would have; and broad brush approach to valuing claim adopted).

[85] Businesses were valued on a going concern basis in *McKenzie v. McKenzie*, 1991 S.L.T. 461 and *Savage v. Savage*, 1997 Fam.L.R. 132. Businesses were valued on a net asset basis in *Bye v. Bye*, 1998 Fam.L.R. 103 and *Brown v. Brown*, 1998 Fam.L.R. 81. A business was valued under reference to a partner's capital interest as indicated from the accounts for the relevant year in *Brown*. The valuation of shares in private limited companies may present formidable difficulties — see *Latter v. Latter*, 1990 S.L.T. 805; *Crockett v. Crockett*, 1992 S.C.L.R. 591; *McConnell v. McConnell*, 1997 Fam.L.R. 97; and *Cordiner v. Cordiner*, 2003 Fam.L.R. 39. As to the valuation of goodwill, see *Rose v. Rose*, 1998 S.L.T. (Sh. Ct.) 56.

[86] A middle valuation was adopted, where the tenant was an unincorporated company in which the husband held virtually all the shares, in *Wilson v. Wilson*, 1999 S.L.T. 249.

[87] Neither method may be held strictly apposite (*Latter v. Latter*, 1990 S.L.T. 805). In *McConnell v. McConnell*, 1997 Fam.L.R. 97, the Lord Ordinary valued the furniture and plenishings in the matrimonial home at their insurance value less an amount reflecting the excess over their probable true and fair value. See also *Cahill v. Cahill*, 1998 S.L.T. (Sh. Ct.) 96. Note that there is a presumption of equal shares in household goods obtained in prospect of or during the marriage other than by gift or succession from a third party — 1985 Act, s. 25.

[88] See *Shipton v. Shipton*, 1992 S.C.L.R. 23.

[89] See *Crockett v. Crockett*, 1992 S.C.L.R. 591 and App. IX.

[90] 1985 Act, s. 10(1), as amended by the Civil Partnership Act 2004, Sched. 28, para. 16.

[91] The words "special circumstances" do not have any technical meaning but refer to any circumstances which are special to the case — *Jacques v. Jacques*, 1997 S.C. (H.L.) 20 at p. 24.

[92] See *Kerrigan v. Kerrigan*, 1988 S.C.L.R. 603 and *White v. White*, 1992 S.C.L.R. 769 (brevity of marriage held in each case to be a special circumstance); *Buczynska v. Buczynski*, 1989 S.L.T. 558; and *Wallis v. Wallis*, 1992 S.C. 455; 1993 S.C. (H.L.) 491

(a)   the terms of any agreement between the persons on the ownership or division of any of the matrimonial or partnership property[93];

(b)   the source of the funds or assets used to acquire any of the matrimonial or partnership property where those funds or assets were not derived from the income or efforts of the persons during the marriage or partnership[94];

(c)   any destruction or dissipation or alienation of property by either spouse[95];

(d)   the nature of the matrimonial or partnership property, the use made of it (including use for business purposes or as a family

---

(post-separation increase in value of matrimonial home held in each case not to be a special circumstance); *Farrell v. Farrell*, 1990 S.C.L.R. 717 (voluntary assumption of co-owning spouse's mortgage liability and low net value of matrimonial home held to be special circumstances); *Jesner v. Jesner*, 1992 S.L.T. 999 (husband's loss of household contents held to be a special circumstance); *Wallis, supra* (mere fact of transfer of property into joint names held not to be a special circumstance); *Burchell v. Burchell*, 1997 Fam.L.R. 137 (husband's lack of candour with the court regarding his assets held to be a special circumstance); and *Trotter v. Trotter*, 2001 S.L.T. (Sh.Ct.) 42 (wife's maintenance of property and payment of all mortgage costs and policy premiums since separation held to be a special circumstance).

[93]   1985 Act, s. 10(6)(a), as amended by the Civil Partnership Act 2004, Sched. 28, para. 16. An agreement to share an asset equally by taking title thereto in joint names may be taken into account as countering the potential effect of other circumstances and reinforcing the presumption in favour of equality — *Jackson v. Jackson*, 2000 S.C.L.R. 81 at p. 95. See also *Anderson v. Anderson*, 1991 S.L.T. (Sh. Ct.) 11 and *Methven v. Methven*, 1999 S.L.T. (Sh. Ct.) 117.

[94]   1985 Act, s. 10(6)(b), as amended by the Civil Partnership Act 2004, Sched. 28, para. 16; for relevant "sources" see, *e.g. Phillip v. Phillip*, 1988 S.C.L.R. 427 (pre-marriage house); *Petrie v. Petrie*, 1988 S.C.L.R. 390 (damages award); *Kerrigan v. Kerrigan*, 1988 S.C.L.R. 603, (pursuer's mother); *Buczynska v. Buczynski*, 1989 S.L.T. 558 (pursuer's mother); *Budge v. Budge*, 1990 S.L.T. 319 (pre-marriage house); *Latter v. Latter*, 1990 S.L.T. 805 (defender's family); *Jesner v. Jesner*, 1992 S.L.T. 999; (pre-marriage house and family trust); *Crockett v. Crockett*, 1992 S.C.L.R. 591 (O.H.) and Extra Division, June 30, 1993, unreported (defender's company); *Davidson v. Davidson*, 1994 S.L.T. 506 (inheritance), *Jackson v. Jackson*, 2000 S.C.L.R. 81 (sale proceeds of shares); *Cunningham v. Cunningham*, 2001 Fam. L.R. 12 (inheritances); *Gray v. Gray*, 2001 S.C.L.R. 681 (pursuer's parents); *Buchan v. Buchan*, 2001 Fam.L.R. 48 (pursuer's parents); *MacLean v. MacLean*, 2001 Fam.L.R. 118 (pre-marriage farm and pursuer's mother); and *Cordiner v. Cordiner*, 2003 Fam.L.R. 39 (pre-marriage investments and house).

[95]   1985 Act, s. 10(6)(c), as amended by the Civil Partnership Act 2004, Sched. 28, para. 16. For dissipation to be established there has to be an element of deliberate and wanton conduct — *Buchan v. Buchan*, 2001 Fam.L.R. 48 (non-payment of mortgage without satisfactory explanation not dissipation). And see *Park v. Park*, 1988 S.C.L.R. 584 (non-payment of mortgage not dissipation); *Short v. Short*, 1994 G.W.D. 21–1300 (encumbering matrimonial home by forging husband's signature was dissipation); and *Russell v. Russell*, 1996 G.W.D. 15–895 (failed business ventures not dissipation).

home) and the extent to which it is reasonable to expect it to be realised or divided or used as security[96];

(e) the actual or prospective liability for any expenses of valuation or transfer of property in connection with the divorce or the dissolution of the civil partnership.[97]

It is for the court of first instance in each case to determine whether an event specified in section 10(6) amounts to special circumstances in the case in question and, if so, whether it justifies a division in proportions other than equal; the court is not required to effect an unequal division of the matrimonial property whenever special circumstances are found to exist.[98]

The court may adopt a global approach in assessing and dividing matrimonial or partnership property, or it may pursue a piecemeal approach, allowing it to divide a particular item from the rest to meet a special circumstance which bears on it primarily; there is room for the scheme of the Act to be applied in different ways in different

---

[96] 1985 Act, s. 10(6)(d), as amended by the Civil Partnership Act 2004, Sched. 28, para. 16, applied in *e.g. Petrie v. Petrie*, 1988 S.C.L.R. 390 (damages award); *Muir v. Muir*, 1989 S.L.T. (Sh. Ct.) 20 (pension); *Cooper v. Cooper*, 1989 S.C.L.R. 347 (matrimonial home); *Budge v. Budge*, 1990 S.L.T. 319 (matrimonial home/croft); *Carpenter v. Carpenter*, 1990 S.L.T. (Sh.Ct.) 68 (pension); *Little v. Little*, 1989 S.C.L.R. 613 (O.H.) and 1990 S.L.T. 785 (I.H.) (motor cars, matrimonial home, pension); *Farrell v. Farrell*, 1990 S.C.L.R. 717 (matrimonial home); *Skarpaas v. Skarpaas*, 1991 S.L.T. (Sh. Ct.) 15 and 1993 S.L.T. 343 (I.H.) (damages claim); *Symon v. Symon*, 1991 S.C.L.R. 414 (pension); *McGuire v. McGuire's Curator Bonis*, 1991 S.L.T. (Sh. Ct.) 76 (criminal injuries compensation award); *Bannon v. Bannon*, 1993 S.L.T. 999 (pension); *Peacock v. Peacock*, 1993 S.C. 88 (matrimonial home); *Davidson v. Davidson*, 1994 S.L.T. 506 (farm); *Stephen v. Stephen*, 1995 S.C.L.R. 175 (pension); *Crosbie v. Crosbie*, 1996 S.L.T. (Sh. Ct.) 86 (pension); *Murphy v. Murphy*, 1996 S.L.T. (Sh. Ct.) 91 (matrimonial home and pension); *Collins v. Collins*, 1997 Fam.L.R. 50 (matrimonial home); *McConnell v. McConnell (No. 2)*, 1997 Fam.L.R. 108 (company shareholding and loans); *Cunniff v. Cunniff*, 1999 S.C. 537 (matrimonial home); *Trotter v. Trotter*, 2001 S.L.T. (Sh. Ct.) 42 (matrimonial home) and *Gray v. Gray*, 2001 S.C.L.R. 681 (matrimonial home). Note that in the case of an interest in a pension scheme, the non-realisable nature of the asset and the deferred rights which it represents may be reflected in different ways: "In some cases an order for the transfer of the rights in such a scheme may be appropriate if those rights are assignable. In others, a discount may be appropriate, although this must depend very much upon the basis upon which the value has been arrived at in the first place. In others, an order for payment by instalments under section 12(3) may be the solution. In others, payment of the value may be deferred in whole or in part to a specified future date under section 12(2)" (*per* the Lord President in *Little v. Little*, 1990 S.L.T. 785 at p. 789). See also now s. 8(1)(ba) and (baa) and s. 12A of the Act (text accompanying nn. 31–49. *supra*). Note further that there may be cases where an equal and instant division of the full actuarial value of the interest is capable of being made by virtue of the availability of other realisable assets (*Little*, at p. 788; *Latter v. Latter*, 1990 S.L.T. 805; *Brooks v. Brooks*, 1993 S.L.T. 184).
[97] 1985 Act, s. 10(6)(e), as amended by the Civil Partnership Act 2004, Sched. 28, para. 16.
[98] *Jacques v. Jacques*, 1997 S.C. (H.L.) 20 at pp. 22 and 24, and *McConnell v. McConnell (No. 2)*, 1997 Fam.L.R. 108 at p. 112.

situations as a matter of discretion.[99] Subparagraphs (b) and (d) of section 10(6) might be thought to invite the latter approach: some items of matrimonial or partnership property might thus, for example, be treated differently from others according to their nature or the use to which they are put.[100]

The question of expenses is bound up intimately with the division of the matrimonial or partnership property and the effects of that division on the parties' resources.[101] The normal principle in petitory actions that expenses should follow success cannot be applied in its full rigour to cases involving such division, particularly where much trouble has been taken to achieve a fair division of the matrimonial or partnership property between the parties with the full co-operation of both sides.[102] The parties' conduct of the litigation rather than the result itself should, accordingly, be the principal criterion on which to proceed.[103] Factors which may be taken into account by the court in exercising its discretion as to expenses, therefore, include the reasonableness of the parties' claims, the extent to which they have co-operated in disclosing, and agreeing the value of, their respective assets, the offers they have made to settle, the extent to which proof could have been avoided and, of course, the final outcome.[104]

---

[99] *Crockett v. Crockett*, Extra Division, June 30, 1993, unreported.

[100] *Crockett v. Crockett*, Extra Division, June 30, 1993, unreported; *Little v. Little*, 1990 S.L.T. 785 at p. 788. "The matrimonial home is one of the clearest examples of a particular item of matrimonial property for which special arrangements may be justified." (*per* the Lord President in *Little*, at p. 788).

[101] *Little v. Little*, 1990 S.L.T. 785 at p. 790.

[102] *ibid.*

[103] *ibid.* See, *e.g. Scott v. Scott*, 1995 G.W.D. 36–1832 (no expenses found due to or by either party).

[104] *Adams v. Adams (No. 2)*, 1997 S.L.T. 150. In *Adams* the Lord Ordinary awarded the husband defender the expenses of the proof and the procedure following thereon, and *quoad ultra* found no expenses due to or by either party, on the footing that the proof was necessitated because the wife insisted throughout on the two points of principle upon which she failed, whereas prior to the diet neither party could adopt a final position on financial matters, full and up-to-date information only being exchanged shortly before the proof. In *Macdonald v. Macdonald*, 1995 S.L.T. 72 (approved on appeal, 1994 G.W.D. 7–404) the Lord Ordinary awarded the wife pursuer the expenses of the action modified to 60 per cent, on the footing that her claims had, for the major part, been successful and that the defender had had no reasonable basis for contesting the issues which had generated much of the expense. In *Whittome v. Whittome (No. 2)*, 1994 S.L.T. 130 the Lord Ordinary awarded the wife defender the expenses of the action modified to 75 per cent, having regard to the fact that she was partly successful, that her conduct throughout the litigation was generally reasonable and that it was reasonable that she should seek a decision from the court in respect of her claim for payment of a capital sum, given the dearth of authority regarding categorisation of assets such as the pursuer's as matrimonial property, and to the practical effect of an award of expenses on the respective assets of the parties. See also *De Winton v. De Winton (No. 2)*, 1997 G.W.D. 2–58 and *Cameron v. Cameron,* 2002 S.L.T. (Sh. Ct.) 23. (*Cf. Ferguson v. Maclennan Salmon Co. Ltd,* 1990 S.L.T. 428 at p. 431, with regard to minutes of tender in divorce actions.)

In applying Principle A, the court must not take account of the conduct of either party to the marriage or as the case may be of either partner unless the conduct has adversely affected the financial resources which are relevant to the decision of the court on a claim for financial provision.[105]

Principle B. Fair account should be taken of any *economic advantage* derived by either person from *contributions* by the other, and of any *economic disadvantage* suffered by either person in the interests of the other person or of the family.[106]

Economic advantage means advantage gained whether before or during the marriage or civil partnership and includes gains in capital, in income and in earning capacity; and *economic disadvantage* is construed accordingly.[107]

Contributions are contributions made whether before or during the marriage or civil partnership, including indirect and non-financial contributions and, in particular, any such contribution made by looking after the family home or caring for the family.[108]

In applying this principle, the court must have regard to the extent to which:

(a) the economic advantages or disadvantages sustained by either person have been balanced by the economic advantages or disadvantages sustained by the other person; and

(b) a resulting imbalance has been or will be corrected by a sharing of the value of the matrimonial property or the partnership property or otherwise.[109]

---

[105] 1985 Act, s. 11(7)(a), as amended by the Civil Partnership Act 2004, Sched. 28, para. 17, applied in *Bremner v. Bremner,* 2000 S.C.L.R. 912 (wife's conduct having adverse effect on health of husband and rendering him unfit for work); *Buchan v. Buchan,* 2001 Fam.L.R. 48 (husband failing to meet his mortgage commitments regularly even where earning a good salary, with no satisfactory explanation of what he did with his money); and *Gray v. Gray,* 2001 S.C.L.R. 681 (husband almost continuously failing to meet his financial responsibilities after separation with respect to aliment for wife and children and mortgage and insurance payments relative to matrimonial home, notwithstanding court orders). *Quaere* whether conduct involving recklessness or carelessness and not deliberate dissipation or alienation of the relevant property is conduct within the meaning of s. 11(7)(a). *Cf. Cunniff v. Cunniff,* 1999 S.C. 537.

[106] Cases in which Principle B was explicitly considered are listed in App. VIII.

[107] 1985 Act, s. 9(2), as amended by the Civil Partnership Act 2004, Sched. 28, para. 15. Economic advantage and economic disadvantage may be evaluated by reference to an extended period of time, part of which may be after the dissolution of the marriage — *Cahill v. Cahill,* 1998 S.L.T. (Sh. Ct.) 96, doubting *Dougan v. Dougan,* 1998 S.L.T. (Sh. Ct.) 27. As to what has been held to amount to "economic advantage" or "economic disadvantage", see cases listed in App. VIII.

[108] 1985 Act, s. 9(2), as amended by the Civil Partnership Act 2004, Sched. 28, para. 15.

[109] 1985 Act, s. 11(2), as amended by the Civil Partnership Act 2004, Sched. 28, para. 17.

The court must not, on the other hand, take account of the conduct of either party to the marriage or as the case may be either partner unless the conduct has adversely affected the financial resources which are relevant to the decision of the court on a claim for financial provision.[110]

For a claim under Principle B to succeed, it is not enough to show that a contribution by the claimant enabled the other spouse or partner to gain an economic advantage; it must also be shown that such an advantage was not balanced by an economic advantage which the claimant had gained.[111] The court has therefore to identify all the economic advantages derived by either party from the contributions of the other and all the economic disadvantages suffered by either party in the interests of the other party or of the family, and only if there is an imbalance can the court then go on further to consider what order is called for.[112]

Principle B does not provide an alternative route to a desired result of unequal sharing of matrimonial or partnership property in terms of Principle A.[113] It is a misuse of Principle B to review the sharing of matrimonial or partnership property by testing it in terms of taking fair account of economic advantage.[114]

Principle C. Any economic burden of caring, (i) after divorce, for a child of the marriage under the age of 16 years should be shared fairly between the persons; (ii) after dissolution of the civil partnership, for a child under that age who has been accepted by both partners as a child of the family.[115]

In applying this principle, the court must have regard to:

    (a)   any decree or arrangement for aliment for the child;
    (b)   any expenditure or loss of earning capacity caused by the need to care for the child[116];
    (c)   the need to provide suitable accommodation for the child;
    (d)   the age and health of the child;
    (e)   the educational, financial and other circumstances of the child;
    (f)   the availability and cost of suitable child-care facilities or services;
    (g)   the needs and resources of the persons; and

---

[110] 1985 Act, s. 11(7)(a), as amended by the Civil Partnership Act 2004, Sched. 28, para. 17. See n. 105 *supra*.

[111] *Petrie v. Petrie*, 1988 S.C.L.R. 390 at p. 394.

[112] *De Winton v. De Winton*, 1998 Fam.L.R. 110 at p. 114.

[113] *Jackson v. Jackson*, 2000 S.C.L.R. 81 at p. 96.

[114] *ibid.*

[115] Cases in which Principle C was explicitly considered are listed in App. VIII.

[116] Expenditure on the child after his or her sixteenth birthday is not to be taken into account (*Monkman v. Monkman*, 1988 S.L.T. (Sh. Ct.) 37); nor should future expenditure on school fees (*Maclachlan v. Maclachlan*, 1998 S.L.T. 693).

(h) all the other circumstances of the case (which *may* include, if the court thinks fit, taking account of any support, financial or otherwise, given by the person who is to make the financial provision to any person whom he maintains as a dependant in his household whether or not he owes an obligation of aliment to that person).[117]

The court must not however take account of the conduct of either party to the marriage or as the case may be of either partner unless the conduct has adversely affected the financial resources which are relevant to the decision of the court on a claim for financial provision.[118]

Principle D. A person who has been dependent to a substantial degree on the financial support of the other person should be awarded such financial provision as is reasonable to enable him to adjust, over a period of not more than three years from (i) the date of the decree of divorce, to the loss of that support on divorce (ii) the date of the decree of dissolution of the civil partnership, to the loss of that support on dissolution.[119]

In applying this principle, the court must have regard to:

(a) the age, health and earning capacity of the person who is claiming the financial provision;

(b) the duration and extent of the dependence of that person prior to divorce or to the dissolution of the civil partnership[120];

(c) any intention of that person to undertake a course of education or training;

(d) the needs and resources of the persons; and

(e) all the other circumstances of the case (which *may* include, if the court thinks fit, taking account of any support, financial or otherwise, given by the person who is to make the financial provision to any person whom he maintains as a dependant in his household whether or not he owes an obligation of aliment to that person).[121]

---

[117] 1985 Act, s. 11(3) and (6).

[118] 1985 Act, s. 11(7)(a), as amended by the Civil Partnership Act 2004, Sched. 28, para. 17. See n. 105 *supra*.

[119] Cases in which Principle D was explicitly considered are listed in App. VIII.

[120] Dependence prior to the marriage or civil partnership may be taken into account — *Petrie v. Petrie*, 1988 S.C.L.R. 390. The level of support afforded to the claimant between the date of separation and the date of divorce or dissolution of the civil partnership may be critical — *Millar v. Millar*, 1990 S.C.L.R. 666 at p. 671; failure to seek any financial support after separation may disentitle the claimant to an award under s. 9(1)(d) — *Gray v. Gray*, 1991 S.C.L.R. 422. *Cf.* n. 124 *infra*.

[121] 1985 Act, s. 11(4) and (6), as amended by the Civil Partnership Act 2004, Sched. 28, para. 17.

The court must not, however, take account of the conduct of either party to the marriage or as the case may be of either partner unless either (a) the conduct has adversely affected the financial resources which are relevant to the decision of the court on a claim for financial provision, or (b) it would be manifestly inequitable to leave the conduct out of account.[122]

Principle E. A person who at the time of the divorce or of the dissolution of the civil partnership seems likely to suffer serious financial hardship as a result of the divorce or dissolution should be awarded such financial provision as is reasonable to relieve him of hardship over a reasonable period.[123]

In applying this principle, the court must have regard to:

(a) the age, health and earning capacity of the person who is claiming the financial provision;

(b) the duration of the marriage or of the civil partnership;

(c) the standard of living of the persons during the marriage or civil partnership;

(d) the needs and resources of the persons; and

(e) all the other circumstances of the case (which *may* include, if the court thinks fit, taking account of any support, financial or otherwise, given by the person who is to make the financial provision to any person whom he maintains as a dependant in his household whether or not he owes an obligation of aliment to that person).[124]

The court must not, though, take account of the conduct of either party to the marriage or as the case may be of either partner unless either (a) the conduct has adversely affected the financial resources which are relevant to the decision of the court on a claim for financial provision, or (b) it would be manifestly inequitable to leave the conduct out of account.[125]

Where any parties have reached agreement in relation to any capital sum order, pension lump sum order or transfer of property order, a joint minute may be entered into expressing that agreement; and the sheriff may grant decree in respect of those parts of the joint minute in

---

[122] 1985 Act, s. 11(7)(a) and (b), as amended by the Civil Partnership Act 2004, Sched. 28, para. 17. See n. 105 *supra*.

[123] Cases in which the application of Principle E was explicitly considered are listed in App. VIII.

[124] 1985 Act, s. 11(5) and (6), as amended by the Civil Partnership Act 2004, Sched. 28, para. 17. Failure to seek financial support after separation does not disentitle the claimant to an award under s. 9(1)(e) — *Haughan v. Haughan*, 2002 S.C. 631. *Cf.* n. 120 *supra*.

[125] 1985 Act, s. 11(7)(a) and (b), as amended by the Civil Partnership Act 2004, Sched. 28, para. 17. See n. 105 *supra*.

relation to which he could otherwise make an order, whether or not such a decree would include a matter for which there was no crave.[126] A joint minute is binding on the parties and cannot be set aside by the court unless: (1) the interests of third parties, such as the child of the marriage, are affected; (2) it is void or voidable on some ground applicable to the general law of contract; or (3) there is specific statutory provision to that effect.[127]

In relation to (3), section 16(1)(b) and (2)(b) of the Family Law (Scotland) Act 1985 provides that where the parties to a marriage or the partners in a civil partnership have entered into an agreement[128] as to the financial provision to be made on divorce or on dissolution of the civil partnership, the court may on granting decree of (or within such time thereafter as the court may specify on granting decree) make an order setting aside or varying the agreement or any term of it where the agreement was not fair and reasonable at the time it was entered into.[129] If the agreement contains a term relating to pension sharing, the court may (i) make the order on granting decree where the order sets aside the agreement or varies the term relating to pension sharing; and (ii) make the order on granting decree or within such time thereafter as the court may specify where the order sets aside or varies any other term of the agreement.[130]

---

[126] r. 33.26(c) or r. 33A.27(c).

[127] *Anderson v. Anderson*, 1989 S.C.L.R. 475 and cases cited therein. See also *Sochart v. Sochart*, 1988 S.L.T. 799; *Horton v. Horton*, 1992 S.L.T. (Sh. Ct.) 37; and *Jongejan v. Jongejan*, 1993 S.L.T. 595 (*cf. Davidson v. Davidson*, 1989 S.L.T. 466 and *Stewart v. Stewart*, 1990 S.C.L.R. 360).

[128] "Agreement" means an agreement entered into before or after the commencement of the 1985 Act — s. 16(5). An agreement recorded in a joint minute falls within s. 16(1)(b) — *Jongejan v. Jongejan*, 1993 S.L.T. 595.

[129] As amended by the Civil Partnership Act 2004, Sched. 28, para. 22. Note that the court cannot make the order prior to granting decree of divorce, a preliminary proof on a crave for such an order is competent — *Gillon v. Gillon*, 1994 S.C. 162. Where (a) the parties to a marriage or the partners in a civil partnership have entered into an agreement as to financial provision to be made on divorce or on dissolution of the civil partnership; and (b) the agreement includes provision in respect of a person's rights or interests or benefits under an occupational pension scheme, the Board of the Pension Protection Fund's subsequently assuming responsibility for the occupational pension scheme in accordance with Chapter 3 or Part 2 of the Pension Act 2004 or any provision in force in Northern Ireland corresponding to that Chapter shall not affect—(a) the power of the court under subs (1)(b) to make an order setting aside or varying the agreement or any term of it; (b) on an appeal, the powers of the appeal court in relation to the order—1985 Act, s. 16(2B) and (2C), as inserted by the Family Law (Scotland) Act 2006, s. 17(5).

[130] 1985 Act, s. 16(2)(b) and (c), as substituted by the Welfare Reform and Pensions Act 1999, Sched. 12, para. 11(1) and (2). A term relating to pension sharing is a term corresponding to provision which may be made in a pension sharing order and satisfying the requirements set out in s. 28(1)(f) or 48(1)(f) of the Welfare Reform and Pensions Act 1999 — 1985 Act, s. 16(2A), as inserted by the 1999 Act, Sched. 12, para. 11(1) and (3).

In considering whether or not the agreement was fair and reasonable at the time it was entered into:

> "the court has to look at all the circumstances prior to and at the time that the agreement was entered into and relevant to its negotiation and signing, to see whether there was some unfair or unconscionable advantage taken of some factor or of some relationship between the parties which enables the court to say that an agreement was not truly entered into by one party or the other as a free agent and that the agreement or any term of it was not in the circumstances fair and reasonable at the time it was entered into. In this determination, the extent of a party's professional qualifications and experience and the nature of any advice received from a professional source may well be important factors to bear in mind in the judgment of what is fair and reasonable. Nevertheless, they cannot in themselves be determinative of the issue where other circumstances suggesting unfair advantage or unreasonable conduct by one party to influence the other in the signing of an agreement which in its terms expressly surrenders rights which that other party would have on divorce are averred."[131]

Any term of an agreement purporting to exclude the right to apply for an order under section 16(1)(b) is void.[132] Application for the order must be made by a crave in the initial writ or defences, as the case may be.[133]

Periodical allowance orders

An order for payment of a periodical allowance may be made on granting decree of divorce or of dissolution of a civil partnership or within such period as the court on granting the decree may specify.[134]

The order may be for a definite or indefinite period or until the happening of a specified event.[135] The order in any event ceases to have

---

[131] *McAfee v. McAfee*, 1990 S.C.L.R. 805 at p. 808, followed in *Gillon v. Gillon (No. 1)*, 1994 S.L.T. 978 at p. 982. In *McAfee*, the order was refused after proof (1993 G.W.D. 28–1782); so also in *Gillon v. Gillon (No. 3)*, 1995 S.L.T. 678 and *Inglis v. Inglis*, 1999 S.L.T. (Sh. Ct.) 59. See also *Anderson v. Anderson*, 1991 S.L.T. (Sh. Ct.) 11; *Young v. Young (No. 2)*, 1991 S.L.T. 869; and *Worth v. Worth*, 1994 S.L.T. (Sh. Ct.) 54.

[132] 1985 Act, s. 16(4).

[133] r. 33.48(1)(a) and (2)(b) or r. 33A.45(1)(a) and (2)(b).

[134] 1985 Act, s. 13(1)(a) and (b), as amended by the Civil Partnership Act 2004, Sched. 28, para. 20. *Cf.* n. 27 *supra*. The order may also be made after the granting of decree (as to which, see n. 161 *infra* and accompanying text).

[135] 1985 Act, s. 13(3). A party is entitled to argue for a restriction in the duration of an order without having given advance notice of the intention so to contend (*Robertson v. Robertson*, 1989 S.C.L.R. 71).

effect on the person receiving payment—(i) and marrying, (ii) entering into a civil partnership, or (iii) dying, except in relation to arrears due under it.[136] If the order is subsisting at the death of the person making the payment, it continues to operate against that person's estate.[137]

Application for a periodical allowance order may be made in similar fashion to an application for a capital sum or transfer of property order, except that the applicant's pleadings must contain an averment stating whether and, if so, when and by whom, a maintenance order has been granted in favour of or against that party or of any other person in respect of whom the order is sought.[138]

The court cannot make a periodical allowance order *unless* (i) the order is justified by Principle C, D or E (detailed *supra*) and (ii) the court is satisfied that an order for payment of a capital sum or for transfer of property or a pension sharing order would be inappropriate or insufficient to satisfy the requirements of section 8(2) of the Act (namely that the order be justified by the principles in section 9 and reasonable having regard to the resources of the parties).[139] The claimant must aver and prove that these conditions are satisfied,[140] even in an undefended action.[141]

---

[136] 1985 Act, s. 13(7)(b), as amended by the Civil Partnership Act 2004, Sched. 28, para. 20.

[137] 1985 Act, s. 13(7)(a), as amended by the Civil Partnership Act 2004, Sched. 28, para. 20, subject to the court's powers under s. 13(4) (nn. 157 and 158, *infra*).

[138] See text accompanying n. 54 *supra* and r. 33.5 or r. 33A.5.

[139] 1985 Act, s. 13(2), as amended by the Welfare Reform and Pensions Act 1999, Sched. 12, para. 10. Cases in which a periodical allowance has been awarded include *Monkman v. Monkman*, 1988 S.L.T. (Sh. Ct.) 37 (for 10 years); *Dever v. Dever*, 1988 S.C.L.R. 352 (for six months); *Petrie v. Petrie*, 1988 S.C.L.R. 390 (for one year); *Atkinson v. Atkinson*, 1988 S.C.L.R. 396 (for three years); *Bell v. Bell*, 1988 S.C.L.R. 457 (until death or remarriage of pursuer or sixtieth birthday of defender); *Park v. Park*, 1988 S.C.L.R. 584 (for one year with an award at a reduced rate for a further year); *McDevitt v. McDevitt*, 1988 S.C.L.R. 206 (for three years); *Muir v. Muir*, 1989 S.L.T. (Sh. Ct.) 20 (for one year); *Tyrrell v. Tyrrell*, 1990 S.L.T. 406 (for one year); *Johnstone v. Johnstone*, 1990 S.L.T. (Sh. Ct.) 79 (until death or remarriage); *Barclay v. Barclay*, 1991 S.C.L.R. 205 (for three years); *Toye v. Toye*, 1992 S.C.L.R. 95 (for three years); *Loudon v. Loudon*, 1994 S.L.T. 381 (for one year); *McConnell v. McConnell* 1997 Fam.L.R. 97 (for three years; reduced on appeal to six months (1997 Fam.L.R. 108)); *Gribb v. Gribb*, 1994 S.L.T. (Sh. Ct.) 43 (until death or remarriage; approved by the Inner House (1996 S.L.T. 719)); *Buckle v. Buckle*, 1995 S.C.L.R. 590 (for one year); *Haughan v. Haughan*, 1996 S.L.T. 321 (until death or remarriage); *Wilson v. Wilson*, 1999 S.L.T. 249 (for 30 months); *Galloway v. Galloway*, 2003 Fam.L.R. 10 (for six years); and *L v. L*, 2003 Fam.L.R. 101 (for three years or until capital sum fully paid, whichever sooner).

[140] *Mackin v. Mackin*, 1991 S.L.T. (Sh. Ct.) 22. See also *Savage v. Savage*, 1997 Fam.L.R. 132 (award refused having regard to the resources which would be available to the husband in the future and the capital payment which was to be made to the wife) and *McConnell v. McConnell (No. 2)*, 1997 Fam.L.R. 108 (award restricted to take account of the fact that the wife was to receive a substantial capital sum and a transfer of property, part of which consisted of a development site from which income could be derived).

[141] *Thirde v. Thirde*, 1987 S.C.L.R. 335.

The rules of law and procedure concerning agreements anent capital payment or transfer of property[142] apply also to agreements anent periodical allowance, with the addition that the court has extra powers to vary the terms of an agreement relating to periodical allowance in certain specified circumstances.[143]

Incidental orders

"An incidental order" is defined by section 14(2) as one or more of the following orders:

(a)   an order for the sale[144] of property[145];

(b)   an order for the valuation[146] of property;

(c)   an order determining any dispute between the parties to the marriage or as the case may be the partners as to their respective property rights by means of a declarator thereof or otherwise;

(d)   an order regulating the occupation of the matrimonial home or the family home of the partnership or the use of furniture and plenishings therein or excluding either person from such occupation[147];

---

[142] See nn. 126–133 and accompanying text, *supra.*

[143] See 1985 Act, s. 16(1)(a) and (2)(a) and (3). See also *Mills v. Mills*, 1990 S.C.L.R. 213 and *Ellerby v. Ellerby*, 1991 S.C.L.R. 608, and r. 33.52 or r. 33A.49.

[144] The order requires to be, at least principally, aimed at financial provision on divorce, so that it cannot be granted just to save the pursuer the trouble of raising a separate action for division and sale (*Reynolds v. Reynolds*, 1991 S.C.L.R. 175, approved in *MacClue v. MacClue*, 1994 S.C.L.R. 933 (motion for order for sale by party not craving financial provision refused as incompetent)). Orders for sale were made in *Reynolds; Lewis v. Lewis*, 1993 S.C.L.R. 32; *Jacques v. Jacques*, 1995 S.C. 327; *Crosbie v. Crosbie*, 1996 S.L.T. (Sh. Ct.) 86; *Thomson v. Thomson*, 2003 Fam.L.R. 22; *Cordiner v. Cordiner*, 2003 Fam.L.R. 39; *McCaskill v. McCaskill*, 2004 Fam.L.R. 123; and *Connolly v. Connolly*, 2005 Fam. L.R. 106.

[145] "Property" in s. 14 can only refer to such property as is property encompassed within the ambit of the Act, *i.e.* the property of one or other or both of the parties to the marriage — *Demarco v. Demarco*, 1990 S.C.L.R. 635 (order for valuation of property owned by company of which defender a shareholder refused).

[146] *cf. McKeown v. McKeown*, 1988 S.C.L.R. 355 and *Demarco v. Demarco*, 1990 S.C.L.R. 635.

[147] As long as such an incidental order remains in force, the former spouse or partner in a civil partnership is deemed to be, except to the extent that the order otherwise provides, a non-entitled spouse or non-entitled partner with occupancy rights in the property as regards (i) certain general powers of management in relation thereto and (ii) protection against certain arrangements intended to defeat those rights (see s. 14(5) or s. 14(5A), as inserted by the Civil Partnership Act 2004, Sched. 28, para. 21). An order under s. 14(2)(d) was granted in *Little v. Little*, 1990 S.L.T. 785 at p. 792, whereby a period of "protected occupation" for one year from the date of decree of divorce was allowed; and in *Symon v. Symon*, 1991 S.C.L.R. 414.

(e) an order regulating liability, as between the persons, for outgoings in respect of the matrimonial home or the family home of the partnership or furniture or plenishings therein[148];

(f) an order that security shall be given for any financial provision[149];

(g) an order that payments shall be made or property transferred to any curator bonis or trustee or other person for the benefit of the person by whom or on whose behalf application has been made under section 8(1) of the Act;

(h) an order setting aside or varying any term in an antenuptial or postnuptial marriage settlement or in any corresponding settlement in respect of the civil partnership[150];

(j) an order as to the date from which any interest on any amount awarded shall run[151];

---

[148] See *e.g. McConnell v. McConnell*, 1997 Fam.L.R. 97 (order made for husband to repay the outstanding mortgage); *Little v. Little*, 1989 G.W.D. 21–887 (order refused *in hoc statu*); and *McCormick v. McCormick*, 1994 G.W.D. 35–2078 (order granted for period until transfer of property order given effect to). In *Macdonald v. Macdonald*, 1995 S.L.T. 72, such order was held incompetent as regards mortgage payments already made.

[149] In *Macdonald v. Macdonald*, 1995 S.L.T. 72, such order was held incompetent as regards alimentary payments. An order was made, however, requiring the defender to grant a standard security over his property in respect of the award of a capital sum to the pursuer. *Cf. Trotter v. Trotter*, 2001 S.L.T. (Sh. Ct.) 42.

[150] "Settlement" includes a settlement by way of a policy of assurance to which s. 2 of the Married Women's Policies of Assurance (Scotland) Act 1880 relates. In *Robertson v. Robertson*, 2003 S.L.T. 208, it was held that a copartnery contract relative to the parties' farming business was not a "marriage settlement".

[151] "[T]he purpose of s. 14(2)(j) is to enable the court to award interest on the whole, or any part, of any amount awarded as a financial provision as from such date as it thinks appropriate, even although this may be a date earlier than the date of payment in terms of the decree … [If] an order for interest is to be made as an incidental order under s. 14(2)(j) it must, as s. 8(2) provides, be justified by the principles set out in s. 9 of the Act and be reasonable having regard to the resources of the parties. It should therefore be seen as an integral part of the order for financial provision, and not as something which is to be added on afterwards once all the exercises to arrive at this provision are complete. The order must also be made having regard to the purpose for which interest is awarded by the court… . What [the court] is required to do, when the capital sum is awarded with reference to the net value of the matrimonial property, is to share fairly the net value of all the matrimonial property as at the relevant date. In most cases this will be the date of the final separation: see s. 10(3)(a). There may be circumstances where a party who has had the sole use or possession of an asset since the relevant date, the whole or part of the value of which is to be shared with the other party on divorce, should be required to pay interest as consideration for the use or possession which he has had between the relevant date and the date of decree. An order for interest may, for example, be appropriate where the use or possession has resulted in a benefit which has been taken into account in some other way in making the order for financial provision. It may also be appropriate where … the amount of the principal sum is fixed by the decree but payment of it, in whole or in

(ja) in relation to a deed relating to moveable property, an order dispensing with the execution of the deed by the grantor and directing the sheriff clerk to execute the deed;[152]

(k) any ancillary order which is expedient to give effect to the principles set out in section 9 of the Act or to any order made under section 8(2) of the Act.[153]

Orders (d) and (e) may only be made on or after the granting of decree; other incidental orders may be made before, on or after the granting or refusal of decree.[154]

Neither an incidental order, nor any rights conferred by such an order, prejudices any rights of any third party in so far as those rights existed immediately before the making of the order.[155]

Section 14 of the 1985 Act gives the court a discretionary power, to be exercised in the circumstances of a particular case.[156] The phrase "an incidental order" means what it says, namely something done by way of order incidental or ancillary to the making of an order under

---

part, is postponed to a later date. Whether interest should be awarded on this basis, and if so on what part of the award, from what date and what the rate of interest should be is in the discretion of the court, bearing in mind that an incidental order for interest under s. 14(2)(j) is an integral part of the order for financial provision under s. 8(2) of the Act" (*per* the Lord President in *Geddes v. Geddes*, 1993 S.L.T. 494 at p. 499 and pp. 500–501). In *Savage v. Savage*, 1997 Fam.L.R. 132 and in *Bolton v. Bolton*, 1995 G.W.D. 14–799 the Lord Ordinary awarded a lump sum under the head of interest to date of decree. In *Welsh v. Welsh*, 1994 S.L.T. 828 the Lord Ordinary awarded interest from the relevant date upon the applicant's share of the equity in the matrimonial home as valued at that date, the non-applicant spouse having had exclusive occupation thereof since the relevant date. In *Gracie v. Gracie*, 1997 S.L.T. (Sh. Ct.) 15 payment of a proportion of the capital sum was deferred and the balance made payable by instalments, with interest on the whole outstanding balance from time to time at the rate of 3 per cent from the date of decree. In *MacLean v. MacLean*, 2001 Fam.L.R. 118 the Lord Ordinary held that, having regard to the fact that the liable party had cared for the parties' children since separation, it was not appropriate to backdate any order for interest. See also *Tahir v. Tahir (No. 2)*, 1995 S.L.T. 451 and *Collins v. Collins*, 1997 Fam.L.R. 50.

[152] As inserted by the Family Law (Scotland) Act 2006, s. 18.

[153] See *e.g. Little v. Little*, 1990 S.L.T. 785 at p. 792 (order made regarding conveyancing expenses).

[154] 1985 Act, s. 14(1) and (3). Application for the order is made by a crave in the initial writ or defences, as the case may be (r. 33.48(1)(a) and (2)(a) or r. 33A.45(1)(a) and (2)(a)) unless made *pendente lite* (see n. 14 *supra*). For an example of an incidental order made after decree of divorce had been granted, see *Walker v. Walker*, 1994 G.W.D. 8–496 (former wife ordained to sign and deliver indemnity and disclaimer forms on insurance policy). Note that an application made after the granting of decree of divorce for an incidental order for the sale of heritable property was held incompetent in *Amin v. Amin,* 2000 S.L.T. (Sh. Ct.) 115.

[155] 1985 Act, s. 15(3).

[156] *McKeown v. McKeown*, 1988 S.C.L.R. 355; *Little v. Little*, 1989 G.W.D. 21–887.

section 8(2) in relation to an order under section 8(1)(a), (aa), (b), (ba) or (baa).[157]

An incidental order may be varied or recalled by subsequent order on cause shown.[158]

ORDERS MADE AFTER THE GRANTING OF DECREE

Certain applications after decree relative to orders for financial provision require to be made by minute lodged in the process of the action to which the application relates.[159] The applications thus provided for include applications after final decree for —

(i) variation of the date or method of payment of a capital sum or the date of transfer of property[160];

(ii) payment by one party to the marriage to the other of a periodical allowance[161];

(iii) variation or recall of an order for a periodical allowance[162];

(iv) conversion of a periodical allowance order into an order for payment of a capital sum or for a transfer of property[163];

(v) recall or variation of a pension lump sum order[164];

---

[157] *Demarco v. Demarco*, 1990 S.C.L.R. 635.

[158] 1985 Act, s. 14(4). Application for such variation or recall must be made by minute in the process of the action to which the application relates — r. 33.51(1)(b) or r. 33A.48(1)(b). Where such minute is lodged, any party may lodge a motion for any interim order which may be made pending the determination of the application — r. 33.51(2) or r. 33A.48(2).

[159] r. 33.51(1)(a) or r. 33A.48(1)(a).

[160] 1985 Act, s. 12(4), requiring that there has since the date of decree been a material change of circumstances (see n. 162 *infra*).

[161] 1985 Act, s. 13(1)(c), as amended by the Civil Partnership Act 2004, para. 20, requiring that there has since the date of decree been a change of circumstances (see n. 162 *infra*). As to an order setting aside or varying any term of an agreement relating to a periodical allowance in terms of s. 16(1)(a) of the 1985 Act, see n. 143 *supra*.

[162] 1985 Act, s. 13(4)(a), as amended by the Civil Partnership Act 2004, para. 20, requiring that since the date of the order there has been a material change of circumstances. Such change is not constituted merely by showing that the court at the time of the earlier award proceeded upon a particular hypothesis which has turned out to be incorrect — *Walker v. Walker*, 1994 S.C. 482. The application may be made by the executor of a party to the former marriage or of a former partner — s. 13(4) as amended by the Civil Partnership Act 2004, para. 20. (see *e.g. Sandison's Exrx. v. Sandison*, 1984 S.L.T. 111 and *Finlayson v. Finlayson's Exrx.*, 1986 S.L.T. 19). The court has power to backdate such variation or recall (s. 13(4)(b)) and in that event to order repayment — s. 13(6).

[163] 1985 Act, s. 13(4)(c), as amended by the Civil Partnership Act 2004, para. 20.

[164] 1985 Act, s. 12A(5), as amended by the Civil Partnership Act 2004, Sched. 28, para. 19, applicable where the liability of the liable party under the capital sum order has been discharged in whole or in part, other than by a payment by the person responsible for the pension arrangement under the pension lump sum order. In that event, on an application by any person having an interest, the court may recall the order or vary the amount specified in the order, as appears to the court appropriate in the circumstances.

(vi)   variation of a pension lump sum order to substitute trustees or managers;[165] and

(vii) an order in terms of section 28(10) or 48(9) of the Welfare Reform and Pensions Act 1999.[166]

Where a minute is lodged, any party may apply by motion for any interim order which may be made pending the determination of the application.[167]

---

[165] 1985 Act, s. 12A(7), as amended by the Civil Partnership Act 2004, Sched. 28, para. 19.
[166] See n. 48 and accompanying text *supra.*
[167] r. 33.51(2) or r. 33A.48(2), applicable to (i) to (iv), inclusive.

SPECIMEN CRAVES AND ASSOCIATED PLEAS-IN-LAW

1. MERITS

C— (i) To divorce the defender from the pursuer on the ground that the marriage has broken down irretrievably as established by the defender's adultery.

(ii) To divorce the defender from the pursuer on the ground that the marriage has broken down irretrievably as established by the defender's behaviour.

(iii) To divorce the defender from the pursuer on the ground that the marriage has broken down irretrievably as established by the parties' non-cohabitation for a continuous period of one year or more and the defender's consent to the granting of decree of divorce.

(iv) To divorce the defender from the pursuer on the ground that the marriage has broken down irretrievably as established by the parties' non-cohabitation for a continuous period of two years or more.

P— The marriage of the parties having broken down irretrievably, the pursuer is entitled to decree of divorce as first craved.

C— (i) To dissolve the civil partnership between the pursuer and the defender on the ground that the civil partnership has broken down irretrievably as established by the defender's behaviour.

(ii) To dissolve the civil partnership between the pursuer and the defender on the ground that the civil partnership has broken down irretrievably as established by the parties' non-cohabitation for a continuous period of one year or more and the defender's consent to the granting of decree of dissolution of the civil partnership.

(iii) To dissolve the civil partnership between the pursuer and the defender on the ground that the civil partnership has broken down irretrievably as established by the parties' non-cohabitation for a continuous period of two years or more.

P—   The civil partnership of the parties having broken down irretrievably, the pursuer is entitled to decree of dissolution of civil partnership as first craved.

C—   To divorce the defender from the pursuer on the ground that an interim gender recognition certificate under the Gender Recognition Act 2004 has, after the date of the marriage, been issued to the pursuer.

P—   An interim gender recognition certificate having after the date of the marriage been issued to the pursuer, the pursuer is entitled to decree of divorce as first craved.

C—   To dissolve the civil partnership between the pursuer and the defender on the ground that an interim gender recognition certificate under the Gender Recognition Act 2004 has, after the date of registration of the civil partnership, been issued to the pursuer.

P—   An interim gender recognition certificate having after the date of the registration of the civil partnership been issued to the pursuer, the pursuer is entitled to decree of dissolution of civil partnership as first craved.

C—   To divorce the defender from the pursuer on the ground that an interim gender recognition certificate under the Gender Recognition Act 2004 has, after the date of the marriage, been issued to the defender.

P—   An interim gender recognition certificate having after the date of the marriage been issued to the defender, the pursuer is entitled to decree of divorce as first craved.

C—   To dissolve the civil partnership between the pursuer and the defender on the ground that an interim gender recognition certificate under the Gender Recognition Act 2004 has, after the date of registration of the civil partnership, been issued to the defender.

P—   An interim gender recognition certificate having after the date of registration of the civil partnership been issued to the defender, the pursuer is entitled to decree of dissolution of civil partnership as first craved.

C—   To postpone the grant of decree of divorce until the defender has given consent to the pursuer's remarriage.

P—   The pursuer being prevented from entering into a religious marriage by virtue of a requirement of that religion and the defender being able to act so as to remove, or enable or contribute to the removal of, the impediment which prevents that marriage, and it being just and reasonable to do so, the grant of decree of divorce should be postponed as   craved.

2. PROTECTIVE MEASURES

C— (1) To interdict the defender from abusing the pursuer by means of violence, harassment, threatening conduct, or any other conduct giving rise, or likely to give rise, to physical or mental injury, fear, alarm or distress; and to attach a power of arrest to the said interdict; and

(2) To interdict the defender from entering or remaining in the pursuer's place of work at 'George's Salon', 35 Leven Street, Geetown; and to attach a power of arrest to the said interdict.

P— The defender having abused the pursuer in the manner condescended on, and having shown an intention to persist therein, the pursuer is entitled to interdict as   craved.

P— A power of arrest being necessary to protect the pursuer from a risk of abuse in breach of the interdicts, should be attached to each of the said interdicts as   craved.

C— To ordain the defender to appear personally before the court on such day and at such hour as the court may appoint to answer to the charge against him of being guilty of contempt of court and breach of the interdict granted by the Sheriff of North Strathclyde at Oban on 5 February 2006, whereby the defender was interdicted from molesting the pursuer by *inter alia* using violence towards her; and failing his appearance before the court as aforesaid, to grant warrant to officers of the court to apprehend the defender and bring him before the court to answer as aforesaid; and, on the charge being admitted or proved, to find that the defender has been guilty of contempt of court and breach of interdict and in respect thereof to visit him with such punishment as to the court shall seem just; and to find the defender liable in expenses.

P— The defender, being in breach of interdict as condescended on, should be found guilty and punished as   craved.

C— (1) To grant an exclusion order suspending the defender's occupancy rights in the matrimonial home at 1 High Street, Seatown;

(2) To grant warrant for the summary ejection of the defender from the matrimonial home at 1 High Street, Seatown;

(3) To interdict the defender from entering the matrimonial home at 1 High Street, Seatown without the express permission of the pursuer; and to attach a power of arrest to the said interdict;

(4) To interdict the defender from entering or remaining in High Street, Seatown; and to attach a power of arrest to the said interdict; and

(5) To interdict the defender from removing, except with the written consent of the pursuer or by a further order of the court, any furniture or plenishings in the matrimonial home at 1 High Street, Seatown.

P— An exclusion order being necessary for the protection of the pursuer from reasonably apprehended conduct of the defender which would be injurious to her health, and the pursuer being entitled to the ancillary orders craved, an exclusion order suspending the defender's occupancy rights in the matrimonial home and orders ancillary thereto should be granted as   craved.

C— (1) To grant an exclusion order suspending the defender's occupancy rights in the family home at 15 Low Street, Efftown;

(2) To grant warrant for the summary ejection of the defender from the family home at 15 Low Street, Efftown;

(3) To interdict the defender from entering the family home at 15 Low Street, Efftown without the express permission of the pursuer; and to attach a power of arrest to the said interdict;

(4) To interdict the defender from entering or remaining in Low Street, Efftown; and to attach a power of arrest to the said interdict; and

(5) To interdict the defender from removing, except with the written consent of the pursuer or by a further order of the court, any furniture or plenishings in the family home at 15 Low Street, Efftown.

P— An exclusion order being necessary for the protection of the pursuer from reasonably apprehended conduct of the defender which would be injurious to her health, and the pursuer being entitled to the ancillary orders craved, an exclusion order suspending the defender's occupancy rights in the family home and orders ancillary thereto should be granted as   craved.

3. PROPERTY ORDERS

C—   To find and declare that the pursuer is entitled to occupy the matrimonial home at 110 High Street, Seatown.

P—   The pursuer being a non-entitled spouse and the said dwelling-house being a matrimonial home, the pursuer is entitled to declarator as   craved.

C—   To find and declare that the pursuer is entitled to occupy the family home at 14 Dover Road, Enntown.

P—   The pursuer being a non-entitled partner and the said dwelling-house being a family home, the pursuer is entitled to declarator as   craved.

C—   To grant leave to the pursuer to enter and occupy the matrimonial home at 110 High Street, Seatown.

P—   The pursuer being a non-entitled spouse and it being just and reasonable for the occupancy rights of the pursuer to be enforced, leave to enter and occupy the matrimonial home should be granted as   craved.

C—   To grant leave to the pursuer to enter and occupy the family home at 14 Dover Road, Enntown.

P   The pursuer being a non-entitled partner and it being just and reasonable for the occupancy rights of the pursuer to be enforced, leave to enter and occupy the family home should be granted as   craved.

C—   To grant to the pursuer the possession and use of the items of furniture and plenishings specified in the schedule hereto in the matrimonial home at 110 High Street, Seatown.

P—   The pursuer being a non-entitled spouse and it being just and reasonable for the pursuer to be granted the possession and use of the specified items owned by the defender in the matrimonial home, decree therefor should be granted as   craved.

C—   To grant to the pursuer the possession and use of the items of furniture and plenishings specified in the schedule hereto in the family home at 14 Dover Road, Enntown.

P   The pursuer being a non-entitled partner and it being just and reasonable for the pursuer to be granted the possession and use of the specified items owned by the defender in the family home, decree therefore should be granted as   craved.

C— To grant decree for the transfer of the tenancy of the matrimonial home at 22 High Street, Seatown from the defender to the pursuer.

P— The pursuer being a non-entitled spouse and it being just and reasonable that the tenancy of the matrimonial home be transferred from the defender to the pursuer, decree therefor should be granted as   craved.

C— To grant decree for the transfer of the tenancy of the family home at 14 Dover Road, Enntown from the defender to the pursuer.

P The pursuer being a non-entitled partner and it being just and reasonable that the tenancy of the family home be transferred from the defender to the pursuer, decree therefore should be granted as   craved.

C— To grant decree for the vesting of the joint tenancy of the matrimonial home the dwellinghouse at 22 Low Street, Seatown in the pursuer solely.

P— The pursuer being a joint tenant of the matrimonial home and it being just and reasonable that the said joint tenancy should be vested in the pursuer solely, decree should be granted as   craved.

C— To grant decree for the vesting of the joint tenancy of the family home at 14 Dover Road, Enntown in the pursuer solely.

P The pursuer being a joint tenant of the family home and it being just and reasonable that the said joint tenancy should be vested in the pursuer solely, decree should be granted as   craved.

4. CHILDREN

C— To make a residence order in respect of John Smith, child under the age of 16 years, whereby he is to live with the pursuer.

P— It being in the best interests of the child that the residence order sought be made, decree should be granted as   craved.

C— To make a contact order in respect of Alexander Robertson, child under the age of 16 years, whereby he is to be with the pursuer each Saturday from 10 a.m. until 6 p.m. and every fourth weekend from 6 p.m. on Friday until 6 p.m. on Sunday.

P— It being in the best interests of the child that the contact order sought be made, decree should be granted as   craved.

C— To make a specific issue order in respect of Thomas Thompson, child under the age of 16 years, whereby he is to attend Millerstone Academy for the academic year commencing 16 August 2005.

P— It being in the best interests of the child that the specific issue order sought be made, decree should be granted as   craved.

C— To vary the interlocutor of the Sheriff of Lothian and Borders at Edinburgh dated 15 July 2000 by making a residence order in respect of Elizabeth Ross, child under the age of 16 years, whereby she is to live with the pursuer.

P— There having been a material change of circumstances and it now being in the best interests of the said child that the residence order sought be made, the said interlocutor should be varied as   craved.

5. MONEY

C— (i) To grant decree against the defender for payment to the pursuer of a capital sum of twenty thousand pounds (£20,000), payable on such date and by such method as the court thinks fit, with interest thereon at such rate and from such date as to the court seems appropriate until payment.

(ii) To grant decree for the transfer of the defender's right, title and interest in the heritable property at 4 Old Street, Avebury; to ordain the defender to make, execute and deliver to the pursuer a valid disposition of the said subjects and such other deeds as may be necessary to give the pursuer a valid title to the subjects, and that within one month of the date of decree to follow hereon; and in the event of the defender failing to make, execute and deliver such disposition and other deeds, to authorise and ordain the sheriff clerk to subscribe on behalf of the defender a disposition of the subjects and such other deeds as may be necessary to give the pursuer a valid title to the subjects, all as adjusted at the sight of the sheriff clerk.

(iii) To grant decree requiring the Standard Assurance Company, as persons responsible for the Island Horse Ltd pension scheme, to pay the whole of any pension lump sum payable to *et separatim* in respect of the death of the defender, when it becomes due, to the pursuer.

(iv)   To grant decree providing that the defender's shareable rights under the John Johnson Ltd pension scheme shall be subject to pension sharing for the benefit of the pursuer and that the sum of one hundred and fifty thousand pounds (£150,000) with interest accrued at eight per cent a year from 1 July 2005 until the date of transfer of the appropriate pension credit into a qualifying scheme for the pursuer be so transferred.

P—   The order   craved being justified by the principle set forth in s. 9(1)(a) of the Family Law (Scotland) Act 1985 and reasonable having regard to the resources of the parties, should be granted.

C—   (i)   To grant an order for the sale of the parties' heritable property at 6 Abbey Street, Perth and for that purpose to grant warrant to such person as the court shall think proper to dispose of the subjects, heritably and irredeemably, by public roup or private bargain, in such manner and under such conditions as the court shall direct; to ordain the pursuer and the defender to execute and deliver to the purchaser or purchasers of the subjects such dispositions and other deeds as shall be necessary for constituting full right thereto in their persons, failing which to dispense with such execution and delivery and to direct the sheriff clerk to execute such dispositions and other deeds all as adjusted at his sight as shall be necessary aforesaid; and to make such order regarding the price of the subjects when sold, after deduction of any debts or burdens affecting the same and all other expenses attending the sale, as to the court seems proper.

(ii)   To find and declare that the pursuer is the sole owner of the Ford Escort motorcar, registration number R123 ABC.

(iii)   To grant an order entitling the pursuer to reside in the heritable property at 5 Low Street, Aberdeen and excluding the defender therefrom for such period following upon the granting of decree as to the court seems proper.

(iv)   To find the defender liable, as between the parties, for such period as to the court seems proper to make all payments due under the standard security granted by the parties in favour of the National Building Society on 5 August 1993 over the heritable property at 4 Princess Road, Carlops.

(v)   To ordain the defender to grant a standard security over
      his heritable property at 6 Royal Mews, Ayr in favour of
      the pursuer for all sums due and to become due to her in
      respect of the order for financial provision   craved
      and failing his doing so within such time as the court
      may specify to authorise and direct the sheriff clerk to
      execute such standard security, as adjusted at his sight.

P—   The order   craved being appropriate in the circum-
      stances, should be granted.

C—   To grant decree against the defender for payment to the
      pursuer of a periodical allowance of fifty pounds (£50)
      per week for a period of three years, or such lesser period
      as the court thinks fit, from the date of decree of divorce
      or until the death or remarriage of the pursuer, if sooner.

C—   To grant decree against the defender for payment to the
      pursuer of a periodical allowance of ninety pounds (£90)
      per week for a period of three years, or such lesser period
      as the court thinks fit, from the date of dissolution of the
      civil partnership of the parties or until the death of, or
      the entering into a civil partnership by, the pursuer, if
      sooner.

P—   The order   craved being justified by the principle set
      forth in s. 9(1)(d) of the Family Law (Scotland) Act 1985
      and reasonable having regard to the resources of the
      parties and an order for payment of a capital sum or for
      transfer of property or a pension sharing order being
      insufficient *et separatim* inappropriate to satisfy the
      requirements of s. 8(2) of the Family Law (Scotland) Act
      1985, the order craved as aforesaid should be granted.

C—   To grant decree against the defender for payment to the
      pursuer of a periodical allowance of seventy-five pounds
      (£75) per week until the death or remarriage of the pursuer
      or for such lesser period as the court thinks fit.

C—   To grant decree against the defender for payment to the
      pursuer of a periodical allowance of one hundred and
      twenty pounds (£120) per week until the death of, or
      entering into a civil partnership by, the pursuer or for
      such lesser period as the court thinks fit.

P—   The order   craved being justified by the principle
      detailed in s. 9(1)(e) of the Family Law (Scotland) Act
      1985 and reasonable having regard to the resources of the
      parties, and an order for payment of a capital sum or for
      transfer of property or a pension sharing order being

insufficient *et separatim* inappropriate to satisfy the requirements of s. 8(2) of the Family Law (Scotland) Act 1985, the order craved as aforesaid should be granted.

C— To interdict the defender from effecting any transfer of, or transaction involving, any redundancy payment received or to be received by him from Rosebank Ltd, 15 Gold Street, Seatown, which has the effect of defeating in whole or in part the pursuer's claim for financial provision as   craved; and to grant such other order as the court thinks fit.

P— The defender being liable to effect a transfer of, or transaction involving, his property which is likely to have the effect of defeating the pursuer's claim for financial provision in whole or in part, interdict should be granted as   craved.

C— To grant an order setting aside the agreement between the parties entered into on 13 March 2003.

P— The agreement between the parties not being fair and reasonable at the time it was entered into, should be set aside as   craved.

C— To vary the interlocutor dated 7 April 2005 insofar as providing for payment by the defender to the pursuer of a capital sum and that by substituting for the date of payment specified therein the date "7 August 2007".

P— There having been a material change of circumstances, the interlocutor should be varied as craved.

C— To recall the decree dated 15 July 2003, in so far as it ordains the defender to make payment to the pursuer of a periodical allowance, with effect from such date as to the court seems appropriate, and to ordain the repayment by the pursuer to the defender of such sum or sums as the court thinks fit.

P— There having been a material change of circumstances the said order should be recalled as craved.

6. MISCELLANEOUS

C— To grant warrant to arrest on the dependence of this action.

C— To grant warrant to intimate this initial writ to Mrs Jane

Jackson, residing at 2 Park Grove, Aytown, mother and one of the next of kin of the defender; and to Mamie Jackson, residing at 52 Maple Terrace, Beetown, daughter of the defender who has reached the age of 16 years.

C— To grant warrant to intimate this initial writ to Miss Mary Black, residing at 2 Glebe Street, Seatown, as a person with whom the defender is alleged to have committed adultery.

C— To grant warrant to intimate this initial writ to Mrs Indira Banda, 5 Calcutta Road, Bombay, as an additional spouse of the defender.

C— To grant warrant to intimate this initial writ to Beetown Council, Central Avenue, Beetown, as a local authority having care of Mark White.

C— To grant warrant to intimate this initial writ to Roger Allan, residing at 1 Main Street, Beetown, as a person liable to maintain Peter Jones.

C— To grant warrant to intimate this initial writ to Henry Smith, residing at 4 Jeffrey Street, Deetown, as a person in fact exercising care or control in respect of Peter Smith.

C— To grant warrant to intimate this initial writ to Deetown Council, The Square, Deetown, as the local authority within which area the pursuer resides.

C— To grant warrant to intimate to Alan Smith, 101 High Road, Efftown, as a child to whom any section 11 order made as craved would relate.

C— To grant warrant to intimate to The Huddersfield Building Society, 123 High Street, Jaytown, as holders of a security in respect of the heritable property at 1 Johnson Terrace, Jaytown.

C— To grant warrant to intimate this initial writ to Peter Evans, 1 Forth Road, Geetown, as a person in whose favour the transfer of the property referred to in the fourth crave was made.

C— To grant warrant to intimate this initial writ to Seatown

Council, Main Square, Seatown, landlords of the matrimonial home at 1 High Street, Seatown.

C— To grant warrant to intimate this initial writ to Hugh White, residing at 4 George Place, Seatown, landlord of the family home at 110 High Street, Seatown.

C— To dispense with intimation to George Banks in respect that his address is not known and cannot reasonably be ascertained.

C— To dispense with intimation to Alan Jones, child under the age of 16 years.

C— To grant warrant to intimate to the Scottish Prudential Co. Ltd, 46 Jones Place, Jaytown, as persons responsible for the White Rose Ltd pension scheme.

C— To find the defender liable in expenses.

SPECIMEN MOTIONS

1. MERITS

The pursuer moves the court to allow proof by affidavit evidence.

The pursuer moves the court to allow proof by affidavit evidence in relation to the merits of the action.

The pursuer moves the court to allow the action to proceed as undefended.

The defender moves the court to prorogate the time for implementing the order of the sheriff dated 24 May 2007 by a further 14 days.

The defender moves the court to grant decree of absolvitor, which failing to dismiss the action, with expenses.

The pursuer moves the court to prorogate the time for lodging a record by a further seven days.

The pursuer moves the court to sist the cause for negotiations.

The pursuer moves the court to recall the sist and re-enrol the cause for further procedure.

2. PROTECTIVE MEASURES

The pursuer moves the court to grant interim interdict against the defender from abusing the pursuer by means of violence, harassment, threatening conduct, or any other conduct giving rise, or likely to give rise, to physical or mental injury, fear, alarm or distress; and to attach a power of arrest to the said interim interdict.

The pursuer moves the court to ordain the defender to appear at the bar to explain his failure to obtemper the interlocutor dated 14 February 2004.

The pursuer moves the court to attach a power of arrest to the interim interdict granted by the sheriff on 23 February 2006.

The pursuer moves the court to grant an interim order suspending the defender's occupancy rights in the matrimonial home at 33 Low Street, Enntown; warrant for the summary ejection of the defender therefrom; interim interdict against the defender from entering the matrimonial home without the express permission of the pursuer, with a power of arrest attached to the said interim interdict; and interim interdict against the defender from removing, except with the written consent of the pursuer or by a further order of the court, any furniture or plenishings in the matrimonial home.

The pursuer moves the court to grant an interim order suspending the defender's occupancy rights in the family home at 16 Parr Street, Eggtown; warrant for the summary ejection of the defender therefrom; interim interdict against the defender from entering the family home without the express permission of the pursuer, with a power of arrest attached to the said interim interdict; and interim interdict against the defender from removing, except with the written consent of the pursuer or by a further order of the court, any furniture or plenishings in the family home.

3. PROPERTY ORDERS

The pursuer moves the court to grant leave to the pursuer to enter the matrimonial home at 63 George Road, Kaytown.

The pursuer moves the court to grant leave to the pursuer to enter the family home at 12 Lennox Street, Kadxtom.

The pursuer moves the court to dispense with the defender's consent to the sale of the heritable subjects at 56 Andrews Road, Peatown by the pursuer to George Smith, residing at 359 Albert Avenue, Teetown, in terms of missives dated 3, 5 and 6 March 2004.

4. CHILDREN

The pursuer moves the court to grant interim interdict against the defender from removing Joyce Jones, child under the age of 16 years, out of the control of the pursuer or furth of the sheriffdom.

The pursuer moves the court to ordain Mrs Eve Stewart to appear at the bar to disclose to the court such information as she has which is relevant to the whereabouts of Alison Brown, child under the age of 16 years.

The pursuer moves the court to appoint a local authority or a reporter to investigate and report to the court on the circumstances of Violet Jones, child under the age of 16 years, and on proposed arrangements for the care and upbringing of the child.

The pursuer moves the court to grant an interim residence order in respect of John Green, child under the age of 16 years, whereby he is to live with the pursuer.

The pursuer moves the court to grant an interim contact order in respect of Alan White, child under the age of 16 years, whereby he is to be with the pursuer each Saturday from 10 a.m. until 6 p.m.

The pursuer moves the court to vary *ad interim* the decree dated 12 November 2003 by making an interim contact order in respect of Alice Main, child under the age of 16 years whereby she is to be with the pursuer each alternate weekend between 6 p.m. on Friday and 6 p.m. on Sunday.

The pursuer moves the court to recall *ad interim* the decree dated 13 August 2003 in so far as it makes a contact order in respect of Joanna Peters, child under the age of 16 years, in favour of the defender.

5. MONEY

The pursuer moves the court to ordain the defender to make payment to her of interim aliment at the rate of £100 per week.

The defender moves the court to vary the interlocutor dated 13 June 2004 by reducing the interim aliment payable thereunder to the sum of £70 per week.

The defender moves the court to recall the interlocutor dated 5 July 2005.

The pursuer moves the court to ordain the defender to provide details of his resources within 21 days.

The pursuer moves the court to grant interim interdict against the defender from effecting any transfer of, or transaction involving, his Mercedes motor vehicle, registration number T21 ACG, or such other order as the court thinks fit.

The pursuer moves the court to grant an incidental order *pendente lite* for the sale of the heritable property at 21 Black Street, Geetown; to that end, to grant warrant to Allan Jones, Solicitor and Estate Agent, 654 Main Street, Geetown, or such other person as the court thinks fit, to dispose of the subjects in such manner and under such conditions as the court shall direct; and to ordain the parties to execute and deliver such disposition and other deeds as shall be necessary to give a valid title to the subjects to the purchaser or purchasers thereof, which failing to authorise the sheriff clerk to execute such disposition and deeds, as adjusted at his sight.

The defender moves the court to vary *ad interim* the decree dated 2 August 2004 by reducing the periodical allowance payable thereunder to the sum of £25 per week.

The defender moves the court to recall *ad interim* the decree dated 23 October 2004 in so far as it ordains the defender to make payment to the pursuer of a periodical allowance.

6. MISCELLANEOUS

The pursuer moves the court to grant warrant to intimate the initial writ to John Jones, 12 High Street, Deetown, as a person with whom the defender is alleged to have had an association.

SPECIMEN WRITS[1]

1. HUME v. HUME

A. Initial Writ

SHERIFFDOM OF NORTH STRATHCLYDE AT PAISLEY

INITIAL WRIT

in the cause

MRS KATHLEEN ALICIA ANDREWS
or HUME (Assisted Person), 331 Main
Street, Paisley

PURSUER

against

EDWARD HUME, 52 Great Queen Street,
Manchester

DEFENDER

The pursuer craves the court:

1. To divorce the defender from the pursuer on the ground that the marriage has broken down irretrievably as established by the defender's adultery.
2. To grant warrant to intimate this initial writ to Racquel Smith, residing at 52 Great Queen Street, Manchester, as a person with whom the defender is alleged to have committed adultery.
3. To find the defender liable in expenses.

---

[1] These are drawn from five fictitious sheriff court processes.

CONDESCENDENCE

1. The pursuer resides at 331 Main Street, Paisley. The defender resides at 52 Great Queen Street, Manchester. The parties were married in Glasgow 1 July 1994. They have two children: Sheila Amy Alicia Hume, born 5 July 1995, and George Hume, born 22 November 1996. Relative marriage and birth certificates are produced.
2. The pursuer has been habitually resident in Scotland throughout the period of one year immediately preceding the raising of this action. She has been resident within the Sheriffdom of North Strathclyde for a period exceeding 40 days immediately preceding the raising of this action. She is unaware of any proceedings continuing in Scotland or elsewhere which are in respect of the marriage or capable of affecting its validity or subsistence.
3. After their marriage the parties lived together until about 4 May 2006. Since then they have not lived together. The defender has formed an adulterous relationship with Racquel Smith, designed in the third crave. Since the said date they have resided together at 52 Great Queen Street, Manchester and have there committed adultery. The marriage has broken down irretrievably. There is no prospect of a reconciliation. The pursuer now seeks decree of divorce.
4. The said children reside with the pursuer. They are happy and well cared for. The pursuer is willing and able to devote her whole time and attention to them and provide them with a good home.

PLEA-IN-LAW

The marriage of the parties having broken down irretrievably, the pursuer is entitled to decree of divorce as first craved.

IN RESPECT
WHEREOF

Enrolled Solicitor
503 Bank Street, Paisley
Solicitor for Pursuer

2. SMART v. SMART

A. Initial Writ, including Minute for Decree

SHERIFFDOM OF GLASGOW AND STRATHKELVIN AT
GLASGOW

INITIAL WRIT

in the cause

JOANNA WYSE or SMART
(Assisted Person), 4 Gardeners Crescent,
Springboig, Glasgow

PURSUER

against

HENRY JOSEPH SMART, 14 Grove
Place, Dennistoun, Glasgow

DEFENDER

The pursuer craves the court:

1. To divorce the defender from the pursuer on the ground that the marriage has broken down irretrievably as established by the defender's behaviour.
2. To interdict the defender from abusing the pursuer by means of violence, harassment, threatening conduct, and any other conduct giving rise, or likely to give rise, to physical or mental injury, fear, alarm or distress; and to attach a power of arrest to the said interdict.
3. To find the defender liable in expenses.

CONDESCENDENCE

1. The pursuer resides at 4 Gardeners Crescent, Springboig, Glasgow. The defender resides at 14 Grove Place, Dennistoun, Glasgow. The parties were married at Glasgow on 20 November 2003. They have no children. Relative marriage certificate is produced.
2. The parties are habitually resident in Scotland. The pursuer has been resident in the Sheriffdom of Glasgow and Strathkelvin for a period exceeding 40 days immediately preceding the raising of this action. She knows of no proceedings continuing in Scotland or elsewhere which are in respect of the marriage or capable of affecting its validity or subsistence.

3. The marriage has broken down irretrievably as established by the defender's behaviour. He developed an alcohol problem. Latterly he drank every day. He would regularly return home drunk late at night. He would become heavily intoxicated at social events to the embarrassment and humiliation of the pursuer. He spent little time at home. He did little to assist in the management of the household. The defender's said behaviour adversely affected the pursuer's health. On or about 6 June 2006, the parties separated. Since then they have not lived together. The pursuer cannot reasonably be expected to cohabit with the defender. There is no prospect of a reconciliation. The pursuer now seeks decree of divorce.

4. Following the parties' separation aforesaid the defender has persistently abused the pursuer. He has frequently abused her by telephone. He has threatened to assault her if she does not resume cohabitation with him. He has followed her in the street demanding a reconciliation. In particular, on or about 5 August 2006, the defender shouted abuse and threats at the pursuer from the street outside her house. The pursuer is apprehensive that he will continue so to act. She is fearful lest he carry out his threats. She accordingly seeks the protection of the interdict and power of arrest second craved.

PLEAS-IN-LAW

1. The marriage of the parties having broken down irretrievably, the pursuer is entitled to decree of divorce as first craved.
2. The defender having abused the pursuer in the manner condescended on, and having shown an intention to persist therein, the pursuer is entitled to interdict as second craved.
3. A power of arrest being necessary to protect the pursuer from a risk of abuse in breach of interdict, should be attached to the said interdict as second craved.

IN RESPECT
WHEREOF

Enrolled Solicitor
692 West George Street,
Glasgow
Solicitor for Pursuer

WADDELL having considered the evidence contained in the affidavits and the other documents all as specified in the schedule hereto and being satisfied that upon the evidence a motion for decree in terms of the first and third craves of the initial writ may properly be made, moves the court accordingly.

IN RESPECT
WHEREOF

Solicitor for Pursuer

SCHEDULE

1. Affidavit of pursuer.
2. Affidavit of Glenda Parkes or Wilson.
3. Marriage certificate no. 5/1/1 of process.

B. Affidavit of Pursuer

SHERIFFDOM OF GLASGOW AND STRATHKELVIN AT GLASGOW

AFFIDAVIT

of the pursuer

in the cause

JOANNA WYSE or SMART
(Assisted Person), 4 Gardeners Crescent,
Springboig, Glasgow

PURSUER

against

HENRY JOSEPH SMART, 14 Grove
Place, Dennistoun, Glasgow
DEFENDER

At Glasgow, the Fifteenth day of December Two Thousand and Six, in the presence of ALLAN WADDELL, Solicitor and Notary Public,

692 West George Street, Glasgow, Compeared: JOANNA WYSE or SMART, residing at 4 Gardeners Crescent, Springboig, Glasgow, who being solemnly sworn, Depones as follows:

1. My full name is Joanna Wyse or Smart. I am 25 years of age, a part-time teller at Citibank, and I reside at 4 Gardeners Crescent, Springboig, Glasgow.
2. I married my husband, Henry Joseph Smart, at present residing at 14 Grove Place, Dennistoun, Glasgow, at Glasgow on 20 November 2003. We have no children. I produce an extract of the entry in the Register of Marriages, no. 5/1/1 of process which I have signed as relative hereto.
3. My husband and I are habitually resident in Scotland. I was resident in the Sheriffdom of Glasgow and Strathkelvin for at least 40 days prior to raising this action of divorce. I do not know of any proceedings continuing in Scotland or elsewhere concerning my marriage or capable of affecting its validity or subsistence.
4. My marriage has broken down irretrievably. I believe that my husband had a drinking problem when we got married but it became progressively worse. Eventually he would never come home without calling in at the pub on the way. When he returned home, he would stay for a short time only before going back out to the pub, where he would stay drinking until closing time. He would then come home drunk. He worked as a TV engineer with Johnsons of Edinburgh Road, Glasgow until he was sacked on account of his drinking.

   My husband's drinking caused me humiliation and embarrassment at the few social events that we attended. My husband behaved so badly at these, because he was hopelessly drunk, that I had to spend almost the entire evening apologising. On one particular occasion, at a disco for a charity held after the death of a friend of mine, I felt particularly bad because my husband had been rude and unpleasant to everybody and had embarrassed and humiliated me in front of a good number of my friends.

   My husband also did virtually nothing to assist with running the house, although I cannot say that he kept me short of money. It was only grudgingly that he ever helped in the decoration of our home, and apart from that he never did anything at all, not even drying the dishes.

   Although my husband never assaulted me, his behaviour certainly affected my health and nerves. I would often get asthmatic attacks because of the stress I felt. Eventually, I felt that I could no longer tolerate his behaviour. On 6 June 2006, I left him and we have not lived together since. I confirm that there is no prospect of a reconciliation between us.

5. Following our separation my husband pestered me by telephone and in the streets, making various threats to hurt me if I did not go back to him. Since I obtained an interim interdict against him to stop him molesting me, I have heard nothing more from him.

All of which is truth as the deponent shall answer to God.

. . . . Deponent

. . . . . Notary Public

C. Affidavit of Glenda Parkes or Wilson

SHERIFFDOM OF GLASGOW AND STRATHKELVIN AT GLASGOW

AFFIDAVIT

of Mrs Glenda Parkes or Wilson

in the cause

JOANNA WYSE or SMART
(Assisted Person), 4 Gardeners Crescent,
Springboig, Glasgow

PURSUER

against

HENRY JOSEPH SMART, 14 Grove
Place, Dennistoun, Glasgow

DEFENDER

At Glasgow, the Fifteenth day of December Two Thousand and Six, in the presence of ALLAN WADDELL, Solicitor and Notary Public, 692 West George Street, Glasgow, Compeared GLENDA PARKES or WILSON, residing at 43 Queen's Road, Springboig, Glasgow, who being solemnly sworn, Depones as follows:

1. My full name is Glenda Parkes or Wilson. I am 27 years of age, a part-time sales assistant and reside at 43 Queen's Road, Springboig, Glasgow.

2. I have been a friend of Joanna Smart, the pursuer in this action, for several years. I came to know her husband pretty well and am able to speak to events during their marriage from my own personal knowledge. I am aware that Mrs Smart and her husband have been separated since about June of this year. I also know why their relationship broke down: it was solely as a result of the defender's increasing addiction to drink. He seemed to drink virtually every day. He often came round to my house to try to persuade my husband to go drinking with him. Usually he had already had a few and was quite drunk.

   I would say that there was a definite effect on Mrs Smart's health. She has asthma and his behaviour affected her asthmatic condition. Before the separation she had to use her inhaler far more than ever before. There were days also when I went to her house and found her sitting in the kitchen in floods of tears. The whole marital relationship slid to rock-bottom as a result of his drinking and its effect on her. I have been at a number of social occasions which they attended before they separated at which he was drunk and I know that she was embarrassed by his behaviour at them. I do not see them ever getting back together again.

All of which is truth as the deponent shall answer to God.

. . . . Deponent

. . . . . Notary Public

3. ANDERSON v. JAMIESON

A. Initial Writ, including Minute for Decree

SHERIFFDOM OF GRAMPIAN, HIGHLAND AND
ISLANDS AT STONEHAVEN

INITIAL WRIT

in the cause

BARBARA ANDERSON, 4 Dundas
Street, Stonehaven

PURSUER

against

OLIVE HANSON or JAMIESON, 4
Nursery Street, Stonehaven

DEFENDER

The pursuer craves the court:

1. To dissolve the civil partnership between the pursuer and the defender on the ground that the civil partnership has broken down irretrievably as established by the parties' non-cohabitation for a continuous period of one year or more and the defender's consent to the granting of decree of dissolution of civil partnership.
2. To grant warrant to intimate this initial writ to Hamish Wilson Robertson, residing at 1 Forge Park, Brechin, Angus as a person who is liable to maintain Peter Robertson.

CONDESCENDENCE

1. The pursuer resides at 4 Dundas Street, Stonehaven. The defender resides at 4 Nursery Street, Stonehaven. The parties registered as civil partners at Edinburgh on 5 December 2005. The defender has a child treated as one of the family by the pursuer: Peter Robertson, born 5 July 2000. Extracts of the relevant entries in the civil partnership register and the register of births are produced. The natural father of the aforesaid child is Hamish Wilson Robertson, designed in the second crave.
2. The parties are habitually resident in Scotland. The pursuer has been resident within the Sheriffdom of Grampian, Highland and

Islands for a period exceeding 40 days immediately preceding the raising of this action. She is unaware of any proceedings continuing in Scotland or elsewhere which are in respect of the civil partnership or capable of affecting its validity or subsistence.

3. After the date of registration of their civil partnership the parties lived together until about 4 January 2006. Since then they have not lived together. The defender is prepared to consent to the granting of decree of dissolution of civil partnership. The civil partnership has broken down irretrievably. There is no prospect of a reconciliation. The pursuer seeks decree of dissolution of civil partnership.

4. The said child resides with the defender and is well looked after. The present arrangements for his care and upbringing are satisfactory.

PLEA-IN-LAW

The civil partnership between the pursuer and the defender having broken down irretrievably, the pursuer is entitled to decree of dissolution of civil partnership as first craved.

IN RESPECT
WHEREOF

Enrolled Solicitor
10 Main Square,
Stonehaven
Solicitor for Pursuer

THOMSON having considered the evidence contained in the affidavits and the other documents all as specified in the schedule hereto and being satisfied that upon the evidence a motion for decree in terms of the first crave of the initial writ may properly be made, moves the court accordingly.

IN RESPECT
WHEREOF

Solicitor for Pursuer

SCHEDULE

1. Affidavit of pursuer.
2. Affidavit of defender.
3. Affidavit of Mrs Jeannie Hogg or Hanson.
4. Certificate of civil partnership, No. 5/1/1 of process.
5. Birth certificate, No. 5/1/2 of process.
6. Notice of Consent, No. 7 of process.

B. Affidavit of Pursuer

SHERIFFDOM OF GRAMPIAN, HIGHLAND AND
ISLANDS AT STONEHAVEN

AFFIDAVIT

of the pursuer

in the cause

BARBARA ANDERSON, 4 Dundas
Street, Stonehaven

PURSUER

against

OLIVE HANSON JAMIESON, 4
Nursery Street, Stonehaven

DEFENDER

At Stonehaven, the Seventh day of September Two Thousand and Seven, in the presence of JOHN THOMSON, Notary Public, 10 Main Square, Stonehaven, Compeared: residing at 4 Dundas Street, Stonehaven, who being solemnly sworn, Depones as follows:

1. My full name is Barbara Anderson. I am aged 42 years and I reside at 4 Dundas Street, Stonehaven. I am unemployed.
2. I registered as a civil partner of Olive Hanson Jamieson, presently residing at 4 Nursery Street, Stonehaven at Edinburgh on 5 December 2005. She has a child from a previous marriage: Peter Robertson, born 5 July 2000, whose natural father is Hamish Wilson Robertson, residing at 1 Forge Park, Brechin, Angus. I treated Peter Robertson as one of the family. I produce extracts of the relevant entries in the civil partnership and birth registers, numbers 5/1/1 and 5/1/2 of process, which I have docqueted as relative hereto.

3. Olive Hanson Jamieson and I are habitually resident in Scotland. I have been resident within the Sheriffdom of Grampian, Highland and Islands for a period exceeding 40 days immediately preceding the raising of this action. I am not aware of any proceedings continuing in Scotland or elsewhere which are in respect of the civil partnership or capable of affecting its validity or subsistence.

4. After registration of our civil partnership Olive Hanson Jamieson and I lived together until about 4 January 2006. Since then we have not lived together. There is no prospect of a reconciliation. Olive Hanson Jamieson consents to the granting of decree of dissolution of civil partnership. I identify her signature on the Form of Consent, No. 7 of process, which I have docqueted as relative hereto.

5. Since the separation I have seen very little of the child, Peter. I am not in a position to speak to the present arrangements for his care and upbringing.

All of which is truth as the Deponent shall answer to God.

. . . . Deponent

. . . . . Notary Public

C. Affidavit of Amy Anderson

SHERIFFDOM OF GRAMPIAN, HIGHLAND AND
ISLANDS AT STONEHAVEN

AFFIDAVIT

of

in the cause

BARBARA ANDERSON, 4 Dundas
Street, Stonehaven

PURSUER

against

OLIVE HANSON JAMIESON, 4
Nursery Street, Stonehaven

DEFENDER

At Stonehaven, the Seventh day of September Two Thousand and Seven, in the presence of JOHN THOMSON, Notary Public, 10 Main Square, Stonehaven, Compeared: Amy Anderson, residing at 4

Dundas Street, Stonehaven, who being solemnly sworn, Depones as follows:

1. My full name is Amy Anderson, I am aged 67 years. I reside at 4 Dundas Street, Stonehaven. I am retired. I am the mother of Barbara Anderson, the pursuer in this action.
2. My daughter lives with me. I am aware that she separated from Olive Hanson Jamieson, her civil partner, on 4 January 2006. She did in fact come to stay with me at that time and has lived with me ever since. I therefore know that she has not lived with Olive Hanson Jamieson since then.

All of which is truth as the Deponent shall answer to God.

. . . . Deponent

. . . . . Notary Public

D. Affidavit of Defender

SHERIFFDOM OF GRAMPIAN, HIGHLAND AND ISLANDS AT STONEHAVEN

AFFIDAVIT

of the defender

in the cause

BARBARA ANDERSON, 4 Dundas Street, Stonehaven

PURSUER

against

OLIVE HANSON JAMIESON, 4 Nursery Street, Stonehaven

DEFENDER

At Stonehaven, the Twenty-First day of September Two Thousand and Seven, in the presence of ALAN MARSH, Notary Public, 11 New Street, Stonehaven, Compeared: OLIVE HANSON JAMIESON, residing at 4 Nursery Street, Stonehaven, who being solemnly sworn, Depones as follows:

1. My full name is Olive Hanson Jamieson. I am aged 32 years and reside at 4 Nursery Street, Stonehaven. I am unemployed.

2. I separated from my civil partner, Barbara Anderson on 4 January 2006. My son Peter Robertson has lived with me since the separation. He stays with me in the former family home at 4 Nursery Street, Stonehaven. The property is a Scottish Homes house and is well furnished. It comprises a livingroom, two bedrooms, kitchenette and bathroom. Peter has one bedroom and I have the other. I always do my best to keep the house clean and tidy. Peter attends St Mark's Primary School near my house and is getting on well there. The school is a 10 minute walk from my home. I accompany my son to and from the school each day. His attendance record is excellent. He has lots of friends with whom he plays regularly.
3. I am unemployed and in receipt of state benefits. I am able to devote my whole time and attention to Peter's care and wellbeing. My mother visits almost every day and helps out where necessary. She also babysits him to allow me to go out from time to time during the evenings. Peter is a happy and healthy boy. He has no contact with my civil partner and does not seem to miss her.

All of which is truth as the Deponent shall answer to God.

. . . . Deponent

. . . . . Notary Public

E. Affidavit of Mrs Jeanette Hogg or Hanson

SHERIFFDOM OF GRAMPIAN, HIGHLAND AND
ISLANDS AT STONEHAVEN

AFFIDAVIT

of Mrs Jeannie Hogg or Hanson

in the cause

BARBARA ANDERSON, 4 Dundas
Street, Stonehaven

PURSUER

against

OLIVE HANSON JAMIESON, 4
Nursery Street, Stonehaven

DEFENDER

At Stonehaven, the Twenty-First day of September, Two Thousand and Seven in the presence of ALAN MARSH, Notary Public, 11 New Street, Stonehaven, Compeared: MRS JEANNIE HOGG or HANSON, residing at 66 Nursery Street, Stonehaven, who being solemnly sworn, Depones as follows:

1. My full name is Jeannie Hogg or Hanson. I am 55 years of age and reside at 66 Nursery Street, Stonehaven. I am a housewife. I am the mother of the defender, Mrs Olive Hanson Jamieson.
2. My daughter and her civil partner, Barbara Anderson, separated on 4 January 2006. Since then my grandson Peter has lived with my daughter in the former family home at 4 Nursery Street, Stonehaven. I visit them virtually every day and usually spend a couple of hours in their presence. We sit around talking or go out to the shops together. My daughter does not work and devotes all her time to looking after Peter. He is always healthy and happy. He adores his mother and is always relaxed and at ease in her company. He is also happy and carefree when with me. He enjoys staying with me whenever I babysit him, which I do to allow my daughter to go out from time to time during the evenings. He does not see Ms Anderson and never asks after her. He does not appear to miss her at all.
3. My daughter and Peter live in a Scottish Homes house which has a livingroom, two bedrooms, kitchenette and bathroom. Peter has his own bedroom and my daughter has the other. The house is always immaculate. My daughter never allows her home to be anything other than extremely clean and tidy.
4. Peter now attends St Mark's Primary School, Stonehaven. The school is only about ten minutes away by foot. My daughter takes her son to and from school herself every day. If she were for any reason unable to do so, I am always available to step in and help out. His attendance record is excellent and I know he enjoys it. He is forever off to play with some new friend or other.

All of which is truth as the Deponent shall answer to God.

. . . . Deponent

. . . . . Notary Public

4. SCOTT v. SCOTT

A. Initial Writ

SHERIFFDOM OF LOTHIAN AND BORDERS AT
EDINBURGH

INITIAL WRIT

in the cause

MRS ANN GEORGE or SCOTT
(Assisted Person), 5 Merton Grove,
Edinburgh

PURSUER

against

PHILIP SCOTT, 14 Elm Grove, Dalkeith
DEFENDER

The pursuer craves the court:

1. To divorce the defender from the pursuer on the ground that the marriage has broken down irretrievably as established by the parties' non-cohabitation for a continuous period of two years or more.
2. To make a residence order in respect of Daphne Scott, child under the age of 16 years, whereby she is to live with the pursuer.
3. Failing an order in terms of the second crave, to make a contact order in respect of Daphne Scott, child under the age of 16 years, whereby she is to be with the pursuer each Saturday from 10 a.m. until 6 p.m. and every fourth weekend from 6 p.m. on Friday until 6 p.m. on Sunday.
4. To grant warrant to intimate this initial writ to Mrs Elspeth Scott, residing at 22 George Place, Dalkeith as a person in fact exercising care or control in respect of Daphne Scott.
5. To grant warrant to intimate to Daphne Scott, 22 George Place, Dalkeith, as a child to whom any section 11 order made as craved would relate.
6. To find the defender liable in expenses.

CONDESCENDENCE

1. The pursuer resides at 5 Merton Grove, Edinburgh. The defender resides at 14 Elm Grove, Dalkeith. The parties were married at Edinburgh on

1 March 1995. They have one child, Daphne Scott born 25 June 1996. Relative marriage and birth certificates are produced.

2. The parties are habitually resident in Scotland. The pursuer has been resident within the Sheriffdom of Lothian and Borders for a period exceeding 40 days immediately preceding the raising of this action. She is unaware of any proceedings continuing in Scotland or elsewhere which are in respect of the marriage or capable of affecting its validity or subsistence. She is unaware of any proceedings continuing or concluded in Scotland or elsewhere which relate to the said child.

3. After the marriage the parties lived together until about June 2004. Since then the parties have not lived together. The marriage has broken down irretrievably. There is no prospect of a reconciliation. The pursuer now seeks decree of divorce.

4. After the parties' separation the child resided with the pursuer. On or about 4 March 2006, at or about 7 p.m., the defender came to the pursuer's house. He demanded to see the child forthwith. The pursuer declined to accede. The defender thereupon assaulted her. He forcibly entered the house and seized the child. He removed the child to the house of his mother, Mrs Elspeth Scott, designed in the third crave. The child remains in the care or control of Mrs Scott. It is not in the best interests of the child to live with Mrs Scott or with the defender. The child was well settled and happy with the pursuer. She attended the local school where she performed well. The child wishes to live with the pursuer. It is in her best interests so to do. It is better for her that the residence order which failing the contact order be made than that no order be made at all.

PLEAS-IN-LAW

1. The marriage of the parties having broken down irretrievably, the pursuer is entitled to decree of divorce as first craved.

2. It being in the best interests of the child that the residence order which failing the contact order sought be made, decree should be granted as second or third craved.

IN RESPECT
WHEREOF

Enrolled Solicitor
42 St Charlotte Street,
Edinburgh
Solicitor for Pursuer

B. Defences

SHERIFFDOM OF LOTHIAN AND BORDERS AT
EDINBURGH

DEFENCES

in the cause

MRS ANN GEORGE or SCOTT
(Assisted Person), 5 Merton Grove,
Edinburgh
PURSUER

against

PHILIP SCOTT, 14 Elm Grove, Dalkeith
DEFENDER

The defender craves the court:

1. To make a residence order in respect of Daphne Scott, child under the age of 16 years, whereby she is to live with the defender.
2. To grant warrant to intimate to Daphne Scott, 22 George Place, Dalkeith, as a child to whom any section 11 order made as craved would relate.

ANSWERS TO CONDESCENDENCE

1. Admitted under explanation that the defender now resides at 22 George Place, Dalkeith.
2. Believed to be true. The defender knows of no such proceedings.
3. Admitted.
4. Admitted that after the parties' separation the child resided with the pursuer. Admitted that on 4 March 2006, at about 7 p.m. the defender came to the pursuer's house. Admitted that he requested access to the child. Admitted that he removed the child to the house of his mother, Mrs Elspeth Scott. Admitted that the child attended the local school. Not known and not admitted how she performed there. *Quoad ultra* denied. Explained and averred that on the said date, when the defender called at the pursuer's house, he requested access to the child. The pursuer thrust the child into the defender's arms. She told him to keep her for good. The pursuer was drunk at the time. The defender believes and avers

that the pursuer is frequently under the influence of alcohol. Her house is dirty. The child was not being properly looked after. Her clothing was torn and filthy. She required to be thoroughly scrubbed at the defender's mother's house where she now lives. There is ample accommodation there for her. She is well looked after by both the defender and his mother. She is happy living with them. She is settling well at her new school. It is in her best interests to live with the defender. It is better for her that the residence order be made than that no order be made at all. The defender believes and avers that it is further in the best interests of the child not to stay overnight with the pursuer.

PLEAS-IN-LAW

1. It being in the best interests of the child that the residence order sought by the defender be made, decree therefor should be pronounced as first craved.
2. It not being in the best interests of the child that the residence order sought by the pursuer be made, decree therefor should not be pronounced as second craved by the pursuer.
3. It not being in the best interests of the child that the contact order sought by the pursuer be made, decree therefor should not be pronounced as third craved by the pursuer.

IN RESPECT
WHEREOF

Enrolled Solicitor
4 Market Street,
Dalkeith
Solicitor for Defender

5. BANKS v. BANKS

A. Initial Writ

SHERIFFDOM OF TAYSIDE, CENTRAL AND FIFE AT DUNDEE

INITIAL WRIT

in the cause

JOHN BANKS, 4 Almond Place,
Liverpool
PURSUER

against

MRS ANNIE ALLISON or BANKS,
1 Park Street, Dundee
DEFENDER

The pursuer craves the court:

1. To divorce the defender from the pursuer on the ground that the marriage has broken down irretrievably as established by the parties' non-cohabitation for a continuous period of two years or more.
2. To grant warrant to intimate this initial writ to Dundee City Council, City Chambers, 21 City Square, Dundee, as a local authority having care of Peter Banks.

CONDESCENDENCE

1. The pursuer resides at 4 Almond Place, Liverpool. The defender resides at 1 Park Street, Dundee. The parties were married at Hamilton on 5 June 1979. There is one child of the marriage under the age of 16 years: Peter Banks, born 5 June 1996. Relative marriage and birth certificates are produced.
2. The defender is habitually resident in Scotland. She has been resident within the Sheriffdom of Tayside, Central and Fife for a period exceeding 40 days immediately preceding the raising of this action. The pursuer is unaware of any proceedings continuing in Scotland or elsewhere which are in respect of the marriage or capable of affecting its validity or subsistence.

3. After their marriage the parties lived together until about January 2005. Since then they have not lived together. The marriage has broken down irretrievably. There is no prospect of a reconciliation. The pursuer seeks decree of divorce.
4. The said child is at present in the care of Dundee City Council, designed in the second crave.

PLEA-IN-LAW

The marriage of the parties having broken down irretrievably, the pursuer is entitled to decree of divorce as first craved.

IN RESPECT
WHEREOF

Enrolled Solicitor,
1 Fleet Street, Glasgow
Solicitor for Pursuer

B. Defences

SHERIFFDOM OF TAYSIDE, CENTRAL AND
FIFE AT DUNDEE

DEFENCES

in the cause

JOHN BANKS, 4 Almond Place,
Liverpool
PURSUER

against

MRS ANNIE ALLISON or BANKS,
1 Park Street, Dundee
DEFENDER

The defender craves the court:

1. To grant decree against the pursuer for payment to the defender of a capital sum of ten thousand pounds (£10,000), payable at such date and by such method as the court thinks fit, with interest on such proportion thereof at such rate and from such date as the court thinks fit until payment.
2. To grant decree against the pursuer for payment to the defender of a periodical allowance of sixty-five pounds (£65) per week for a period of three years, or such lesser period as the court thinks fit, from the date of decree of divorce or until the death or remarriage of the defender, if sooner.

Answers to Condescendence

1. Admitted.
2. Admitted. The defender knows of no such proceedings.
3. Admitted.
4. Admitted.
5. The defender seeks orders for financial provision on divorce as first and second craved. As at the date of separation the pursuer had savings of £20,000 and the defender had no capital. The defender is in employment as a clerkess and earns about £120 per week. She is in receipt of maintenance from the pursuer at the rate of £65 per week. She has no capital. She has been dependent on the pursuer for financial support throughout the marriage. In all the circumstances, the sums first and second craved represent, respectively, a fair sharing of the matrimonial property and reasonable financial provision enabling the defender to adjust to the loss of support upon divorce. In these circumstances decree should be granted as first and second craved.

Pleas-in-Law

1. The order first craved being justified by the principle set forth in s. 9(1)(a) of the Family Law (Scotland) Act 1985 and reasonable having regard to the parties' resources, should be granted.
2. The order second craved being justified by the principle set forth in s. 9(1)(d) of the Family Law (Scotland) Act 1985 and reasonable having regard to the parties' resources and an order for payment of a capital sum being insufficient to satisfy the requirements of s. 8(2) of the Act, the order second craved should be granted.

IN RESPECT
WHEREOF

Enrolled Solicitor,
42 Ainslie Street,
Dundee
Solicitor for Defender

C. Joint Minute for Parties

SHERIFFDOM OF TAYSIDE, CENTRAL AND
FIFE AT DUNDEE

JOINT MINUTE

for the parties

in the cause

JOHN BANKS, 4 Almond Place,
Liverpool

PURSUER

against

MRS ANNIE ALLISON or BANKS,
1 Park Street, Dundee

DEFENDER

JONES for the pursuer and
ADAMS for the defender concurred and hereby concur in stating to
the court that in the event of decree of divorce being granted and subject
to the approval of the court the parties have agreed and hereby agree
as follows:

1. The pursuer shall pay to the defender a capital sum of eight thousand
   pounds (£8,000), payable upon the granting of decree of divorce,
   with interest thereon at the rate of eight per cent a year from the
   date of decree to follow hereon until payment; and
2. The pursuer shall pay to the defender a periodical allowance of
   sixty five pounds (£65) per week for a period of two years from

the date of decree of divorce or until the death or remarriage of the
defender, if sooner.
The parties therefore craved and hereby crave the court to interpone
authority hereto and grant decree in terms hereof.

IN RESPECT
WHEREOF

Enrolled Solicitor,
1 Fleet Street, Glasgow
Solicitor for Pursuer

Enrolled Solicitor,
42 Ainslie Street,
Dundee
Solicitor for Defender

PRACTICE NOTE RE AFFIDAVITS IN FAMILY ACTIONS[1]

When affidavits may be lodged

1. Once the period within which a notice of intention to defend requires to be lodged has expired without such notice having been lodged, affidavits may be prepared and lodged without any order of the court.

Person before whom sworn or affirmed

2. An affidavit is admissible if it is sworn (or affirmed) before a notary public, justice of the peace, or any person having authority to administer oaths for the place where the affidavit is sworn, such as a commissioner for oaths or a British diplomatic officer or consul abroad. A solicitor acting for a party to the action may act in a notarial capacity when an affidavit is sworn. Any person before whom an affidavit is sworn (referred to below as "the notary") must observe all the normal rules in this connection and must satisfy himself or herself as to the capacity of the witness to swear an affidavit.

Importance of affidavits

3. The witness should be made to appreciate the importance of the affidavit and that the affidavit constitutes his or her evidence in the case. The possible consequences of giving false evidence should be explained to the witness. Before the witness signs the affidavit he or she must have read it or the notary must have read it over to the witness.

Oath or affirmation

4. The witness must be placed on oath or must affirm.

Form and signature of the affidavit

5. The document should be on A4 paper. The affidavit should commence with the words "At   the   day of   20   , in the presence of
I   having been solemnly sworn/having affirmed give evidence as follows:". The affidavit should be drafted in the first person and should take the form of numbered paragraphs. The full name, age, address and occupation of the witness should be given in the first paragraph. The affidavit should end with the

---

[1] This Practice Note has been issued in each of the Sheriffdoms.

words "All of which is the truth as I shall answer to God" or "All of which is affirmed by me to be true", as appropriate. Any blanks in the affidavit must be filled in. Any insertion, deletion or other amendment to the affidavit requires to be initialled by the witness and the notary. Each page must be signed by both the witness and the notary. It is not necessary for the affidavit to be sealed by the notary.

Drafting the affidavit

6. An affidavit should be based on a reliable and full precognition of the witness.

7. The drafter of an affidavit should provide himself or herself, before drawing it, with an up-to-date copy of the pleadings, a copy of the appropriate precognition and the relative productions. The affidavit should be drawn so as to follow the averments in the pleadings to the extent that these are within the knowledge of that particular witness and in the same order.

8. Affidavits should be expressed in the words of the person whose affidavit it is, should be accurate as at the date of the affidavit and should not consist of a repetition of passages in the pleadings. It should be clear from the terms of the affidavit whether the witness is speaking from his or her own knowledge, as when the witness was present and saw what happened, or whether the witness is relying on what he or she was told by a particular person.

Productions

9. Productions already lodged in process must be borrowed up, and put to the party or to the witness who refers to them in his or her affidavit. Each production will require to be referred to in the affidavit by its number of process and must be docqueted and signed by the witness and the notary. If a production has not yet been lodged when the affidavit is sworn, it will require to be identified by the witness in the affidavit, should be docqueted with regard to the affidavit and signed by the witness and the notary. It must then be lodged as a production. Some productions will necessarily be docqueted with regard to more than one affidavit.

10. In consent cases, the defender's written consent form will have to be put to the pursuer in his or her affidavit, and be identified, docqueted and signed in the same way as other productions.

11. In adultery cases, photographs of both the pursuer and the defender may require to be produced, put to the appropriate witnesses and be identified, docqueted and signed in the manner already described.

Date of affidavit

12. All affidavits lodged must be of recent date. This factor is particularly important in cases involving children, cases in which financial craves are involved and in any other circumstances where the evidence of a witness or circumstances to which the wit-

ness speaks are liable to change through the passage of time. The notary must take particular care in such cases to ensure that the affidavit evidence as to such matters is correct as at the time the affidavit is sworn. Affidavits relating to the welfare of children which have been sworn more than three months prior to lodging a minute for decree are likely to be rejected by the court as out of date.

Applications relating to parental responsibilities and rights (See OCR 33.28)
13. In actions in which an application in terms of s. 11 of the Children (Scotland) Act 1995 is before the court not fewer than two affidavits dealing with the welfare of the child(ren) should be provided, at least one of them from a person who is neither a parent nor a party to the action. These affidavits should present the court with a full picture of the arrangements for the care of the child(ren) along the lines set out in paragraph 15, adapted to suit the circumstances of the particular case. The affidavits should set out reasons why it is better that the s. 11 order be made than not. The pursuer's affidavit should deal fully with the arrangements which have been made for their care, so far as within his or her knowledge. If the pursuer cannot give substantial evidence as to that it is likely to be necessary to obtain such evidence from the person who is responsible for their care.

14. In actions of divorce or judicial separation in which there are children of the marriage or children treated by the parties as a child of their family but in which no order in terms of s. 11 in terms of the Children (Scotland) Act 1995 is sought, the court, in terms of s. 12, requires to consider whether to exercise the powers set out in ss. 11 or 54 of that Act in light of the information before it as the arrangements for the child(ren)'s upbringing. Information accordingly requires to be before the court as to these arrangements. As a minimum, the affidavits of the witnesses should include the information set out in paragraphs 15 (*a*) to (*e*) below.
15. An affidavit dealing with the arrangements for the care of children should, where relevant, include the following:
   (*a*) the qualifications of the witness, if not a parent, to speak about the child; how often, and in what circumstances the witness normally sees the child;
   (*b*) the ability of those with whom the child lives to provide proper care for him or her;
   (*c*) observations as to the relationship between the child and the other members of the household, the child's general appearance, interests, state of health and well-being;
   (*d*) a description of the home conditions in which the child lives;
   (*e*) the arrangements for contact between the child and any parent (and siblings) who do not live in the same household as the child;

(f) information about the school the child attends; whether the child attends school regularly; and

(g) details of child care arrangements during working hours, including the arrangements for such care outwith school hours.

Affidavit relating to disclosure of the whereabouts of children
16. An affidavit sworn or affirmed in compliance with an order to disclose the whereabouts of children (in terms of the Family Law Act 1986, s. 33 and OCR 33.23) will require to be drafted in such a way as to meet the requirements of the court in the circumstances of the particular case. The form of the affidavit should be as above.

Financial and other ancillary craves
17. Affidavit evidence in support of financial craves is necessary in an undefended action. (See *Ali v Ali,* 2001 S.C. 618; 2001 S.L.T. 602; 2001 S.C.L.R. 485). Where financial craves are involved, the evidence should be as full, accurate and up to date as possible. If the evidence is insufficient the court may require supplementary evidence to be provided. If, after an affidavit has been sworn and the solicitor concerned has parted with it, a material change of circumstances occurs before decree has been granted the court must be informed forthwith. A further affidavit may have to be sworn.
18. The pursuer should give evidence as to his or her own financial position at the date of the affidavit. Where the pursuer gives evidence in an affidavit as to the financial position of the defender, the affidavit should state the date, as precisely as possible, at which the information was valid. The court must be provided with information which is as up to date as possible as to the defender's ability to pay the sums the pursuer is seeking. Where the pursuer cannot obtain recent information as to the defender's means the affidavit should state that that is the case but should contain as much material information relating to the defender's means as possible. If the pursuer is unable to provide sufficient evidence to justify the orders craved in full, in the minute for decree, after the words "in terms of crave(s) (number(s)...) of the initial writ", there may be added words such as "or such other sum (or sums) as the court may think proper".
19. Where the pursuer has craved a capital sum, an order for the sale of the matrimonial home, a periodical allowance, interdict or expenses, for example, and in the minute for decree does not seek decree for one or more of these, the reasons for that should be given in his or her affidavit.

Joint minutes
20. When parties record their agreement in a joint minute as to how financial and other ancillary craves should be dealt with by the court, the pursuer's affidavit should refer to the joint minute and indicate that he or she is

content that the agreement set out in it should be given effect.

Minute for decree

21. The minute for decree must be signed by a solicitor who has examined the affidavits and other documents. That solicitor takes responsibility therefor, whether or not he or she is the person who drew the initial writ or affidavits. The minute for decree should not be signed seeking decree of divorce or separation unless the evidence consists of or includes evidence other than that of a party to the marriage (Civil Evidence (Scotland) Act 1988, s. 8(3); *Taylor v Taylor,* 2000 S.L.T. 1419; 2001 S.C.L.R. 16).

CONVENTION ON THE RIGHTS OF THE CHILD

Adopted by the General Assembly of the United Nations on 20
November 1989

PREAMBLE

The States Parties to the present Convention,

Considering that, in accordance with the principles proclaimed in
the Charter of the United Nations, recognition of the inherent dignity
and of the equal and inalienable rights of all members of the human
family is the foundation of freedom, justice and peace in the world,

Bearing in mind that the peoples of the United Nations have, in the
Charter, reaffirmed their faith in fundamental human rights and in the
dignity and worth of the human person, and have determined to promote
social progress and better standards of life in larger freedom,

Recognizing that the United Nations has, in the Universal
Declaration of Human Rights and in the International Covenants on
Human Rights, proclaimed and agreed that everyone is entitled to all
the rights and freedoms set forth therein, without distinction of any
kind, such as race, colour, sex, language, religion, political or other
opinion, national or social origin, property, birth or other status,

Recalling that, in the Universal Declaration of Human Rights, the
United Nations has proclaimed that childhood is entitled to special
care and assistance,

Convinced that the family, as the fundamental group of society and
the natural environment for the growth and well-being of all its
members and particularly children, should be afforded the necessary
protection and assistance so that it can fully assume its responsibilities
within the community,

Recognizing that the child, for the full and harmonious development
of his or her personality, should grow up in a family environment, in
an atmosphere of happiness, love and understanding.

Considering that the child should be fully prepared to live an
individual life in society, and brought up in the spirit of the ideals
proclaimed in the Charter of the United Nations, and in particular
in the spirit of peace, dignity, tolerance, freedom, equality and
solidarity,

Bearing in mind that the need to extend particular care to the child has been stated in the Geneva Declaration of the Rights of the Child of 1924 and in the Declaration of the Rights of the Child adopted by the General Assembly on 20 November 1959 and recognized in the Universal Declaration of Human Rights, in the International Covenant on Civil and Political Rights (in particular in articles 23 and 24), in the International Covenant on Economic, Social and Cultural Rights (in particular in article 10) and in the statutes and relevant instruments of specialized agencies and international organizations concerned with the welfare of children,

Bearing in mind that, as indicated in the Declaration of the Rights of the Child, "the child, by reason of his physical and mental immaturity, needs special safeguards and care, including appropriate legal protection, before as well as after birth",

Recalling the provisions of the Declarations on Social and Legal Principles relating to the Protection and Welfare of Children, with Special Reference to Foster Placement and Adoption Nationally and Internationally; the United Nations Standard Minimum Rules for the Administration of Juvenile Justice (The Beijing Rules); and the Declaration on the Protection of Women and Children in Emergency and Armed Conflict,

Recognizing that, in all countries in the world, there are children living in exceptionally difficult conditions, and that such children need special consideration,

Taking due account of the importance of the traditions and cultural values of each people for the protection and harmonious development of the child,

Recognizing the importance of international co-operation for improving the living conditions of children in every country, in particular in the developing countries,

Have agreed as follows:

PART I

ARTICLE I

For the purposes of the present Convention, a child means every human being below the age of eighteen years unless, under the law applicable to the child, majority is attained earlier.

ARTICLE 2

1. States Parties shall respect and ensure the rights set forth in the present Convention to each child within their jurisdiction without discrimination of any kind, irrespective of the child's or his or her

parent's or legal guardian's race, colour, sex, language, religion, political or other opinion, national, ethnic or social origin, property, disability, birth or other status.

2. States Parties shall take all appropriate measures to ensure that the child is protected against all forms of discrimination or punishment on the basis of the status, activities, expressed opinions, or beliefs of the child's parents, legal guardians, or family members.

ARTICLE 3

1. In all actions concerning children, whether undertaken by public or private social welfare institutions, courts of law, administrative authorities or legislative bodies, the best interests of the child shall be a primary consideration.

2. States Parties undertake to ensure the child such protection and care as is necessary for his or her well-being, taking into account the rights and duties of his or her parents, legal guardians, or other individuals legally responsible for him or her, and, to this end, shall take all appropriate legislative and administrative measures.

3. States Parties shall ensure that the institutions, services and facilities responsible for the care or protection of children shall conform with the standards established by competent authorities, particularly in the areas of safety, health, in the number and suitability of their staff, as well as competent supervision.

ARTICLE 4

States Parties shall undertake all appropriate legislative, administrative, and other measures for the implementation of the rights recognized in the present Convention. With regard to economic, social and cultural rights, States Parties shall undertake such measures to the maximum extent of their available resources and, where needed, within the framework of international co-operation.

ARTICLE 5

States Parties shall respect the responsibilities, rights and duties of parties or, where applicable, the members of the extended family or community as provided for by local custom, legal guardians or other persons legally responsible for the child, to provide, in a manner consistent with the evolving capacities of the child, appropriate direction and guidance in the exercise by the child of the rights recognized in the present Convention.

ARTICLE 6

1. States Parties recognize that every child has the inherent right to life.
2. States Parties shall ensure to the maximum extent possible the survival and development of the child.

ARTICLE 7

1. The child shall be registered immediately after birth and shall have the right from birth to a name, the right to acquire a nationality and, as far as possible, the right to know and be cared for by his or her parents.
2. States Parties shall ensure the implementation of these rights in accordance with their national law and their obligations under the relevant international instruments in this field, in particular where the child would otherwise be stateless.

ARTICLE 8

1. States Parties undertake to respect the right of the child to preserve his or her identity, including nationality, name and family relations as recognized by law without unlawful interference.
2. Where a child is illegally deprived of some or all of the elements of his or her identity, States Parties shall provide appropriate assistance and protection, with a view to speedily re-establishing his or her identity.

ARTICLE 9

1. States parties shall ensure that a child shall not be separated from his or her parents against their will, except when competent authorities subject to judicial review determine, in accordance with applicable law and procedures, that such separation is necessary for the best interests of the child. Such determination may be necessary in a particular case such as one involving abuse or neglect of the child by the parents, or one where the parents are living separately and a decision must be made as to the child's place of residence.
2. In any proceedings pursuant to paragraph 1 of the present article, all interested parties shall be given an opportunity to participate in the proceedings and make their views known.
3. States Parties shall respect the right of the child who is separated from one or both parents to maintain personal relations and direct contact with both parents on a regular basis, except if it is contrary to the child's best interests.
4. Where such separation results from any action initiated by a State Party, such as the detention, imprisonment, exile, deportation or death

(including death arising from any cause while the person is in the custody of the State) of one or both parents or of the child, that State Party shall, upon request, provide the parents, the child or, if appropriate, another member of the family with the essential information concerning the whereabouts of the absent member(s) of the family unless the provision of the information would be detrimental to the well-being of the child. States Parties shall further ensure that the submission of such a request shall of itself entail no adverse consequences for the person(s) concerned.

Article 10

1. In accordance with the obligation of States Parties under article 9, paragraph 1, applications by a child or his or her parents to enter or leave a State Party for the purposes of family reunification shall be dealt with by States Parties in a positive, humane and expeditious manner. States Parties shall further ensure that the submission of such a request shall entail no adverse consequences for the applicants and for the members of their family.

2. A child whose parents reside in different States shall have the right to maintain on a regular basis, save in exceptional circumstances personal relations and direct contacts with both parents. Towards that end and in accordance with the obligation of States Parties under article 9, paragraph 1, States Parties shall respect the right of the child and his or her parents to leave any country, including their own, and to enter their own country. The right to leave any country shall be subject only to such restrictions as are prescribed by law and which are necessary to protect the national security, public order (*ordre public*), public health or morals or the rights and freedoms of others and are consistent with the other rights recognized in the present Convention.

Article 11

1. States Parties shall take measures to combat the illicit transfer and non-return of children abroad.

2. To this end, States Parties shall promote the conclusion of bilateral or multilateral agreements or accession to existing agreements.

Article 12

1. States Parties shall assure to the child who is capable of forming his or her own views the right to express those views freely in all matters affecting the child, the views of the child being given due weight in accordance with the age and maturity of the child.

2. For this purpose, the child shall in particular be provided the opportunity to be heard in any judicial and administrative proceedings affecting the child, either directly, or through a representative or an appropriate body, in a manner consistent with the procedural rules of national law.

ARTICLE 13

1. The child shall have the right to freedom of expression; this right shall include freedom to seek, receive and impart information and ideas of all kinds, regardless of frontiers, either orally, in writing or in print, in the form of art, or through any other media of the child's choice.
2. The exercise of this right may be subject to certain restrictions, but these shall only be such as are provided by law and are necessary:
(a) For respect of the rights or reputations of others; or
(b) For the protection of national security or of public order (*ordre public*), or of public health or morals.

ARTICLE 14

1. States Parties shall respect the right of the child to freedom of thought, conscience and religion.
2. States Parties shall respect the rights and duties of the parents and, when applicable, legal guardians, to provide direction to the child in the exercise of his or her right in a manner consistent with the evolving capacities of the child.
3. Freedom to manifest one's religion or beliefs may be subject only to such limitations as are prescribed by law and are necessary to protect public safety, order, health or morals, or the fundamental rights and freedom of others.

ARTICLE 15

1. States Parties recognize the rights of the child to freedom of association and to freedom of peaceful assembly.
2. No restrictions may be placed on the exercise of these rights other than those imposed in conformity with the law and which are necessary in a democratic society in the interests of national security or public safety, public order (*ordre public*), the protection of public health or morals or the protection of the rights and freedoms of others.

ARTICLE 16

1. No child shall be subjected to arbitrary or unlawful interference with his or her privacy, family, home or correspondence, nor to unlawful attacks on his or her honour and reputation.

2. The child has the right to the protection of the law against such interference or attacks.

ARTICLE 17

States Parties recognize the important function performed by the mass media and shall ensure that the child has access to information and material from a diversity of national and international sources, especially those aimed at the promotion of his or her social, spiritual and moral well-being and physical and mental health. To this end, States Parties shall:

(a) Encourage the mass media to disseminate information and material of social and cultural benefit to the child and in accordance with the spirit of article 29;

(b) Encourage international co-operation in the production, exchange and dissemination of such information and material from a diversity of cultural, national and international sources;

(c) Encourage the production and dissemination of children's books;

(d) Encourage the mass media to have particular regard to the linguistic needs of the child who belongs to a minority group or who is indigenous;

(e) Encourage the development of appropriate guidelines for the protection of the child from information and material injurious to his or her well-being, bearing in mind the provisions of articles 13 and 18.

ARTICLE 18

1. States Parties shall use their best efforts to ensure recognition of the principle that both parents have common responsibilities for the upbringing and development of the child. Parents or, as the case may be, legal guardians, have the primary responsibility for the upbringing and development of the child. The best interests of the child will be their basic concern.

2. For the purpose of guaranteeing and promoting the rights set forth in the present Convention, States Parties shall render appropriate assistance to parents and legal guardians in the performance of their child-rearing responsibilities and shall ensure the development of institutions, facilities and services for the care of children.

3. States Parties shall take all appropriate measures to ensure that children of working parents have the right to benefit from child-care services and facilities for which they are eligible.

ARTICLE 19

1. States Parties shall take all appropriate legislative, administrative, social and educational measures to protect the child from all forms of

physical or mental violence, injury or abuse, neglect or negligent treatment, maltreatment or exploitation, including sexual abuse, while in the care of parent(s), legal guardian(s) or any other person who has the care of the child.

2. Such protective measures should, as appropriate, include effective procedures for the establishment of social programmes to provide necessary support for the child and for those who have the care of the child, as well as for other forms of prevention and for identification, reporting, referral, investigation, treatment and follow-up of instances of child maltreatment described heretofore, and, as appropriate, for judicial involvement.

ARTICLE 20

1. A child temporarily or permanently deprived of his or her family environment, or in whose own best interests cannot be allowed to remain in that environment, shall be entitled to special protection and assistance provided by the State.

2. States Parties shall in accordance with their national laws ensure alternative care for such a child.

3. Such care could include, *inter alia*, foster placement, *kafalah* of Islamic law, adoption or if necessary placement in suitable institutions for the care of children. When considering solutions, due regard shall be paid to the desirability of continuity in a child's upbringing and to the child's ethnic, religious, cultural and linguistic background.

ARTICLE 21

States Parties that recognize and/or permit the system of adoption shall ensure that the best interests of the child shall be the paramount consideration and they shall:

(a) Ensure that the adoption of a child is authorized only by competent authorities who determine, in accordance with applicable law and procedures and on the basis of all pertinent and reliable information, that the adoption is permissible in view of the child's status concerning parents, relatives and legal guardians and that, if required, the persons concerned have given their informed consent to the adoption on the basis of such counselling as may be necessary;

(b) Recognize that inter-country adoption may be considered as an alternative means of child's care, if the child cannot be placed in a foster or an adoptive family or cannot in any suitable manner be cared for in the child's country of origin;

(c) Ensure that the child concerned by inter-country adoption enjoys safeguards and standards equivalent to those existing in the case of national adoption;

(d)   Take all appropriate measures to ensure that, in inter-country adoption, the placement does not result in improper financial gain for those involved in it;

(e)   Promote, where appropriate, the objectives of the present article by concluding bilateral or multilateral arrangements or agreements, and endeavour, within this framework, to ensure that the placement of the child in another country is carried out by competent authorities or organs.

ARTICLE 22

1. States Parties shall take appropriate measures to ensure that a child who is seeking refugee status or who is considered a refugee in accordance with applicable international or domestic law and procedures shall, whether unaccompanied or accompanied by his or her parents or by any other person, receive appropriate protection and humanitarian assistance in the enjoyment of applicable rights set forth in the present Convention and in other international human rights or humanitarian instruments to which the said States are Parties.

2. For this purpose, States Parties shall provide, as they consider appropriate, co-operation in any efforts by the United Nations and other competent intergovernmental organizations or non-governmental organizations co-operating with the United Nations to protect and assist such a child and to trace the parents or other members of the family of any refugee child in order to obtain information necessary for reunification with his or her family. In cases where no parents or other members of the family can be found, the child shall be accorded the same protection as any other child permanently or temporarily deprived of his or her family environment for any reason, as set forth in the present Convention.

ARTICLE 23

1. States Parties recognize that a mentally or physically disabled child should enjoy a full and decent life, in conditions which ensure dignity, promote self-reliance and facilitate the child's active participation in the community.

2. States Parties recognize the right of the disabled child to special care and shall encourage and ensure the extension, subject to available resources, to the eligible child and those responsible for his or her care, of assistance for which application is made and which is appropriate to the child's condition and to the circumstances of the parents or others caring for the child.

3. Recognizing the special needs of a disabled child, assistance extended in accordance with paragraph 2 of the present article shall

be provided free of charge, whenever possible, taking into account the financial resources of the parents or others caring for the child, and shall be designed to ensure that the disabled child has effective access to and receives education, training, health care services, rehabilitation services, preparation for employment and recreation opportunities in a manner conducive to the child's achieving the fullest possible social integration and individual development, including his or her cultural and spiritual development.

4. States Parties shall promote, in the spirit of international co-operation, the exchange of appropriate information in the field of preventive health care and of medical, psychological and functional treatment of disabled children, including dissemination and access to information concerning methods of rehabilitation, education and vocational services, with the aim of enabling States Parties to improve their capabilities and skills and to widen their experience in these areas. In this regard, particular account shall be taken of the needs of developing countries.

ARTICLE 24

1. States Parties recognize the right of the child to the enjoyment of the highest attainable standard of health and to facilities for the treatment of illness and rehabilitation of health. States Parties shall strive to ensure that no child is deprived of his or her right of access to such health care services.

2. States Parties shall pursue full implementation of this right and, in particular, shall take appropriate measures:

(a) To diminish infant and child mortality;

(b) To ensure the provision of necessary medical assistance and health care to all children with emphasis on the development of primary health care;

(c) To combat disease and malnutrition, including within the framework of primary health care, through, *inter alia*, the application of readily available technology and through the provision of adequate nutritious foods and clean drinking-water, taking into consideration the dangers and risks of environmental pollution;

(d) To ensure appropriate pre-natal and post-natal health care for mothers;

(e) To ensure that all segments of society, in particular parents and children, are informed, have access to education and are supported in the use of basic knowledge of child health and nutrition, the advantages of breast-feeding, hygiene and environmental sanitation and the prevention of accidents;

(f) To develop preventive health care, guidance for parents and family planning education and services.

3. States Parties shall take all effective and appropriate measures with a view to abolishing traditional practices prejudicial to the health of children.

4. States Parties undertake to promote and encourage international co-operation with a view to achieving progressively the full realization of the right recognized in the present article. In this regard, particular account shall be taken of the needs of developing countries.

ARTICLE 25

State Parties recognize the right of a child who has been placed by the competent authorities for the purposes of care, protection or treatment of his or her physical or mental health, to a periodic review of the treatment provided to the child and all other circumstances relevant to his or her placement.

ARTICLE 26

1. States Parties shall recognize for every child the right to benefit from social security, including social insurance, and shall take the necessary measures to achieve the full realization of this right in accordance with their national law.

2. The benefits should, where appropriate, be granted, taking into account the resources and the circumstances of the child and persons having responsibility for the maintenance of the child, as well as any other consideration relevant to an application for benefits made by or on behalf of the child.

ARTICLE 27

1. States Parties recognize the right of every child to a standard of living adequate for the child's physical, mental, spiritual, moral and social development.

2. The parent(s) or others responsible for the child have the primary responsibility to secure, within their abilities and financial capacities, the conditions of living necessary for the child's development.

3. States Parties, in accordance with national conditions and within their means, shall take appropriate measures to assist parents and others responsible for the child to implement this right and shall in case of need provide material assistance and support programmes, particularly with regard to nutrition, clothing and housing.

4. States Parties shall take all appropriate measures to secure the recovery of maintenance for the child from the parents or other persons having financial responsibility for the child, both within the State Party and from abroad. In particular, where the person having financial

responsibility for the child lives in a State different from that of the child, States Parties shall promote the accession to international agreements or the conclusion of such agreements, as well as the making of other appropriate arrangements.

ARTICLE 28

1. States Parties recognize the right of the child to education, and with a view to achieving this right progressively and on the basis of equal opportunity, they shall, in particular:
(a) Make primary education compulsory and available free to all;
(b) Encourage the development of different forms of secondary education, including general and vocational education, make them available and accessible to every child, and take appropriate measures such as the introduction of free education and offering financial assistance in case of need;
(c) Make higher education accessible to all on the basis of capacity by every appropriate means;
(d) Make educational and vocational information and guidance available and accessible to all children;
(e) Take measures to encourage regular attendance at schools and the reduction of drop-out rates.
2. States Parties shall take all appropriate measures to ensure that school discipline is administered in a manner consistent with the child's human dignity and in conformity with the present Convention.
3. States Parties shall promote and encourage international co-operation in matters relating to education, in particular with a view to contributing to the elimination of ignorance and illiteracy throughout the world and facilitating access to scientific and technical knowledge and modern teaching methods. In this regard, particular account shall be taken of the needs of developing countries.

ARTICLE 29

1. States Parties agree that the education of the child shall be directed to:
(a) The development of the child's personality, talents and mental and physical abilities to their fullest potential;
(b) The development of respect for human rights and fundamental freedoms, and for the principles enshrined in the Charter of the United Nations;
(c) The development of respect for the child's parents, his or her own cultural identity, langauge and values, for the national values of the country in which the child is living, the country from which he or she may originate, and for civilizations different from his or her own;

(d) The preparation of the child for responsible life in a free society, in the spirit of understanding, peace, tolerance, equality of sexes, and friendship among all peoples, ethnic, national and religious groups and persons of indigenous origin;

(e) The development of respect for the natural environment.

2. No part of the present article or article 28 shall be construed so as to interfere with the liberty of individuals and bodies to establish and direct educational institutions, subject always to the observance of the principles set forth in paragraph 1 of the present article and to the requirements that the education given in such institutions shall conform to such minimum standards as may be laid down by the State.

ARTICLE 30

In those States in which ethnic, religious or linguistic minorities or persons of indigenous origin exist, a child belonging to such a minority or who is indigenous shall not be denied the right, in community with other members of his or her group, to enjoy his or her own culture to profess and practise his or her own religion, or to use his or her own language.

ARTICLE 31

1. States Parties recognize the right of the child to rest and leisure, to engage in play and recreational activities appropriate to the age of the child and to participate freely in cultural life and the arts.

2. States Parties shall respect and promote the right of the child to participate fully in cultural and artistic life and shall encourage the provision of appropriate and equal opportunities for cultural, artistic, recreational and leisure activity.

ARTICLE 32

1. States Parties recognize the right of the child to be protected from economic exploitation and from performing any work that is likely to be hazardous or to interfere with the child's education, or to be harmful to the child's health or physical, mental, spiritual, moral or social development.

2. States Parties shall take legislative, administrative, social and educational measures to ensure the implementation of the present article. To this end, and having regard to the relevant provisions of other international instruments, States Parties shall in particular:

(a) Provide for a minimum age or minimum ages for admission to employment;

(b) Provide for appropriate regulation of the hours and conditions of employment;

(c) Provide for appropriate penalties or other sanctions to ensure the effective enforcement of the present article.

ARTICLE 33

States Parties shall take all appropriate measures, including legislative, administrative, social and educational measures, to protect children from the illicit use of narcotic drugs and psychotropic substances as defined in the relevant international treaties, and to prevent the use of children in the illicit production and trafficking of such substances.

ARTICLE 34

States Parties undertake to protect the child from all forms of sexual exploitation and sexual abuse. For these purposes, States Parties shall in particular take all appropriate national, bilateral and multilateral measures to prevent:
(a) The inducement or coercion of a child to engage in any unlawful sexual activity;
(b) The exploitative use of children in prostitution or other unlawful sexual practices;
(c) The exploitative use of children in pornographic performances and materials.

ARTICLE 35

States Parties shall take all appropriate national, bilateral and multilateral measures to prevent the abduction of, the sale of or traffic in children for any purpose or in any form.

ARTICLE 36

States Parties shall protect the child against all other forms of exploitation prejudicial to any aspects of the child's welfare.

ARTICLE 37

States Parties shall ensure that:
(a) No child shall be subjected to torture or other cruel, inhuman or degrading treatment or punishment. Neither capital punishment nor life imprisonment without possibility of release shall be imposed for offences committed by persons below eighteen years of age;

(b) No child shall be deprived of his or her liberty unlawfully or arbitrarily. The arrest, detention or imprisonment of a child shall be in conformity with the law and shall be used only as a measure of last resort and for the shortest appropriate period of time;

(c) Every child deprived of liberty shall be treated with humanity and respect for the inherent dignity of the human person, and in a manner which takes into account the needs of persons of his or her age. In particular, every child deprived of liberty shall be separated from adults unless it is considered in the child's best interest not to do so and shall have the right to maintain contact with his or her family through correspondence and visits, save in exceptional circumstances;

(d) Every child deprived of his or her liberty shall have the right to prompt access to legal and other appropriate assistance, as well as the right to challenge the legality of the deprivation of his or her liberty before a court or other competent, independent and impartial authority, and to a prompt decision on any such action.

ARTICLE 38

1. States Parties undertake to respect and to ensure respect for rules of international humanitarian law applicable to them in armed conflicts which are relevant to the child.

2. States Parties shall take all feasible measures to ensure that persons who have not attained the age of fifteen years do not take a direct part in hostilities.

3. States Parties shall refrain from recruiting any person who has not attained the age of fifteen years into their armed forces. In recruiting among those persons who have attained the age of fifteen years but who have not attained the age of eighteen years, States Parties shall endeavour to give priority to those who are oldest.

4. In accordance with their obligations under international humanitarian law to protect the civilian population in armed conflicts, States Parties shall take all feasible measures to ensure protection and care of children who are affected by an armed conflict.

ARTICLE 39

States Parties shall take all appropriate measures to promote physical and psychological recovery and social reintegration of a child victim of: any form of neglect, exploitation, or abuse; torture or any other form of cruel, inhuman or degrading treatment or punishment; or armed conflicts. Such recovery and reintegration shall take place in an environment which fosters the health, self-respect and dignity of the child.

ARTICLE 40

1. States Parties recognize the right of every child alleged as, accused of, or recognized as having infringed the penal law to be treated in a manner consistent with the promotion of the child's sense of dignity and worth, which reinforces the child's respect for the human rights and fundamental freedoms of others and which takes into account the child's age and the desirability of promoting the child's reintegration and the child's assuming a constructive role in society.

2. To this end, and having regard to the relevant provisions of international instruments, States Parties shall, in particular, ensure that:

(a) No child shall be alleged as, be accused of, or recognized as having infringed the penal law by reason of acts or omissions that were not prohibited by national or international law at the time they were committed;

(b) Every child alleged as or accused of having infringed the penal law has at least the following guarantees:

  (i) To be presumed innocent until proven guilty according to law;

  (ii) To be informed promptly and directly of the charges against him or her, and, if appropriate, through his or her parents or legal guardians, and to have legal or other appropriate assistance in the preparation of presentation of his or her defence;

  (iii) To have the matter determined without delay by a competent, independent and impartial authority or judicial body in a fair hearing according to law, in the presence of legal or other appropriate assistance and, unless it is considered not to be in the best interests of the child, in particular, taking into account his or her age or situation, his or her parents or legal guardians;

  (iv) Not to be compelled to give testimony or to confess guilt; to examine or have examined adverse witnesses and to obtain the participation and examination of witnesses on his or her behalf under conditions of equality;

  (v) If considered to have infringed the penal law, to have this decision and any measures imposed in consequence thereof reviewed by a higher competent, independent and impartial authority or judicial body according to law;

  (vi) To have the free assistance of an interpreter if the child cannot understand or speak the language used;

  (vii) To have his or her privacy fully respected at all stages of the proceedings.

3. States Parties shall seek to promote the establishment of laws, procedures, authorities and institutions specifically applicable to children alleged as, accused of, or recognized as having infringed the penal law, and, in particular:

(a)   The establishment of a minimum age below which children shall be presumed not to have the capacity to infringe the penal law;

(b)   Whenever appropriate and desirable, measures for dealing with such children without resorting to judicial proceedings, providing that human rights and legal safeguards are fully respected.

4. A variety of dispositions, such as care, guidance and supervision orders; counselling; probation; foster care; education and vocational training programmes and other alternatives to institutional care shall be available to ensure that children are dealt with in a manner appropriate to their well-being and proportionate both to their circumstances and the offence.

ARTICLE 41

Nothing in the present Convention shall affect any provisions which are more conducive to the realization of the rights of the child and which may be contained in:

(a)   The law of a State Party; or

(b)   International law in force for that State.

PART II

ARTICLE 42

States Parties undertake to make the principles and provisions of the Convention widely known, by appropriate and active means, to adults and children alike.

ARTICLE 43

1. For the purpose of examining the progress made by States Parties in achieving the realization of the obligations undertaken in the present Convention, there shall be established a Committee on the Rights of the Child, which shall carry out the functions hereinafter provided.

2. The Committee shall consist of ten experts of high moral standing and recognized competence in the field covered by this Convention. The members of the Committee shall be elected by States Parties from among their nationals and shall serve in their personal capacity, consideration being given to equitable geographical distribution, as well as to the principal legal systems.

3. The members of the Committee shall be elected by secret ballot from a list of persons nominated by States Parties. Each State Party may nominate one person from among its own nationals.

4. The initial election to the Committee shall be held no later than six months after the date of the entry into force of the present Convention and thereafter every second year. At least four months before the date of each election, the Secretary-General of the United Nations shall address a letter to States Parties inviting them to submit their nominations within two months. The Secretary-General shall subsequently prepare a list in alphabetical order of all persons thus nominated, indicating States Parties which have nominated them and shall submit it to the States Parties to the present Convention.

5. The elections shall be held at meetings of States Parties convened by the Secretary-General at United Nations Headquarters. At those meetings, for which two thirds of States Parties shall constitute a quorum, the persons elected to the Committee shall be those who obtain the largest number of votes and an absolute majority of the votes of the representatives of States Parties present and voting.

6. The members of the Committee shall be elected for a term of four years. They shall be eligible for re-election if renominated. The term of five of the members elected at the first election shall expire at the end of two years; immediately after the first election, the names of these five members shall be chosen by lot by the Chairman of the meeting.

7. If a member of the Committee dies or resigns or declares that for any other cause he or she can no longer perform the duties of the Committee, the State Party which nominated the member shall appoint another expert from among its nationals to serve for the remainder of the term, subject to the approval of the Committee.

8. The Committee shall establish its own rules of procedure.

9. The Committee shall elect its officers for a period of two years.

10. The meetings of the Committee shall normally be held at United Nations Headquarters or at any other convenient place as determined by the Committee. The Committee shall normally meet annually. The duration of the meetings of the Committee shall be determined, and reviewed, if necessary, by a meeting of the States Parties to the present Convention, subject to the approval of the General Assembly.

11. The Secretary-General of the United Nations shall provide the necessary staff and facilities for the effective performance of the functions of the Committee under the present Convention.

12. With the approval of the General Assembly, the members of the Committee established under the present Convention shall receive emoluments from United Nations resources on such terms and conditions as the Assembly may decide.

ARTICLE 44

1. States Parties undertake to submit to the Committee, through the Secretary-General of the United Nations, reports on the measures they

have adopted which give effect to the rights recognized herein and on the progress made on the enjoyment of those rights:

(a)   Within two years of the entry into force of the Convention for the State Party concerned;

(b)   Thereafter every five years.

2. Reports made under the present article shall indicate factors and difficulties, if any, affecting the degree of fulfilment of the obligations under the present Convention. Reports shall also contain sufficient information to provide the Committee with a comprehensive understanding of the implementation of the Convention in the country concerned.

3. A State Party which has submitted a comprehensive initial report to the Committee need not, in its subsequent reports submitted in accordance with paragraph 1(b) of the present article, repeat basic information previously provided.

4. The Committee may request from States Parties further information relevant to the implementation of the Convention.

5. The Committee shall submit to the General Assembly, through the Economic and Social Council, every two years, reports on its activities.

6. States Parties shall make their reports widely available to the public in their own countries.

ARTICLE 45

In order to foster the effective implementation of the Convention and to encourage international co-operation in the field covered by the Convention:

(a)   The specialised agencies, the United Nations Children's Fund, and other United Nations organs shall be entitled to be represented at the consideration of the implementation of such provisions of the present Convention as fall within the scope of their mandate. The Committee may invite the specialized agencies, the United Nations Children's Fund and other competent bodies as it may consider appropriate to provide expert advice on the implementation of the Convention in areas falling within the scope of their respective mandates. The Committee may invite the specialized agencies, the United Nations Children's Fund, and other United Nations organs to submit reports on the implementation of the Convention in areas falling within the scope of their activities;

(b)   The Committee shall transmit, as it may consider appropriate, to the specialized agencies, the United Nations Children's Fund and other competent bodies, any reports from States Parties that contain a request, or indicate a need, for technical advice or assistance, along with the Committee's observations and suggestions, if any, on these requests or indications;

(c) The Committee may recommend to the General Assembly to request the Secretary-General to undertake on its behalf studies on specific issues relating to the rights of the child;

(d) The Committee may make suggestions and general recommendations based on information received pursuant to articles 44 and 45 of the present Convention. Such suggestions and general recommendations shall be transmitted to any State Party concerned and reported to the General Assembly, together with comments, if any, from States Parties.

PART III

ARTICLES 46

The present Convention shall be open for signature by all States.

ARTICLE 47

The present Convention is subject to ratification. Instruments of ratification shall be deposited with the Secretary-General of the United Nations.

ARTICLE 48

The present Convention shall remain open for accession by any State. The instruments of accession shall be deposited with the Secretary-General of the United Nations.

ARTICLE 49

1. The present Convention shall enter into force on the thirtieth day following the date of deposit with the Secretary-General of the United Nations of the twentieth instrument of ratification or accession.

2. For each State ratifying or acceding to the Convention after the deposit of the twentieth instrument of ratification or accession, the Convention shall enter into force on the thirtieth day after the deposit by such State of its instrument of ratification or accession.

ARTICLE 50

1. Any State Party may propose an amendment and file it with the Secretary-General of the United Nations. The Secretary-General shall thereupon communicate the proposed amendment to States Parties, with a request that they indicate whether they favour a conference of

States Parties for the purpose of considering and voting upon the proposals. In the event that, within four months from the date of such communication, at least one third of the States Parties favour such a conference, the Secretary-General shall convene the conference under the auspices of the United Nations. Any amendment adopted by a majority of States Parties present and voting at the conference shall be submitted to the General Assembly for approval.

2. An amendment adopted in accordance with paragraph 1 of the present article shall enter into force when it has been approved by the General Assembly of the United Nations and accepted by a two-thirds majority of States Parties.

3. When an amendment enters into force, it shall be binding on those States Parties which have accepted it, other States Parties still being bound by the provisions of the present Convention and any earlier amendments which they have accepted.

ARTICLE 51

1. The Secretary-General of the United Nations shall receive and circulate to all States the text of reservations made by States at the time of ratification or accession.

2. A reservation incompatible with the object and purpose of the present Convention shall not be permitted.

3. Reservations may be withdrawn at any time by notification to that effect addressed to the Secretary-General of the United Nations, who shall then inform all States. Such notification shall take effect on the date on which it is received by the Secretary-General.

ARTICLE 52

A State Party may denounce the present Convention by written notification to the Secretary-General of the United Nations. Denunciation becomes effective one year after the date of receipt of the notification by the Secretary-General.

ARTICLE 53

The Secretary-General of the United Nations is designated as the depositary of the present Convention.

ARTICLE 54

The original of the present Convention, of which the Arabic, Chinese, English, French, Russian and Spanish texts are equally authentic, shall be deposited with the Secretary-General of the United Nations.

In witness thereof the undersigned plenipotentiaries, being duly authorized thereto by their respective Governments, have signed the present Convention.

APPENDIX VI

REPORTED CASES INVOLVING
SECTION 11 ORDERS

(1) *McGhee v. McGhee,* 1998 Fam.L.R. 122 (Sheriff T. Scott)
    Parties married in January 1988 and living apart at date of
proof (June 1998)—Husband accepting wife's child (F, born
April 1983)—Parties having two children (RAM, born
November 1988, and RVM, born June 1990)—Wife always
principal carer and having children with her during periods of
separation—Husband awarded custody of children on 16 April
1996 on joint motion after parties' reconciliation—Parties
having another child (M, born 13 May 1996)—Parties separating finally about one year later, wife leaving matrimonial home
with M and being prevented from taking the other three
children by husband relying upon his award of custody—Wife
seeking variation of custody award, claiming husband
assaulted her while she was pregnant, drove while unfit through
drink, encouraged children to consume alcohol, kept RAM
up late talking until the early hours and gave RAM (when
aged nine) a box of matches to play with—Husband arguing
that many of wife's complaints were historical and that she
was obliged to show a change of circumstances since granting
of joint motion for custody—Wife held entitled to residence
order, it being of little value where interlocutor sought to be
varied was not the product of a full judicial investigation to
look for a change of circumstances since agreement was made.
(2) *Fourman v. Fourman,* 1998 Fam. L.R. 98 (Sheriff N.M.P.
Morrison Q.C.)
    Parties married in November 1982 and living apart at date
of proof (September 1998)—Parties having three children (PF,
born July 1984, MF, born September 1989 and RF, born May
1992)—Parties separating in February 1998, wife leaving
matrimonial home with children—Children living with each
parent for equal amount of time ever since separation and
wanting to spend equal time with both parents—Wife an
Australian with dual nationality—Wife seeking specific issue
order to be allowed to remove children to Australia to live

there, claiming that life for her and the children would be cheaper, easier and better than in Scotland and that she would be more capable there of pursuing her career ambition to train and practise in acupuncture—Wife held not entitled to specific issue order, her wanting to take the children to Australia really because she wanted to go rather than because it was in their best interests to go; and it not seeming that stability, security and predictability were more apparent or more likely in Australia than they were in Scotland.

(3)　*G v. G,* 1999 Fam. L.R. 30 (Sheriff Principal C. G. B. Nicholson Q.C.)

Parties married in August 1995 and living apart at date of motion (January 1999)—Parties having a child (K, born January 1997)—Parties separating in April 1997, husband leaving matrimonial home—Child living with wife in happy and settled environment ever since separation—Husband granted a variety of contact orders—Wife failing to comply with orders and as a result being found guilty of contempt of court on three occasions—Husband seeking interim residence order—Husband held not entitled to interim residence order, it being better for K that no order be made at all in respect that the ordering of a change in a child's residence would always be something which should be approached with care particularly where, as here, the existing arrangements appeared to be above reproach; and even greater care had to be exercised when it was proposed to remove a child from a happy and settled environment.

(4)　*Dosoo v. Dosoo (No 2),* 1999 Fam.L.R. 130 (Sheriff J. M. S. Horsburgh Q.C.)

Parties married in October 1980 and living apart at date of proof (October 1999)—Parties having three children (K, born May 1984, F, born November 1986, and B, born July 1994)—Parties living separate lives within matrimonial home from April 1998 and husband thereafter removing—Children living with wife ever since separation—Husband seeking contact order in relation to B only, K and F being unwilling to see him—Husband arguing that B had good relationship with him, that loss of contact could harm B's development and that as the product of a mixed race marriage contact with him was particularly important to B—Husband held not entitled to contact order, the evidence of a strong relationship with B not being convincing; husband seeming disinterested in imparting knowledge to his children about their Ghanaian background; his interest in the two older children having waned as they grew older; and B being likely to acquire from him negative influences.

(5)   *H v. H,* 2000 Fam.L.R. 73 (Sheriff Principal D. J. Risk Q.C.)

Parties married in 1992 and living apart at date of proof (July 1998)—Husband accepting wife's child (A, born August 1986)—Parties having a child (N, born January 1995) after separation in March 1993—Husband seeking orders relating to N in separate proceedings conjoined with divorce action—Husband seeking contact order in relation to A, who suffered from attention deficit disorder, Asperger's syndrome and Tourette's syndrome—Motion granted to allow A to be sisted as a party and A allowed to lead evidence from professionals that he was of sufficient understanding to be competent witness and to lodge affidavit stating his opposition to contact—Husband held not entitled to contact order, there being expert evidence that affidavit a true representation of A's views rather than an echo of his mother with whom he lived.

(6)   *M v. M,* 2000 Fam.L.R. 84 (Lord Kingarth)

Parties divorced in January 1996 and living apart at date of proof (June 2000)—Parties having three children (AM, born January 1988, HM, born February 1990, and EM, born February 1992)—Children living with wife in Ross-shire ever since separation—Husband residing in Edinburgh and having contact with children two out of three weekends in summer and alternate weekends in winter, in addition to half the school holidays, the parties driving to a halfway point to transfer children for each visit—Wife seeking residence and specific issue orders to allow her to remove children from Scotland to reside with her in the United States, wishing to live in the US to look after her elderly mother, to protect her stake in the family property business (which stake would increase upon her mother's death) and to take up a well remunerated post within the business—Wife held entitled to residence and specific issue orders, she having good reason to make the proposed move to the United States and making her plans over a substantial period (though there was nothing approaching an absolute need for her to go there); there being a reasonable expectation that she and her new husband would be able to provide a materially better life for the children in the US; the children being better able to generally grow in a stable environment compared with their life in Scotland which was punctuated by weekend contact visits and long travel to Edinburgh; their inheritance being likely to be better protected by wife living in the US; AM expressing a clear desire to go to the US; and there being a clear risk that if wife and her new husband's plans were thwarted it would leave a strong sense of regret affecting family atmosphere—Husband held entitled to contact order allowing nine weeks' residential contact in the UK every summer and two further weeks in Scotland each Christmas, it being desirable to maintain a degree of regularity in contact.

(7) *White v. White,* 2001 S.C. 689 (First Division; Sheriff C. G. B. Nicholson Q.C.; Sheriff K. A. Ross)

Parties divorced in August 1997 and living apart at date of proof (May 1999)—Parties having two children (K, born November 1985, and V, born July 1991)—Children living with wife ever since parties' separation in 1995—Husband having good relationship with children prior to separation and no evidence that his relationship with them was in any way detrimental or harmful to them—Husband having contact with children after separation, although K sometimes reluctant to see him, until early 1997 when relations between parties broke down and wife took steps to prevent contact taking place—Husband seeking contact with children every alternate Saturday—Husband dropping application for contact with K after her expressing desire not to see him—Husband held entitled to contact with V every alternate Saturday, it generally being conducive to welfare of children if their absent parents maintain personal relations and direct contact with them on a regular basis.

(8) *Cunningham v. Cunningham,* 2001 Fam.L.R. 12 (Lord Macfadyen)

Parties married and living apart at date of proof (November 2000)—Parties having a child (M, born July 1988)—Child living with wife ever since parties' separation—Husband having regular contact with child but on occasions exhibiting argumentative and aggressive behaviour in relation to contact, thereby upsetting and frightening M—Parties agreed that arrangements relating to M should continue but husband opposing residence order in wife's favour lest he thereby be excluded to some extent from his proper parenting role—Wife held entitled to residence order, it being better for M that an order be made than that there be no such order in respect that (i) order would put on a formal basis the agreed arrangement; (ii) it would reassure M that she was to stay with her mother and alleviate feelings of insecurity and uncertainty; and (iii) it would provide a secure platform for development of contact between husband and M.

(9) *Bailey v. Bailey,* 2001 Fam.L.R. 133 (Sheriff Principal J. C. McInnes Q.C.)

Parties divorced in 1998 and living apart at date of proof (July 2001)—Parties having three children (C, L and D)—

Children living with wife ever since separation in 1995—
Husband having contact with children until October 1999—
Wife rarely making children available thereafter, despite court
orders—Children, though upset and confused as a result of
the anxiety seemed to have developed in relation to contact,
appearing to have enjoyed and benefited from contact on the
few occasions when it had taken place—Reporter appointed
by court to supervise and report on period of contact between
husband and children on 4 November 2000 in order to assist
court in reaching a decision as to whether there should be an
order for contact—Report wholly favourable to husband but
not available until after proof concluded and not taken into
consideration—Husband held at first instance not entitled to
contact but, after appeal, cause remitted back to sheriff to hear
submissions in relation to report.

(10) *S v. S,* 2002 S.C. 246 (Extra Division)

Parties married and living apart at date of proof (May 2001)—
Parties having a child (D, born April 1992)—Parties separating
in 1999—Child living with wife ever since separation and
husband having generous overnight contact—Wife wishing to
further her career by taking promoted post in Australia for three
years—Wife seeking residence order and specific issue order
to allow her to take D to Australia—Court dispensing with
intimation by way of Form F9 to child when action raised in
November 1999 and not subsequently taking steps to ascertain
views of child—Appeal court obtaining report which concluded
that child did not want to go to Australia—Wife held not entitled
to residence order or specific issue order.

(11) *G v. G,* 2002 Fam.L.R. 120 (Extra Division; Lord Hardie of
Blackford)

Parties married and living apart at date of motion (May
2002)—Parties having two children (EJ and A)—Children
living with wife ever since parties' separation—Parties not
having made any clear decision about children's education at
time of separation—Wife seeking interim specific issue order
in relation to EJ, aged 12 at date of motion, providing that she
attend a boarding school and ordaining husband to make
payment of all school fees and outlays save insofar as met by
scholarship award or relating to riding expenses and stabling
costs—EJ attending day school but awarded scholarship for
boarding school, meeting 50 per cent of annual school fees
and livery for horse for period of six years from autumn term
of 2002—Entrance to school under award able to be deferred
for one year on same terms—EJ, who had a talent for
horseriding, wished to go to the boarding school—Husband

not consulted prior to application being made on EJ's behalf for scholarship and disputing appropriateness of boarding school education—Husband's financial circumstances not straightforward as he was presently living off capital—Wife held not entitled to interim specific issue order, there not being a sufficient basis to make it reasonable to disturb the status quo; the husband's views as to which school was more appropriate being entitled to be taken into account; and the proper weight to be given to EJ's views and the relevance of any decision for A's future schooling being matters which had to be considered, best done at proof.

(12) *M v C,* 2002 S.L.T. (Sh. Ct.) 82 (Sheriff A.L. Stewart Q.C.)

Parties married in July 1994 and living apart at date of proof (March 2002)—Parties having a child (M, born August 1996)—Parties separating in July 1999—Child living with wife ever since separation—Wife reverting to using maiden name after parties' separation, wishing M to use that name also and enrolling him at school under changed name—Wife a practising Roman Catholic and wanting M to be brought up in that faith, attending catechism classes—Husband seeking specific issue orders (1) that wife could not alter M's surname; and (2) that M should not be required to attend classes in religious instruction, in each case without husband's consent— Husband held entitled to specific issue order that wife could not alter M's surname without his consent, it being as a general rule quite inappropriate for either parent to take a unilateral decision to change a child's name and there being no overwhelming reasons why M's surname should be changed without husband's consent, even though eight months had elapsed since M registered at school under changed name— Husband held not entitled to specific issue order that M should not be required to attend classes in religious instruction, the catechism classes being a normal part of the education of a child brought up as a Catholic who did not attend a denominational school for which husband's consent was not required or, in any event, able reasonably to be withheld.

(13) *Ellis v. Ellis,* 2003 Fam.L.R. 77 (Sheriff G. J. Evans)

Parties married and living apart at date of proof (November 2002)—Parties having two children (J, born July 1994, and R, born January 1997)—Parties separating in September 1997, with J residing primarily with husband and R with wife until summer 2000 when children's residence shared between parties—Children residing primarily from April 2001 with wife, who showed level of commitment to children which had initially been absent from husband in persevering with pregnancies despite strong opposition from him and had been consistent in her willingness to give full consideration to them—J's behaviour at school showing marked improvement once wife had become his primary carer—Parties' relationship acrimonious—Husband awarded interim contact on two nights each week, on weekends from Friday at 5.30 p.m. until 10 a.m. on Sunday and residential contact of at least one week during school holidays—Husband living with new Finnish partner (K) with whom he had child aged 7-8 months, but future of their relationship uncertain and possibility of their moving to Finland—Husband seeking residence order in relation to children—J expressing wish to live with him but view based on transitory circumstances such as the effect on wife of post natal depression and the fact that she was a stronger disciplinarian than husband, his house was materially better equipped than wife's and he had promised rewards to J if he was awarded residence—Wife held entitled to residence order, the fact that wife the primary carer of J and R being a very strong factor in wife's favour; there being a greater degree of certainty about wife's circumstances; and children's residing with her not being so detrimental to their welfare that the advantages that they had gained from continuity and stability in their circumstances should be sacrificed to unknown and untested future with husband and K—Husband held entitled to contact on basis of existing interim arrangements.

(14) *G v. G*, 2003 Fam.L.R. 118 (Sheriff W. Holligan)

Parties divorced and living apart at date of proof (July 2003)—Parties having a child (G, born April 1997)—Parties separating in June 1999, husband leaving matrimonial home—Husband initially having overnight contact with child twice a week, midweek and at weekend, subsequently stopping overnight midweek contact and, in September 2002, ceasing midweek contact altogether—Child not making as much progress at school as he ought to although no cause had been identified and his difficulties might resolve with time or might require learning support— Husband seeking residence order—Child's views not sought, having regard to opinion of psychologist that not practicable to seek child's views in relation to residence—Husband held not entitled to residence order, it being in child's best interests to continue to reside with wife and it being better that no order for residence be made than that an order be made.

(15) *J v. J*, 2004 Fam.L.R. 20 (Second Division)

Parties divorced and living apart at date of proof (February 2003)—Parties having two children (N, born July 1992, and

R, born July 1995)—Parties separating in March 1995—
Children living with wife ever since separation—Husband
having contact with children on an informal basis with both
children—Husband obtaining new job, his hours of work
tending to conflict with contact arrangements which were often
cancelled at short notice—Parties' relationship becoming
acrimonious and informal contact arrangements breaking
down—Husband ceasing from late 1997 to attempt to maintain
contact with children—Children expressing wishes in 2001
not to have contact—Husband held entitled to contact order
in relation to children in terms providing for gradual
resumption of contact, consideration being given to weight to
be attached to children's wishes, their being liable to be upset
at the outset if contact were resumed and the long term
considerations which worked entirely to their benefit.

(16) *K v. K*, 2004 Fam.L.R. 25 (Sheriff A. M. Bell)

Parties married in July 1993 and living apart at date of proof
(August 2003)—Parties having three children (M, born
December 1993, K, born July 1995, and X, born December
1998)—Parties separating in July 2001—Children living with
wife until January 2002 when they went to live with husband—
Wife suffering from depression for many years and abusing
alcohol and drugs—Husband initially willing to allow wife to
have contact but she having no contact for nearly 18 months
during which time she underwent psychiatric treatment and
alcohol detoxification—Wife twice taking drugs overdose in
2002—Wife beginning a relationship with a man in July 2002
and living with him at date of proof—Wife on probation and
subject to community service order and sentence deferred for
good behaviour—Wife attempting suicide in December
2002—Wife re-establishing contact with children at contact
centre in May 2003, seeing them twice—M expressing a wish
to continue to see her, K being obviously unhappy at present
and unsure whether she wanted to see her, and X not expressing
any wish to give a view as to whether he wished to see her—
Wife held entitled to contact order in relation to M and X,
contact to take place for one hour per week at a contact centre.

REPORTED CASES INVOLVING PRINCIPLE A[1]

Cases in which Principle A was explicitly considered include the following:

(1) *Petrie v. Petrie*, 1988 S.C.L.R. 390 (Sheriff D. J. Risk)
   Parties married in June 1983 and separated in November 1985 — Husband seriously injured in March 1983 and receiving damages in October 1986 — Damages held not to be matrimonial property — Opinion that, having regard to the special circumstances mentioned in s. 10(6)(b) and (d), wife's share of the compensation payment would probably have been discounted to a very great extent, if not entirely.

(2) *Phillip v. Phillip*, 1988 S.C.L.R. 427 (Sheriff E. F. Bowen)
   Parties married in December 1952 and separated in summer 1976 — Matrimonial property at relevant date comprising husband's savings, life policy and retirement gratuity together with reduced pension rights as well as matrimonial home owned by husband — Proportion of matrimonial home's purchase price (assessed at £4,000 as at the date of separation) coming from property which husband owned prior to the marriage — Value of matrimonial property at relevant date held to be £39,200 — Held that, having regard to the special circumstances mentioned in s. 10(6)(b), the sum of £4,000 should be deducted from net value of matrimonial property at relevant date and that resulting balance, namely £35,200, should be shared equally.

(3) *Bell v. Bell*, 1988 S.C.L.R. 457 (Sheriff J. C. M. Jardine)
   Parties married in July 1960 and separated in June 1986 — Matrimonial property at relevant date comprising (i) jointly owned matrimonial home and household goods therein; (ii) wife's savings; and (iii) husband's savings, insurance policies and occupational pension — Matrimonial home valued on basis of actual sale price shortly after relevant date — Household goods and husband's interest in occupational

[1]See Chap. 7, nn. 57–105 and accompanying text.

pension scheme referable to the period of the marriage up to relevant date valued on broad axe basis — Matrimonial property at relevant date valued at £99,484, comprising £70,692 (husband) and £28,792 (wife) — Wife receiving payments and goods from husband after separation valued at £38,584 — Wife held entitled to equal division of matrimonial property, namely (after deduction of £38,584) to capital sum of £11,158, restricted to £10,000 to comply with the terms of her crave.

(4) *Park v. Park*, 1988 S.C.L.R. 584 (Sheriff D. Kelbie)

Parties married in December 1980 and separated in October 1985 — Matrimonial property at relevant date comprising (i) jointly owned matrimonial home (subject to mortgage), insurance policies and household furniture and furnishings; and (ii) husband's interest in occupational pension scheme — Arrears of mortgage payments accumulating — Husband keeping household furniture and furnishings — Wife held entitled to capital sum representing one-half of agreed value of furniture and furnishings and one-half of husband's probable interest in occupational pension scheme — Failure to make mortgage payments held not to amount to special circumstances in terms of s. 10(6)(c).

(5) *Kerrigan v. Kerrigan*, 1988 S.C.L.R. 603 (Sheriff G. J. Evans)

Parties married in August 1984 and separated in September 1985 — Matrimonial property at relevant date comprising jointly owned matrimonial home — Matrimonial home purchased in contemplation of marriage with building society loan and gift of money from husband's mother — Husband making mortgage payments — Husband held entitled to transfer of property order in respect of wife's one-half *pro indiviso* share of matrimonial home.

(6) *Buczynska v. Buczynski*, 1989 S.L.T. 558 (Lord Morton of Shuna)

Parties married in July 1969 and separated in May 1987 — Separation held to have occurred when husband's solicitor sent a letter requesting wife to leave the house by which time parties had ceased to share a bedroom and wife had ceased to cook for the husband — Wife owning flat at relevant date — Husband owning matrimonial home valued at £80,000 at relevant date — Wife acquiring flat with building society loan and gift from mother — Held that if wife's flat was matrimonial property, special circumstances existed as provided for in s. 10(6)(b) — Wife held entitled to capital sum of £35,000.

(7) *Little v. Little*, 1989 S.C.L.R. 613; 1990 S.L.T. 785 (First Division; Lord Cameron of Lochbroom)

Parties married in October 1961 and separated in April 1986 — Matrimonial property at relevant date comprising matrimonial home owned by husband (valued at £66,500 and subject to mortgage of £20,800), furniture and furnishings therein (valued at £2,500), timeshares held in joint names, contents of joint bank account (£840), personal possessions, two cars (used for professional purposes), speedboat owned by husband (valued at £600), six endowment policies in husband's name (valued at £27,501) and interests held by each party in certain other policies and pension schemes — Husband's pension interests exceeding wife's in value by £70,996 — Husband keeping contents of joint bank account — Husband making payment of £2,616 towards timeshare after separation — Wife held entitled to (i) transfer of property order in respect of a one-half *pro indiviso* share of matrimonial home and furniture and furnishings therein; and (ii) an award of capital sum of £38,260, comprising (a) the sum of £35,498, representing the difference in value of parties' interests in their respective pension schemes at relevant date; and (b) the sum of £2,763, representing one-half of the value of endowment policies, speedboat and joint bank account (£14,470) less one-half of mortgage outstanding at relevant date and one-half of timeshare payment made after separation (£11,708) — Extract superseded in respect of one-half of capital sum for a period of six years.

(8) *Walker v. Walker*, 1989 S.C.L.R. 625; 1991 S.L.T. 157 (First Division; Lord Morton of Shuna)

Parties married in July 1960 and separated in October 1986 — Matrimonial property at relevant date comprising (i) jointly owned matrimonial home; and (ii) other substantial heritable and moveable assets owned by husband — Wife held entitled to transfer of property orders reflecting one-half of net value of the matrimonial property at relevant date as well as husband's advantage and wife's disadvantage in terms of future income arising from business built up by contributions made by both parties during the marriage.

(9) *Muir v. Muir*, 1989 S.L.T. (Sh. Ct.) 20 (Sheriff I. A. Macmillan)

Parties married in September 1964 and separated in November 1984 — Matrimonial property at relevant date comprising matrimonial home owned by husband and his interest in insurance policies and pension fund — Wife held entitled to capital sum reflecting one-half of net value of matrimonial home, one-half of surrender value of insurance policies and two-fifths of value of pension fund, all as valued as at relevant date.

(10) *Cooper v. Cooper*, 1989 S.C.L.R. 347 (Sheriff Principal R. D. Ireland Q.C.; Sheriff N. McPartlin)

Parties separated in 1987 after several years of marriage — Matrimonial property at relevant date comprising jointly owned matrimonial home, household contents and cash — Husband keeping cash and sharing household contents — Wife living in matrimonial home with children of marriage and husband living in sheltered accommodation — Wife assuming responsibility for repaying loans on house — Wife held entitled to transfer of property order with respect to husband's one-half share, having regard to the special circumstances specified in s. 10(6)(d).

(11) *Morrison v. Morrison*, 1989 S.C.L.R. 574 (Sheriff G. H. Gordon Q.C.)

Parties married in March 1971 and separated in September 1987 — Matrimonial property at relevant date comprising (i) jointly owned matrimonial home, household contents and endowment policy; (ii) taxi business owned by husband; and (iii) car owned by wife — Wife contributing to taxi business — Children of marriage living with wife — Wife held entitled to capital sum reflecting (a) two-thirds of total value of matrimonial home and contents less husband's share of wife's car and wife's half-share of matrimonial home as joint owner; and (b) one-half of net value of taxi business.

(12) *Budge v. Budge*, 1990 S.L.T. 319 (Lord Cameron of Lochbroom)

Parties married in April 1980 and separated in July 1985 — Matrimonial property at relevant date comprising caravan owned by wife (valued at £100) and lease of croft owned by husband (valued at £9,500) — Lease originally acquired by husband with £7,000 obtained from sale of property owned by him before marriage — Wife assisting husband in maintaining and improving croft during the parties' cohabitation — Wife held entitled to capital sum of £1,200, assessing fair sharing of the matrimonial property in croft at £1,250 less £50 for value of wife's caravan.

(13) *Tyrrell v. Tyrrell*, 1990 S.L.T. 406 (Lord Sutherland)

Parties married in September 1964 and separated in October 1982 — Matrimonial property at relevant date comprising (i) assets distributed by agreement between parties upon separation; (ii) husband's cash, shares, life assurance policies and interest in pension fund (valued at £67,496); and (iii) wife's jewellery and fur (valued at £12,432) — Net value of total matrimonial property at relevant date therefore £79,928 — Wife held entitled to capital sum of £27,532, reflecting an equal division of the undistributed assets less those retained by her — Wife held not entitled to any share of husband's redundancy payment received by him in June 1986.

(14) *Latter v. Latter*, 1990 S.L.T. 805 (Lord Marnoch)

Parties separated in March 1987 after several years of marriage — Matrimonial property at relevant date comprising (a) husband's pension rights (valued at £169,000); (b) husband's interest in insurance policies (valued at £2,050); (c) husband's shares in Marks & Spencer plc (valued at £2,670); (d) debt due to husband by family trust (£4,655); (e) furniture and contents of matrimonial home (valued at £12,000 on a basis close to willing buyer/willing seller); (f) husband's shareholding of 4,150 shares in private family company, M & H Latter (Holdings) Ltd (valued at £626,650 on a net asset basis without any deduction for notional capital gains tax liability); and (g) various undisclosed assets (valued at about £229,000) — Debts at relevant date comprising (i) debt due by husband to family company of £5,000; and (ii) arrears of tax amounting to £41,000 — Net value of matrimonial property at relevant date therefore about £1,000,000 — Matrimonial home, purchased with funds paid by wife's parents direct to solicitors as gift to wife, held not to be matrimonial property — Shareholding in M & H Latter (Holdings) Ltd deriving from series of shareholdings gifted to, or inherited or purchased with gifted funds by, husband in what were now subsidiary companies and following on an overall company reconstruction — Special circumstances relied on by wife (for which husband debited with figure of £25,000) were that (a) some of capital of wife's family trust had been lent unprofitably by husband to his companies; (b) husband's conduct had resulted in unnecessary financial hardship to wife; and (c) some of parties' furniture replaced furniture originally donated by wife's parents — Special circumstances relied on by husband were that (a) substantial sums were spent by husband's family on matrimonial home (for which husband credited with sum of £90,000); (b) pension was not realisable (for which no credit given, standing availability of other liquid assets); and (c) shareholding emanated in substance if not in form from donation or inheritance (for which net value of matrimonial property discounted by around half the value of those shares, namely by sum of £320,000) — Wife held entitled to capital sum of £275,000, representing (i) one-half of discounted net value of matrimonial property, namely £340,000 (50% of £680,000), less (ii) net credit due to husband, namely £65,000 (£90,000 less £25,000), with extract superseded for two months.

(15) *Carpenter v. Carpenter*, 1990 S.L.T. (Sh. Ct.) 68 (Sheriff R.H. Dickson)

Parties married in June 1964 and separated in October 1983 — Matrimonial property at relevant date comprising husband's interest in pension fund and life policies — Wife held entitled to capital sum reflecting one-half of value of life policies and three-eighths of value of interest in pension fund at relevant date.

(16) *Main v. Main*, 1990 S.C.L.R. 165 (Sheriff Principal Sir Frederick O'Brien Q.C.)

Parties married in April 1967 and separated in September 1986 — Matrimonial property at relevant date comprising jointly owned matrimonial home and other assets in respect of which a payment of £1,400 by husband to wife would produce an equal sharing — Wife making payments of about £2,000 in respect of parties' joint mortgage since date of separation — Wife not wishing to sell matrimonial home where she had resided with her daughters for many years — Held that wife was entitled to capital sum of £5,400, comprising (i) £1,400 to produce an equal sharing; (ii) £1,000 in respect of the mortgage payments; and (iii) £3,000 to facilitate purchase of matrimonial home, having regard to the special circumstances mentioned in s. 10(6)(d).

(17) *Farrell v. Farrell*, 1990 S.C.L.R. 717 (Sheriff C. N. Stoddart)

Parties married in August 1981 and separated in July 1986 — Matrimonial property at relevant date comprising jointly owned matrimonial home (with low net value) and furniture and plenishings therein — Wife continuing to occupy matrimonial home — Husband leaving wife with burden of keeping up mortgage after separation — Wife held entitled to transfer of property order in respect of husband's one-half share of matrimonial home and furniture and plenishings therein so far as not in her sole ownership, there being special circumstances present.

(18) *Thomson v. Thomson*, 1991 S.L.T. 126 (Lord Cameron of Lochbroom)

Parties separated in May 1986 after several years of marriage — Matrimonial property at relevant date comprising husband's life insurance policies and shares in two private companies with total value of £15,000 — Husband subsequently transferring the shares to his brother purportedly for value — Transfer held to be collusive arrangement to defeat the wife's claim in which no money actually changed hands and husband's resources therefore assessed on the basis that he had as yet received no payment for shares — Wife held entitled to capital sum of £7,500.

(19) *McKenzie v. McKenzie*, 1991 S.L.T. 461 (Lord Prosser)

Parties married in 1971 and separated in December 1987 — Matrimonial property at relevant date comprising jointly owned matrimonial home, husband's interest in pension fund valued at £70,900 and wife's business valued on a going concern basis at £16,000 — Wife held entitled to capital sum representing the difference between one-half of value of husband's pension and one-half of value of her business, namely £27,450.

(20) *Anderson v. Anderson*, 1991 S.L.T. (Sh. Ct.) 11 (Sheriff W. C. Henderson)

Parties married in July 1967 and separated in April 1987 — Matrimonial property at relevant date comprising household contents, cash, shares, personal items and car — Husband taking personal items and signing document narrating "I sign everything over to my wife i.e. household contents, money in bank, shares" upon separation — Husband subsequently claiming capital sum, conceding wife's entitlement to car — Held that husband had effectively ousted the jurisdiction of the court; and that, in any event, even if the matter fell to be approached from the standpoint of an agreement between the parties, s. 10(6)(a) entitled the court to make no award.

(21) *Skarpaas v. Skarpaas*, 1991 S.L.T. (Sh. Ct.) 15; 1993 S.L.T. 343 (First Division; Sheriff Principal R.A. Bennett Q.C.; Sheriff A. L. Stewart)

Parties married in August 1984 and separated in July 1988 — Matrimonial property at relevant date comprising husband's claim for damages for personal injuries sustained during the course of the marriage less certain debts — Decree granted in husband's favour after relevant date for such damages, including sums for solatium, past loss of earnings, interest and loss of future earning capacity — No evidence led as to value of damages claim if offered for sale in the market place at relevant date — Held that in the absence of such evidence value of damages claim as quantified by the court less debts should be shared, under deduction of interest on sums for solatium and past loss of earnings referable to period after relevant date and, having regard to the special circumstances mentioned in s. 10(6)(d), under further deduction of sums for solatium and loss of future earning capacity.

(22) *Pryde v. Pryde*, 1991 S.L.T. (Sh. Ct.) 26 (Sheriff A .M. Bell)

Parties married in August 1980 and separated in August 1987 — Matrimonial property at relevant date comprising husband's interest in pension fund, valued at £550 — Wife held entitled to capital sum of £200, it being clear that sole item of matrimonial property was something which was not easily realised and husband having no other resources — Husband's contention that certain furniture was also matrimonial property rejected, there being in any event no evidence led as to the value thereof.

(23) *McGuire v. McGuire's Curator Bonis*, 1991 S.L.T. (Sh. Ct.) 76 (Sheriff W.C. Henderson)

Parties married in November 1955 and separated in November 1987 — Matrimonial property at relevant date comprising the sum of at least £40,000 held by husband's curator bonis, being residue of husband's original award of criminal injuries compensation in total sum of £45,000, including £25,000 for solatium — Husband requiring permanent residential care — £32,000 still held by curator bonis at date of proof — Husband entitled to state assistance for cost of his care if and when his capital fell below £8,000 — Wife held entitled to capital sum of £20,000, with some, albeit fairly slight regard to personal element of solatium factor in the award as a special circumstance in terms of s. 10(6)(d).

(24) *Wallis v. Wallis*, 1991 S.C.L.R. 192; 1992 S.C. 455; 1993 S.C. (H.L.) 49 (House of Lords; First Division; Sheriff A. B. Wilkinson)

Parties married in March 1986 and separated in March 1987 — Matrimonial property at relevant date comprising (i) jointly owned matrimonial home (valued at £17,400 net) and furniture and plenishings therein (valued at £13,500); and (ii) husband's car (valued at £8,000) — Matrimonial home increasing in value by £24,000 by date of proof — Husband held entitled to transfer of property order in respect of wife's one-half share of matrimonial home and furniture and plenishings therein, subject to payment by him of capital sum of £19,450, representing (i) one-half of net value of matrimonial home at relevant date (£8,700); (ii) one-half of value of furniture and plenishings therein (£6,750); and (iii) one-half of value of motor car (£4,000).

(25) *Symon v. Symon*, 1991 S.C.L.R. 414 (Sheriff A. M. G. Russell Q.C.)

Parties married in 1976 and separated in October 1987 — Matrimonial property at relevant date comprising (i) jointly owned property, namely matrimonial home, household contents (valued at £3,000) and contents of building society account; and (ii) property owned by husband, namely car, insurance policies and pension rights (valued at £27,000) — Husband removing some of household contents after separation — Wife held entitled to one-half of value of car and insurance policies, the sum of £6,000 as her share of husband's pension rights and the sum of £500 to balance the division of household contents — Order granted for sale of matrimonial home.

(26) *Jesner v. Jesner*, 1992 S.L.T. 999 (Lord Osborne)

Parties separated after several years of marriage — Matrimonial property at relevant date comprising (i) jointly owned property, namely a derelict farmhouse with adjoining land (valued at £30,000), household furnishings, a 60% share of an area of surrounding farmland (valued at £24,000) and three motor cars (valued at £4,500); and (ii) shares in a private company owned by husband (valued at £12,000) — Husband contriving to lose household furnishings — Farmhouse with adjoining land purchased with loan of £30,000, which was still outstanding at relevant date, and the proceeds of sale of house owned by husband prior to marriage — Assets of husband's company purchased by the use of money put in trust for husband by his father — Husband held entitled to transfer of property order in respect of wife's one-half share of the farmhouse with adjoining land, thus leaving wife with marginally under 30% of net value of matrimonial property.

(27) *Crockett v. Crockett*, 1992 S.C.L.R. 591; 30 June 1993, unreported (Extra Division; Lord McCluskey)

Parties married in August 1984 and separated in August 1988 — Matrimonial property at relevant date comprising jointly owned matrimonial home, insurance policy in joint names, husband's shares in private company (valued by reference to future maintainable earnings), wife's 38.03% interest in company's pension fund, husband's 61.97% interest therein, husband's interest in other insurance and pension policies and husband's cash — Parties each liable for bank debt at relevant date — Net value of matrimonial property at relevant date amounting to £390,387.90, comprising £142,175.29 (wife) and £248,212.61 (husband) — Husband's company insolvent by date of proof — Husband accepting substantial liability to aliment child of marriage — Wife held entitled to capital sum of £17,500, having regard to need for husband to apply remaining resources to try to save business or give it marketability.

(28) *Gulline v. Gulline*, 1992 S.L.T. (Sh. Ct.) 71 (Sheriff G. J. Evans)

Parties married in August 1973 and separated in July 1984 — Matrimonial property at relevant date comprising (i) assets distributed by agreement between parties upon separation and (ii) husband's interest in pension fund (valued at £34,590) — Joint debt of about £1,000 met by husband after separation — Wife held entitled to capital sum reflecting one-half of husband's interest in pension fund less about half of joint debt, namely £17,000, payable on date of husband's retirement, with interest at the rate of 7.5 per cent per annum (the projected rate of return on investment) from date of decree of divorce.

(29) *Shipton v. Shipton*, 1992 S.C.L.R. 23 (Sheriff N.E.D. Thomson)

Parties married in September 1978 and separated in September 1987 — Matrimonial property at relevant date comprising (i) jointly owned matrimonial home (valued at £53,000) and furnishings therein (valued at £1,375); and (ii) husband's interest in pensions and insurance policy, shares and loan outstanding to him as director (valued at £17,195, discounting book value of loan by £27,000) — Matrimonial home purchased with assistance from husband's father by way of gift or loan of £4,800 — Matrimonial property at relevant date valued at £66,770, after deduction of the sum of £4,800 — Wife held entitled to capital sum of £9,285, payable within four weeks of date of sale of the matrimonial home.

(30) *Toye v. Toye*, 1992 S.C.L.R. 95 (Sheriff A. S. Jessop)

Parties married in March 1969 and separated in December 1988 — Matrimonial property at relevant date comprising (i) jointly owned matrimonial home and furniture and plenishings therein; (ii) jointly owned endowment policies; and (iii) husband's interest in pension policies — Total net value of matrimonial property at date of proof amounting to £149,542, comprising £86,000 (net value of matrimonial home); £11,000 (endowment policies); and £52,542 (pension policies) — Wife living in matrimonial home with child of marriage — Wife held entitled to transfer of property order in respect of husband's one-half share of (a) matrimonial home and furniture and plenishings therein; and (b) endowment policies, subject to taking responsibility for mortgage payments and insurance premiums and relinquishing in exchange all right, title and interest in husband's pension policies, there being special circumstances justifying an unequal division of matrimonial property and economic disadvantage suffered by wife.

(31) *White v. White*, 1992 S.C.L.R. 769 (Temporary Sheriff J. Gilmour)

Parties married in January 1991 and separated in February 1991 — Matrimonial property at relevant date comprising matrimonial home purchased shortly before marriage by husband in own name with his own funds and a loan obtained by him — Parties only cohabiting for a few weeks — Wife held not entitled to any financial provision.

(32) *Peacock v. Peacock*, 1993 S.C. 88 (Second Division)

Parties separated in August 1989 after several years of marriage — Matrimonial property at relevant date comprising matrimonial home and life assurance policy jointly owned by parties — Matrimonial home valued at relevant date at £29,000, subject to mortgage of £13,949, and at date of proof at £32,000, subject to a mortgage of £14,562 — Life assurance policy having surrender value of £643.75 — Wife in employment and continuing to occupy matrimonial home with parties' children after separation and making all but one of mortgage payments — Husband unemployed and making no financial contribution to children's maintenance — Wife held entitled, subject to assignation to husband of her share of life assurance policy, to transfer of property order in respect of husband's one-half share of matrimonial home, having regard to the special circumstances mentioned in s. 10(6)(d), in particular that transfer was necessary for children's welfare.

(33) *Brooks v. Brooks*, 1993 S.L.T. 184 (Lord Marnoch)

Parties separated in November 1988 after several years of marriage — Matrimonial property at relevant date comprising (i) jointly owned heritable properties; (ii) wife's assets (valued at £48,626); and (iii) husband's assets (valued at £100,974, inclusive of pension entitlement valued at £86,974) — Debt outstanding by husband to wife's mother amounting to £4,580 — Wife held entitled to capital sum of £23,884, representing one-half of difference in value between parties' respective matrimonial property less the debt, with extract superseded for a period of four months.

(34) *Bannon v. Bannon*, 1993 S.L.T. 999 (Lord Cameron of Lochbroom)

Parties married in September 1971 and separated in August 1988 — Matrimonial property at relevant date comprising husband's interest in pension fund, valued at £46,000 — Husband without resources — Wife held entitled to capital sum of £32,000, with extract superseded until date upon which husband would be entitled to retire on full pension, over six years thence.

(35) *Macdonald v. Macdonald*, 1993 S.C.L.R. 132 (Lord Caplan)

Parties separated in May 1990 after several years of marriage — Matrimonial property at relevant date comprising (i) jointly owned matrimonial home (valued at £247,000 and subject to mortgage of £39,000) and joint building society account (£900); (ii) wife's pension (valued at £22,000); and (iii) husband's pension (valued at £14,708) and endowment policies (valued at £38,203) less his bank debt of £7,000 — Matrimonial property owned by wife at relevant date therefore valued at £126,450 and husband's at £150,361 — Matrimonial property of parties at relevant date accordingly valued in total at £276,811 — Wife held entitled to equalisation payment of about £12,000 (being one-half of total matrimonial property less wife's share) under s. 9(1)(a).

(36) *Lewis v. Lewis*, 1993 S.C.L.R. 32 (Sheriff Principal J. S. Mowat Q.C.)

Parties separated in November 1985 after several years of marriage — Matrimonial property at relevant date comprising (i) jointly owned matrimonial home; (ii) husband's savings of £4,300; and (iii) wife's savings of £6,800 — Order made for sale of matrimonial home — Husband held entitled to capital sum of £700.

(37) *Loudon v. Loudon,* 1994 S.L.T. 381 (Lord Milligan)

Parties married in 1973 and separated in February 1991 — Matrimonial property at relevant date comprising assets valued at £834,119, although high degree of suspicion that husband had not disclosed all relevant assets — Wife arguing for unequal division on that basis and for her economic disadvantage — Wife held entitled to capital sum of £308,765, being the balance left after allowance made for sum of £150,000 already advanced to her by husband, the total (£458,765.45) representing 55% of the value of matrimonial property at relevant date.

(38) *Shand v. Shand*, 1994 S.L.T. 387 (Lord Coulsfield)

Parties married in August 1969 and separated in March 1985 — Matrimonial property at relevant date comprising assets valued at £259,951 but husband subsequently sequestrated — Both parties in receipt of income support at date of proof, but suspicions that husband in one way or another enjoyed some supplement to that income — Sole identified asset not falling under sequestration a pension policy in which husband had an interest with present transfer value of £12,207 — Pension policy capable of being realised forthwith to produce capital sum of £3,000 and income of £900 per annum or, if allowed to mature for a further period of seven or eight years, possible capital sum of £6,000 with income of £2,400 per annum to follow — Wife held entitled to capital sum of £12,000, with extract superseded until the likely date of conclusion of the sequestration, a period of almost two years.

(39) *Davidson v. Davidson*, 1994 S.L.T. 506 (Lord MacLean)

Parties married in July 1988 and separated in September 1991 — Matrimonial property at relevant date comprising farm valued at £177,000 — Farm purchased with money realised by wife from her substantial inherited shareholdings to enable her to carry on a farming business — Husband likely to suffer considerable financial hardship as a result of divorce — Husband held entitled to capital sum of £60,000, there being special circumstances why the matrimonial property should not be shared equally.

(40) *Welsh v. Welsh*, 1994 S.L.T. 828 (Lord Osborne)

Parties married in April 1969 and separated in December 1987 — Matrimonial property at relevant date comprising jointly owned matrimonial home (valued at £29,000 and subject to mortgage of £19,280), furniture and plenishings (valued at £1,500), husband's interest in a superannuation scheme (valued at £15,850), motor car (valued at £500), cash in bank (£71.91) and an endowment policy (valued at £321.20) — Total net value of matrimonial property at relevant date therefore £27,963.11 — Wife consenting to transfer of property order in respect of her one-half share of matrimonial home — Wife held entitled to balancing capital payment of £13,981, representing an equal sharing of the matrimonial property as at the relevant date.

(41) *Gribb v. Gribb*, 1994 S.L.T. (Sh. Ct.) 43; 1996 S.L.T. 719 (Second Division; Sheriff J. C. McInnes Q.C.)

Parties married in March 1953 and separated in February 1991 — Matrimonial property at relevant date comprising jointly owned matrimonial home (valued at £52,000), the contents thereof (valued at £6,195) and husband's interest in his pension scheme (valued at £100,800) — Wife held entitled to transfer of property order in respect of husband's one-half share of matrimonial home.

(42) *Jacques v. Jacques*, 1995 S.C. 327; 1997 S.C.(H.L.) 20 (House of Lords; First Division)

Parties married in January 1987 and separated in September 1990 — Matrimonial property at relevant date comprising jointly owned matrimonial home (valued at £55,000) and various other items — Matrimonial home purchased for £30,000, the source of funds being the sale proceeds of house owned by husband and occupied by parties before their marriage — Matrimonial home requiring certain repairs, financed by balance of sale proceeds and bank loan taken out by husband, with both parties giving up employment to renovate the property, thus contributing to increase in value of property — Husband still liable as at relevant date in respect of loan in the sum of £5,000 but retaining after separation items of matrimonial property of broadly equivalent value — Husband using matrimonial home for unsuccessful bed and breakfast business — Husband held not entitled to transfer of property order, there being no special circumstances present justifying departure from equal sharing — Wife held entitled to order for sale of matrimonial home, with extract superseded for six months.

(43) *Tahir v. Tahir (No. 2)*, 1995 S.L.T. 451 (Lord Clyde)

Parties married in 1979 and separated in August 1985 — Matrimonial property at relevant date comprising matrimonial home (valued at £13,500), the contents thereof (valued at £200), certain other items (valued at £2,385) and funds of £17,000 — Debts at relevant date comprising £10,000 in respect of mortgage and £2,526.59 in respect of repairs bill — Debt alleged to be due by husband to third party for which a sheriff court decree existed held to be fictitious and sheriff court decree accordingly reduced — Net value of matrimonial property at relevant date therefore a round total of £20,000 — Wife held entitled to one-half thereof in terms of s. 9(1)(a), namely £10,000.

(44) *Mayor v. Mayor*, 1995 S.L.T. 1097 (Lord Marnoch)

Parties separated in 1983 after several years of marriage — Matrimonial property at relevant date comprising (i) wife's savings of £1,000; and (ii) husband's interest in family business (valued at £4,358), ownership of premises thereof (valued at £65,000) and cash (£3,252) — Husband transferring other properties into name of his mother, who had since died, his entitlement on her intestacy amounting to £31,000 — Wife held entitled to capital sum of £50,000, with extract superseded for six months, it being unavoidable that family business premises be sold in order to do justice between the parties.

(45) *Buckle v. Buckle*, 1995 S.C.L.R. 590 (Sheriff N. McPartlin)

Parties married for thirty years — Matrimonial property at relevant date comprising husband's pension rights, valued at £76,000 — Wife held entitled to capital sum of £15,000, payable by monthly instalments of £250 over five years.

(46) *Crosbie v. Crosbie*, 1996 S.L.T. (Sh. Ct.) 86 (Sheriff Principal G. L. Cox Q.C.)

Parties married in 1957 and separated in October 1991 — Matrimonial property at relevant date comprising (i) jointly owned matrimonial home; and (ii) husband's interest in pension fund (valued at £78,000) and certain assets retained by him (valued at £40,000) less debt of £1,832; and (iii) certain assets retained by wife (valued at £23,230) — Wife held entitled to capital sum of £36,469 (of which £7,469 payable within seven days, £19,000 within six months and the balance of £10,000 by monthly instalments of £416), comprising (i) £7,469, representing equal sharing of matrimonial property except for the pension interest; and (ii) £29,000, representing fair sharing of pension interest having regard to its non-realisability.

(47) *Murphy v. Murphy*, 1996 S.L.T. (Sh. Ct.) 91 (Sheriff A. M. Bell)

Parties married in October 1969 and separated in January 1991 — Matrimonial property at relevant date comprising (i) jointly owned matrimonial home; and (ii) husband's interest in pensions (valued at £28,301.13), insurance policy (valued at £354), car (valued at £1,000) and cash (£3,147.13) — Wife receiving about £2,500 after separation — Wife living in matrimonial home with children of marriage — Matrimonial home having net value of £36,370.19 at date of proof — Wife held entitled to transfer of property order in respect of husband's one-half share of matrimonial home.

(48) *Cunniff v. Cunniff*, 1997 Fam.L.R. 42; 1999 S.C. 537 (Extra Division; Lord Abernethy)

Parties married in May 1971 and separated after divorce proceedings were raised in March 1991 — Matrimonial property at relevant date comprising jointly owned matrimonial home (valued at £80,000), family car (valued at £2,500), husband's pension interest (valued at £8,600), cash held by wife (£1,272) and cash held by husband (£9) — Total value of matrimonial property at relevant date therefore £92,381 — Debts at relevant date comprising mortgage of £39,500 and matrimonial debts of £11,460, not including Irish tax debt which husband did not intend to pay and which was unenforceable — Net value of matrimonial property at relevant date accordingly £41,421 — Wife retaining family car — Husband unemployed and unable to pay matrimonial debts for which he alone was liable — Wife living in matrimonial home with child under 16 (and being visited by older children), paying mortgage, unable to afford alternative accommodation and prone to ill health — Sale of matrimonial home sought by husband liable to result in claim by Scottish Legal Aid Board against sale proceeds, not leaving husband necessarily better off — Wife held entitled to transfer of property order in respect of husband's one-half share of matrimonial home, there being special circumstances justifying unequal division of matrimonial property — Husband's earning capacity and increase in value of his pension fund held to be resources for the purposes of financial provision on divorce.

(49) *Graham v. Graham*, 1997 Fam.L.R. 117 (Second Division)

Parties separated in February 1993 after several years of marriage — Matrimonial property at relevant date comprising matrimonial home jointly owned by them along with third party — Matrimonial home valued at £28,000 and subject to mortgage of £14,000 at relevant date — Parties' combined interest in matrimonial home therefore valued at £9,332 — Parties also having debts at relevant date amounting to £9,278 for which husband had assumed responsibility — Wife held not entitled to transfer of property order in respect of husband's one-third share of matrimonial home.

(50) *McConnell v. McConnell*, 1997 Fam.L.R. 97; 1997 Fam.L.R. 108 (Second Division; Lord Osborne)

Parties separated in November 1990 after several years of marriage — Matrimonial property at relevant date comprising jointly owned matrimonial home and contents therein (valued by discounting their insurance value) and various other assets held jointly or by one or other party (including husband's shares in private company valued under reference to company's net assets) — Total matrimonial property at relevant date valued at £1,450,044, whereof property valued at £331,622 in wife's hands and property valued at £1,118,422 in husband's — Debts at relevant date (excluding certain contingent tax liabilities but including tax liability arising in relation to income enjoyed during year preceding relevant date) amounting to £141,337, whereof wife liable for £18,728 (being one-half of outstanding mortgage over matrimonial home of £37,456) and husband for £122,609 — Net value of total matrimonial property at relevant date therefore £1,308,707, whereof £312,894 in wife's hands and £995,813 in husband's — Wife held entitled to (i) transfer of property order in respect of husband's one-half share of matrimonial home and contents therein (valued at £272,500); (ii) an incidental order for payment by husband of outstanding mortgage over matrimonial home (inclusive of wife's one-half liability in the sum of £18,728); and (iii) capital sum of £50,000, the total value of orders for financial provision thereby made in favour of wife being £341,228, representing in round figures one-half of net value of the matrimonial property at relevant date less net value of matrimonial property in wife's hands, there being no special circumstances justifying an unequal division of matrimonial property.

(51) *Adams v. Adams (No. 1)*, 1997 S.L.T. 144 (Lord Gill)

Parties married in September 1978 and separated in September 1991 — Matrimonial property at relevant date comprising jointly owned matrimonial home and insurance policy on joint lives and various other assets (valued at £44,380) — Wife living in matrimonial home with children — Order for sale of matrimonial home granted — Wife held entitled to capital sum of £22,190, representing an equal sharing of matrimonial property, payable on receipt by husband of his half share of sale proceeds.

(52) *Savage v. Savage,* 1997 Fam.L. R. 132 (Lord Sutherland)

Parties separated in June 1990 after several years of marriage — Matrimonial property at relevant date comprising (i) jointly owned matrimonial home; and (ii) husband's savings (£49,300) and business (valued on a going concern basis at £75,000) — Parties agreeing sale of matrimonial home and division of proceeds — Wife receiving proceeds of insurance policies amounting to £2,100 — Net value of undistributed matrimonial property therefore amounting to £122,200 — Wife held entitled to capital sum of £63,600 (with extract superseded *quoad* the sum of £18,600 for three months), comprising (i) £61,100, representing equal sharing of matrimonial property; and (ii) £2,500, representing interest thereon from relevant date.

(53) *Gracie v. Gracie*, 1997 S.L.T. (Sh. Ct.) 15 (Sheriff R. G. Craik Q.C.)

Parties married in February 1975 and separated in February 1994 — Matrimonial property at relevant date comprising jointly owned matrimonial home, joint endowment policy and husband's interest in pension scheme (valued at £30,000) — Wife held entitled to capital sum of £15,000, payable by 11 annual instalments of £1,000 until date of husband's entitlement to pension, when balance due.

(54) *Collins v. Collins*, 1997 Fam.L.R. 50 (Sheriff J. R. Smith)

Parties married in August 1980 and separated in January 1988 — Matrimonial property at relevant date comprising jointly owned matrimonial home (valued at £14,400 net), furniture (valued at £4,700) and cash (£911) — Husband retaining furniture and cash — Value of matrimonial property at relevant date therefore £20,011, whereof £12,811 retained by husband and £7,200 retained by wife — Debts at relevant date amounting to £858, paid by wife — Husband suffering from multiple sclerosis with reduced life expectancy and requiring constant professional care in matrimonial home (adapted into what resembled nursing home) — Wife's conduct adversely affecting parties' resources — Husband held entitled to transfer of property order in respect of wife's one-half share of matrimonial home, having regard to special circumstances mentioned in s. 10(6)(d) — Wife held entitled to capital sum of £9,927.54 (secured by standard security over matrimonial home and with extract superseded until date of husband's death, with no interest thereon), comprising (i) £3,234, representing an equal sharing of the net value of the matrimonial property; and (ii) £7,200, representing net value of wife's one-half share of matrimonial home at relevant date, restricted to £9,927.54 to comply with terms of wife's crave.

(55) *Maclachlan v. Maclachlan*, 1998 S.L.T. 693 (Lord Macfadyen)

Parties separated in March 1995 after several years of marriage — Matrimonial property at relevant date comprising jointly owned matrimonial home subject to a joint mortgage, household contents, parties' respective interests in pension funds and certain other assets, including funds in wife's hands derived from a redundancy payment — Parties sharing household contents by agreement — Parties' pension interests broadly comparable in value — Wife's other assets at relevant date valued at £25,294.60 and husband's at £5,523.13 — Husband held entitled to equal sharing of balance of matrimonial property, namely £9,885.74 (being one-half of £30,817.73, less £5,523.13), there being no special circumstances present to justify sharing other than equally.

(56) *Wilson v. Wilson*, 1999 S.L.T. 249 (Lord Marnoch)

Parties married in February 1979 and separated in February 1996 — Matrimonial property at relevant date comprising assets having net value of £804,122, whereof wife's assets valued at £93,452 — Husband failing to discharge onus of proof that certain monies inherited — Property held by husband's company held not to be matrimonial property — Wife held entitled to the sum of £308,609, representing equal division of matrimonial property.

(57) *Jackson v. Jackson*, 2000 S.C.L.R. 81 (Lord Macfadyen)

Parties married in 1986 and separated after divorce proceedings were raised in October 1996 — Matrimonial property at relevant date comprising various agreed items of property, valued at £163,190 (wife) and £232,906 (husband), and various other items of property, namely wife's jewellery (valued at £10,448), wife's share of contents of matrimonial home (valued at £9,460), husband's share thereof (valued at £780), wife's pension (valued at £6,039), husband's pension (valued at £51,744), wife's shareholding in private family company, P & B Enterprises Ltd (valued at £436,205) and husband's shareholding therein (valued at £440,942) — Total value of matrimonial property at relevant date therefore £1,351,714, comprising £625,342 (wife) and £726,372 (husband) — Husband's debts at relevant date, including tax debt subsequently paid by him, amounting to £23,532 — Total net value of matrimonial property at relevant date accordingly £1,328,182, comprising £625,342 (wife) and £702,840 (husband) — Funds used to acquire shareholding in P & B

Enterprises Ltd to some extent derived from husband's efforts before marriage but unclear as to how much so derived and husband in any event choosing to invest those funds in that company on basis that shares taken almost equally between wife and himself — Wife held entitled to capital sum of £38,750, representing equal sharing of net value of matrimonial property, there being no special circumstances present justifying unequal sharing — Extract superseded until sale of shares in P & B Enterprises Ltd effected.

(58) *R v. R*, 2000 Fam.L.R. 43 (Lord Eassie)

Parties married in April 1988 and separated in March 1998 — Matrimonial property at relevant date comprising farm and other assets with total value of £1,204,635 (excluding furniture and plenishings divided by agreement), whereof husband owned everything except for three horses belonging to wife valued at £5,000 — Great bulk of matrimonial property stemming from assets inherited by or given to husband — Wife having care of children of marriage and suffering economic disadvantage — Wife held entitled to capital sum of £380,000, there being special circumstances in terms of s. 10(6)(b) justifying an unequal division of matrimonial property.

(59) *Stuart v. Stuart*, 2001 S.L.T. (Sh. Ct.) 20 (Sheriff Principal J.C. McInnes Q.C.)

Parties married in June 1989 and separated in July 1995— Matrimonial property at relevant date comprising jointly owned matrimonial home and its contents, a car, husband's interest in an occupational pension scheme and an insurance policy with a negative value—Matrimonial home purchased at discount from development corporation in June 1995 for £26,840, funded by building society loan of £27,000, and valued at relevant date at £45,000—Varying proportions of discount repayable in the event of resale within three years— Other assets valued at relevant date at £6,733.18—Matrimonial home valued at £46,000 and subject to loan of £27,050.07 in May 1999—Matrimonial home remaining unsold at date of proof, husband paying mortgage costs and policy premiums since separation—Wife held entitled to capital sum of £12,336.59, comprising (i) £9,000, being her share of the net proceeds of sale of the matrimonial home at relevant date (ignoring contingent liability to repay discount); and (ii) £3,366.59, representing equal sharing of the other assets.

(60) *Trotter v. Trotter*, 2001 S.L.T. (Sh. Ct.) 42 (Sheriff Principal C.G.B. Nicholson Q.C.)

Parties separated in December 1997 after several years of marriage—Matrimonial property date comprising jointly owned matrimonial home and contents, two endowment policies in joint names securing mortgage over matrimonial home, wife's interest in pension fund and husband's three pension policies and cash in bank—Net value of matrimonial property at relevant date amounting to just under £66,900—Wife occupying matrimonial home since separation with daughters of the marriage aged 16 and 18 at date of proof, maintaining the property and paying all mortgage costs and policy premiums, and requiring to provide a home for daughters for at least a few years; and liable to be left in very vulnerable position if house sold—Wife held entitled to transfer of property orders in respect of husband's interest in matrimonial home and contents and relative endowment policies (leaving wife with property to the value of just over £40,000 and husband with property worth a little over £26,000), there being special circumstances justifying an unequal division of net value of matrimonial property at relevant date.

(61) *Cunningham v. Cunningham*, 2001 Fam.L.R. 12 (Lord Macfadyen)

Parties separated in 1998 after several years of marriage—Matrimonial property at relevant date comprising assets with an aggregate value of £1,285,376, whereof £390,056 in hands of wife and £895,320 in hands of husband—Matrimonial property in wife's hands including assets acquired with inherited funds totalling £50,000—Husband using inherited capital of £214,100 to fund matrimonial property to the extent of (i) a holiday home in his own name, valued at £68,000; (ii) a contribution of £100,000 to the purchase price of the jointly owned matrimonial home; and (iii) an unidentified contribution of £50,000 to matrimonial property in his own hands—Wife held entitled to capital sum of £218,632 (less payment to account of £25,000), representing an equal division of value of matrimonial property after (i) deduction from matrimonial property in wife's hands of £50,000 (being the value of matrimonial property in her own hands acquired with her inherited funds); and (ii) deduction from matrimonial property in husband's hands of £118,000 (being the sum of (a) £68,000, being the value of his holiday home funded by his inherited capital; and (b) £50,000, being his contribution to matrimonial property in his own hands from his inherited capital), no credit being given to husband for contribution of £100,000 to purchase of matrimonial home.

(62) *McHugh v. McHugh*, 2001 Fam.L.R. 30 (Lord Macfadyen)

Parties separated in July 1999 after several years of marriage—Matrimonial property at relevant date comprising matrimonial home in joint names, subject to secured loan, and sundry items of incorporeal property—Husband held beneficially entitled to only one-half of shares in limited company issued in his name—Net value of matrimonial property at relevant date accordingly amounting to £461,749, whereof £112,992 held by wife and £348,757 held by husband—Wife held entitled to (1) in return for discharge of his whole liabilities under the standard security over the matrimonial home and indemnification by wife of husband in respect of all liabilities arising under standard security after decree but before such discharge, transfer of property order in respect of husband's one-half *pro indiviso* share in matrimonial home, valued at £20,191; and (2) capital sum of £97,700, with interest on unpaid balance thereof from time to time outstanding at five per cent a year from date of decree, all by the following instalments, *viz.* (i) one instalment of £25,000 payable within one month of date of decree, and (ii) annual instalments of £20,000 (or such lesser amount as shall remain outstanding) on 1 May each year until the whole has been paid.

(63) *Gray v. Gray*, 2001 S.C.L.R. 681 (Sheriff A.L. Stewart Q.C.)

Parties separated in May 1999 after several years of marriage—Matrimonial property at relevant date comprising matrimonial home, with a net value of £24,023.09, and other items valued at £9,814.95—Wife using £6,000 gifted by her parents as deposit for parties' first home—Wife continuing to reside in matrimonial home after separation along with the two children of the marriage—Matrimonial home reasonably close to wife's parents' house and to children's school, so that it would be disruptive for children to move—Wife's parents giving her financial assistance towards maintaining mortgage payments whereas husband almost continuously failing to meet financial responsibilities after separation with respect to aliment for wife and children and mortgage and insurance payments relative to matrimonial home, notwithstanding court orders—Wife held entitled, subject to consent of mortgagor, to transfer of property order in respect of husband's interest in matrimonial home, there being special circumstances justifying unequal sharing of net value of matrimonial property at relevant date.

(64) *Buchan v. Buchan*, 2001 Fam.L.R. 48 (Sheriff A. Pollock)

Parties separated in January 1995 after several years of marriage—Matrimonial property at relevant date comprising jointly owned matrimonial home valued at £127,500 and relative endowment policy, wife's pension entitlement valued at £57,869.21 and husband's pension valued as at August 1995 at £11,223.46—Wife's parents gifting £20,000 towards cost of first matrimonial home in exchange for undertaking that they would be housed by parties for the rest of their lives— Wife keeping the family financially for five years through teaching post when husband lost his job; matrimonial home repossessed through husband failing to maintain mortgage payments, and wife contributing £13,000 towards deposit for new matrimonial home; and husband thereafter leading independent social life and having affairs, spending £22,000 in two years and providing little support for family other than sporadic payments towards mortgage and life insurance premiums, which were in arrears at relevant date—Wife held entitled to transfer of property orders in respect of husband's interest in matrimonial home and endowment policy associated therewith, wife's parents' gift amounting to special circumstances, husband deriving economic advantage from wife's various roles throughout marriage as joint breadwinner, housekeeper, mother and teacher, and husband's conduct adversely affecting parties' financial resources.

(65) *MacLean v. MacLean*, 2001 Fam.L.R. 118 (Lord Rodger of Earlsferry)

Parties married in October 1980 and separated in May 1993—Matrimonial property at relevant date comprising assets with an aggregate net value of £1,035,985, whereof £1,008,557 (including personal equity plan worth £27,897) owned by wife and £27,428 (a personal equity plan) owned by husband— Wife applying mother's gift of £40,000 to purchase of farm— Other matrimonial property deriving more or less directly from funds provided by wife out of property owned by her prior to marriage—Wife an extremely hard-working, able and dedicated farmer—Husband also contributing to farm work, being very able at what he did—Wife having sole responsibility for care and maintenance of children of marriage since separation—Husband held entitled to capital sum of £235,000, being 25% (rounded down) of net value of matrimonial property at relevant date after deduction of parties' personal equity plans and mother's gift (*i.e.* £940,660), but, having regard in particular to fact that wife had had all the responsibility for care and maintenance of children since separation, order for backdating of interest on capital sum to relevant date refused.

(66) *Fraser v. Fraser*, 2002 Fam.L.R. 53 (Extra Division)

Parties separated in September 1989 after several years of marriage—Matrimonial property at relevant date comprising husband's interest in occupational pension scheme valued at £105,395—Husband's sole capital resource at date of proof held to be a one-half share in a joint bank account with cohabitant—Wife held entitled to capital sum of £1,000, being one-half of the sum at credit in the bank account, payment to be made six months from the date of decree with interest at the legal rate.

(67) *Pressley v. Pressley*, 2002 S.C.L.R. 804 (Sheriff Principal Sir Stephen S.T. Young Q.C.)

Parties married in November 1995 and separated in May 2000—Matrimonial property at relevant date comprising wife's shares (acquired during marriage by way of employee sharesave accounts commenced prior to marriage), savings and pension interest, valued at £40,134—Shares falling in value since relevant date—Wife having other readily realisable capital assets and house—Husband held entitled to capital sum of £20,067, there being no special circumstances justifying departure from principle of equal sharing.

(68) *Thomson v. Thomson*, 2003 Fam.L.R. 22 (Sheriff C. J. Harris Q.C.)

Parties married in June 1994, separated in April 1996 and divorced in September 2002—Matrimonial property at relevant date comprising jointly owned matrimonial home, valued at £52,000 and subject to mortgage of £33,731.95, and husband's pension valued at £3,550—Matrimonial home worth £57,500 and subject to mortgage of £27,370.96 at date of proof (December 2002)—Wife occupying matrimonial home since separation along with child of the marriage aged seven at date of proof and unable to afford to buy or rent property in locality—Husband paying half the mortgage since separation while living elsewhere—Husband held entitled to order for sale of matrimonial home, postponed for four and a half years until completion of child's primary education at local school, with net free proceeds of sale split equally in respect that husband's continuing liability to make mortgage payments offset any special circumstances supporting unequal division of proceeds.

(69) *Cordiner v. Cordiner*, 2003 Fam.L.R. 39 (Sheriff Principal Sir Stephen S.T. Young Q.C.)

Parties married in December 1985 and separated in late 1997—Matrimonial property at relevant date comprising jointly owned matrimonial home with a net value of £126,000 and other assets with an aggregate value of £99,000 whereof savings of £5,000 (only) in wife's sole name—Husband owning assets at date of marriage worth £107,000—Wife held entitled to sale of matrimonial home and division of free proceeds into 126 parts with 69.5 parts to be paid to husband and 56.5 parts to wife, representing equal division of value of matrimonial property at relevant date after deduction of value of (i) husband's assets at date of marriage; and (ii) wife's only capital asset at date of separation.

(70) *L v. L*, 2003 Fam.L.R. 101 (Lord Bonomy)

Parties married in April 1985 and separated in June 1998—Matrimonial property at relevant date comprising matrimonial home valued at £220,000 and contents thereof and other assets—Net value of matrimonial property at relevant date amounting to £1,789,340, whereof husband owned assets worth £1,781,132 and wife owned £8,208—Wife held entitled to (i) transfer of property order, of consent, in respect of matrimonial home and contents thereof; and (ii) capital sum of £650,000, representing one-half of value of matrimonial property at relevant date (*i.e.* £894,670) less (a) £8,208, being wife's assets at relevant date; (b) £220,000, being value of matrimonial home at relevant date; and (c) £16,462 in respect of household contents.

(71) *Carrol v. Carrol*, 2003 Fam.L.R. 108 (Sheriff A. S. Jessop)

Parties separated in August 1997 after several years of marriage—Matrimonial property at relevant date comprising (i) jointly owned matrimonial home, with a net value of £39,969; (ii) jointly owned insurance policy, with a net value of £5,900; (iii) part of husband's personal injury damages claim arising from accident in the course of his employment in 1993 in which he was seriously injured, valued at £63,397.14; (iv) husband's personal pension policy, valued at £8,101; and (v) furniture, valued at £1,062, less debts totalling £39,308—Net value of matrimonial property at relevant date amounting to £79,121.14—Husband's damages claim settled on a global basis for £240,000 following upon tender for £210,000 broken down into various heads—Claim valued on a fairly broad brush approach, excluding *solatium* and loss of future earnings and deducting repayable benefits and fees but not discounting for assignation, there being no proof that claim had value if offered for sale in market place or what value such a claim would have—Husband's prospects of employment in the future remote—Wife residing in matrimonial home with children of marriage, it being in younger child's best interests to continue to live in same house and attend same school—Wife held entitled to (i) transfer of property order in respect of husband's interests in matrimonial home and insurance policy; and (ii) capital sum of £1,000, payable by monthly instalments of £25, an equal division of matrimonial property not being possible given husband's financial circumstances.

(72) *Coyle v. Coyle*, 2004 Fam.L.R. 2 (Lady Smith)

Parties married in February 1975 and separated in February 1995—Matrimonial property at relevant date comprising matrimonial home, valued at £270,000, and other assets— Net value of matrimonial property at relevant date amounting to £1,157,913 or £1,182,913, whereof wife owned asset worth £21,053—Matrimonial home subsequently valued at £500,000 but wife suffering economic disadvantage in interests of husband and children by refraining from pursuing her career— Wife held entitled to (i) transfer of property order in respect of matrimonial home; and (ii) capital sum of £295,000, there being no special circumstances justifying unequal sharing of net value of matrimonial property at relevant date.

(73) *Christie v. Christie*, 2004 S.L.T. (Sh. Ct.).95 (Sheriff Principal B. A. Kerr Q.C.)

Parties separated in November 2001 after several years of marriage—Matrimonial property at relevant date comprising jointly owned matrimonial home, endowment policies relative to the heritable loan secured over the house, pensions and other savings—Net value of matrimonial property at relevant date amounting to £73,260.74—Matrimonial home increasing in value by 15% since separation during which period husband residing in matrimonial home and funding heritable loan whilst wife elsewhere with 15-year-old daughter—Wife held entitled to transfer of property orders in respect of husband's interest in matrimonial home and relative endowment policies (giving her £31,882 or 43.5% of the net value of the matrimonial property at relevant date), the need for the child and her mother to return as soon as possible to the matrimonial home being a powerful and compelling reason for granting the orders.

(74) *Kennedy v. Kennedy*, 2004 S.L.T. (Sh. Ct.) 102 (Sheriff Principal B. A. Kerr Q.C.)

Parties separated in June 1996 after several years of marriage—Matrimonial property at relevant date comprising (i) endowment policy in joint names worth £8,320; (ii) contents of matrimonial home retained by wife, valued at £1,000, wife's pension, valued at £1,910, and wife's savings of £760; and (iii) husband's pension, valued at £36,750 with additional voluntary contributions worth £3,540, husband's savings of £3,400 and husband's reversionary interest in matrimonial home, valued at £17,000—Net value of matrimonial property at relevant date accordingly £72,680—Wife held entitled to (1) transfer of property orders in respect of matrimonial home and husband's one-half share of endowment policy, valued at £21,160 in total; and (2) capital sum of £7,350, with no order made in respect of remaining matrimonial property, resulting in equal sharing of net value of matrimonial property at relevant date.

(75) *W v. W,* 2004 Fam.L.R. 54 (Lord Clarke)

Parties married in March 1981 and separated in May 1999—Matrimonial property at relevant date comprising jointly owned matrimonial home, valued at £150,000, and other assets—Net value of matrimonial property at relevant date amounting to £460,649—Wife encashing after separation bond for £20,000 forming part of matrimonial property —Wife residing in matrimonial home with four children of marriage whose best interests served by continuing to reside there—Matrimonial home valued at £225,000 at date of proof—Wife held entitled to (i) transfer of property order in respect of husband's interest in matrimonial home; and (ii) capital sum of £22,824.50, account being taken of bond encashed by wife (£20,000) and increase in value of defender's interest in matrimonial home since separation (£37,500), resulting in equal sharing of net value of matrimonial property at relevant date.

(76) *McCaskill v. McCaskill*, 2004 Fam.L.R. 123 (Sheriff Principal I. D. Macphail Q.C.)

Parties separated in August 1998 after several years of marriage—Matrimonial property at relevant date comprising (i) jointly owned matrimonial home, valued at £45,000; and (ii) husband's pension interest, valued at £21,460—Matrimonial home valued at £100,000 at date of proof—Wife caring for child of the marriage—Husband making certain payments in relation to property—Wife held entitled to (1) capital sum of £14,570, comprising (i) £10,820, being one-half of husband's pension interest, and (ii) £3,750, to enable fair sharing of economic burden of caring for child; and (2) order for sale of matrimonial home and for equal division of proceeds of sale after deduction of husband's payments.

(77) *Connolly v. Connolly,* 2005 Fam. L.R.106 (First Division)

Parties separated after several years of marriage—Matrimonial property at relevant date *inter alia* comprising jointly owned properties in Scotland and Ireland—Net value of matrimonial property, excluding Irish property, at relevant date amounting to £342,386, whereof wife owned assets worth £238,742 and husband owned assets worth £103,644—Husband in arrears of aliment at date of proof—Continuing hostility between parties creating potential difficulties in achieving co-operation over sale of Irish property—Husband held entitled to capital sum of £69,677, being one-half of the differential between the parties' respective assets (apart from the Irish property), subject to certain adjustments the effect of which was to add the sum of £2,128—Husband's capital sum to be under deduction of outstanding arrears of aliment—Wife held entitled to an order requiring husband to execute a disposition in her favour of his one-half share of the Irish property and husband held entitled to order for the sale of the Irish property immediately thereafter with the sale proceeds deposited at the disposal of the court.

(78) *Russell, v. Russell,* 2005 Fam. L.R. 96 (Sheriff Principal R A Dunlop Q.C.)

Parties separated after several years of marriage—Net value of matrimonial property at relevant date amounting to £24,272.88, comprising matrimonial home owned by wife (valued at £48,000 and subject to loan of £10,480.32) less husband's bank debt of £12,500 and parties' joint debts of £746.80—Husband held entitled to capital sum of £24,400 in order that the parties should be left with net assets of approximately the same value, measured at the date of separation.

(79) *Sweeney v. Sweeney (No 2),* 2006 S.C. 82 (Extra Division; Lord Kingarth)

Parties married in October 1981 and separated in December 1998—Net value of matrimonial property at relevant date amounting to £4,432,419.43, whereof husband owned assets valued at £3,316,728.16 (of which assets valued at £1,037,622.16 were reasonable to realise and assets valued at £2,279,106 were not reasonable to realise) and wife owned assets valued at £1,115, 691.27 (of which assets valued at £348,634 were reasonable to realise and assets valued at £769,614 were not reasonable to realise)—Wife accepting that husband's business interest should be apportioned otherwise than equally, thus restricting her entitlement upon a fair sharing of the net value of the matrimonial property to the sum of £1,066,338, less advance payment of £350,000—Wife held entitled to capital sum of £950,000 (the outstanding balance of £600,000 being payable in five instalments over a period of just over three and a half years), having regard to the fact that if the husband was required to pay the wife's entitlement in full he would be left with no funds available to preserve or develop his business if required.

REPORTED CASES INVOLVING PRINCIPLES B TO E

PRINCIPLE B[2]

Cases in which Principle B was explicitly considered include the following:

(1) *Petrie v. Petrie*, 1988 S.C.L.R. 390 (Sheriff D.J. Risk) (husband held not to have derived economic advantage from presence of wife in the home).

(2) *Kerrigan v. Kerrigan*, 1988 S.C.L.R. 603 (Sheriff G. J. Evans) (wife held to have derived economic advantage from husband's mortgage payments by increase in value of jointly owned matrimonial home).

(3) *Muir v. Muir*, 1989 S.L.T. (Sh. Ct.) 20 (Sheriff I. A. Macmillan) (husband held not to have derived economic advantage from wife's occupation of his house since separation).

(4) *Little v. Little*, 1989 S.C.L.R. 613 (Lord Cameron of Lochbroom) (wife held to have suffered economic disadvantage in the family interest by the interruption of her professional career in order to look after house and family for a period).

(5) *Walker v. Walker*, 1989 S.C.L.R. 625 (Lord Morton of Shuna) (wife held to have suffered an economic disadvantage and husband a corresponding economic advantage in terms of future income arising from the business built up by the contributions both parties made during the marriage).

(6) *Tyrrell v. Tyrrell*, 1990 S.L.T. 406 (Lord Sutherland) (husband held not to have derived any economic advantage from any contribution by wife by way of increase in value of his pension since separation).

(7) *Farrell v. Farrell*, 1990 S.C.L.R. 717 (Sheriff C. N. Stoddart) (wife held to have suffered an economic disadvantage and the husband a corresponding economic advantage from contributions made by her since the parties' separation in terms of mortgage, rates and insurance payments relative to the matrimonial home).

---

[2]See Chap. 7, text accompanying nn. 106–114.

(8) *Skarpaas v. Skarpaas*, 1991 S.L.T. (Sh. Ct.) (Sheriff A. L. Stewart) (wife held to have suffered economic disadvantage in relation to her business because of need to look after injured husband).

(9) *Jesner v. Jesner*, 1992 S.L.T. 999 (Lord Osborne) (husband held to have derived economic advantage from wife's contribution in looking after family home and caring for family).

(10) *Shipton v. Shipton*, 1992 S.C.L.R. 23 (Sheriff N. E. D. Thomson) (wife held to have suffered economic disadvantage through her inability to work during the marriage).

(11) *Toye v. Toye*, 1992 S.C.L.R. 95 (Sheriff A. S. Jessop) (wife held to have suffered economic disadvantage by giving up work which she could not readily resume).

(12) *Macdonald v. Macdonald*, 1993 S.C.L.R. 132 (Lord Caplan) (wife held to have suffered economic disadvantage through having assumed greater economic burden of caring for children than husband hitherto).

(13) *Davidson v. Davidson*, 1994 S.L.T. 506 (Lord MacLean) (husband held to have derived economic advantage from gifts of money from wife).

(14) *Ranaldi v. Ranaldi*, 1994 S.L.T. (Sh. Ct.) 25 (Sheriff R. G. Craik Q.C.) (husband held to have derived economic advantage through wife having taken in lodgers throughout marriage).

(15) *Loudon v. Loudon*, 1994 S.L.T. 381 (Lord Milligan) (wife held to have suffered economic disadvantage by giving up work and losing earning potential).

(16) *Welsh v. Welsh*, 1994 S.L.T. 828 (Lord Osborne) (wife's economic disadvantage in giving up well-paid employment to look after husband and children held to have been balanced by economic advantage from being maintained by husband and from enjoying the results of mortgage payments made exclusively by him in respect of jointly owned matrimonial home and by economic disadvantage suffered by him accordingly; but economic advantage held to have been enjoyed by husband in having exclusive use of house after separation with corresponding economic disadvantage to wife).

(17) *Tahir v. Tahir (No. 2)*, 1995 S.L.T. 451 (Lord Clyde) (husband held to have gained economic advantage, and the wife a corresponding economic disadvantage, by his forcibly dispossessing her of her jewellery).

(18) *Hunter v. Hunter*, 1996 S.C.L.R. 329 (Sheriff Principal D.J. Risk Q.C.) (wife held not to have suffered economic disadvantage during the course of the marriage through the husband's payment of aliment for his children by a previous marriage).

(19) *Adams v. Adams (No. 1)*, 1997 S.L.T. 144 (Lord Gill) (wife's economic disadvantage in prejudicing her career by bringing up the parties' children held to have been counterbalanced by husband's greater contribution to household finances).

(20) *McVinnie v. McVinnie (No. 2)* 1997 S.L.T. (Sh. Ct.) 12 (Sheriff Principal C.G.B. Nicholson Q.C.) (husband held to have derived economic advantage through child-caring contribution by wife and from portion of wife's receipts from sale of her interest in two houses).

(21) *De Winton v. De Winton*, 1998 Fam.L.R. 110 (Lord Cameron of Lochbroom) (husband held to have gained economic advantage from wife's financial investment in farming partnership which had allowed the firm overdraft to be lowered and certain improvements to be carried out at the expense of disabling her from dealing with her own money to her own profit — an advantage not cancelled out by her receiving her share of the partnership assets — and from her management of holiday cottages which had enhanced their revenue earning capacity to his financial benefit; but wife's contribution to the children's school fees not an economic disadvantage to wife nor, in any event, a corresponding economic advantage to husband).

(22) *Cahill v. Cahill*, 1998 S.L.T. (Sh. Ct.) 96 (Sheriff Principal E. F. Bowen Q.C.) (wife held to have derived economic advantage through improvements carried out to her cottage by the husband during the marriage).

(23) *Wilson v. Wilson*, 1999 S.L.T. 249 (Lord Marnoch) (husband's economic advantage gained through the wife's looking after the family home and the parties' children whilst he ploughed back considerable profits into his company held not to have been balanced throughout the marriage by an economic advantage to her such as a better lifestyle).

(24) *Cunniff v. Cunniff*, 1999 S.C. 537; 1997 Fam.L.R. 42 (Extra Division; Lord Abernethy) (husband's economic advantage in working full time and gaining additional qualifications whilst wife had given up work and raised the family held to have resulted in an imbalance of economic advantage and disadvantage which warranted correction, albeit that the wife's economic disadvantage could not be quantified).

(25) *R v. R*, 2000 Fam.L.R. 43 (Lord Eassie) (wife held to have suffered economic disadvantage through being unable to pursue an independent economic activity because of her natural commitment to care of the children of marriage and organis-ation of family home, including in particular her design input and de facto superintendence of its refurbishment).

(26) *Cunningham v. Cunningham*, 2001 Fam.L.R. 12 (Lord Macfadyen) (wife held not to have suffered any quantifiable economic disadvantage in interrupting her career as a paediatric physiotherapist for some six years when children were young in order to care for them).

(27) *Buchan v. Buchan*, 2001 Fam.L.R. 48 (Sheriff A. Pollock) (wife held to have suffered economic disadvantage and husband to have derived an economic advantage from wife's various roles throughout marriage as joint breadwinner, housekeeper, mother and teacher).

(28) *Pressley v. Pressley*, 2002 S.C.L.R. 804 (Sheriff Principal Sir Stephen S. T. Young) (wife held not to have suffered economic disadvantage nor husband an economic advantage from fact that wife's earnings higher than husband's during marriage).

(29) *Carrol v. Carrol*, 2003 Fam.L.R. 108 (Sheriff A. S. Jessop) (wife held to have suffered economic disadvantage to a slight extent through having to give up her employment and losing career prospects and possible pension in order to look after parties' four children while husband at work).

(30) *Coyle v. Coyle*, 2004 Fam.L.R. 2 (Lady Smith) (husband held not to have gained economic advantage from wife's management of house and children, but wife held to have suffered economic disadvantage in interests of husband and children by refraining, at husband's request, from pursuing her career).

(31) *Symanski v. Symanski (No 2)*, 2005 Fam. L.R. 2 (Sheriff Principal C G B Nicholson Q.C.) (husband held to have gained economic advantage from wife's injections of capital into his failed businesses prior to the marriage).

PRINCIPLE C[3]

Cases in which Principle C was explicitly considered include the following:

(1) *Monkman v. Monkman*, 1988 S.L.T. (Sh. Ct.) 37 (Sheriff Principal P. I. Caplan, Q.C.) (economic burden held to be shared fairly by periodical allowance under s. 9(1)(c) for wife until child about 20 years old).

(2) *Morrison v. Morrison*, 1989 S.C.L.R. 574 (Sheriff G. H. Gordon Q.C.) (economic burden held to be shared fairly by award to wife under s. 9(1)(c) of two-thirds of value of matrimonial home and contents).

---

[3]See Chap. 7, nn. 115–118 and accompanying text.

(3) *Millar v. Millar*, 1990 S.C.L.R. 666 (Sheriff Principal C. G. B. Nicholson Q.C.; Sheriff R. G. Craik Q.C.) (economic burden held to be shared fairly under reference to alimentary award in child's favour).

(4) *Shipton v. Shipton*, 1992 S.C.L.R. 23 (Sheriff N. E. D. Thomson) (economic burden held to be shared fairly by award of greater share of matrimonial property).

(5) *Toye v. Toye*, 1992 S.C.L.R. 95 (Sheriff A. S. Jessop) (economic burden held to be shared fairly by award of periodical allowance for three years).

(6) *Macdonald v. Macdonald*, 1993 S.C.L.R. 132 (Lord Caplan) (economic burden held to be shared fairly by award of capital sum to enable need to provide accommodation for children to be met).

(7) *Adams v. Adams (No. 1)*, 1997 S.L.T. 144 (Lord Gill) (economic burden held to be shared fairly by resumption of alimentary payments by husband).

(8) *Maclachlan v. Maclachlan*, 1998 S.L.T. 693 (Lord Macfadyen) (economic burden held to be shared fairly by substantial adjustment of capital in wife's favour — cancelled out by husband's entitlement under s. 9(1)(a)).

(9) *McCaskill v. McCaskill*, 2004 Fam. L.R. 123 (Sheriff Principal I. D. Macphail Q.C.) (economic burden held to be shared fairly by enhanced award of capital sum).

PRINCIPLE D[4]

Cases in which Principle D was explicitly considered include the following:

(1) *Dever v. Dever*, 1988 S.C.L.R. 352 (Sheriff Principal S. E. Bell Q.C.) (wife aged 27 years and married living with husband for six years, no children, in receipt of state benefits, claimed no maintenance since separation 18 months prior to diet of proof, awarded periodical allowance under s. 9(1)(d) for six months from date of decree).

(2) *Petrie v. Petrie*, 1988 S.C.L.R. 390 (Sheriff D. J. Risk) (wife aged 42 years and married and living with husband for two years, one child, cohabited with husband for several years before marriage, in receipt of state benefits, no skills or qualifications but fit for work, claimed no maintenance since

---

[4]See Chap. 7, nn. 119–122 and accompanying text.

separation in belief that her adultery disentitled her, awarded periodical allowance under s. 9(1)(d) for one year from date of decree).

(3) *Atkinson v. Atkinson*, 1988 S.C.L.R. 396 (Sheriff Principal R. R. Taylor Q.C.) (wife earning salary insufficient for her upkeep in the standard of life she enjoyed during marriage, awarded a periodical allowance under s. 9(1)(d) for three years from date of decree).

(4) *Park v. Park*, 1988 S.C.L.R. 584 (Sheriff D. Kelbie) (wife married and living with husband for five years, no children, earning one-fifth of the total amount earned by the parties, awarded a periodical allowance under s. 9(1)(d) to increase her "share" to one-third and allow her to adjust back to one-fifth, award being made for one year and at reduced rate for further year).

(5) *Muir v. Muir*, 1989 S.L.T. (Sh. Ct.) 20 (Sheriff I. A. Macmillan) (wife aged 47 years, no dependent children, in receipt of invalidity benefit, hoping to resume work as shop assistant, separated for four years and in receipt of maintenance during last of those years, awarded a periodical allowance under s. 9(1)(d) for one year from date of decree).

(6) *Tyrrell v. Tyrrell*, 1990 S.L.T. 406 (Lord Sutherland) (wife married and living with husband for 18 years, in part-time employment and in receipt of maintenance for seven years after separation until date of proof, awarded a periodical allowance under s. 9(1)(d) for one year from date of decree).

(7) *Sheret v. Sheret*, 1990 S.C.L.R. 799 (Sheriff N. McPartlin) (wife married and living with husband for two years, aged 42 years, with no immediate prospects of employment, supported only periodically by husband, awarded a periodical allowance under s. 9(1)(d) for 13 weeks from date of decree).

(8) *Millar v. Millar*, 1990 S.C.L.R. 666 (Sheriff Principal C. G. B. Nicholson Q.C.; Sheriff R. G. Craik Q.C.) (wife married and living with husband for 10 years, one child in joint custody, wife in part-time employment and in receipt of interim aliment for herself and child, awarded aliment in larger amount for child leaving small shortfall, held not entitled to a periodical allowance under s. 9(1)(d)).

(9) *Thomson v. Thomson*, 1991 S.L.T. 126 (Lord Cameron of Lochbroom) (wife dependent wholly for her financial support on husband for five years before separation, awarded interim aliment three years later against husband held to have taken every opportunity to avoid his financial responsibilities since separation, awarded a periodical allowance under s. 9(1)(d) for three years).

(10) *Barclay v. Barclay*, 1991 S.C.L.R. 205 (Sheriff I. C. Cameron) (wife aged 29 years, married and living with husband for some three years, no children, permanently disabled by multiple sclerosis and resident in a nursing home, not envisaged that she would ever be able to resume life in the community, awarded a periodical allowance under s. 9(1)(d) for three years).

(11) *Gray v. Gray*, 1991 S.C.L.R. 422 (Sheriff T. Russell) (wife dependent to substantial degree on husband's financial support prior to separation, since then not provided with, nor had she sought, financial support from husband, held to have adjusted to withdrawal of support and no award made).

(12) *Loudon v. Loudon*, 1994 S.L.T. 381 (Lord Milligan) (wife aged 45 years, married and living with husband for 17 years, one child (aged 17), wife unemployed and requiring to retrain to "get back on employment ladder", awarded a periodical allowance under s. 9(1)(d) for one year).

(13) *Buckle v. Buckle*, 1995 S.C.L.R. 590 (Sheriff N. McPartlin) (wife financially dependent on husband after 30 years marriage but undergoing one-year college course in office technology, held entitled to capital sum payable by instalments over five years, awarded a periodical allowance for one year under s. 9(1)(d)).

(14) *McConnell v. McConnell*, 1997 Fam.L.R. 97; 1997 Fam.L.R. 108 (Second Division; Lord Osborne) (wife married and living with husband for 16 years, three children, wife almost exclusively dependent upon income from husband, held reasonable for her to have period of time to adjust to new circumstances created by determination of the litigation, awarded a periodical allowance under s. 9(1)(d) for three years, reduced on appeal to six months).

(15) *Wilson v. Wilson*, 1999 S.L.T. 249 (Lord Marnoch) (wife married and living with husband for 17 years, two children aged 18 and 16, dependent on husband for financial support, requiring to retrain in order to get back on employment ladder, awarded a periodical allowance under s. 9(1)(d) for 30 months).

(16) *L v. L*, 2003 Fam.L.R. 101 (Lord Bonomy) (wife married and living with husband for 13 years, three children (aged 17, 15 and six), dependent to a substantial degree on husband's financial support pending settlement of the capital sum awarded to her, held entitled to periodical allowance under s. 9(1)(d) of £1,000 per month for a period of three years or until the capital sum fully paid, whichever was sooner).

PRINCIPLE E[5]

Cases in which the application of Principle E was explicitly considered include the following:

(1) *Atkinson v. Atkinson*, 1988 S.C.L.R. 396 (Sheriff Principal R. R. Taylor Q.C.) (wife with salary insufficient for her upkeep in the standard of life she enjoyed during marriage, but her income and substantial capital made it "quite out of the question" to make award under s. 9(1)(e)).

(2) *Bell v. Bell*, 1988 S.C.L.R. 457 (Sheriff J. C. M. Jardine) (wife aged 51 years, married and living with husband for 26 years, no dependent children, a qualified teacher but a full-time housewife and mother dependent on husband's support throughout the marriage, unlikely to find work affording reasonable remuneration, with sufficient capital to retain a nice house but with no income after divorce, awarded a periodical allowance under s. 9(1)(e) until husband's sixtieth birthday or her own death or remarriage).

(3) *Muir v. Muir*, 1989 S.L.T. (Sh. Ct.) 20 (Sheriff I. A. Macmillan) (wife aged 47 years, no dependent children, in receipt of invalidity benefit, hoping to resume work as shop assistant, separated for four years and in receipt of maintenance during last of those years, awarded a periodical allowance under s. 9(1)(d) for one year from date of decree, but s. 9(1)(e) held inapplicable).

(4) *Tyrrell v. Tyrrell*, 1990 S.L.T. 406 (Lord Sutherland) (wife married and living with husband for 18 years, in part-time employment and in receipt of maintenance for seven years after separation until date of proof, had received substantial capital at time of separation, with further capital sum upon decree, held entitled to award of a periodical allowance under s. 9(1)(d), but to no award under s. 9(1)(e)).

(5) *Johnstone v. Johnstone*, 1990 S.L.T. (Sh. Ct.) 79 (Sheriff R. D. Ireland Q.C.) (wife aged 35 years, married and living with husband for 13 years, one child, unfit for work because of epilepsy, awarded a periodical allowance until her death or remarriage under s. 9(1)(e)).

(6) *McKenzie v. McKenzie*, 1991 S.L.T. 461 (Lord Prosser) (wife aged nearly 60 years, married and living with husband for 16 years, no dependent children, ran small business with low income with possibility of income from lodger, entitled to

---

[5]See Chap. 7, nn. 123–125 and accompanying text.

small pension at 60, held liable to be "seriously short of money" notwithstanding award of capital sum if no maintenance awarded, awarded a periodical allowance until death or remarriage under s. 9(1)(e)).

(7) *Barclay v. Barclay*, 1991 S.C.L.R. 205 (Sheriff I. C. Cameron) (wife aged 29 years, married and living with husband for some three years, no children, permanently disabled by multiple sclerosis and resident in a nursing home, not envisaged that she would ever be able to resume life in the community, awarded a periodical allowance under s. 9(1)(d) for three years from date of decree but, requiring substantial support anyway from public funds, given award under s. 9(1)(e)).

(8) *Davidson v. Davidson*, 1994 S.L.T. 506 (Lord MacLean) (husband aged 46 years with very restricted earning capacity and without sound mental health, wife a very wealthy woman, marriage of five years' duration, husband awarded capital sum under s. 9(1)(e) in respect of loss of home and "considerable financial comfort" of wife's money).

(9) *Gribb v. Gribb*, 1994 S.L.T. (Sh. Ct.) 43; 1996 S.L.T. 719 (Second Division; Sheriff J. C. McInnes) (wife aged 62 years, married and living with her husband for 38 years, in part-time employment and in receipt of modest pension payments, awarded transfer of property order in respect of husband's interest in the matrimonial home and held entitled to award of a periodical allowance until her death or remarriage under s. 9(1)(e)).

(10) *Buckle v. Buckle*, 1995 S.C.L.R. 590 (Sheriff N. McPartlin) (wife financially dependent on husband after 30 years marriage but undergoing one-year college course in office technology, awarded a capital sum payable by instalments over five years, held entitled to a periodical allowance for one year under s. 9(1)(d) but any financial hardship occasioned by the divorce held to be mitigated by capital award and so no award under s. 9(1)(e)).

(11) *Haughan v. Haughan*, 1996 S.L.T. 321; 2002 S.C. 631 (Extra Division; Lord Marnoch) (wife aged 51 years, married and living with husband for 26 years, suffering impaired hearing, chronic high blood pressure and fibrositis and moderate to severe depression, in penurious circumstances with very restricted earning capacity, held entitled to award of a periodical allowance until her death or remarriage under s. 9(1)(e)).

(12) *Savage v. Savage*, 1997 Fam.L.R. 132 (Lord Sutherland) (wife unfit for work and unlikely to find employment, but awarded

a "not insubstantial" capital sum, husband's business drawings at very modest level, no award under s. 9(1)(e)).

(13) *Galloway v. Galloway*, 2003 Fam.L.R. 10 (Temporary Judge T. G. Coutts Q.C.) (wife aged 55 years, no dependent children, in part-time employment, husband with very substantial income, awarded a periodical allowance under s. 9(1)(e) until her sixtieth birthday or her death or remarriage, whichever was the earlier).

TABLE OF MATRIMONIAL PROPERTY AND RESOURCES[1]

PURSUER	£	DEFENDER	£
At relevant date:		*At relevant date:*	
(i) one half-interest in matrimonial home	96,937	(i) one-half interest in matrimonial home	96,937
(ii) one-half interest in Scottish Widows Insurance Policy . . .	3,684	(ii) one-half interest in Scottish Widows Insurance Policy . . .	3,684
(iii) 38.03% interest in C.C. Hornig & Son Ltd Executive Pension Fund . . .	43,318	(iii) 61.97% interest in C.C. Hornig & Son Ltd Executive Pension Fund . . .	70,588
		(iv) interest in Legal & General Pension Plan Policy . . .	4,000
		(v) interest in Liverpool and Victoria Insurance Policy . . .	2,200
		(vi) cash in Bank of Scotland . . .	3,567.32
		(vii) shares in C.C. Hornig & Son Ltd	69,000
SUBTOTAL	**143,939**	**SUBTOTAL**	**249,976.32**
Less		*Less*	
(a) one-half liability to Bank of Scotland . . .	1,763.71	(a) one-half liability to Bank of Scotland . . .	1,763.71
TOTAL	**142,175.29**	**TOTAL**	**248,212.61**

[1]This is the table (revised) presented to the court on behalf of the defender in *Crockett v. Crockett*, 1992 S.C.L.R. 591.

At present date:	£	At present date:	£
(i) 14 Glenorchy Terrace, Edinburgh . . .	100,000	(i) 10 Ventnor Terrace, Edinburgh . . .	90,000
(ii) one-half interest in Scottish Widows Insurance Policy . . .	6,449	(ii) one-half interest in Scottish Widows Insurance Policy . . .	6,449
[(iii) 38.03% interest in C.C. Hornig & Son Ltd Executive Pension Fund . . .	54,390]	[(iii) 61.97% interest in C.C. Hornig & Son Ltd Executive Pension Fund . . .	88,628]
[(iv) personal jewellery	8,000]	[(iv) interest in Legal & General Pension Plan Policy . . .	7,444]
		(v) interest in Liverpool and Victoria Insurance Policy	10,343
		(vi) shares in Abbey National . . .	2,000
		(vii) cash in Bank of Scotland . . .	3,567.22
		(viii) cash in Bank of Scotland . . .	41,136.52
		(ix) shares in C.C. Hornig & Son Ltd	nil
		[(x) personal jewellery	8,000)]
	--------------		--------------
SUBTOTAL	**106,449***	**SUBTOTAL**	**153,495.74***
Less (a) mortgage . . .	16,000	*Less* (a) mortgage . . .	30,312
(b) one-half liability to Bank of Scotland . . .	273.39	(b) one-half liability to Bank of Scotland . . .	273.39
(c) cheque account overdraft with Bank of Scotland . . .	2,000	(c) current account overdraft with Bank of Scotland . . .	8,620
(d) legal fees . . .	10,000	(d) legal fees . . .	10,000
	--------------		--------------
	28,273.39		49,205.39
TOTAL	**78,175.61**	**TOTAL**	**104,290.35**
*excludes (illiquid) pension(s) and personal jewellery			

PENSIONS ON DIVORCE REGULATIONS

A. The Divorce etc. (Pensions) (Scotland) Regulations 2000[1]
(S.S.I. 2000 No. 112)

The Scottish Ministers, in exercise of the powers conferred upon them by section 10(8) and (8A) of the Family Law (Scotland) Act 1985 and of all other powers enabling them in that behalf, hereby make the following Regulations:

Citation, commencement and application

1.—(1) These Regulations may be cited as the Divorce etc. (Pensions) (Scotland) Regulations 2000 and shall come into force on 1st December 2000.

(2) These Regulations shall not affect any action for divorce commenced before 1st December 2000 or any action for declarator of nullity of marriage commenced before that date.

---

[1]As amended by S.S.I. 2000 No. 392.

(3) For the purposes of these Regulations an action for divorce or action for declarator of nullity of marriage shall commence on the date of service of the summons.

Interpretation

2.—(1) In these Regulations —
"the Act" means the Family Law (Scotland) Act 1985;
"the 1993 Act" means the Pension Schemes Act 1993;
"the 1995 Act" means the Pensions Act 1995;
"the 1999 Act" means the Welfare Reform and Pensions Act 1999;
"active member" has the same meaning as in section 124(1) of the 1995 Act;
"benefits under a pension arrangement" has the same meaning as in section 27(1), subject to section 12A(10) and any reference to the rights or interests which a party has or may have in benefits under a pension arrangement includes a reference to the rights or interests which a party has or may have in such benefits which are payable in respect of the death of either party;
"deferred member" has the meaning given by section 124(1) of the 1995 Act;
"a party" means a party to a marriage;
"occupational pension scheme" has the same meaning as in section 1 of the 1993 Act;
"pension arrangement" has the same meaning as in section 46(1) of the 1999 Act;
"person responsible for a pension arrangement" has the same meaning as in section 46(2) of the 1999 Act;
"personal pension scheme" has the same meaning as in section 1 of the 1993 Act but as if the reference to employed earners in that definition were to any earner;
"matrimonial property" has the same meaning as in section 10(4) and (5);
"relevant date" has the same meaning as in section 10(3);
"salary related occupational pension scheme" has the meaning given in regulation 1A of the Occupational Pension Schemes (Transfer Values) Regulations 1996.
(2) Any reference in these Regulations to —

(*a*) a numbered section is to a section bearing that number in the Act;
(*b*) a numbered regulation is to a regulation bearing that number in these Regulations.

Valuation

3.—(1) The value of any benefits under a pension arrangement shall be calculated and verified for the purposes of the Act, in accordance with this regulation and regulation 4.

(2) The value, as at the relevant date, of the rights or interests which a party has or may have in any benefit under a pension arrangement as at that date shall be calculated as follows and in accordance with —

- (*a*) paragraph (3), if the party with pension rights is a deferred member of an occupational pension scheme;
- (*b*) paragraph (4), if the party with pension rights is an active member of an occupational pension scheme;
- (*c*) paragraphs (5) and (6), if —
  - (i) the party with pension rights is a member of a personal pension scheme; or
  - (ii) those rights are contained in a retirement annuity contract; or
- (*d*) paragraphs (7) to (9), if —
  - (i) the pension of the party with pension rights is in payment;
  - (ii) the party with the pension rights holds an annuity other than a retirement annuity contract; or
  - (iii) the rights of the party with pension rights are contained in a deferred annuity contract other than a retirement annuity contract.

(3) Where the party with pension rights is a deferred member of an occupational pension scheme, the value of the benefits which he has under that scheme shall be taken to be —

- (*a*) in the case of an occupational pension scheme other than a salary related scheme, the cash equivalent to which he acquired a right under section 94(1)(a) of the 1993 Act (right to cash equivalent) on the termination of his pensionable service, calculated on the assumption that he has made an application under section 95 of that Act (ways of taking right to cash equivalent) on the date on which the request for the valuation was received; or
- (*b*) in the case of a salary related occupational pension scheme, the guaranteed cash equivalent to which he would have acquired a right under section 94(1)(aa) of the 1993 Act if he had made an application under section 95(1) of that Act, calculated on the assumption that he has made an application under section 95 of that Act on the date on which the request for the valuation was received.

(4) Where the party with pension rights is an active member of an occupational pension scheme, the valuation of the benefits which he has accrued under that scheme shall be calculated and verified —

(*a*) on the assumption that the member has made a request for an estimate of the cash equivalent that would be available to him were his pensionable service to terminate on the date on which the request for valuation was received; and

(*b*) in accordance with regulation 11 and Schedule 1 to the Occupational Pension Schemes (Transfer Values) Regulations 1996 (disclosure).

(5) Where the party with pension rights is a member of a personal pension scheme, or those rights are contained in a retirement annuity contract, the value of the benefits which he has under that scheme or contract shall be taken to be the cash equivalent to which he would have acquired a right under section 94(1)(b) of the 1993 Act, if he had made an application under section 95(1) of that Act on the date on which the request for the valuation was received.

(6) In relation to a personal pension scheme which is comprised in a retirement annuity contract made before 4th January 1988, paragraph (5) shall apply as if such were not excluded from the scope of Chapter IV of Part IV of the 1993 Act by section 93(1)(b) of that Act (scope of Chapter IV).

(7) Except in a case to which, or to the extent to which, paragraph (9) applies, the cash equivalent of benefits in respect of a person referred to in paragraph (2)(d) shall be calculated and verified in such a manner as may be approved in particular cases by —

(*a*) a Fellow of the Institute of Actuaries;

(*b*) a Fellow of the Faculty of Actuaries; or

(*c*) a person with actuarial qualifications who is approved by the Scottish Ministers, at the request of the person responsible for the pension arrangement in question, as being a proper person to act for the purposes of this regulation in connection with that arrangement.

(8) Except in a case to which paragraph (9) applies, cash equivalents are to be calculated and verified by adopting methods and making assumptions which —

(*a*) if not determined by the person responsible for the pension arrangement in question, are notified to him by the actuary referred to in paragraph (7); and (*b*) are certified by the actuary to the person responsible for the pension arrangement in question as being consistent with the "Retirement Benefit Scheme-Transfer Values (GN11)" published by the Institute of Actuaries and the Faculty of Actuaries and current at the date on which the request for valuation is received.

(9) Where the cash equivalent, or any portion of it represents rights to money purchase benefits under the pension arrangement in question of the party with pension rights, and those rights do not fall, either wholly or in part, to be valued in a manner which involves making estimates of the value of benefits, then that cash equivalent, or that portion of it, shall be calculated and verified in such manner as may be approved in particular cases by the person responsible for the pension arrangement in question, and by adopting methods consistent with the requirement of Chapter IV of Part IV of the 1993 Act (protection for early leavers-transfer values).

(10) For the purposes of paragraph (3), (4), (7) or (9), section 93(1)(a)(i) of the 1993 Act (scope of Chapter IV) shall be construed as if the words "at least one year" had been omitted from that provision.

(11) For the purposes of paragraphs (3), (4) and (5), where the date on which the request for valuation was received is more than 12 months after the relevant date then the date for the purpose of valuing the benefits shall be the relevant date.

Valuation of relevant state scheme rights

3A. — (1) The value of any benefits in relevant state scheme rights shall be calculated and verified for the purposes of the Act in accordance with this regulation and regulation 4.

(2) The value, as at the relevant date, of the rights or interests which a party has or may have in any benefits in relevant state scheme rights shall be calculated and verified in such manner as may be approved by the Government Actuary.

(3) For the purposes of this regulation the date for the purposes of valuing any benefits in relevant state scheme rights shall be the date on which the request for valuation was received except where the date on which the request for valuation was received is more than 12 months after the relevant date where the date for the purpose of valuing the benefits shall be the relevant date.

Apportionment

4. The value of the proportion of any rights or interests which a party has or may have in any benefits under a pension arrangement or in relevant state scheme rights as at the relevant date and which forms part of the matrimonial property by virtue of section 10(5) shall be calculated in accordance with the following formula —

$$\frac{A \ \times \ B}{C}$$

where —

A is the value of these rights or interests in any benefits under the pension arrangement which is calculated, as at the relevant date, in accordance with paragraph (2) of regulation 3 above; and

B is the period of C which falls within the period of the marriage of the parties before the relevant date and, if there is no such period, the amount shall be zero; and

C is the period of the membership of that party in the pension arrangement before the relevant date.

Revocation and saving

5.—(1) Subject to paragraph (2), there are hereby revoked:

(*a*) regulation 3, and regulations 1 and 2 thereof insofar as they relate to regulation 3, of the Divorce etc. (Pensions) (Scotland) Regulations 1996;

(*b*) regulation 4, and regulations 1, 2 and 3 thereof insofar as they relate to regulation 4, of the Divorce etc. (Pensions) (Scotland) Amendment Regulations 1997.

(2) Notwithstanding paragraph (1), the Regulations specified in paragraph (1) shall continue to apply to any action for divorce commenced before 1st December 2000 or any action for declarator of nullity of marriage commenced before that date.

B. The Divorce etc. (Notification and Treatment of Pensions) (Scotland) Regulations 2000 (S.I. 2000/1050)

The Secretary of State for Social Security, in exercise of the powers conferred upon him by section 23(1)(a)(ii) of the Welfare Reform and Pensions Act 1999 and sections 10(8) and (10) and 12A(8) of the Family Law (Scotland) Act 1985, and of all other powers enabling him in that behalf hereby makes the following Regulations:

Citation, commencement and interpretation

1.—(1) These Regulations may be cited as the Divorce etc. (Notification and Treatment of Pensions) (Scotland) Regulations 2000 and shall come into force on 1st December 2000.

(2) These Regulations shall not affect any action for divorce commenced before 1st December 2000 or any action for declarator of nullity of marriage commenced before that date.

(3) In these Regulations —

"the 1985 Act" means the Family Law (Scotland) Act 1985;

"the 1999 Act" means the Welfare Reform and Pensions Act 1999;

"the other party" means the other party to a marriage;

"pension arrangement" has the meaning given by section 46(1) of the 1999 Act,

and any expression used in these Regulations to which a meaning is assigned in section 12A of the 1985 Act shall have the same meaning in these Regulations as in that section

Notices under section 12A of the 1985 Act

2.—(1) This regulation applies in the circumstances set out in section 12A (6)(a) of the 1985 Act.

(2) Where this regulation applies, the person responsible for the first pension arrangement shall, within 21 days after the date of the transfer, give notice in accordance with the following paragraphs of this regulation to: —

(*a*) the person responsible for the new pension arrangement; and

(*b*) the other party.

(3) The notice to the person responsible for the new pension arrangement shall consist of a copy of the following documents: —

(*a*) every order made under section 12A(2) or (3) of the 1985 Act imposing any requirement upon the person responsible for the first pension arrangement;

(*b*) any order under section 12A(7) of the 1985 Act varying such an order;

(*c*) any notice given by any other party to the person responsible for the first pension arrangement under regulation 5 of these Regulations; and

(*d*) where the rights of the liable party under the first pension arrangement were derived in whole or in part from a transfer from a previous pension arrangement, any notice under paragraph (2)(a) of this regulation given on the occasion of that transfer.

(4) The notice to the other party shall contain the following particulars —

    (*a*) the fact that all the accrued rights of the liable party under the first pension arrangement have been transferred to the new pension arrangement;

    (*b*) the date on which the transfer takes effect;

    (*c*) the name and address of the person responsible for the new pension arrangement; and

    (*d*) the fact that the order made under section 12A(2) or (3) of the 1985 Act is to have effect as if it had been made instead of respect of the person responsible for the new pension arrangement.

3.—(1) This regulation applies where —

    (*a*) section 12A(6) of the 1985 Act has already applied; and

    (*b*) the liable party has transferred all his accrued rights for the second or any subsequent time to another new pension arrangement.

(2) Where this regulation applies, the person responsible for the pension arrangement from which the transfer is made to the other new pension arrangement shall, within 21 days after the date of the transfer, give notice to the other party of —

    (*a*) the fact that all accrued rights of the liable party have been transferred to the other new pension arrangement;

    (*b*) the date on which the transfer takes effect;

    (*c*) the name and address of the person responsible for the other new pension arrangement; and

    (*d*) the fact that the court may, on an application by any person having interest, vary any order under section 12A(2) or (3) of the 1985 Act.

4.—(1) This regulation applies where —

    (*a*) an order under section 12A(2) or (3) of the 1985 Act has been made imposing any requirement on the person responsible for the pension arrangement; and

    (*b*) some but not all of the accrued rights of the liable party have been transferred from the pension arrangement.

(2) Where this regulation applies, the person responsible for the pension arrangement from which the transfer is made shall, within 21 days after the date of the transfer, give notice to the other party of —

(*a*) the likely extent of the reduction in the benefits payable under the arrangement as a result of the transfer;

(*b*) the name and address of the person responsible for the pension arrangement under which the liable party has acquired transfer of credits as a result of the transfer;

(*c*) the date on which the transfer takes effect; and

(*d*) the fact that the court may, on an application by any person having an interest, vary an order under section 12A(2) or (3) of the 1985 Act.

5.—(1) This regulation applies where —

(*a*) an order under section 12A(2) or (3) of the 1985 Act has been made imposing any requirements on the person responsible for the pension arrangement; and

(*b*) there has been a change in the name or address of the other party.

(2) Where this regulation applies, the other party shall, within 21 days of the occurrence of the change mentioned in paragraph (1)(b) of this regulation, give notice of that change to the person responsible for the pension arrangement.

6.—(1) This regulation applies where —

(*a*) a transfer of accrued rights has taken place in the circumstances set out in section 12A(6)(a) of the 1985 Act;

(*b*) notice has been given in accordance with regulation 2(2)(a) and (b) of these Regulations; and

(*c*) there has been a change in the name or address of the other party but the other party has not, before receiving notice under regulation (2)(2)(b), given notice of that change to the person responsible for the first pension arrangement under regulation 5(2) of these Regulations.

(2) Where this regulation applies, the reference in regulation 5(2) to the person responsible for the pension arrangement shall be construed as a reference to the person responsible for the new pension arrangement and not the person responsible for the first pension arrangement.

(3) Subject to paragraph (4), where this regulation applies and the other party, within one year from the transfer, gives to the person responsible for the first pension arrangement notice of that change in purported compliance with regulation 5(2), the person responsible for the first pension arrangement shall —

(*a*) send that notice to the person responsible for the new pension arrangement; and

(*b*) give the other party a second notice under regulation 2(2)(b),

and the other party shall thereupon be deemed to have given notice under regulation 5(2) to the person responsible for the new pension arrangement.

(4) Upon complying with paragraph (3) above, the person responsible for the first pension arrangement shall be discharged from any further obligation under that paragraph, whether in relation to the change in question or any further change in the name or address of the other party which may be notified to them by the other party.

7. A notice under these Regulations may be sent by ordinary first class post to the last known address of the intended recipient and shall be deemed to have been received on the seventh day following the date of posting.

Revocations

8.—(1) Subject to paragraph (2), there are hereby revoked: —

(*a*) regulations 4 to 10 of the Divorce etc. (Pensions) (Scotland) Regulations 1996, and regulations 1 and 2 thereof insofar as they relate to regulations 4 to 10; and

(*b*) regulations 5 to 8 of the Divorce etc. (Pensions) (Scotland) Amendment Regulations 1997, and regulations 1, 2 and 3 thereof insofar as they relate to regulations 5 to 8.

(2) Notwithstanding paragraph (1), the regulations specified in paragraph (1) shall continue to apply to any action for divorce commenced before 1st December 2000 and any action for declarator of marriage commenced before that date.

C. The Pensions on Divorce etc. (Provision of Information) Regulations 2000[2] (S.I. 2000/1048)

The Secretary of Sate for Social Security, in exercise of the powers conferred upon him by sections 168(1) and (4), 181(1) and 182(2) and (3) of the Pension Schemes Act 1993 and sections 23(1)(a), (b)(i), (c)(i) and (2), 34(1)(b)(ii), 45(1) and 83(4) and (6) of the Welfare Reform and Pensions Act 1999 and of all other powers enabling him in that behalf, after consulting such persons as he considered appropriate, hereby makes the following Regulations:

---

[2]As amended by S.I. 2000/2691.

Citation, commencement and interpretation

1.—(1) These Regulations may be cited as the Pensions on Divorce etc. (Provision of Information) Regulations 2000 and shall come into force on 1st December 2000.

(2) In these Regulations —

"the 1993 Act" means the Pension Schemes Act 1993;

"the 1995 Act" means the Pensions Act 1995;

"the 1999 Act" means the Welfare Reform and Pensions Act 1999;

"the Charging Regulations" means the Pensions on Divorce etc. (Charging) Regulations 2000;

"the Implementation and Discharge of Liability Regulations" means the Pension Sharing (Implementation and Discharge of Liability) Regulations 2000;

"the Valuation Regulations" means the Pension Sharing (Valuation) Regulations 2000;

"active member" has the meaning given by section 124(1) of the 1995 Act;

"day" means any day other than —

(*a*) Christmas Day or Good Friday; or

(*b*) a bank holiday, that is to say, a day which is, or is to be observed as, a bank holiday or a holiday under Schedule 1 to the Banking and Financial Dealings Act 1971;

"deferred member" has the meaning given by section 124(1) of the 1995 Act;

"implementation period" has the meaning given by section 34(1) of the 1999 Act;

"member" means a person who has rights to future benefits, or has rights to benefits payable, under a pension arrangement;

"money purchase benefits" has the meaning given by section 181(1) of the 1993 Act;

"normal benefit age" has the meaning given by section 101B of the 1993 Act;

"notice of discharge of liability" means a notice issued to the member and his former spouse by the person responsible for a pension arrangement when that person has discharged his liability in respect of a pension credit in accordance with Schedule 5 to the 1999 Act;

"notice of implementation" means a notice issued by the person responsible for a pension arrangement to the member and his former spouse at the beginning of the implementation period notifying them of the day on which the implementation period for the pension credit begins;

"occupational pension scheme" has the meaning given by section 1 of the 1993 Act;

"the party with pension rights" and "the other party" have the meanings given by section 25D(3) of the Matrimonial Causes Act 1997;

"pension arrangement" has the meaning given in section 46(1) of the 1999 Act;

"pension credit" means a credit under section 29(1)(b) of the 1999 Act;

"pension credit benefit" means the benefits payable under a pension arrangement or a qualifying arrangement to or in respect of a person by virtue of rights under the arrangement in question which are attributable (directly or indirectly) to a pension credit;

"pension credit rights" means rights to future benefits under a pension arrangement or a qualifying arrangement which are attributable (directly or indirectly) to a pension credit;

"pension sharing order or provision" means an order or provision which is mentioned in section 28(1) of the 1999 Act;

"pensionable service" has the meaning given by section 124(1) of the 1995 Act;

"person responsible for a pension arrangement" has the meaning given by section 46(2) of the 1999 Act;

"personal pension scheme" has the meaning given by section 1 of the 1993 Act;

"qualifying arrangement" has the meaning given by paragraph 6 of Schedule 5 to the 1999 Act;

"retirement annuity contract" means a contract or scheme approved under Chapter III of Part XIV of the Income and Corporation Taxes Act 1988;

"salary related occupational pension scheme" has the meaning given by regulation 1A of the Occupational Pension Schemes (Transfer Values) Regulations 1996;

"the Regulatory Authority" means the Occupational Pensions Regulatory Authority;

"transfer day" has the meaning given by section 29(8) or the 1999 Act;

"transferee" has the meaning given by section 29(8) of the 1999 Act;

"transferor" has the meaning given by section 29(8) of the 1999 Act;

"trustees or managers" has the meaning given by section 46(1) of the 1999 Act.

Basic information about pensions and divorce

2.—(1) The requirements imposed on a person responsible for a pension arrangement for the purposes of section 23(1)(a) of the 1999 Act (supply of pension information in connection with divorce etc.) are that he shall furnish —

(*a*) on request from a member, the information referred to in paragraphs (2) and (3)(b) to (f);

(*b*) on request from the spouse of a member, the information referred to in paragraph (3); or

(*c*) pursuant to an order of the court, the information referred to in paragraph (2), (3) or (4),

to the member, the spouse of the member, or, as the case may be, to the court.

(2) The information in this paragraph is a valuation of pension rights or benefits accrued under that member's pension arrangement.

(3) The information in this paragraph is —

(*a*) a statement that on request from the member, or pursuant to an order of the court, a valuation of pension rights or benefits accrued under that member's pension arrangement, will be provided to the member, or, as the case may be, to the court;

(*b*) a statement summarising the way in which the valuation referred to in paragraph (2) and sub-paragraph (a) is calculated;

(*c*) the pension benefits which are included in a valuation referred to in paragraph (2) and sub-paragraph (a);

(*d*) whether the person responsible for the pension arrangement offers membership to a person entitled to a pension credit, and if so, the types of benefits available to pension credit members under that arrangement;

(*e*) whether the person responsible for the pension arrangements intends to discharge his liability for a pension credit other than by offering membership to a person entitled to a pension credit; and

(*f*) the schedule of charges which the person responsible for the pension arrangement will levy in accordance with regulation 2(2) of the Charging Regulations (general requirements as to charges).

(4) The information in this paragraph is any other information relevant to any power with respect to the matters specified in section 23(1)(a) of the 1999 Act and which is not specified in Schedule 1 or 2 to the Occupational Pension Schemes (Disclosure of Information) Regulations 1996 (basic information about the scheme and information to be made available to individuals), or in Schedule 1 or 2 to the Personal Pension Schemes (Disclosure of Information) Regulations 1987 (basic information about the scheme and information to be made available to individuals), in a case where either of those Regulations applies.

(5) Where the member's request for, or the court order for the provision of, information includes a request for, or an order for the

provision of, a valuation under paragraph (2), the person responsible for the pension arrangement shall furnish all the information requested, or ordered, to the member —

(a) within 3 months beginning with the date the person responsible for the pension arrangement receives that request or order for the provision of the information;

(b) within 6 weeks beginning with the date the person responsible for the pension arrangement receives that request, or order, for the provision of the information, if the member has notified that person on the date of the request or order that the information is needed in connection with proceedings commenced under any of the provisions referred to in section 23(1)(a) of the 1999 Act; or

(c) within such shorter period specified by the court in an order requiring the person responsible for the pension arrangement to provide a valuation in accordance with paragraph (2).

(6) Where —

(a) the member's request for, or the court order for the provision of, information does not include a request or an order for a valuation under paragraph (2); or

(b) the member's spouse requests the information specified in paragraph (3),

the person responsible for the pension arrangement shall furnish that information to the member, his spouse, or the court as the case may be, within one month beginning with the date that person responsible for the pension arrangement receives the request for, or the court order for the provision of, the information.

(7) At the same time as furnishing the information referred to in paragraph (1), the person responsible for a pension arrangement may furnish the information specified in regulation 4(2) (provision of information in response to a notification that a pension sharing order or provision may be made).

Information about pensions and divorce: valuation of pension benefits

3.—(1) Where an application for financial relief under any of the provisions referred to in section 23(1)(a)(i) or (iii) of the 1999 Act (supply of pension information in connection with domestic and overseas divorce etc. in England and Wales and corresponding Northern Ireland powers) has been made or is in contemplation, the valuation of benefits under a pension arrangement shall be calculated and verified for the purposes of regulation 2 of these Regulations in accordance with —

(*a*) paragraph (3), if the person with pension rights is a deferred member of an occupational pension scheme;

(*b*) paragraph (4), if the person with pension rights is an active member of an occupational pension scheme;

(*c*) paragraphs (5) and (6), if —

    (i) the person with pension rights is a member of a personal pension scheme; or

    (ii) those pension rights are contained in a retirement annuity contract; or

(*d*) paragraphs (7) to (9), if —

    (i) the pension of the person with pension rights is in payment;

    (ii) the rights of the person with pension rights are contained in an annuity contract other than a retirement annuity contract; or

    (iii) the rights of the person with pension rights are contained in a deferred annuity contract other than a retirement annuity contract.

(2) Where an application for financial provision under any of the provisions referred to in section 23(1)(a)(ii) of the 1999 Act (corresponding Scottish powers) has been made, or is in contemplation, the valuation of benefits under a pension arrangement shall be calculated and verified for the purposes of regulation 2 of these Regulations in accordance with regulation 3 of the Divorce etc. (Pensions) (Scotland) Regulations 2000 (valuation).

(3) Where the person with pension rights is a deferred member of an occupational pension scheme, the value of the benefits which he has under that scheme shall be taken to be —

(*a*) in the case of an occupational pension scheme other than a salary related scheme, the cash equivalent to which he acquired a right under section 94(1)(a) of the 1993 Act (right to cash equivalent) on the termination of his pensionable service, calculated on the assumption that he has made an application under section 95 of that Act (ways of taking right to cash equivalent) on the date on which the request for the valuation was received; or

(*b*) in the case of a salary related occupational pension scheme, the guaranteed cash equivalent to which he would have acquired a right under section 94(1)(aa) of the 1993 Act if he had made an application under section 95(1) of that Act, calculated on the assumption that he has made such an application on the date on which the request for the valuation was received.

(4) Where the person with pension rights is an active member of an occupational pension scheme, the valuation of the benefits which he has accrued under that scheme shall be calculated and verified —

    (*a*)   on the assumption that the member had made a request for an estimate of the cash equivalent that would be available to him were his pensionable service to terminate on the date on which the request for the valuation was received; and

    (*b*)   in accordance with regulation 11 of and Schedule 1 to the Occupational Pension Schemes (Transfer Values) Regulations 1996 (disclosure).

(5) Where the person with pension rights is a member of a personal pension scheme, or those rights are contained in a retirement annuity contract, the value of the benefits which he has under that scheme or contract shall be taken to be the cash equivalent to which he would have acquired a right under section 94(1)(b) of the 1993 Act, if he had made an application under section 95(1) of that Act on the date on which the request for the valuation was received.

(6) In relation to a personal pension scheme which is comprised in a retirement annuity contract made before 4th January 1988, paragraph (5) shall apply as if such a scheme were not excluded from the scope of Chapter IV of Part IV of the 1993 Act by section 93(1)(b) of that Act (scope of Chapter IV).

(7) Except in a case to which, or to the extent to which, paragraph (9) applies, the cash equivalent of benefits in respect of a person referred to in paragraph (1)(d) shall be calculated and verified in such manner as may be approved in a particular case by —

    (*a*)   a Fellow of the Institute of Actuaries;

    (*b*)   a Fellow of the Faculty of Actuaries; or

    (*c*)   a person with other actuarial qualifications who is approved by the Secretary of State, at the request of the person responsible for the pension arrangement in question, as being a proper person to act for the purposes of this regulation in connection with that arrangement.

(8) Except in a case to which paragraph (9) applies, cash equivalents are to be calculated and verified by adopting methods and making assumptions which —

(*a*) if not determined by the person responsible for the pension arrangement in question, are notified to him by an actuary referred to in paragraph (7); and

(*b*) are certified by the actuary to the person responsible for the pension arrangement in question as being consistent with "Retirement Benefit Schemes — Transfer Values (GN11)" published by the Institute of Actuaries and the Faculty of Actuaries and current at the date on which the request for the valuation is received.

(9) Where the cash equivalent, or any portion of it represents rights to money purchase benefits under the pension arrangement in question of the person with pension rights, and those rights do not fall, either wholly or in part, to be valued in a manner which involves making estimates of the value of benefits, then that cash equivalent, or that portion of it, shall be calculated and verified in such manner as may be approved in a particular case by the person responsible for the pension arrangement in question, and by adopting methods consistent with the requirements of Chapter IV of Part IV of the 1993 Act (protection for early leavers — transfer values).

(10) Where paragraph (3), (4) or (9) has effect by reference to provisions of Chapter IV of Part IV of the 1993 Act, section 93(1)(a)(i) of that Act (scope of Chapter IV) shall apply to those provisions as if the words "at least one year" had been omitted from section 93(1)(a)(i).

Provision of information in response to a notification that a pension sharing order or provision may be made

4.—(1) A person responsible for a pension arrangement shall furnish the information specified in paragraph (2) to the member or to the court, as the case may be —

(*a*) within 21 days beginning with the date that the person responsible for the pension arrangement received the notification that a pension sharing order or provision may be made; or

(*b*) if the court has specified a date which is outside the 21 days referred to in sub-paragraph (a), by that date.

(2) The information referred to in paragraph (1) is —

(*a*) the full name of the pension arrangement and address to which any order or provision referred to in section 28(1) of the 1999 Act (activation of pension sharing) should be sent;

(*b*) in the case of an occupational pension scheme, whether the scheme is winding up, and, if so, —

      (i)   the date on which the winding up commenced; and

     (ii) the name and address of the trustees who are dealing with the winding up;

(*c*) in the case of an occupational pension scheme, whether a cash equivalent of the member's pension rights, if calculated on the date the notification referred to in paragraph (1)(a) was received by the trustees or managers of that scheme, would be reduced in accordance with the provisions of regulation 8(4), (6) or (12) of the Occupational Pension Schemes (Transfer Values) Regulations 1996 (further provisions as to reductions of cash equivalents);

(*d*) whether the person responsible for the pension arrangement is aware that the member's rights under the pension arrangement are subject to any, and if so, to specify which, of the following —

      (i)   any order or provision specified in section 28(1) of the 1999 Act;

     (ii) an order under section 23 of the Matrimonial Causes Act 1973 (financial provision orders in connection with divorce etc.), so far as it includes provision made by virtue of section 25B or 25C of that Act (powers to include provisions about pensions);

    (iii) an order under section 12A(2) or (3) of the Family Law (Scotland) Act 1985 (powers in relation to pensions lump sums when making a capital sum order) which relates to benefits or future benefits to which the member is entitled under the pension arrangement;

    (iv) an order under Article 25 of the Matrimonial Causes (Northern Ireland) Order 1978, so far as it includes provision made by virtue of Article 27B or 27C of that Order (Northern Ireland powers corresponding to those mentioned in paragraph (2)(d)(ii));

     (v) a forfeiture order;

    (vi) a bankruptcy order;

   (vii) an award of sequestration on a member's estate or the making of the appointment on his estate of a judicial factor under section 41 of the Solicitors (Scotland) Act 1980 (appointment of judicial factor);

(*e*) whether the member's rights under the pension arrangement include rights specified in regulation 2 of the Valuation Regulations (rights under a pension arrangement which are not shareable);

(*f*) if the person responsible for the pension arrangement has not at an earlier stage provided the following information, whether that person requires the charges specified in regulation 3 (charges recoverable in respect of the provision of basic information), 5 (charges in respect of pension sharing activity), or 6 (additional amounts recoverable in respect of pension sharing activity) of the Charging Regulations to be paid before the commencement of the implementation period, and if so, —

    (i) whether that person requires those charges to be paid in full; or

    (ii) the proportion of those charges which he requires to be paid;

(*g*) whether the person responsible for the pension arrangement may levy additional charges specified in regulation 6 of the Charging Regulations, and if so, the scale of the additional charges which are likely to be made;

(*h*) whether the member is a trustee of the pension arrangement;

(*i*) whether the person responsible for the pension arrangement may request information about the member's state of health from the member if a pension sharing order or provision were to be made;

(*j*) (repealed); and

(*k*) whether the person responsible for the pension arrangement requires information additional to that specified in regulation 5 (information required by the person responsible for the pension arrangement before the implementation period may begin) in order to implement the pension sharing order or provision.

Information required by the person responsible for the pension arrangement before the implementation period may begin

5. The information prescribed for the purposes of section 34(1)(b) of the 1999 Act (information relating to the transferor and the transferee which the person responsible for the pension arrangement must receive) is —

(*a*) in relation to the transferor —

    (i) all names by which the transferor has been known;

    (ii) date of birth;

    (iii) address;

    (iv) National Insurance number;

    (v) the name of the pension arrangement to which the pension sharing order or provision relates; and

    (vi) the transferor's membership or policy number in that pension arrangement;

(*b*) in relation to the transferee —

    (i) all names by which the transferee has been known;

    (ii) date of birth;

     (iii) address;

     (iv) National Insurance number; and

     (v) if the transferee is a member of the pension arrangement from which the pension credit is derived, his membership or policy number in that pension arrangement;

  (*c*) where the transferee has given his consent in accordance with paragraph 1(3)(c), 3(3)(c) or 4(2)(c) of Schedule 5 to the 1999 Act (mode of discharge of liability for a pension credit) to the payment of the pension credit to the person responsible for a qualifying arrangement —

     (i) the full name of that qualifying arrangement;

     (ii) its address;

     (iii) if known, the transferee's membership number or policy number in that arrangement; and

     (iv) the name or title, business address, business telephone number, and, where available, the business facsimile number and electronic mail address of a person who may be contacted in respect of the discharge of liability for the pension credit;

  (*d*) where the rights from which the pension credit is derived are held in an occupational pension scheme which is being wound up, whether the transferee has given an indication whether he wishes to transfer his pension credit rights which may have been reduced in accordance with the provisions of regulation 16(1) of the Implementation and Discharge of Liability Regulations (adjustments to the amount of the pension credit — occupational pension schemes which are underfunded on the valuation day) to a qualifying arrangement; and

  (*e*) any information requested by the person responsible for the pension arrangement in accordance with regulation 4(2)(i) or (k).

Provision of information after the death of the person entitled to the pension credit before liability in respect of the pension credit has been discharged

6.—(1) Where the person entitled to the pension credit dies before the person responsible for the pension arrangement has discharged his liability in respect of the pension credit, the person responsible for the pension arrangement shall, within 21 days of the date of receipt of the notification of the death of the person entitled to the pension credit, notify in writing any person whom the person responsible for the pension arrangement considers should be notified of the matters specified in paragraph (2).

(2) The matters specified in this paragraph are —

(*a*) how the person responsible for the pension arrangement intends to discharge his liability in respect of the pension credit;

(*b*) whether the person responsible for the pension arrangement intends to recover charges from the person nominated to receive pension credit benefits, in accordance with regulations 2 to 9 of the Charging Regulations, and if so, a copy of the schedule of charges issued to the parties to pension sharing in accordance with regulation 2(2)(b) of the Charging Regulations (general requirements as to charges); and

(*c*) a list of any further information which the person responsible for the pension arrangement requires in order to discharge his liability in respect of the pension credit.

Provision of information after receiving a pension sharing order or provision

7.—(1) A person responsible for a pension arrangement who is in receipt of a pension sharing order or provision relating to that arrangement shall provide in writing to the transferor and transferee, or, where regulation 6(1) applies, to the person other than the person entitled to the pension credit referred to in regulation 6 of the Implementation and Discharge of Liability Regulations (discharge of liability in respect of a pension credit following the death of the person entitled to the pension credit), as the case may be, —

(*a*) a notice in accordance with the provisions of regulation 7(1) of the Charging Regulations (charges in respect of pension sharing activity — postponement of implementation period);

(*b*) a list of information relating to the transferor or the transferee, or, where regulation 6(1) applies, the person other than the person entitled to the pension credit referred to in regulation 6 of the Implementation and Discharge of Liability Regulations, as the case may be, which —

  (i)   has been requested in accordance with regulation 4(2)(i) and (k), or, where appropriate, 6(2)(c), or should have been provided in accordance with regulation 5;

  (ii) the person responsible for the pension arrangement considers he needs in order to begin to implement the pension sharing order or provision; and

  (iii) remains outstanding;

(*c*) a notice of implementation; or

(*d*) a statement by the person responsible for the pension arrangement explaining why he is unable to implement the pension sharing order or agreement.

(2) The information specified in paragraph (1) shall be furnished in accordance with that paragraph within 21 days beginning with —

(*a*) in the case of sub-paragraph (a), (b) or (d) of that paragraph, the day on which the person responsible for the pension arrangement receives the pension sharing order or provision; or

(*b*) in the case of sub-paragraph (c) of that paragraph, the later of the days specified in section 34(1)(a) and (b) of the 1999 Act (implementation period).

Provision of information after the implementation of a pension sharing order or provision

8.—(1) The person responsible for the pension arrangement shall issue a notice of discharge of liability to the transferor and the transferee, or, as the case may be, the person entitled to the pension credit by virtue of regulation 6 of the Implementation and Discharge of Liability Regulations no later than the end of the period of 21 days beginning with the day on which the discharge of liability in respect of the pension credit is completed.

(2) In the case of a transferor whose pension is not in payment, the notice of discharge of liability shall include the following details —

(*a*) the value of the transferor's accrued rights as determined by reference to the cash equivalent value of those rights calculated and verified in accordance with regulation 3 of the Valuation Regulations (calculation and verification of cash equivalents for the purposes of the creation of pension debits and credits);

(*b*) the value of the pension debit;

(*c*) any amount deducted from the value of the pension rights in accordance with regulation 9(2)(c) of the Charging Regulations (charges in respect of pension sharing activity — method of recovery);

(*d*) the value of the transferor's rights after the amounts referred to in sub-paragraphs (b) and (c) have been deducted; and

(*e*) the transfer day.

(3) In the case of a transferor whose pension is in payment, the notice of discharge of liability shall include the following details —

(*a*) the value of the transferor's benefits under the pension arrangement as determined by reference to the cash equivalent value of those rights calculated and verified in accordance with regulation 3 of the Valuation Regulations;

(*b*)   the value of the pension debit;

(*c*)   the amount of the pension which was in payment before liability in respect of the pension credit was discharged;

(*d*)   the amount of pension which is payable following the deduction of the pension debit from the transferor's pension benefits;

(*e*)   the transfer day;

(*f*)   if the person responsible for the pension arrangement intends to recover charges, the amount of any unpaid charges —

    (i)   not prohibited by regulation 2 of the Charging Regulations (general requirements as to charges); and

    (ii)   specified in regulations 3 and 6 of those Regulations;

(*g*)   how the person responsible for the pension arrangement will recover the charges referred to in sub-paragraph (f), including —

    (i)   whether the method of recovery specified in regulation 9(2)(d) of the Charging Regulations will be used;

    (ii)   the date when payment of those charges in whole or in part is required; and

    (iii)   the sum which will be payable by the transferor, or which will be deducted from his pension benefits, on that date.

(4) In the case of a transferee —

(*a*)   whose pension is not in payment; and

(*b*)   who will become a member of the pension arrangement from which the pension credit rights were derived,

the notice of discharge of liability to the transferee shall include the following details —

    (i)   the value of the pension credit;

    (ii)   any amount deducted from the value of the pension credit in accordance with regulation 9(2)(b) of the Charging Regulations;

    (iii)   the value of the pension credit after the amount referred to in sub-paragraph (b)(ii) has been deducted;

    (iv)   the transfer day;

    (v)   any periodical charges the person responsible for the pension arrangement intends to make, including how and when those charges will be recovered from the transferee; and

    (vi)   information concerning membership of the pension arrangement which is relevant to the transferee as a pension credit member.

(5) In the case of a transferee who is transferring his pension credit rights out of the pension arrangement from which those rights were

derived, the notice of discharge of liability to the transferee shall include the following details —

(*a*) the value of the pension credit;

(*b*) any amount deducted from the value of the pension credit in accordance with regulation 9(2)(b) of the Charging Regulations;

(*c*) the value of the pension credit after the amount referred to in sub-paragraph (b) has been deducted;

(*d*) the transfer day; and

(*e*) details of the pension arrangement, including its name, address, reference number, telephone number, and, where available, the business facsimile number and electronic mail address, to which the pension credit has been transferred.

(6) In the case of a transferee, who has reached normal benefit age on the transfer day, and in respect of whose pension credit liability has been discharged in accordance with paragraph 1(2), 2(2), 3(2) or 4(4) of Schedule 5 to the 1999 Act (pension credits: mode of discharge — funded pension schemes, unfunded public service pension schemes, other unfunded pension schemes, or other pension arrangements), the notice of discharge of liability to the transferee shall include the following details —

(*a*) the amount of pension credit benefit which is to be paid to the transferee;

(*b*) the date when the pension credit benefit is to be paid to the transferee;

(*c*) the transfer day;

(*d*) if the person responsible for the pension arrangement intends to recover charges, the amount of any unpaid charges —
   (i)   not prohibited by regulation 2 of the Charging Regulations; and
   (ii) specified in regulations 3 and 6 of those Regulations; and

(*e*) how the person responsible for the pension arrangement will recover the charges referred to in sub-paragraph (d), including —
   (i)   whether the method of recovery specified in regulation 9(2)(e) of the Charging Regulations will be used;
   (ii) the date when payment of those charges in whole or in part is required; and
   (iii) the sum which will be payable by the transferee, or which will be deducted from his pension credit benefits, on that date.

(7) In the case of a person entitled to the pension credit by virtue of regulation 6 of the Implementation and Discharge of Liability Regulations, the notice of discharge of liability shall include the following details —

(a) the value of the pension credit rights as determined in accordance with regulation 10 of the Implementation and Discharge of Liability Regulations (calculation of the value of appropriate rights);

(b) any amount deducted from the value of the pension credit in accordance with regulation 9(2)(b) of the Charging Regulations;

(c) the value of the pension credit;

(d) the transfer day; and

(e) any periodical charges the person responsible for the pension arrangement intends to make, including how and when those charges will be recovered from the payments made to the person entitled to the pension credit by virtue of regulation 6 of the Implementation and Discharge of Liability Regulations.

Penalties

9. Where any trustee or manager of an occupational pension scheme fails, without reasonable excuse, to comply with any requirement imposed under regulation 6, 7 or 8, the Regulatory Authority may require that trustee or manager to pay within 28 days from the date of its imposition, a penalty which shall not exceed —

(a) £200 in the case of an individual, and

(b) £1,000 in any other case.

Provision of information after receipt of an earmarking order

10.—(1) The person responsible for the pension arrangement shall, within 21 days beginning with the day that he receives —

(a) an order under section 23 of the Matrimonial Causes Act 1973, so far as it includes provision made by virtue of section 25B or 25C of that Act (powers to include provision about pensions);

(b) an order under section 12A(2) or (3) of the Family Law (Scotland) Act 1985; or

(c) an order under Article 25 of the Matrimonial Causes (Northern Ireland) Order 1978, so far as it includes provision made by virtue of Article 27B or 27C of that Order (Northern Ireland powers corresponding to those mentioned in sub-paragraph (a)), issue to the party with pension rights and the other party a notice which includes the information specified in paragraphs (2) and (5), or (3), (4) and (5), as the case may be.

(2) Where an order referred to in paragraph (1)(a), (b) or (c) is made in respect of the pension rights or benefits of a party with pension rights whose pension is not in payment, the notice issued by the person responsible for a pension arrangement to the party with pension rights and the other party shall include a list of the circumstances in respect of any changes of which the party with pension rights or the other party must notify the person responsible for the pension arrangement.

(3) Where an order referred to in paragraph (1)(a) or (c) is made in respect of the pension rights or benefits of a party with pension rights whose pension is in payment, the notice issued by the person responsible for a pension arrangement to the party with pension rights and the other party shall include —

(*a*) the value of the pension rights or benefits of the party with pension rights;

(*b*) the amount of the pension of the party with pension rights after the order has been implemented;

(*c*) the first date when a payment pursuant to the order is to be made; and

(*d*) a list of the circumstances, in respect of any changes of which the party with pension rights or the other party must notify the person responsible for the pension arrangement.

(4) Where an order referred to in paragraph (1)(a) or (c) is made in respect of the pension rights of a party with pension rights whose pension is in payment, the notice issued by the person responsible for a pension arrangement to the party with pension rights shall, in addition to the items specified in paragraph (3), include —

(*a*) the amount of the pension of the party with pension rights which is currently in payment; and

(*b*) the amount of pension which will be payable to the party with pension rights after the order has been implemented.

(5) Where an order referred to in paragraph (1)(a), (b) or (c) is made the notice issued by the person responsible for a pension arrangement to the party with pension rights and the other party shall include —

(*a*) the amount of any charges which remain unpaid by —
    (i)   the party with pension rights; or
    (ii) the other party,

in respect of the provision by the person responsible for the pension arrangement of information about pensions and divorce pursuant to regulation 3 of the Charging Regulations, and in respect of complying with an order referred to in paragraph (1)(a), (b) or (c); and

> (*b*) information as to the manner in which the person responsible for the pension arrangement will recover the charges referred to in sub-paragraph (a), including —
> > (i) the date when payment of those charges in whole or in part is required;
> > (ii) the sum which will be payable by the party with pension rights or the other party, as the case may be; and
> > (iii) whether the sun will be deducted from payments of pension to the party with pension rights, or, as the case may be, from payments to be made to the other party pursuant to an order referred to in paragraph (1)(a), (b) or (c).

D. The Pensions on Divorce etc. (Charging) Regulations 2000[3] (S.I. 2000/1049)

The Secretary of State for Social Security, in exercise of the powers conferred upon him by sections 23(1)(d) and (3), 24, 41(1) and (2) and 83(4) and (6) of the Welfare Reform and Pensions Act 1999 and of all other powers enabling him in that behalf, after consulting such persons as he considered appropriate hereby makes the following Regulations:

Citation, commencement and interpretation

1.—(1) These Regulations may be cited as the Pensions on Divorce etc. (Charging) Regulations 2000 and shall come into force on 1st December 2000.

(2) In these Regulations, unless the context otherwise requires —

"the 1999 Act" means the Welfare Reform and Pensions Act 1999;
"the Provision of Information Regulations" means the Pensions on Divorce etc. (Provision of Information) Regulations 2000;
"day" means any day other than —
(*a*) Christmas Day or Good Friday; or
(*b*) a bank holiday, that is to say, a day which is, or is to be observed as, a bank holiday or a holiday under Schedule 1 to the Banking and Financial Dealings Act 1971;

---

[3]As amended by S.I. 2000/2691.

"implementation period" has the meaning given by section 34(1) of the 1999 Act;

"normal pension age" has the meaning given by section 180 of the Pension Schemes Act 1993;

"notice of implementation" has the meaning given by regulation 1(2) of the Provision of Information Regulations;

"pension arrangement" has the meaning given to that expression in section 46(1) of the 1999 Act;

"pension credit" means a credit under section 29(1)(b) of the 1999 Act;

"pension credit benefit" has the meaning given by section 101B of the Pensions Schemes Act 1993;

"pension credit rights" has the meaning given by section 101B of the Pension Schemes Act 1993;

"pension sharing activity" has the meaning given by section 41(5) of the 1999 Act;

"pension sharing order or provision" means an order or provision which is mentioned in section 28(1) of the 1999 Act;

"person responsible for a pension arrangement" has the meaning given to that expression in section 46(2) of the 1999 Act;

"the Regulatory Authority" means the Occupational Pensions Regulatory Authority;

"the relevant date" has the meaning given by section 10(3) of the Family Law (Scotland) Act 1985;

"trustees or managers" has the meaning given by section 46(1) of the 1999 Act.

General requirements as to charges

2.—(1) Subject to paragraph (8), a person responsible for a pension arrangement shall not recover any charges incurred in connection with —

(*a*) the provision of information under —
   (i) regulation 2 of the Provision of Information Regulations (basic information about pensions and divorce);
   (ii) regulation 4 of those Regulations (provision of information in response to a notification that a pension sharing order or provision may be made); or
   (iii) regulation 10 of those Regulations (provision of information after receipt of an earmarking order);
(*b*) complying with any order specified in section 24 of the 1999 Act (charges by pension arrangements in relation to earmarking orders); or
(*c*) any descriptions of pension sharing activity specified in regulation 5 of these Regulations,

unless he has complied with the requirements of paragraphs (2) to (5).

(2) The requirements mentioned in paragraph (1) are that the person responsible for a pension arrangement shall, before a pension sharing order or provision is made —

(*a*) inform the member or his spouse, as the case may be, in writing of his intention to recover costs incurred in connection with any of the matters specified in sub-paragraph (a), (b) or (c) of paragraph (1); and

(*b*) provide the member or his spouse, as the case may be, with a written schedule of charges in accordance with paragraphs (3) and (4) in respect of those matters specified in sub-paragraph (a) or (c) of paragraph (1) for which a charge may be recoverable.

(3) No charge shall be recoverable in respect of any of the items mentioned in paragraph (4) unless the person responsible for a pension arrangement has specified in the written schedule of charges mentioned in paragraph (2)(b) that a charge may be recoverable in respect of that item.

(4) The items referred to in paragraph (3) are —

(*a*) the provision of a cash equivalent other than one which is provided in accordance with the provisions of —
  (i)   section 93A or 94 of the 1993 Act (salary related schemes: right to statement of entitlement, and right to cash equivalent);
  (ii) regulation 11(1) of the Occupational Pension Schemes (Transfer Values) Regulations 1996 (disclosure); or
  (iii) regulation 5 (information to be made available to individuals) of, and paragraph 2(b) of Schedule 2 (provision of cash equivalent) to the Personal Pension Schemes (Disclosure of Information) Regulations 1987;

(*b*) subject to regulation 3(2)(b) or (c), as the case may be, the provision of a valuation in accordance with regulation 2(2) of the Provision of Information Regulations;

(*c*) whether a person responsible for a pension arrangement intends to recover the cost of providing membership of the pension arrangement to the person entitled to a pension credit, before or after the pension sharing order is implemented;

(*d*) whether the person responsible for a pension arrangement intends to recover additional charges in the circumstances prescribed in regulation 6 of these Regulations in respect of pension sharing activity described in regulation 5 of these Regulations;

(*e*) whether the charges are inclusive or exclusive of value added tax, where the person responsible for a pension arrangement is required to charge value added tax in accordance with the provisions of the Value Added Tax Act 1994;

(*f*) periodical charges in respect of pension sharing activity which the person responsible for a pension arrangement may make when a person entitled to a pension credit becomes a member of the pension arrangement from which the pension credit is derived;

(*g*) whether the person responsible for a pension arrangement intends to recover charges specified in regulation 10 of these Regulations.

(5) In the case of the cost referred to in paragraph (4)(c) or the charges to be imposed in respect of pension sharing activity described in regulation 5 of these Regulations, the person responsible for a pension arrangement shall provide —

(*a*) a single estimate of the overall cost of the pension sharing activity;

(*b*) a range of estimates of the overall cost of the pension sharing activity which is dependent upon the complexity of an individual case; or

(*c*) a breakdown of the cost of each element of pension sharing activity for which a charge shall be made.

(6) Subject to regulation 9(3) and (4), a person responsible for a pension arrangement shall recover only those sums which represent the reasonable administrative expenses which he has incurred or is likely to incur in connection with any of the activities mentioned in paragraph (1), or in relation to a pension sharing order having been made the subject of an application for leave to appeal out of time.

(7) The requirements of paragraph (2) do not apply in connection with the recovery by a person responsible for a pension arrangement of costs incurred in relation to a pension sharing order having been made the subject of an application for leave to appeal out of time.

(8) The information specified in regulation 2(2) and (3) of the Provision of Information Regulations shall be provided to the member or his spouse without charge unless —

(*a*) the person responsible for the pension arrangement has furnished the information to the member, his spouse or the court within a period of 12 months immediately prior to the date of the request or the court order for the provision of that information;

(*b*) the member has reached normal pension age on or before the date of the request or the court order for the provision of the information;

(*c*) the request or the court order for the provision of the information is made within 12 months prior to the member reaching normal pension age; or

(*d*) the circumstances referred to in regulation 3(2)(b)(i) apply.

Charges recoverable in respect of the provision of basic information

3.—(1) Subject to paragraph (2), the charges prescribed for the purposes of section 23(1)(d) of the 1999 Act (charges which a person responsible for a pension arrangement may recover in respect of supplying pension information in connection with divorce etc.) are any charges incurred by the person responsible for the pension arrangement in connection with the provision of any of the information set out in —

(*a*) regulation 2 of the Provision of Information Regulations which may be recovered in accordance with regulation 2(8) of these Regulations;

(*b*) regulation 4 of those Regulations; or

(*c*) regulation 10 of those Regulations.

(2) The charges mentioned in paragraph (1) shall not include any costs incurred by a person responsible for a pension arrangement in respect of the matters specified in sub-paragraphs (a) to (f) —

(*a*) any costs incurred by the person responsible for a pension arrangement which are directly related to the fulfilment of his obligations under regulation 2(3) of the Provision of Information Regulations, other than charges which may be recovered in the circumstances described in regulation 2(8) of these Regulations;

(*b*) any costs incurred by the person responsible for the pension arrangement as a result of complying with a request for, or an order of the court requiring, a valuation under regulation 2(2) of the Provision of Information Regulations, unless —

   (i) he is required by a member or a court to provide that valuation in less than 3 months beginning with the date the person responsible for the pension arrangement receives that request or order for the valuation;

   (ii) the valuation is requested by a member who is not entitled to a cash equivalent under any of the provisions referred to in regulation 2(4)(a);

   (iii) a member has requested a cash equivalent in accordance with any of those provisions within 12 months immediately prior to the date of the request for a valuation under regulation 2(2) of the Provision of Information Regulations;

(c) any costs incurred by the person responsible for the pension arrangement as a result of providing a valuation of benefits calculated and verified in accordance with regulation 3 of the Divorce etc. (Pensions) (Scotland) Regulations 2000 (valuation), unless —

   (i) he is required by the court to provide that valuation in less than 3 months beginning with the date the person responsible for the pension arrangement receives that order;

   (ii) the valuation is requested by a member who is not entitled to a cash equivalent under any of the provisions referred to in regulation 2(4)(a);

   (iii) a member has requested a cash equivalent in accordance with any of those provisions within 12 months immediately prior to the date of the request for a valuation under regulation 2(2) of the Provision of Information Regulations; or

   (iv) the relevant date is more than 12 months immediately prior to the date the person responsible for the pension arrangement receives the request for the valuation;

(d) any costs incurred by the trustees or managers of —

   (i) an occupational pension scheme in connection with the provision of information under regulation 4 of the Occupational Pension Schemes (Disclosure of Information) Regulations 1996 (basic information about the scheme); or

   (ii) a personal pension scheme in connection with the provision of information under regulation 4 of the Personal Pension Schemes (Disclosure of Information) Regulations 1987 (basic information about the scheme),

which the trustees or managers shall provide to the member free of charge under those Regulations;

(e) any costs incurred by the trustees or managers of an occupational pension scheme, or a personal pension scheme, as the case may be, in connection with the provision of a transfer value in accordance with the provisions of —

   (i) section 93A or 94 of the 1993 Act;

   (ii) regulation 11(1) of the Occupational Pension Schemes (Transfer Values) Regulations 1996; or

   (iii) regulation 5 of, and paragraph 2(b) of Schedule 2 to, the Personal Pension Schemes (Disclosure of Information) Regulations 1987; or (*f*) any costs not specified by the person responsible for a pension arrangement in the information on charges provided to the member pursuant to regulation 2 of the Provision of Information Regulations with the exception of any additional amounts under regulation 6(1)(a) of these Regulations.

Charges in respect of the provision of information — method of recovery

4.—A person responsible for a pension arrangement may recover the charges specified in regulation 3(1) by using either of the methods described in sub-paragraph (a) or (b) —

(*a*) requiring payment of charges at any specific time between the request for basic information and the completion of the implementation of a pension sharing order or provision, or the compliance with an order specified in section 24 of the 1999 Act, as the case may be; or

(*b*) subject to paragraph (2), requiring as a condition of providing information in accordance with —

(i) regulation 2 of the Provision of Information Regulations; or

(ii) regulation 10 of those Regulations,

that payment of the charges to which regulation 3(1) refers shall be made in full by the member before the person responsible for the pension arrangement becomes obliged to provide the information.

(2) Paragraph (1)(b) shall not apply —

(*a*) where a court has ordered a member to obtain the information specified in regulation 2 of the Provision of Information Regulations;

(*b*) where, in accordance with regulation 2(8) of these Regulations, the person responsible for the pension arrangement shall provide that information without charge, or

(*c*) where the person responsible for the pension arrangement is required to supply that information by virtue of regulation 4 of the Provision of Information Regulations.

Charges in respect of pension sharing activity

5.—(1) The charges prescribed in respect of prescribed descriptions of pension sharing activity for the purposes of section 41(1) of the 1999 Act (charges in respect of pension sharing costs) are any costs reasonably incurred by the person responsible for the pension arrangement in connection with pension sharing activity other than those costs specified in paragraph (3).

(2) The descriptions of pension sharing activity prescribed for the purposes of section 41(1) of the 1999 Act are any type of activity which fulfills the requirements of section 41(5) of the 1999 Act.

(3) The costs specified in this paragraph are any costs which are not directly related to the costs which arise in relation to an individual case.

Additional amounts recoverable in respect of pension sharing activity

6.—(1) The circumstances in which a person responsible for a pension arrangement may recover additional amounts are —

(*a*) where a period of more than 12 months has elapsed between the person responsible for the pension arrangement supplying information in accordance with regulation 2 of the Provision of Information Regulations and the taking effect of an order or provision specified in subsection (1) of section 28 of the 1999 Act (activation of pension sharing); or

(*b*) in the case of an occupational pension scheme, where the trustees or managers of that scheme undertake activity from time to time associated with pension credit rights or pension credit benefit in that scheme which belong to a member.

(2) For the purposes of section 41(2)(d) of the 1999 Act, the additional amounts are —

(*a*) in the circumstances described in paragraph (1)(a), interest calculated at a rate not exceeding increases in the retail prices index on the amounts of any charges not yet due, or of any charges requested but yet to be recovered, which are specified in the schedule of charges issued to the member in accordance with regulation 2(2)(b) of these Regulations; and

(*b*) in the circumstances described in paragraph (1)(b), an amount not exceeding an increase calculated by reference to increases in the retail prices index on the amounts which relate to the costs referred to in regulation 2(4)(d) and which are specified in the schedule of charges provided to the member and his spouse in accordance with regulation 2(2)(b).

(3) Where a person responsible for a pension arrangement intends to recover an additional amount specified in paragraph (2)(a) in the circumstances described in paragraph (1)(a), he shall set out this intention, the rate of interest to be used, and the total costs recoverable in the notice of implementation and final costs issued in accordance

with regulation 7 of the Provision of Information Regulations (provision of information after receiving a pension sharing order or provision).

(4) Where the trustees or managers of an occupational pension scheme intend to recover an additional amount specified in paragraph (2)(b) in the circumstances described in paragraph (1)(b), they shall inform the parties involved in pension sharing in writing of this intention in the schedule of charges issued in accordance with regulation 2(2)(b) of these Regulations.

Charges in respect of pension sharing activity — postponement of implementation period

7.—(1) The circumstances when the start of the implementation period may be postponed are when a person responsible for a pension arrangement —

(*a*) issues a notice to the member and the person entitled to the pension credit no later than 21 days after the day on which the person responsible for the pension arrangement receives the pension sharing order or provision; and

(*b*) in that notice, requires the charges specified in regulation 3, 5 or 6 to be paid before the implementation of the pension sharing order or provision is commenced.

(2) Paragraph (1) shall apply only if the person responsible for the pension arrangement has specified at a stage no later than in his response to the notification that a pension sharing order or provision may be made, issued in accordance with regulation 4 of the Provision of Information Regulations —

(*a*) that he requires the charges mentioned in paragraph (1) to be paid before the implementation period is commenced; and either

(*b*) whether he requires those charges to be paid in full; or

(*c*) the proportion of those charges which he requires to be paid as full settlement of those charges.

(3) Once payment of the charges mentioned in paragraph (1) has been made in accordance with the requirements of the person responsible for the pension arrangement —

(*a*) that person shall —

(i) issue the notice of implementation in accordance with regulation 7(1)(c) of the Provision of Information Regulations, and

(ii) begin the implementation period for the pension credit, within 21 days from the date the charges are paid, provided that the person responsible for the pension arrangement would otherwise be able to begin to implement the pension sharing order or provision, and

(*b*) subject to paragraph (4), that person shall not be entitled to recover any further charges in respect of the pension sharing order or provision in question.

(4) Paragraph (3)(b) shall not apply —

(*a*) in relation to the recovery of charges referred to in regulations 2(4)(d) and 6(2)(b); or
(*b*) where the pension credit depends on a pension sharing order and the order is the subject of an application for leave to appeal out of time.

Charges in respect of pension sharing activity — reimbursement as between the parties to pension sharing

8.—A payment in respect of charges recoverable under regulation 3, 5 or 6 made by one party to pension sharing on behalf of the other party to pension sharing, shall be recoverable by the party who made the payment from that other party as a debt.

Charges in respect of pension sharing activity — method of recovery

9.—(1) Subject to paragraphs (7) and (8), a person responsible for a pension arrangement may recover the charges specified in regulations 3, 5 and 6 by using any of the methods described in paragraph (2).

(2) The methods of recovery described in this paragraph are —

(*a*) subject to regulation 7 requiring the charges referred to in paragraph (1) to be paid before the implementation period for the pension sharing order or provision is commenced;
(*b*) deduction from a pension credit;
(*c*) deduction from the accrued rights of the member;
(*d*) where a pension sharing order or provision is made in respect of a pension which is in payment, deduction from the member's pension benefits;
(*e*) where liability in respect of a pension credit is discharged by the person responsible for the pension arrangement in accordance with paragraph 1(2), 2(2), or 3(2) of Schedule 5 to the 1999 Act (mode of discharge of liability for pension

credits), deduction from payments of pension credit benefit; or

(*f*) deduction from the amount of a transfer value which is calculated in accordance with —

    (i) regulation 7 of the Occupational Pension Schemes (Transfer Values) Regulations 1996 (manner of calculation and verification of cash equivalents); or

    (ii) regulation 3 of the Personal Pension Schemes (Transfer Values) Regulations 1987 (manner of calculation and verification of cash equivalents).

(3) A person responsible for a pension arrangement shall not recover charges referred to in paragraph (1) by using any of the methods described in paragraph (2)(b), (c), (d), (e) or (f) unless —

(*a*) a pension sharing order or provision corresponding to any order or provision specified in subsection (1) of section 28 of the 1999 Act has been made;

(*b*) the implementation period has commenced;

(*c*) where a pension sharing order has been made, the person responsible for a pension arrangement is not aware of an appeal against the order having begun on or after the day on which the order takes effect;

(*d*) there are charges which are unpaid and for which the party, to whom paragraph (2)(b), (c), (d), (e) or (f) applies, is liable;

(*e*) the person responsible for the pension arrangement has issued a notice of implementation in accordance with regulation 7 of the Provision of Information Regulations;

(*f*) the person responsible for a pension arrangement specifies in the notice of implementation that recovery of the charges may be made by using any of those methods; and

(*g*) 21 days have elapsed since the notice of implementation was issued to the parties to pension sharing in accordance with the requirements of regulation 7 of the Provision of Information Regulations.

(4) If a pension sharing order or provision includes provision about the apportionment between the parties to pension sharing of any charge under section 41 of the 1999 Act or under corresponding Northern Ireland legislation, by virtue of section 24D of the Matrimonial Causes Act 1973 (pension sharing orders: apportionment of charges) or section 8A of the Family Law (Scotland) Act 1985 (pension sharing orders: apportionment of charges), the recovery of charges using any of the methods described in paragraph (2) by the person responsible for the pension arrangement shall comply with the terms of the order or provision.

(5) A person responsible for a pension arrangement shall not recover charges referred to in paragraph (1) by using any of the methods described in paragraph (2), from a party to pension sharing, if that party has paid in full the proportion of the charges for which he is liable.

(6) A person responsible for a pension arrangement may recover charges by using any of the methods described in paragraph (2)(b), (c) or (d) —

(*a*) at any time within the implementation period prescribed by section 34 of the 1999 Act ("implementation period");

(*b*) following an application by the trustees or managers of an occupational pension scheme, such longer period as the Regulatory Authority may allow in accordance with section 33(4) of the 1999 Act (extension of time for discharge of liability); or

(*c*) within 21 days after the end of the period referred to in sub-paragraph (a) or (b).

(7) Where the commencement of the implementation period is postponed, or its operation ceases in accordance with regulation 4 of the Pension Sharing (Implementation and Discharge of Liability) Regulations 2000 (postponement or cessation of implementation period where an application is made for leave to appeal out of time) a person responsible for a pension arrangement may require any outstanding charges referred to in paragraph (1) to be paid immediately, in respect of —

(*a*) all costs which have been incurred prior to the date of postponement or cessation; or

(*b*) any reasonable costs related to —
    (i) the application for leave to appeal out of time; or
    (ii) the appeal out of time itself.

(8) Paragraph (7) applies even if, prior to receiving the notification of the application for leave to appeal out of time, a person responsible for a pension arrangement has indicated to the parties to pension sharing that he will not be using the method of recovery specified in paragraph (2)(a).

Charges in relation to earmarking orders

10.—The prescribed charges which a person responsible for a pension arrangement may recover in respect of complying with an order specified in section 24 of the 1999 Act are those charges which represent the reasonable administrative expenses which he has incurred or is likely to incur by reason of the order.

E. The Pensions on Divorce etc. (Pension Sharing) (Scotland) Regulations 2000 (S.I. 2000/1051)

The Secretary of State for Social Security, in exercise of the powers conferred upon him by sections 28(1)(f)(ii) and (3)(a) and 48(1)(f)(ii) and (3)(a) of the Welfare Reform and Pensions Act 1999 and of all other powers enabling him in that behalf, after consulting such persons as he considered appropriate, hereby makes the following Regulations:

Citation, commencement and interpretation

1.—(1) These Regulations may be cited as the Pensions on Divorce etc. (Pension Sharing) (Scotland) Regulations 2000 and shall come into force on 1st December 2000.

(2) In these Regulations —

"the 1985 Act" means the Family Law (Scotland) Act 1985;
"the 1999 Act" means the Welfare Reform and Pensions Act 1999;
"pension arrangement" has the meaning given by section 46(1) of the 1999 Act;
"qualifying arrangement" has the meaning given by paragraph 6 of Schedule 5 to the 1999 Act;
"transferee" and "transferor" have, in regulations 2 and 3, the meaning given by section 29(8), and, in regulations 4 and 5, the meaning given by section 49(6), of the 1999 Act.

Sharing of Rights under Pension Arrangements

Prescribed form of provision corresponding to provision in a pension sharing order under the 1985 Act

2. For the purposes of section 28(1)(f)(ii) of the 1999 Act, the provision which corresponds to the provision which may be made by a pension sharing order under the 1985 Act shall be in a form which contains in an annex to, and which is separable from, the qualifying agreement referred to in section 28(1)(f)(i) of the 1999 Act, the following information —

(*a*) in relation to the party who is the transferor —
    (i) all names by which the transferor has been known;
    (ii) date of birth;
    (iii) address;
    (iv) national insurance number;

  (v) the name and address of the pension arrangement to which the pension sharing provision relates, and

  (vi) the transferor's membership number or policy number in that pension arrangement;

(*b*) in relation to the party who is the transferee —

  (i) all names by which the transferee has been known;

  (ii) date of birth;

  (iii) address;

  (iv) national insurance number, and

  (v) if the transferee is a member of the pension arrangement from which a pension credit is derived, his membership number in that pension arrangement;

(*c*) details of —

  (i) the amount to be transferred to the transferee, or

  (ii) the specified percentage of the cash equivalent of the relevant benefits on the valuation day to be transferred to the transferee;

(*d*) where the transferee has given his consent, in accordance with paragraph 1(3)(c), 3(3)(c), or 4(2)(c) of Schedule 5 to the 1999 Act (mode of discharge of liability for a pension credit), to the payment of a pension credit to the person responsible for a qualifying arrangement —

  (i) the full name of that qualifying arrangement;

  (ii) its address;

  (iii) if known, the transferee's membership number or policy number in that arrangement, and

  (iv) the name or title, business address, business telephone number and, where available, the business facsimile number and electronic mail address of a person who may be contacted in respect of the discharge of liability for the pension credit;

(*e*) details of the provision about the apportionment (if any) made by the transferor and the transferee of liability for any charges levied by the person responsible for the pension arrangement in relation to pension sharing under Chapter I of Part IV of the 1999 Act, and

(*f*) confirmation by the transferor that he has intimated to the pension arrangement his intention with respect to pension sharing and that the pension arrangement has acknowledged receipt of the intimation.

Circumstances in which an agreement is to be entered into, in order to be considered a "qualifying agreement" under section 28(1)(f) of the 1999 Act

3. A qualifying agreement is, for the purposes of section 28(1)(f) of the 1999 Act, one which the transferor and transferee have entered into in order to determine the financial settlement on divorce and in respect of which the transferor has intimated to the person responsible for a pension arrangement prior to the making of the agreement the intention to have the transferor's pension rights under the pension arrangement shared with the transferee.

Sharing of State Scheme Rights

Prescribed form of provision corresponding to provision in a pension sharing order under the 1985 Act

4. For the purposes of section 48(1)(f)(ii) of the 1999 Act, the provision which corresponds to the provision which may be made by a pension sharing order under the 1985 Act shall be in a form which contains in an annex to, and which is separable from, the qualifying agreement referred to in section 48(1)(f)(i) of the 1999 Act, the following information —

    (*a*) in relation to the party who is the transferor —
        (i) full name;
        (ii) date of birth;
        (iii) address;
        (iv) national insurance number, and
        (v) details of the specified amount or, as appropriate, the specified percentage of the cash equivalent on the transfer day of the transferor's relevant state scheme rights immediately before that day;
    (*b*) in relation to the party who is the transferee —
        (i) full name by which the transferee is or will be known;
        (ii) date of birth;
        (iii) address, and
        (iv) national insurance number, and
    (*c*) a statement by the transferor and the transferee that they have received confirmation from the Secretary of State that shareable state scheme rights are held in the name of the transferor and that on the grant of decree of divorce or declarator of nullity of marriage a pension-sharing agreement will be implemented.

Circumstances in which an agreement is to be entered into, in order to be considered a "qualifying agreement" under section 48(1)(f) of the 1999 Act

5. A qualifying agreement is, for the purposes of section 48(1)(f) of the 1999 Act, one which the transferor and transferee have entered into in order to determine the financial settlement on divorce and in respect of which they have received confirmation from the Secretary of State that shareable state scheme rights are held in the name of the transferor.

F. The Pension Sharing (Valuation) Regulations 2000[4]
(S.I. 2000/1052)

The Secretary of State for Social Security, in exercise of the powers conferred upon him by sections 27(2), 30(1) and (2) and 83(4) and (6) of the Welfare Reform and Pensions Act 1999, and of all other powers enabling him in that behalf, after consulting such persons as he considered appropriate, hereby makes the following Regulations:

Citation, commencement and interpretation

1.—(1) These Regulations may be cited as the Pension Sharing (Valuation) Regulations 2000 and shall come into force on 1st December 2000.

(2) In these Regulations —

"the 1993 Act" means the Pension Schemes Act 1993;
"the 1995 Act" means the Pensions Act 1995;
"the 1999 Act" means the Welfare Reform and Pensions Act 1999;
"employer" has the meaning given by section 181(1) of the 1993 Act;
"occupational pension scheme" has the meaning given by section 1 of the 1993 Act;
"pension arrangement" has the meaning given by section 46(1) of the 1999 Act;
"relevant arrangement" has the meaning given by section 29(8) of the 1999 Act;
"relevant benefits" has the meaning given by section 612 of the Income and Corporation Taxes Act 1988;
"scheme" means an occupational pension scheme;

---

[4]As amended by S.I. 2000/2691.

"scheme actuary", in relation to a scheme to which section 47(1)(b) of the 1995 Act applies, means the actuary mentioned in section 47(1)(b) of that Act;

"transfer credits" has the meaning given by section 181(1) of the 1993 Act;

"transfer day" has the meaning given by section 29(8) of the 1999 Act;

"transferor" has the meaning given by section 29(8) of the 1999 Act;

"trustees or managers" has the meaning given by section 46(1) of the 1999 Act;

"valuation day" has the meaning given by section 29(7) of the 1999 Act.

Rights under a pension arrangement which are not shareable

2.—(1) Rights under a pension arrangement which are not shareable are —

(*a*) subject to paragraph (2), any rights accrued between 1961 and 1975 which relate to contracted-out equivalent pension benefit within the meaning of section 57 of the National Insurance Act 1965 (equivalent pension benefits, etc.);

(*b*) any rights in respect of which a person is in receipt of —

 (i) a pension;

 (ii) an annuity;

 (iii) payments under an interim arrangement within the meaning of section 28(1A) of the 1993 Act (ways of giving effect to protected rights); or

 (iv) income withdrawal within the meaning of section 630(1) of the Income and Corporation Taxes Act 1988 (interpretation),

by virtue of being the widow, widower or other dependant of a deceased person with pension rights under a pension arrangement; and

(*c*) any rights which do not result in the payment of relevant benefits.

(2) Paragraph (1)(a) applies only when those rights are the only rights held by a person under a pension arrangement.

Calculation and verification of cash equivalents for the purposes of the creation of pension debits and credits

3. For the purposes of section 29 of the 1999 Act (creation of pension debits and credits), cash equivalents may be calculated and verified —

(*a*)	where the relevant arrangement is an occupational pension scheme in accordance with regulations 4 and 5; or

(*b*)	in any other case, in accordance with regulations 6 and 7.

Occupational pension schemes: manner of calculation and verification of cash equivalents

4.—(1) In a case to which, or to the extent to which, paragraph (2) or (5) does not apply, cash equivalents are to be calculated and verified in such manner as may be approved in a particular case by the scheme actuary or, in relation to a scheme to which section 47(1)(b) of the 1995 Act (professional advisers) does not apply, by —

(*a*)	a Fellow of the Institute of Actuaries;

(*b*)	a Fellow of the Faculty of Actuaries; or

(*c*)	a person with other actuarial qualifications who is approved by the Secretary of State, at the request of the trustees or managers of the scheme in question, as being a proper person to act for the purposes of these Regulations in connection with that scheme

and, subject to paragraph (2), in the following paragraphs of this regulation and in regulation 5 "actuary" means the scheme actuary or, in relation to a scheme to which section 47(1)(b) of the 1995 Act does not apply, the actuary referred to in sub-paragraph (a), (b) or (c) of this paragraph.

(2) Where the transferor in respect of whose rights a cash equivalent is to be calculated and verified, is a member of a scheme having particulars from time to time set out in regulations made under section 7 of the Superannuation Act 1972 (superannuation of persons employed in local government service, etc.), that cash equivalent shall be calculated and verified in such manner as may be approved by the Government Actuary or by an actuary authorised by the Government Actuary to act on his behalf for that purpose and in such a case "actuary" in this regulation and in regulation 5 means the Government Actuary or the actuary so authorised.

(2A) Where the person with pension rights is a deferred member of an occupational pension scheme on the transfer day, the value of the benefits which he has accrued under that scheme shall be taken to be —

(*a*)	in the case of an occupational pension scheme other than a salary related scheme, the cash equivalent to which he acquired a right under section 94(1)(a) of the 1993 Act (right to cash equivalent) on the termination of his pensionable service, calculated on the assumption that he has made an application under section 95(1) of that Act (ways of taking right to cash equivalent); or

(b) in the case of a salary related occupational pension scheme, the guaranteed cash equivalent to which he would have acquired a right under section 94(1)(aa) of the 1993 Act if he had made an application under section 95(1) of that Act.

(2B) Where the person with pension rights is an active member of an occupational pension scheme on the transfer day, the value of the benefits which he has accrued under that scheme shall be calculated and verified —

(a) on the assumption that the member had made a request for an estimate of the cash equivalent that would be available to him were his pensionable service to terminate on the transfer day; and

(b) in accordance with regulation 11 of, and Schedule 1 to, the Occupational Pension Schemes (Transfer Values) Regulations 1996 (disclosure).

(3) Except in a case to which paragraph (5) applies, cash equivalents are to be calculated and verified by adopting methods and making assumptions which —

(a) if not determined by the trustees or managers of the scheme in question, are notified to them by the actuary; and

(b) are certified by the actuary to the trustees or managers of the scheme —

(i) as being consistent with "Retirement Benefit Schemes — Transfer Values (GN11)" published by the Institute of Actuaries and the Faculty of Actuaries and current on the valuation day;

(ii) as being consistent with the methods adopted and assumptions made, at the time when the certificate is issued, in calculating the benefits to which entitlement arises under the rules of the scheme in question for a person who is acquiring transfer credits under those rules; and

(iii) in the case of a scheme to which section 56 of the 1995 Act (minimum funding requirement) applies as providing as a minimum an amount, consistent with the methods adopted and assumptions made in calculating, for the purposes of section 57 of that Act (valuation and certification of assets and liabilities), the liabilities mentioned in section 73(3)(a), (aa), (b), (c)(i) and (d) of that Act (preferential liabilities on winding up), subject, in any case where the cash equivalent calculation is made on an individual and not a collective basis, to any adjustments which are appropriate to take account of that fact.

(4) If, by virtue of Schedule 5 to the Occupational Pension Schemes (Minimum Funding Requirement and Actuarial Valuations) Regulations 1996 (modifications), section 56 of the 1995 Act applies to a section of a scheme as if that section were a separate scheme, paragraph (3)(b)(iii) shall apply as if that section were a separate scheme and as if the reference therein to a scheme were accordingly a reference to that section.

(5) Where a cash equivalent or any portion of a cash equivalent relates to money purchase benefits which do not fall to be valued in a manner which involves making estimates of the value of benefits, then that cash equivalent or that portion shall be calculated and verified in such manner as may be approved in particular cases by the trustees or managers of the scheme, and by adopting methods consistent with the requirements of Chapter IV of Part IV of the 1993 Act (protection for early leavers — transfer values).

Occupational pension schemes: further provisions as to the calculation of cash equivalents and increases and reductions of cash equivalents

5.—(1) Where it is the established custom for additional benefits to be awarded from the scheme at the discretion of the trustees or managers or the employer, the cash equivalent shall, unless the trustees or managers have given a direction that cash equivalents shall not take account of such benefits, take account of any such additional benefits as will accrue to the transferor if the custom continues unaltered.

(2) The trustees or managers shall not make a direction such as is mentioned in paragraph (1) unless, within 3 months before making the direction, they have consulted the actuary and have obtained the actuary's written report on the implications for the state of funding of the scheme of making such a direction, including the actuary's advice as to whether or not in the actuary's opinion there would be any adverse implications for the funding of the scheme should the trustees or managers not make such a direction.

(3) Subject to paragraph (6), in the case of a scheme to which section 56 of the 1995 Act applies, each respective part of the cash equivalent which relates to liabilities referred to in section 73(3)(a), (aa), (b), (c)(i) or (d) of the 1995 Act may be reduced by the percentage which is the difference between —

(*a*) 100 per cent; and

(*b*) the percentage of the liabilities mentioned in the relevant paragraph of section 73(3) which the actuarial valuation shows the scheme assets as being sufficient to satisfy

where the actuarial valuation is the latest actuarial valuation obtained in accordance with section 57 of the 1995 Act before the valuation day.

(4) If, by virtue of Schedule 5 to the Occupational Pension Schemes (Minimum Funding Requirement and Actuarial Valuations) Regulations 1996, section 56 of the 1995 Act applies to a section of a scheme as if that section were a separate scheme, paragraph (3) shall apply as if that section were a separate scheme, and as if the reference therein to a scheme were accordingly a reference to that section.

(5) The reduction referred to in paragraph (3) shall not apply to a case where liability in respect of a pension credit is to be discharged in accordance with —

(*a*) paragraph 1(2) of Schedule 5 to the 1999 Act (pension credits: mode of discharge — funded pension schemes); or

(*b*) paragraph 1(3) of that Schedule, in a case where regulation 7(2) of the Pension Sharing (Implementation and Discharge of Liability) Regulations 2000 applies.

(6) Where a scheme has begun to be wound up, a cash equivalent may be reduced to the extent necessary for the scheme to comply with sections 73 and 74 of the 1995 Act (discharge of liabilities by insurance, etc.), and the Occupational Pension Schemes (Winding Up) Regulations 1996.

(7) If, by virtue of the Occupational Pension Schemes (Winding Up) Regulations 1996, section 73 of the 1995 Act applies to a section of a scheme as if that section were a separate scheme, paragraph (6) shall apply as if that section were a separate scheme and as if the references therein to a scheme were accordingly references to that section.

(8) Where all or any of the benefits to which a cash equivalent relates have been surrendered, commuted or forfeited before the date on which the trustees or managers discharge their liability in respect of the pension credit in accordance with the provisions of Schedule 5 to the 1999 Act, the cash equivalent of the benefits so surrendered, commuted or forfeited shall be reduced to nil.

(9) In a case where two or more of the paragraphs of this regulation fall to be applied to a calculation, they shall be applied in the order in which they occur in this regulation.

Other relevant arrangements: manner of calculation and verification of cash equivalents

6.—(1) Except in a case to which paragraph (3) applies, cash equivalents are to be calculated and verified in such manner as may be approved in a particular case by —

(*a*) a Fellow of the Institute of Actuaries;
(*b*) a Fellow of the Faculty of Actuaries; or
(*c*) a person with other actuarial qualifications who is approved by the Secretary of State, at the request of the person responsible for the relevant arrangement, as being a proper person to act for the purposes of this regulation and regulation 7 in connection with that arrangement,

and in paragraph (2) "actuary" means any person such as is referred to in sub-paragraph (a), (b) or (c) of this paragraph.

(1A) Where the person with pension rights is a member of a personal pension scheme, or those rights are contained in a retirement annuity contract, the value of the benefits which he has accrued under that scheme or contract on the transfer day shall be taken to be the cash equivalent to which he would have acquired a right under section 94(1)(b) of the 1993 Act, if he had made an application under section 95(1) of that Act on the date on which the request for the valuation was received.

(1B) In relation to a personal pension scheme which is comprised in a retirement annuity contract made before 4th January 1988, paragraph (2) shall apply as if such a scheme were not excluded from the scope of Chapter IV of Part IV of the 1993 Act by section 93(1)(b) of that Act (scope of Chapter IV).

(2) Except in a case to which paragraph (3) applies, cash equivalents are to be calculated and verified by adopting methods and making assumptions which —

(*a*) if not determined by the person responsible for the relevant arrangement, are notified to them by an actuary; and
(*b*) are certified by an actuary to the person responsible for the relevant arrangement as being consistent with "Retirement Benefit Schemes — Transfer Values (GN11)", published by the Institute of Actuaries and the Faculty of Actuaries and current on the valuation day.

(3) Where a transferor's cash equivalent, or any portion of it —

(*a*) represents his rights to money purchase benefits under the relevant arrangement; and (*b*) those rights do not fall, either wholly or in part, to be valued in a manner which involves making estimates of the value of benefits,

then that cash equivalent, or that portion of it, shall be calculated and verified in such manner as may be approved in a particular case by the person responsible for the relevant arrangement, and by adopting methods consistent with the requirements of Chapter IV of Part IV of the 1993 Act.

(4) This regulation and regulation 7 apply to a relevant arrangement other than an occupational pension scheme.

Other relevant arrangements: reduction of cash equivalents

7. Where all or any of the benefits to which a cash equivalent relates have been surrendered, commuted or fortified before the date on which the person responsible for the relevant arrangement discharges his liability for the pension credit in accordance with the provisions of Schedule 5 to the 1999 Act, the cash equivalent of the benefits so surrendered, commuted or fortified shall be reduced in proportion to the reduction in the total value of the benefits.

G. The Pension Sharing (Implementation and Discharge of Liability) Regulations 2000[5] (S.I. 2000/1053)

ARRANGEMENT OF REGULATIONS

PART I
General
1. Citation, commencement and interpretation

PART II
Extension, Postponement or Cessation of Implementation Period
2. Time period for notification to the Regulatory Authority of failure by the trustees or managers of an occupational pension scheme to discharge their liability in respect of a pension credit
3. Circumstances in which an application for an extension of the implementation period may be made
4. Postponement or cessation of implementation period when an application is made for leave to appeal out of time
5. Civil penalties

---

[5]As amended by S.I. 2000/2691.

PART III

Death of person entitled to a Pension Credit before liability in respect of the Pension Credit is discharged

6. Discharge of liability in respect of a pension credit following the death of the person entitled to the pension credit

PART IV

Discharge of liability in respect of a Pension Credit

7. Funded pension schemes
8. Unfunded occupational pension schemes other than public service pension schemes
9. Other pension arrangements
10. Calculation of the value of appropriate rights
11. Qualifying arrangements
12. Disqualification as a destination for pension credit — general
13. Disqualification as a destination for pension credit — contracted-out or safeguarded rights
14. Disqualification as a destination for pension credit — occupational pension schemes
15. Disqualification as a destination for pension credit — annuity contracts and insurance policies
16. Adjustments to the amount of the pension credit — occupational pension schemes which are underfunded on the valuation day
17. Adjustments to the amount of the pension credit — payment made without knowledge of the pension debit
18. Adjustments to the amount of the pension credit — increasing the amount of the pension credit

The Secretary of State for Social Security, in exercise of the powers conferred upon him by sections 10(2)(b), 124(1) and 174(2) and (3) of the Pensions Act 1995, sections 33(2)(a) and (4), 34(4)(c), 35(2)(b) and 83(4) and (6) of, and paragraphs 1(2)(b), (3)(c), 3(3)(c), 4(2)(c), (4), 5(b), 6(2)(b), 7(1)(b), (2)(a), (2)(b), (3), (4), (6), 8(1), (2), 9, 10, and 13 of Schedule 5 to, the Welfare Reform and Pensions Act 1999, and of all other powers enabling him in that behalf, after consulting such persons as he considered appropriate, hereby makes the following Regulations:

PART I
GENERAL

Citation, commencement and interpretation

1.—(1) These Regulations may be cited as the Pension Sharing (Implementation and Discharge of Liability) Regulations 2000 and shall come into force on 1 December 2000.

(2) In these Regulations —

"the 1993 Act" means the Pension Schemes Act 1993;

"the 1995 Act" means the Pensions Act 1995;

"the 1999 Act" means the Welfare Reform and Pensions Act 1999;

"base rate" means the base rate for the time being quoted by the reference banks or, where there is for the time being more than one such base rate, the base rate which, when the base rate quoted by each bank is ranked in a descending sequence of seven, is fourth in the sequence;

"the implementation period" has the meaning given by section 34 of the 1999 Act;

"the Inland Revenue" means the Commissioners of Inland Revenue;

"normal benefit age" has the meaning given by section 101B of the 1993 Act;

"occupational pension scheme" has the meaning given by section 1 of the 1993 Act;

"pension arrangement" has the meaning given by section 46(1) of the 1999 Act;

"pension credit" means a credit under section 29(1)(b) of the 1999 Act;

"pension sharing order" means an order which is mentioned in section 28(1) of the 1999 Act;

"pension sharing order or provision" means an order or provision which is mentioned in section 28(1) of the 1999 Act;

"personal pension scheme" has the meaning given by section 1 of the 1993 Act;

"person responsible for a pension arrangement" has the meaning given to that expression in section 46(2) of the 1999 Act;

"the reference banks" means the seven largest institutions for the time being which —

(a) are authorised by the Financial Services Authority under the Banking Act 1987;

(b) are incorporated in and carrying on within the United Kingdom a deposit-taking business (as defined in section 6, but subject to any order under section 7 of that Act); and

(c) quote a base rate in sterling;

and for the purpose of this definition the size of an institution at any time is to be determined by reference to the gross assets denominated in sterling of that institution, together with any subsidiary (as defined in section 736 of the companies Act 1985), as shown in the audited end of year accounts last published before that time;

"the Regulatory Authority" means the Occupational Pensions Regulatory Authority;

"safeguarded rights" has the meaning given in section 68A(1) of the 1993 Act;

"scheme actuary", in relation to a scheme to which section 47(1)(b) of the 1995 Act applies, means the actuary mentioned in section 47(1)(b) of that Act;

"section 9(2B) rights" has the meaning given in regulation 1(2) of the Occupational Pension Schemes (Contracting-out) Regulations 1996;

"transferee" has the meaning given by section 34(5) of the 1999 Act;

"transferor" has the meaning given by section 34(5) of the 1999 Act;

"trustees or mangers", in relation to an occupational pension scheme or a personal pension scheme means —

(a) in the case of a scheme established under a trust, the trustees of the scheme, and

(b) in any other case, the managers of the scheme;

"the valuation day" has the meaning given in section 29(7) of the 1999 Act.

PART II
EXTENSION, POSTPONEMENT OR CESSATION OF
IMPLEMENTATION PERIOD

Time period for notification to the Regulatory Authority of failure by the trustees or managers of an occupational pension scheme to discharge their liability in respect of a pension credit

2. The period prescribed for the purposes of section 33(2)(a) of the 1999 Act (period within which notice must be given of non-discharge of pension credit liability) is the period of 21 days beginning with the day immediately following the end of the implementation period.

Circumstances in which an application for an extension of the implementation period may be made

3. The circumstances in which an application may be made for the purposes of section 33(4) of the 1999 Act (application for extension of period within which pension credit liability is to be discharged) are that the application is made to the Regulatory Authority before the end of the implementation period; and —

(*a*) the Regulatory Authority is satisfied that —
    (i) the scheme is being wound up or is about to be wound up;
    (ii) the scheme is ceasing to be a contracted-out scheme;

    (iii) the financial interests of the members of the scheme generally will be prejudiced if the trustees or managers do what is needed to discharge their liability for the pension credit within that period;

    (iv) the transferor or the transferee has not taken such steps as the trustees or managers can reasonably expect in order to satisfy them of any matter which falls to be established before they can properly discharge their liability for the pension credit;

    (v) the trustees or managers have not been provided with such information as they reasonably require properly to discharge their liability for the pension credit within the implementation period;

    (vi) the transferor or the transferee has disputed the amount of the cash equivalent calculated and verified for the purposes of section 29 of the 1999 Act (creation of pension debits and credits);

(*b*) the provisions of section 53 of the 1993 Act (supervision: former contracted-out schemes) apply; or

(*c*) the application has been made on one or more of the grounds specified in paragraph (a) or (b), and the Regulatory Authority's consideration of the application cannot be completed before the end of the implementation period.

Postponement or cessation of implementation period when an application is made for leave to appeal out of time

4.—(1) The modification to the operation of section 34 of the 1999 Act ("implementation period") where the pension credit depends on a pension sharing order and the order is the subject of an application for leave to appeal out of time are —

(*a*) where the implementation period has not commenced, its commencement shall be postponed; or

(*b*) where the implementation period has commenced, its operation shall cease and it shall not commence afresh until the person responsible for the pension arrangement has received the documents referred to in paragraph (2).

(2) The postponement or cessation referred to in paragraph (1)(a) or (b) shall continue until the person responsible for the pension arrangement is in receipt of —

(*a*) confirmation from the court that the order which was the subject of the application for leave to appeal out of time has not been varied or discharged; or

(*b*) a copy of the varied pension sharing order.

(3) Where the person responsible for the pension arrangement has discharged his liability in respect of the pension credit which depends on a pension sharing order and that person subsequently receives notification of an application for leave to appeal out of time in respect of that order, he shall inform the court within 21 days from the date on which he received the notification that liability in respect of that pension credit has been discharged.

Civil penalties

5. For the purpose of section 33(2)(b) or (3) of the 1999 Act, the maximum amount of the penalty which may be imposed by the Regulatory Authority under section 10(2)(b) of the 1995 Act is —

    (*a*) £1,000 in the case of an individual, and
    (*b*) £10,000 in any other case.

PART III

DEATH OF PERSON ENTITLED TO A PENSION CREDIT BEFORE LIABILITY IN RESPECT OF THE PENSION CREDIT IS DISCHARGED

Discharge of liability in respect of a pension credit following the death of the person entitled to the pension credit

6.—(1) The person responsible for the pension arrangement shall following the death of the person entitled to the pension credit discharge his liability in respect of a pension credit in accordance with this regulation.

(2) Where the rules or provisions of a pension arrangement so provide and provided that any requirements of the Inland Revenue under Part XIV of the Income and Corporation Taxes Act 1988 are satisfied, the person responsible for the pension arrangement shall discharge his liability in respect of a pension credit by undertaking to —

    (*a*) make —
        (i) a payment of a lump sum; or
        (ii) payments of a pension; or
        (iii) payments of both a lump sum and a pension,

to one or more persons; or

    (*b*) enter into an annuity contract or take out a policy of insurance with an insurance company for the benefit of one or more persons; or (*c*) make a payment or, as the case may be, payments under sub-paragraph (a) and enter into an annuity contract or take out an insurance policy under sub-paragraph (b).

(3) Where paragraph (2)(b) or (c) applies, the annuity contract entered into or insurance policy taken out must satisfy the requirements of paragraph 6(2) of Schedule 5 to the 1999 Act (qualifying arrangements) and regulation 11 of these Regulations.

(4) Where the provisions of paragraph (2) do not apply, liability in respect of a pension credit shall be discharged by retaining the value of the pension credit in the pension arrangement from which that pension credit was derived.

(5) Where —

(*a*) liability in respect of a pension credit has been discharged in accordance with paragraph (2); and

(*b*) the value of the payment or payments made, the annuity contract entered into or the insurance policy taken out, as the case may be, is less than the value of the pension credit,

the value of an amount equal to the difference between the value of the pension credit and the value of that payment or those payments, that contract or policy, as the case may be, shall be retained in the pension arrangement from which that pension credit was derived.

PART IV
DISCHARGE OF LIABILITY IN RESPECT OF A
PENSION CREDIT

Funded pension schemes

7.—(1) The circumstances in which the trustees or managers of a scheme, to which paragraph 1 of Schedule 5 to the 1999 Act applies, may discharge their liability in respect of a pension credit in accordance with sub-paragraph (2)(b) of that paragraph are where —

(*a*) the person entitled to the credit has failed to provide his consent in accordance with paragraph 1(2)(a) and (4) of that Schedule; and

(*b*) the circumstances set out in paragraph 1(3) of that Schedule do not apply.

(2) The circumstances in which the trustees or managers of a scheme, to which paragraph 1 of Schedule 5 to the 1999 Act applies, may discharge their liability in respect of a pension credit in accordance with sub-paragraph (3)(c) of that paragraph are where —

(*a*) the person entitled to the credit has failed to provide his consent in accordance with paragraph 1(3)(c) of that Schedule; and

(*b*) either —

    (i) the person entitled to the pension credit has failed to provide his consent in accordance with paragraph 1(2)(a) and (4) of that Schedule; or

    (ii) the trustees or managers of the scheme have not discharged their liability in accordance with paragraph (1) above.

Unfunded occupational pension schemes other than public service pension schemes

8.—(1) The circumstances in which the trustees or managers of a scheme, to which paragraph 3 of Schedule 5 to the 1999 Act applies, may discharge their liability in respect of a pension credit in accordance with sub-paragraph (3)(c) of that paragraph are those specified in —

(*a*) sub-paragraphs (a) and (b) of paragraph (2), in the case of an approved scheme; and

(*b*) sub-paragraphs (a), (b) and (c) of paragraph (2), in the case of an unapproved scheme.

(2) The circumstances specified in this paragraph are —

(*a*) the liability of the trustees or managers has not been discharged in accordance with the provisions of paragraph 3(2) of that Schedule;

(*b*) the person entitled to the pension credit has not consented to the discharge of liability in accordance with paragraph 3(3) of that Schedule; and

(*c*) the employer who is associated with the scheme from which the pension credit derives —

    (i) consents to the trustees or managers discharging their liability for the credit in accordance with paragraph 3(3) of that Schedule; and

    (ii) agrees to compensate the person entitled to the credit fully for any tax liability which he may incur as a result of the trustees or managers of the scheme discharging their liability for the credit in accordance with paragraph 3(3) of that Schedule.

(3) In this regulation "approved scheme" means an occupational pension scheme which is approved for the purposes of Part XIV of the Income and Corporation Taxes Act 1988 and an "unapproved scheme"

means an occupational pension scheme which is not approved for those purposes.

Other pension arrangements

9.—(1) The circumstances in which the person responsible for a pension arrangement, to which paragraph 4 of Schedule 5 to the 1999 Act applies, may discharge his liability in respect of a pension credit in accordance with sub-paragraph (2)(c) of that paragraph are where his liability has not been discharged in accordance with the provisions of paragraph 4(3) or (4) of that Schedule.

(2) The circumstances in which the person responsible for the pension arrangement may discharge his liability in respect of the pension credit under paragraph 4(4) of Schedule 5 to the 1999 Act are where the person responsible for the pension arrangement has not discharged his liability in accordance with the provisions of —

- (*a*) paragraph (1) above;
- (*b*) paragraph 4(2) of that Schedule; or
- (*c*) paragraph 4(3) of that Schedule.

Calculation of the value of appropriate rights

10.—(1) Except in a case to which paragraph (4) applies, the value of the rights conferred on a person entitled to a pension credit shall be calculated by adopting methods and making assumptions which the scheme actuary or, in relation to a scheme to which section 47(1)(b) of the 1995 Act (professional advisers) does not apply, by a person referred to in paragraph (2), has certified to the person responsible for the pension arrangement as being consistent with —

- (*a*) the methods adopted and assumptions made when transfers of other pension rights are received by the person responsible for the pension arrangement; and
- (*b*) the Guidance Note 11 "Retirement Benefit Schemes — Transfer Values" published by the Institute of Actuaries and the Faculty of Actuaries and which is current on the valuation day.

(2) A person referred to in this paragraph is —

- (*a*) a Fellow of the Institute of Actuaries;
- (*b*) a Fellow of the Faculty of Actuaries; or
- (*c*) a person with other actuarial qualifications who is approved by the Secretary of State, at the request of the person responsible for the pension arrangement in question, as being a proper

person to act for the purposes of these Regulations in connection with that scheme.

(3) Where the person entitled to a pension credit in respect of whom a cash equivalent is to be calculated and verified is a member of a scheme having particulars from time to time set out in regulations made under section 7 of the Superannuation Act 1972 (superannuation of persons employed in local government service, etc.), that cash equivalent shall be calculated and verified in such manner as may be approved by the Government Actuary or by an actuary authorised by the Government Actuary to act on his behalf for that purpose.

(4) Where the rights conferred on a person entitled to a pension credit are derived from money purchase rights in whole or in part, the value of those rights shall be calculated by the person responsible for the pension arrangement in a manner consistent with the methods adopted and assumptions made when transfers of other pension rights are received by the person responsible for the pension arrangement, and by adopting methods consistent with the requirements of Chapter IV of Part IV of the 1993 Act (protection for early leavers — transfer values).

Qualifying arrangements

11.—(1) The requirements referred to in paragraph 6(2)(b) of Schedule 5 to the 1999 Act (requirements applying to annuity contracts or policies of insurance for the purpose of sub-paragraph (1) of that paragraph) are that the annuity contract is entered into or the insurance policy is taken out with an insurance company which is —

(*a*) authorised under section 3 or 4 of the Insurance Companies Act 1982 (authorisation of insurance business) to carry on long term business (within the meaning of section 1 of that Act (classification));

(*b*) in the case of a friendly society authorised under section 32 of the Friendly Societies Act 1992 (grant of authorisation by Commission: general) to carry out long term business under any of the Classes specified in Head A of Schedule 2 to that Act (the activities of a friendly society: long term business); or

(*c*) an EC company as defined in section 2 of the Insurance Companies Act 1982 (restriction on carrying on insurance business), and which falls within paragraph (2).

(2) An EC company falls within this paragraph if it —

(*a*) carries on ordinary long term insurance business (within the meaning of section 96(1) of the Insurance Companies Act 1982) in the United Kingdom through a branch in respect of which such of the requirements of Part I of Schedule 2F to that Act (recognition in the United Kingdom of EC and EFTA companies: EC companies carrying on business etc. in the United Kingdom) as are applicable have been complied with; or

(*b*) provides ordinary long term insurance in the United Kingdom and such of the requirements of Part I of Schedule 2F to that Act as are applicable have been complied with in respect of insurance.

Disqualification as a destination for pension credit — general

12. The requirements referred to in paragraph 7(1)(b) of Schedule 5 to the 1999 Act (requirements to be satisfied to qualify pension arrangements as destinations for pension credits) are that the pension arrangement —

(*a*) is an arrangement which carries on pension business as defined by section 431B of the Income and Corporation Taxes Act 1988 (meaning of "pension business");

(*b*) is an overseas arrangement within the meaning given by regulation 1(2) of the Contracting-out (Transfer and Transfer Payment) Regulations 1996 (citation, commencement and interpretation); or

(*c*) is an overseas scheme within the meaning given by regulation 1(2) of the Contracting-out (Transfer and Transfer Payment) Regulations 1996.

Disqualification as a destination for pension credit — contracted-out or safeguarded rights

13.—(1) The descriptions of pension arrangements referred to in paragraph 7(2)(a) of Schedule 5 to the 1999 Act (pension arrangements which qualify as destinations for pension credits, where the rights by reference to which the amount of the credits are determined are or include contracted-out rights or safeguarded rights) are —

(*a*) a contracted-out salary related occupational pension scheme which satisfies the requirements of section 9(2) of the 1993 Act (requirements for certification of occupational salary related schemes);

(*b*) a contracted-out money purchase occupational pension scheme which satisfies the requirements of section 9(3) of the 1993

Act (requirements for certification of occupational money purchase schemes);

(*bb*) a contracted-out occupational pension scheme to which section 149 of the 1995 Act (hybrid occupational pension schemes) applies;

(*c*) an appropriate personal pension scheme within the meaning of section 7(4) of the 1993 Act (issue of appropriate scheme certificates);

(*d*) an annuity contract or an insurance policy which satisfies the requirements of paragraph 6 of Schedule 5 to the 1999 Act (qualifying arrangements);

(*e*) an overseas arrangement within the meaning given by regulation 1(2) of the Contracting-out (Transfer and Transfer Payment) Regulations 1996; or

(*f*) an overseas scheme within the meaning given by regulation 1(2) of the Contracting-out (Transfer and Transfer Payment) Regulations 1996.

(2) The requirements referred to in paragraph 7(2)(b) of Schedule 5 to the 1999 Act (requirements to be satisfied by a pension arrangement which qualifies as a destination for a pension credit, where the rights by reference to which the amount of the credit are determined are or include contracted-out rights or safeguarded rights) are —

(*a*) in relation to the descriptions of pension arrangement referred to in paragraph (1)(a) to (d), the requirements specified in the Pension Sharing (Safeguarded Rights) Regulations 2000 to be met by an occupational pension scheme or a personal pension scheme;

(*b*) in relation to the descriptions of pension arrangement referred to in paragraph (1)(e), the requirements specified in regulation 15 (disqualification as a destination for pension credit — annuity contracts and insurance policies) and regulation 7(3) and (4) of the Pension Sharing (Safeguarded Rights) Regulations 2000 (the pension and annuity requirements — money purchase schemes);

(*c*) in relation to the descriptions of pension arrangement referred to in paragraph (1)(f) and (g), the requirements specified in regulation 11 of the Contracting-out (Transfer and Transfer Payment) Regulations 1996 (transfer payments to overseas schemes or arrangements in respect of section 9(2B) rights), as if the references in that regulation to —

(i) "earner" were to "the person entitled to a pension credit"; and

(ii) "accrued section 9(2B) rights" were to "safeguarded rights".

(3) The rights for the purposes of paragraph 7(6) of Schedule 5 to the 1999 Act (meaning of "contracted-out" rights under or derived from an occupational pension scheme or a personal pension scheme) are those which fall within the categories specified in regulation 2 of the Pension Sharing (Safeguarded Rights) Regulations 2000 (definition of contracted-out rights).

Disqualification as a destination for pension credit — occupational pension schemes

14. The calculation of the value of the rights of the person entitled to the pension credit for the purposes of paragraph 7(3) of Schedule 5 to the 1999 Act shall be made in accordance with the methods adopted and assumptions made by the scheme which are consistent with the methods adopted and assumptions made by that scheme when transfers of other pension rights are received by the scheme.

Disqualification as a destination for pension credit — annuity contracts and insurance policies

15.—(1) The circumstances referred to in paragraph 7(4) of Schedule 5 to the 1999 Act (circumstances in which an annuity contract or insurance policy is disqualified as a destination for pension credit) are where the requirements specified in paragraphs (2) to (7) are not satisfied.

(2) The annuity contract or insurance policy must provide that that contract or policy, as the case may be, may not be assigned or surrendered unless —

(*a*) the person entitled to the pension credit; or
(*b*) if the person entitled to the pension credit has died, his widow or widower,

has consented to the assignment or surrender.

(3) The benefits previously secured by the annuity contract or insurance policy become secured, or are replaced by benefits which are secured by another qualifying arrangement.

(4) The annuity contract or insurance policy, as the case may be, must provide that the benefits secured by that contract or policy may be commuted if either —

(*a*) the conditions set out in paragraph (5) are satisfied; or
(*b*) the conditions set out in paragraph (6) are satisfied.

(5) The conditions referred to in paragraph (4)(a) are —

(*a*) the benefits secured by the annuity contract or insurance policy have become payable, and the aggregate of those benefits does not exceed £260 per annum;

(*b*) an actuary certifies that the methods and assumptions to be used to calculate any benefit in a lump sum form will result in the benefit being broadly equivalent to the annual amount of benefits which would have been payable in pension benefits; and

(*c*) all of the interest of the person entitled to the pension credit under the annuity contract or insurance policy is discharged upon payment of a lump sum.

(6) The conditions referred to in paragraph (4)(b) are —

(*a*) the benefits secured by the annuity contract or insurance policy have become payable and the person entitled to the pension credit requests or consents to the commutation;

(*b*) the person entitled to the pension credit is suffering from serious ill health prior to normal benefit age; and

(*c*) the insurance company with which the annuity contract is entered into, or with which the insurance policy is taken out, assumes an obligation to pay the benefits secured by the annuity contract or insurance policy to —

  (i) the person entitled to the pension credit;

  (ii) the trustees of a trust for the benefit of the person entitled to the pension credit; or

  (iii) the trustees of a trust for the benefit of the dependants of the person entitled to the pension credit.

(7) The annuity contract or insurance policy must contain, or be endorsed with, terms so as to provide for any increase in accordance with regulation 32 of the Pension Sharing (Pension Credit Benefit) Regulations 2000 (increase of relevant pension) which would have been applied to the benefits which have become secured or been replaced by the annuity contract or insurance policy had the discharge of liability not taken place.

(8) In this regulation —

> "serious ill health" means ill health which is such as to give rise to a life expectancy of less than one year from the date on which commutation of the benefits secured by the annuity contract or insurance policy is applied for.

Adjustments to the amount of the pension credit — occupational pension schemes which are underfunded on the valuation day

16.—(1) The circumstances referred to in paragraph 8(1)(d) of Schedule 5 to the 1999 Act (adjustments to amount of pension credit) are —

(a) the discharge of liability in respect of the pension credit in accordance with paragraph 1(3) of Schedule 5 to the 1999 Act is at the request, or with the consent, of the person entitled to the pension credit;

(b) the person entitled to the pension credit has refused an offer by the trustees or managers of the occupational pension scheme from which the pension credit is derived to discharge their liability in respect of the pension credit, without any reduction in the amount of the credit, in accordance with the provisions of paragraph 1(2) of Schedule 5 to the 1999 Act (conferring appropriate rights in that scheme on the person entitled to the pension credit); and

(c) prior to making his request or giving his consent in accordance with sub-paragraph (a) the person entitled to the pension credit has received from the trustees or managers of the occupational pension scheme from which the pension credit is derived, a written statement which provides the following information —

    (i) the reasons why the amount of the pension credit has been reduced;

    (ii) the amount by which the pension credit has been reduced; and

    (iii) where possible, an estimate of the date by which it will be possible to pay the full, unadjusted amount of the pension credit.

(2) The lesser amount referred to in paragraph 8(1) of Schedule 5 to the 1999 Act may be determined for the purposes of that paragraph by reducing the amount of the pension credit which relates to liabilities referred to in section 73(3)(a), (aa), (b), (c)(i) or (d) of the 1995 Act (preferential liabilities on winding-up) by the percentage which is the difference between —

(a) 100 per cent; and

(b) the percentage of the pension credit which the actuarial valuation shows the scheme assets as being sufficient to satisfy,

where the actuarial valuation is the latest actuarial valuation obtained in accordance with section 57 of the 1995 Act (valuation and certification of assets and liabilities) before the valuation day.

(3) If, by virtue of Schedule 5 to the Occupational Pension Schemes (Minimum Funding Requirement and Actuarial Valuations) Regulations 1996, section 56 of the 1995 Act (minimum funding requirement) applies to a section of a scheme as if that section were a separate scheme, paragraph (2) shall apply as if that section were a separate scheme, and as if the reference therein to a scheme were accordingly a reference to that section.

Adjustments to the amount of the pension credit — payments made without knowledge of the pension debit

17. For the purposes of paragraph 9 of Schedule 5 to the 1999 Act (adjustments to amount of pension credit), where the cash equivalent of the member's shareable rights after deduction of the payment referred to in sub-paragraph (b) of that paragraph, is less than the amount of the pension debit, the pension credit shall be reduced to that lesser amount.

Adjustments to the amount of the pension credit — increasing the amount of the pension credit

18.—(1) For the purposes of paragraph 10 of Schedule 5 to the 1999 Act (adjustments to amount of pension credit) the trustees or managers of an occupational pension scheme to which paragraph 1(3) or 3(3) of Schedule 5 to the 1999 Act applies shall increase the amount of the pension credit by —

    (*a*) the amount, if any, by which the amount of that pension credit falls short of what it would have been if the valuation day had been the day on which the trustees or managers make the payment; or

    (*b*) if it is greater, interest on the amount of that pension credit calculated on a daily basis over the period from the valuation day to the day on which the trustees or managers make the payment, at an annual rate of one per cent above the base rate.

(2) For the purposes of paragraph 10 of Schedule 5 to the 1999 Act the trustees or managers of a personal pension scheme to which paragraph 1(3) of Schedule 5 to the 1999 Act applies, or a person responsible for a pension arrangement to which paragraph 4(2) of Schedule 5 to the 1999 Act applies, shall increase the amount of the pension credit by —

    (*a*) the interest on the amount of that pension credit, calculated on a daily basis over the period from the valuation day to the day on which the trustees or managers or the person responsible for the pension arrangement make the payment, at the same rate as that payable for the time being on judgment debts by virtue of section 17 of the Judgments Act 1838; or

(b) if it is greater, the amount, if any, by which the amount of that pension credit falls short of what it would have been if the valuation day had been the day on which the trustees or managers or the person responsible for the pension arrangement make the payment.

H. The Sharing of State Scheme Rights (Provision of Information and Valuation) (No. 2) Regulations 2000 (S.I. 2000/2914)

The Secretary of State for Social Security, in exercise of the powers conferred upon him by sections 45B(7), 55A(6), 55B(7), 122(1) and 175(3) and (4) of the Social Security Contributions and Benefits Act 1992 and sections 23(1)(a), (b)(ii) and (c)(i) and (2), 49(4) and 83(4) and (6) of the Welfare Reform and Pensions Act 1999 and of all other powers enabling him in that behalf, after agreement by the Social Security Advisory Committee that proposals to make regulation 4 of these Regulations should not be referred to it and after consulting such person as he considered appropriate, hereby makes the following Regulations:

Citation, commencement and interpretation

1.—(1) These Regulations may be cited as the Sharing of State Scheme Rights (Provision of Information and Valuation) (No. 2) Regulations 2000 and shall come into force on 1st December 2000.

(2) In these Regulations —

"the 1992 Act" means the Social Security Contributions and Benefits Act 1992;

"the 1999 Act" means the Welfare Reform and Pensions Act 1999;

"shareable state scheme rights" has the meaning given by section 47(2) of the 1999 Act.

Basic information about the sharing of state scheme rights and divorce

2.—(1) The requirements imposed on the Secretary of State for the purposes of section 23(1)(a) of the 1999 Act (supply of pension information in connection with divorce etc.) are that he shall furnish —

(a) the information specified in paragraphs (2) and (3) —
 (i) to a person who has shareable state scheme rights on request from that person; or
 (ii) to the court, pursuant to an order of the court; or

(*b*) the information specified in paragraph (3) to the spouse of a person who has shareable state scheme rights, on request from that spouse.

(2) The information specified in this paragraph is a valuation of the person's shareable state scheme rights.

(3) The information in this paragraph is an explanation of —

(*a*) the state scheme rights which are shareable;
(*b*) how a pension sharing order or provision will affect a person's shareable state scheme rights; and
(*c*) how a pension sharing order or provision in respect of a person's shareable state scheme rights will result in the spouse of the person who has shareable state scheme rights becoming entitled to a shared additional pension.

(4) The Secretary of State shall furnish the information specified in paragraphs (2) and (3) to the court, or as the case may be, to the person who has shareable state scheme rights within —

(*a*) 3 months beginning with the date the Secretary of State receives the request or, as the case may be, the order for the provision of that information;
(*b*) 6 weeks beginning with the date the Secretary of State receives the request or, as the case may be, the order for the provision of the information, if the person who has shareable state scheme rights has notified the Secretary of State on the date of the request or order that the information is needed in connection with proceedings commenced under any of the provisions referred to in section 23(1)(a) of the 1999 Act; or
(*c*) such shorter period specified by the court in an order requiring the Secretary of State to provide a valuation in accordance with paragraph (2).

(5) Where —

(*a*) the request made by the person with shareable state scheme rights for, or the court order requiring, the provision of information does not include a request or, as the case may be, an order for a valuation under paragraph (2); or
(*b*) the spouse of the person with shareable state scheme rights requests the information specified in paragraph (3),

the Secretary of State shall furnish that information to the person who has shareable state scheme rights, his spouse, or the court, as the case may be, within one month beginning with the date the Secretary of State receives the request or the court order for the provision of that information.

Information about the sharing of state scheme rights and divorce: valuation of shareable state scheme rights

3. Where an application for financial relief or financial provision under any of the provisions referred to in section 23(1)(a) of the 1999 Act has been made or is in contemplation, the valuation of shareable state scheme rights shall be calculated and verified for the purposes of regulation 2(2) of these Regulations in such manner as may be approved by or on behalf of the Government Actuary.

Calculation and verification of cash equivalents for the purposes of the creation of state scheme pension debits and credits

4. For the purposes of —

- (*a*) section 49 of the 1999 Act (creation of state scheme pension debits and credits);
- (*b*) section 45B of the 1992 Act (reduction of additional pension in Category A retirement pension: pension sharing);
- (*c*) section 55A of the 1992 Act (shared additional pension); and
- (*d*) section 55B of the 1992 Act (reduction of shared additional pension: pension sharing),

cash equivalents shall be calculated and verified in such manner as may be approved by or on behalf of the Government Actuary.

Revocation

5. The Sharing of State Scheme Rights (Provision of Information and Valuation) Regulations 2000 are revoked.

INDEX